03

by COFFEE

WANDANCE

CHARACTERS

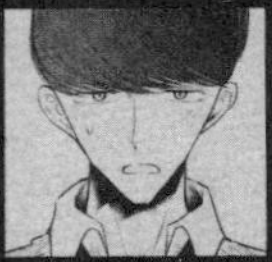

Kaboku Kotani

First-year member of the dance club. Has trouble talking in front of people because of his stutter. It was Wanda who drew him into the dance club.

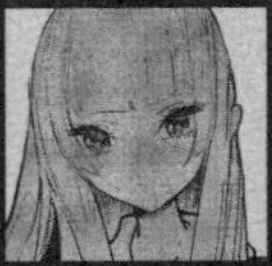

Hikari Wanda

First-year member of the dance club. Loves dancing. Not very muscular, but has excellent physical intuition.

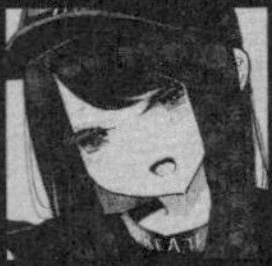

On Miyao

Third-year member and president of the dance club. Goes by "On-chan." Answers questions and gives guidance to the less-experienced members.

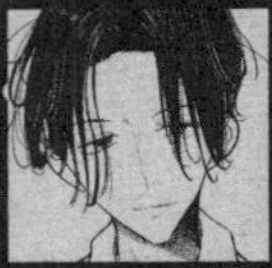

Iori Itsukushima

Second-year member of the dance club. Has excellent dance skills, but never attends club. Has a sweet tooth.

CONTENTS

Ch. 9: First Contest (Pt. 1)

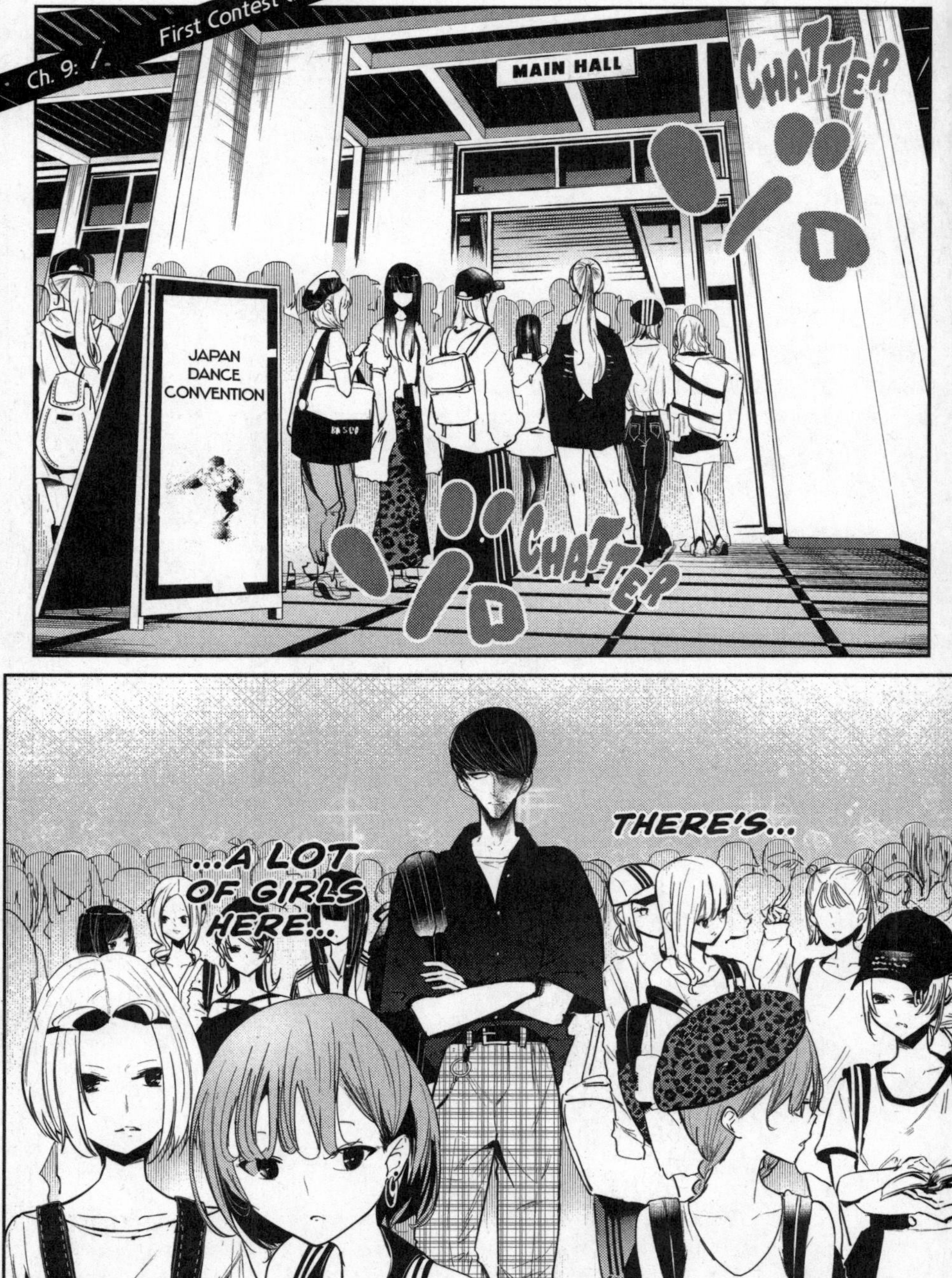
CHATTER
MAIN HALL
JAPAN DANCE CONVENTION
CHATTER
THERE'S...
...A LOT OF GIRLS HERE...

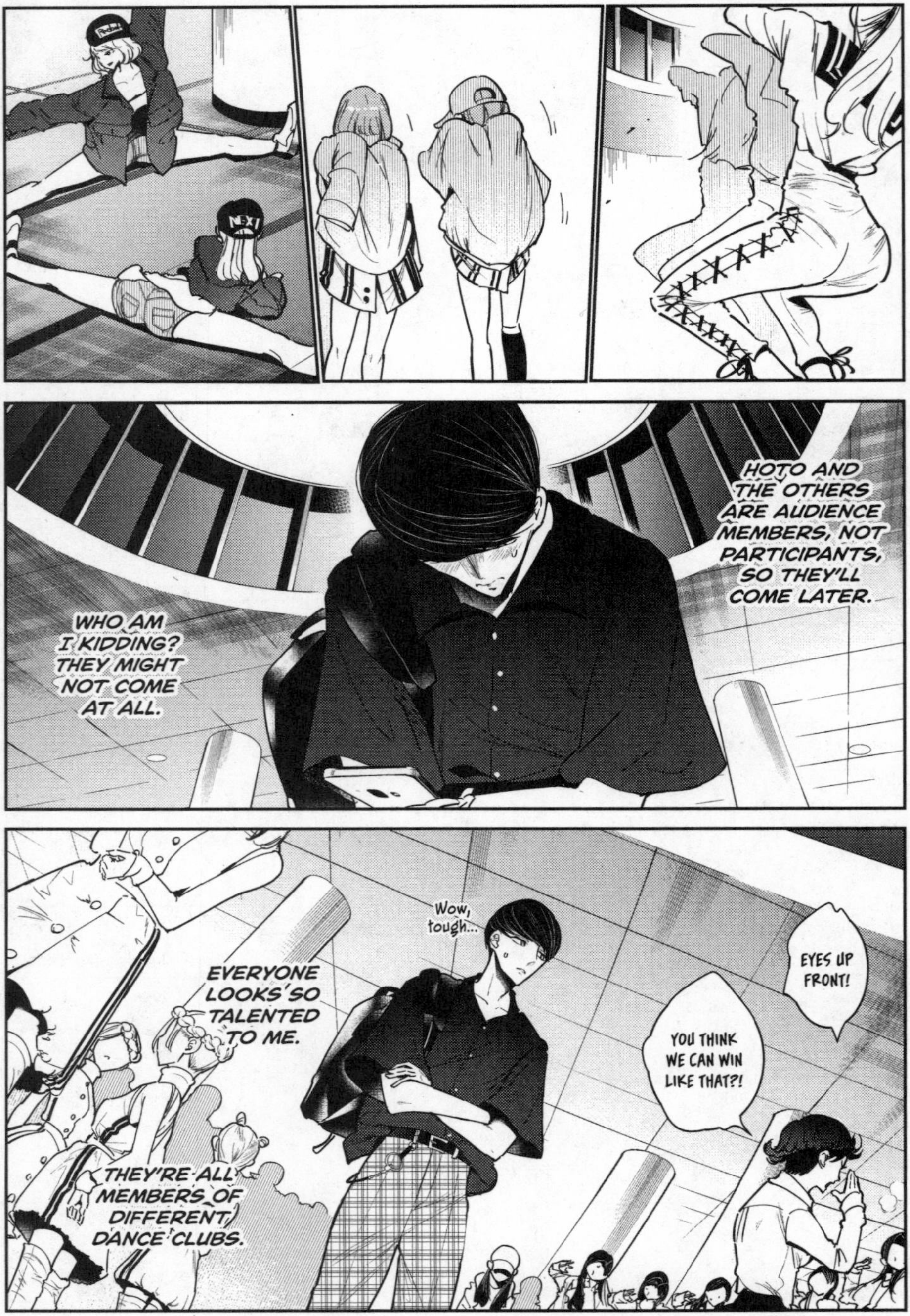
HOTO AND THE OTHERS ARE AUDIENCE MEMBERS, NOT PARTICIPANTS, SO THEY'LL COME LATER.
WHO AM I KIDDING? THEY MIGHT NOT COME AT ALL.
EYES UP FRONT!
YOU THINK WE CAN WIN LIKE THAT?!
Wow, tough...
EVERYONE LOOKS SO TALENTED TO ME.
THEY'RE ALL MEMBERS OF DIFFERENT DANCE CLUBS.

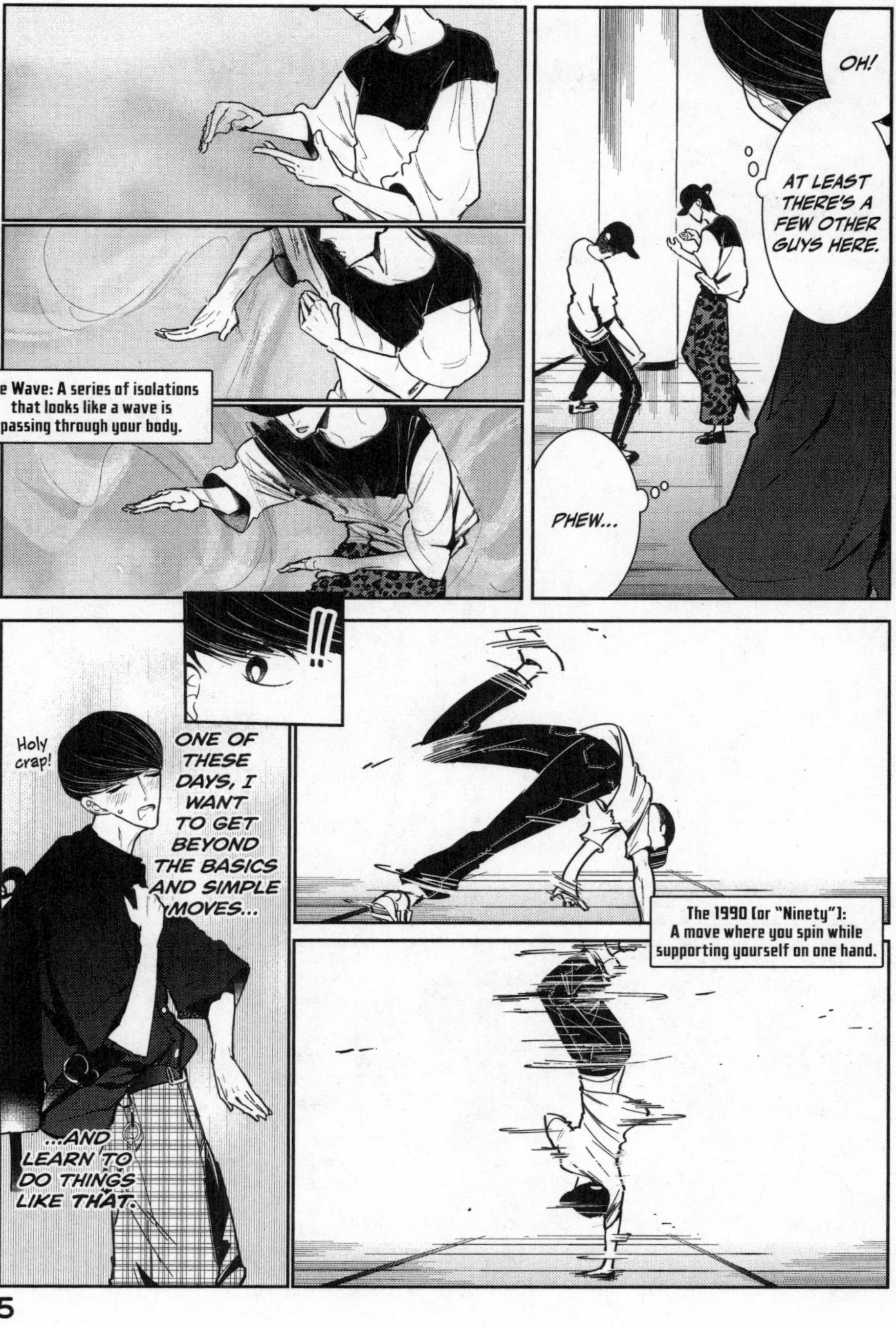
OH!
AT LEAST THERE'S A FEW OTHER GUYS HERE.
PHEW...
The Wave: A series of isolations that looks like a wave is passing through your body.
The 1990 (or "Ninety"): A move where you spin while supporting yourself on one hand.
!!
Holy crap!
ONE OF THESE DAYS, I WANT TO GET BEYOND THE BASICS AND SIMPLE MOVES...
...AND LEARN TO DO THINGS LIKE THAT.

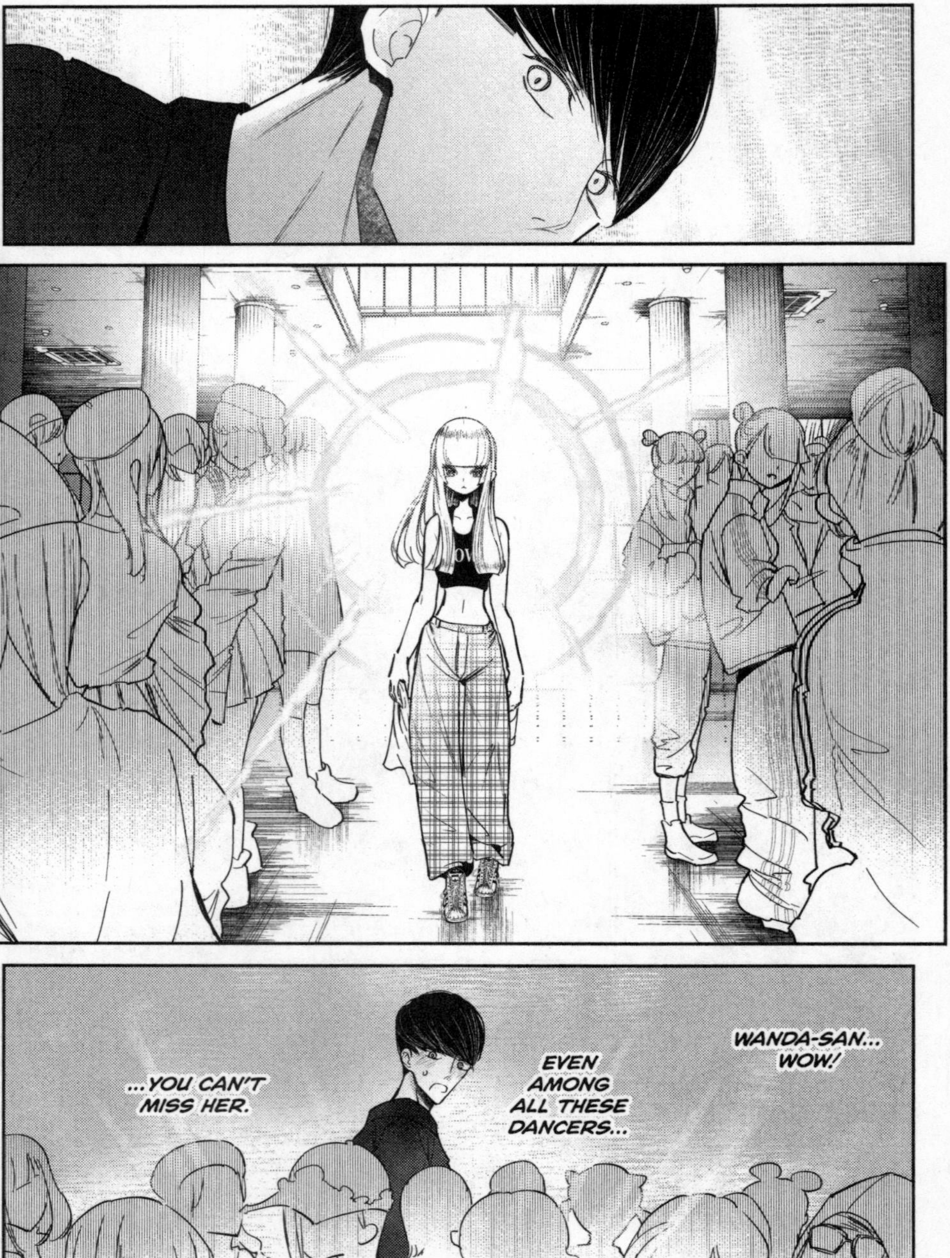
WANDA-SAN... WOW!
EVEN AMONG ALL THESE DANCERS...
...YOU CAN'T MISS HER.

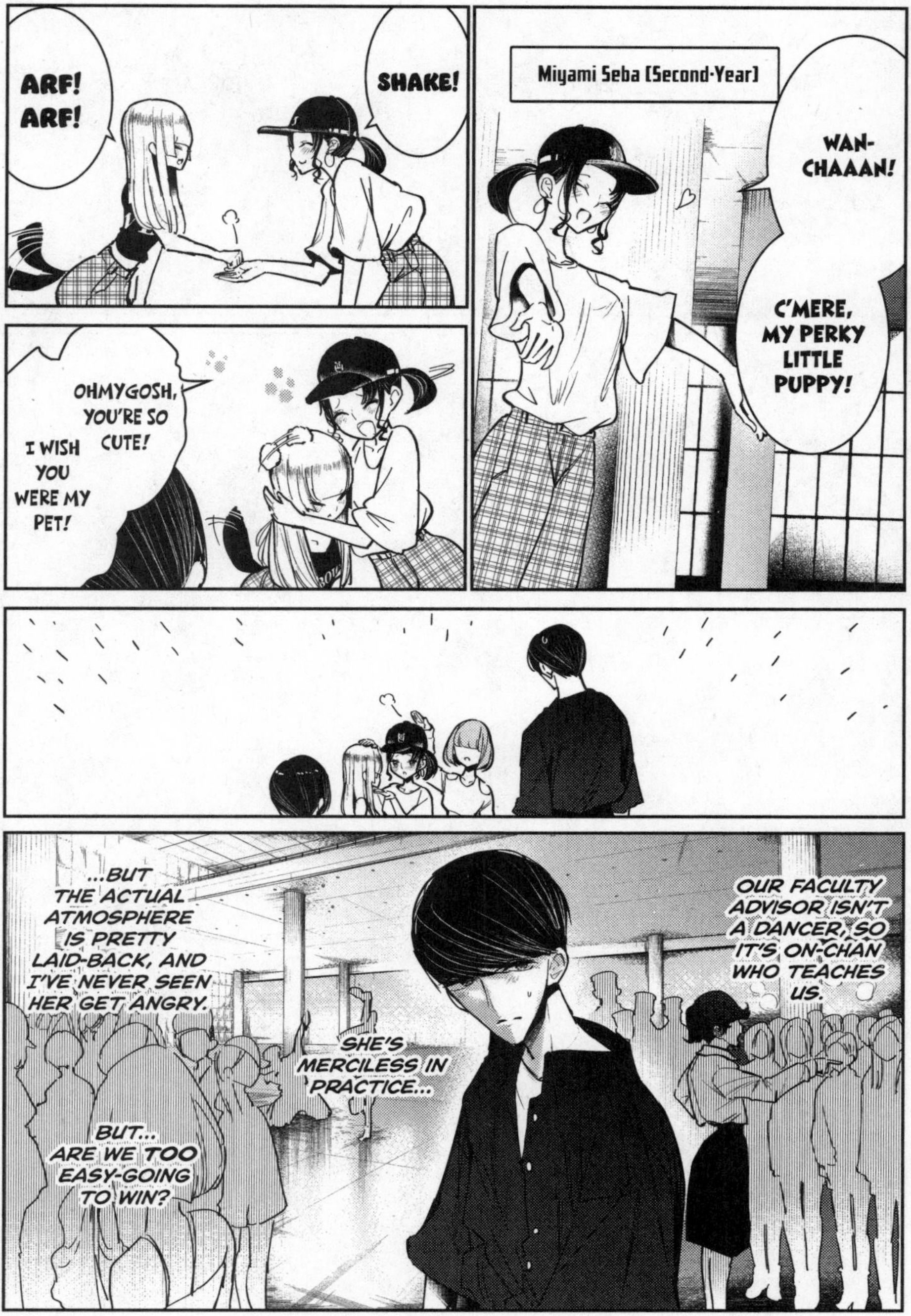
Miyami Seba (Second-Year)
WAN-CHAAAN!
C'MERE, MY PERKY LITTLE PUPPY!
SHAKE!
ARF! ARF!
OHMYGOSH, YOU'RE SO CUTE!
I WISH YOU WERE MY PET!
OUR FACULTY ADVISOR ISN'T A DANCER, SO IT'S ON-CHAN WHO TEACHES US.
SHE'S MERCILESS IN PRACTICE...
...BUT THE ACTUAL ATMOSPHERE IS PRETTY LAID-BACK, AND I'VE NEVER SEEN HER GET ANGRY.
BUT... ARE WE TOO EASY-GOING TO WIN?

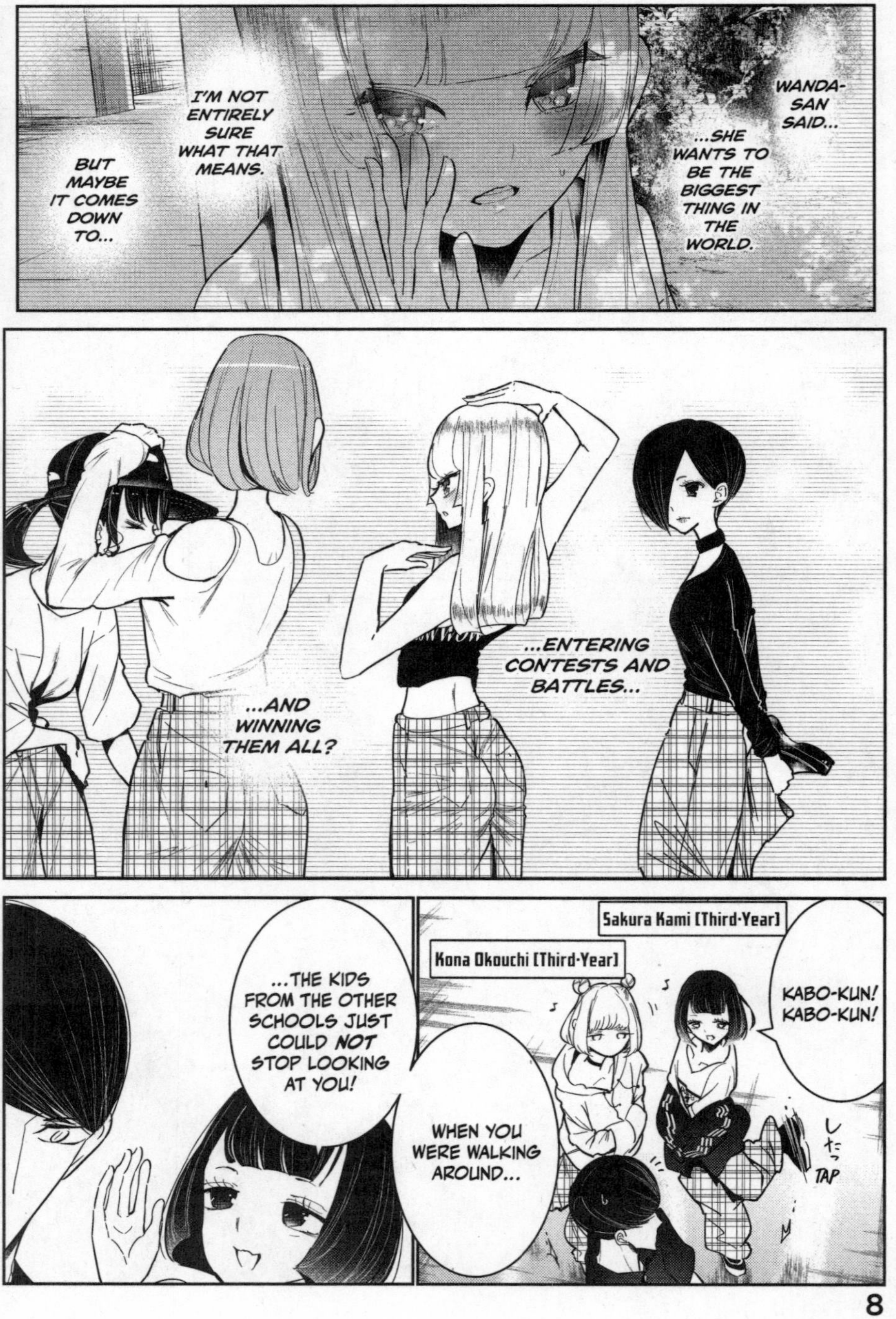
WANDA-SAN SAID...
...SHE WANTS TO BE THE BIGGEST THING IN THE WORLD.
I'M NOT ENTIRELY SURE WHAT THAT MEANS.
BUT MAYBE IT COMES DOWN TO...
...ENTERING CONTESTS AND BATTLES...
...AND WINNING THEM ALL?
Sakura Kami [Third-Year]
Kona Okouchi [Third-Year]
KABO-KUN! KABO-KUN!
したっ
TAP
WHEN YOU WERE WALKING AROUND...
...THE KIDS FROM THE OTHER SCHOOLS JUST COULD NOT STOP LOOKING AT YOU!

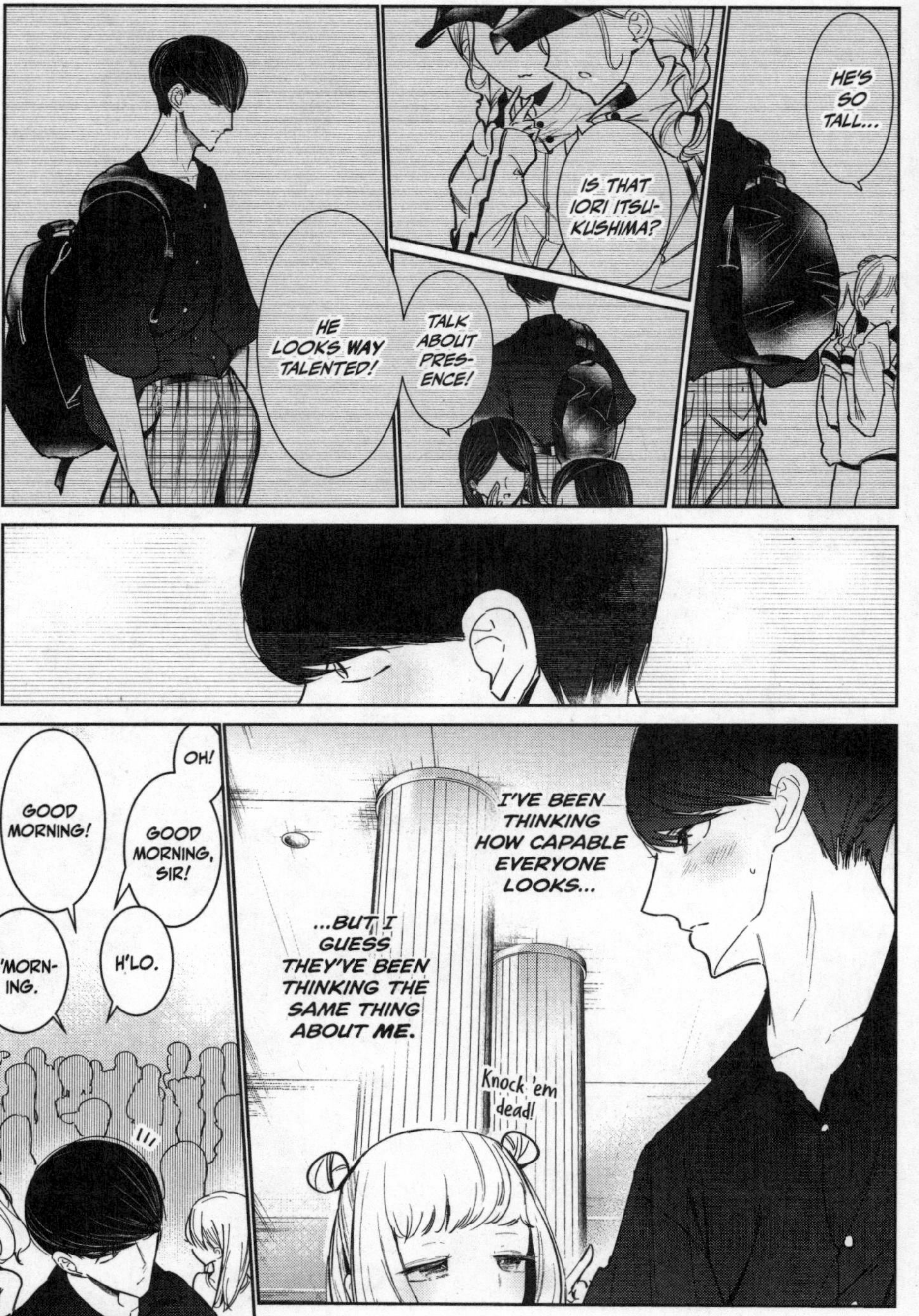
HE'S SO TALL...
IS THAT IORI ITSU-KUSHIMA?
TALK ABOUT PRES-ENCE!
HE LOOKS WAY TALENTED!
I'VE BEEN THINKING HOW CAPABLE EVERYONE LOOKS...
...BUT I GUESS THEY'VE BEEN THINKING THE SAME THING ABOUT ME.
Knock 'em dead!
OH!
GOOD MORNING, SIR!
GOOD MORNING!
H'LO.
G'MORN-ING.

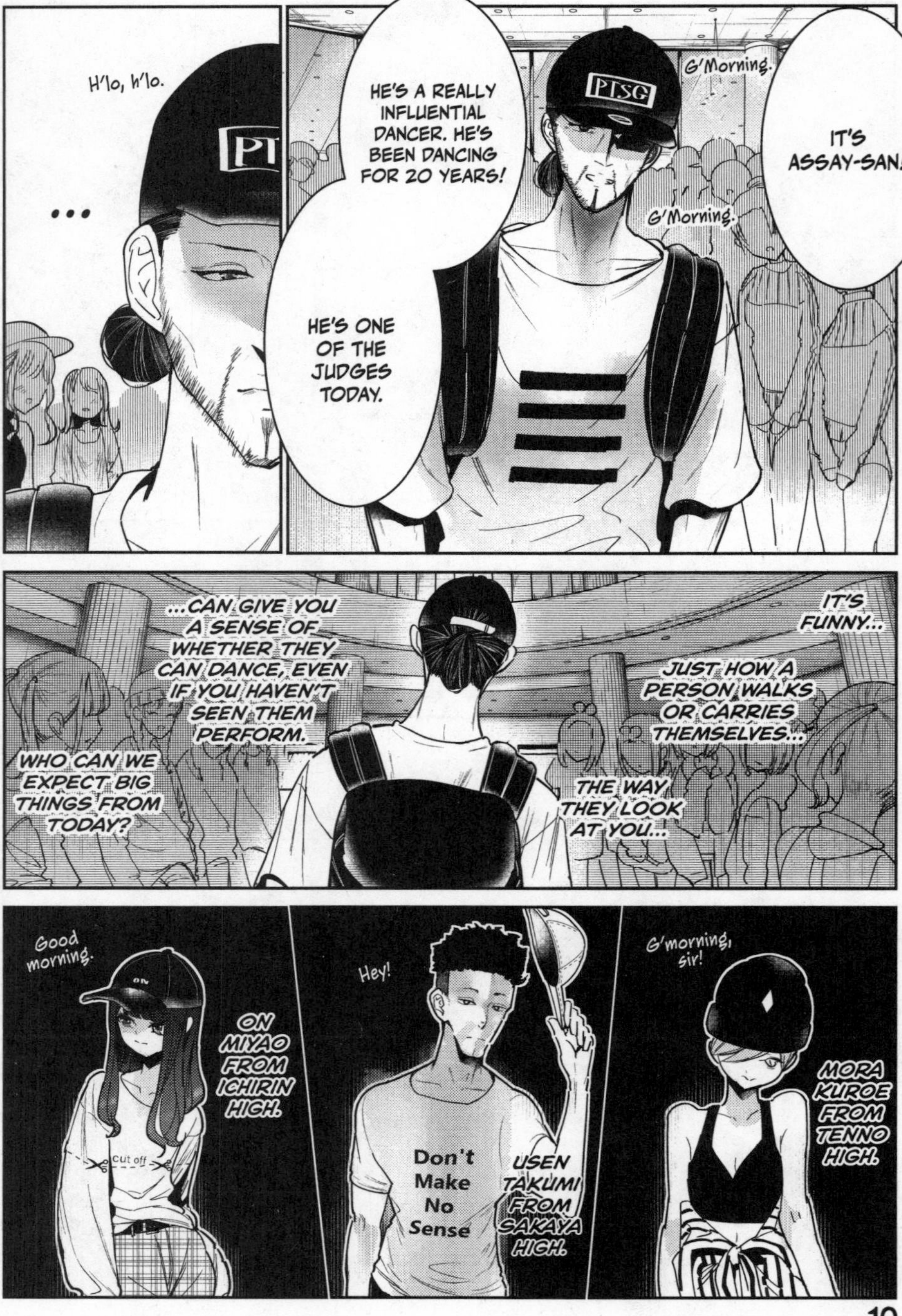
IT'S ASSAY-SAN!
G'Morning.
HE'S A REALLY INFLUENTIAL DANCER. HE'S BEEN DANCING FOR 20 YEARS!
G'Morning.
HE'S ONE OF THE JUDGES TODAY.
H'lo, h'lo.
...
IT'S FUNNY...
JUST HOW A PERSON WALKS OR CARRIES THEMSELVES...
THE WAY THEY LOOK AT YOU...
...CAN GIVE YOU A SENSE OF WHETHER THEY CAN DANCE, EVEN IF YOU HAVEN'T SEEN THEM PERFORM.
WHO CAN WE EXPECT BIG THINGS FROM TODAY?
G'morning, sir!
MORA KUROE FROM TENNO HIGH.
Hey!
Don't Make No Sense
USEN TAKUMI FROM SAKAYA HIGH.
Good morning.
ON MIYAO FROM ICHIRIN HIGH.
Cut off

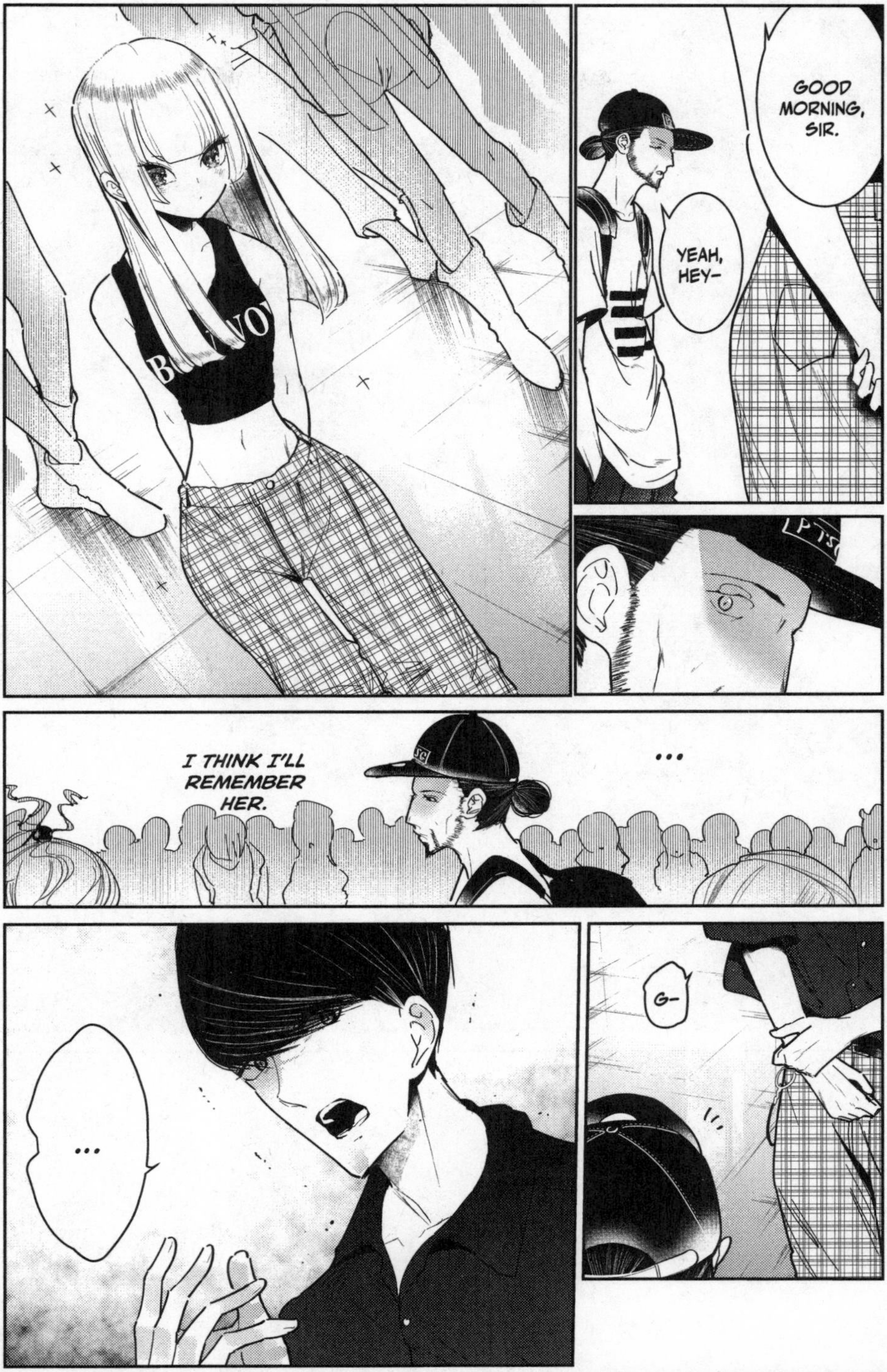
GOOD MORNING, SIR.
YEAH, HEY–
...
I THINK I'LL REMEMBER HER.
G–
...

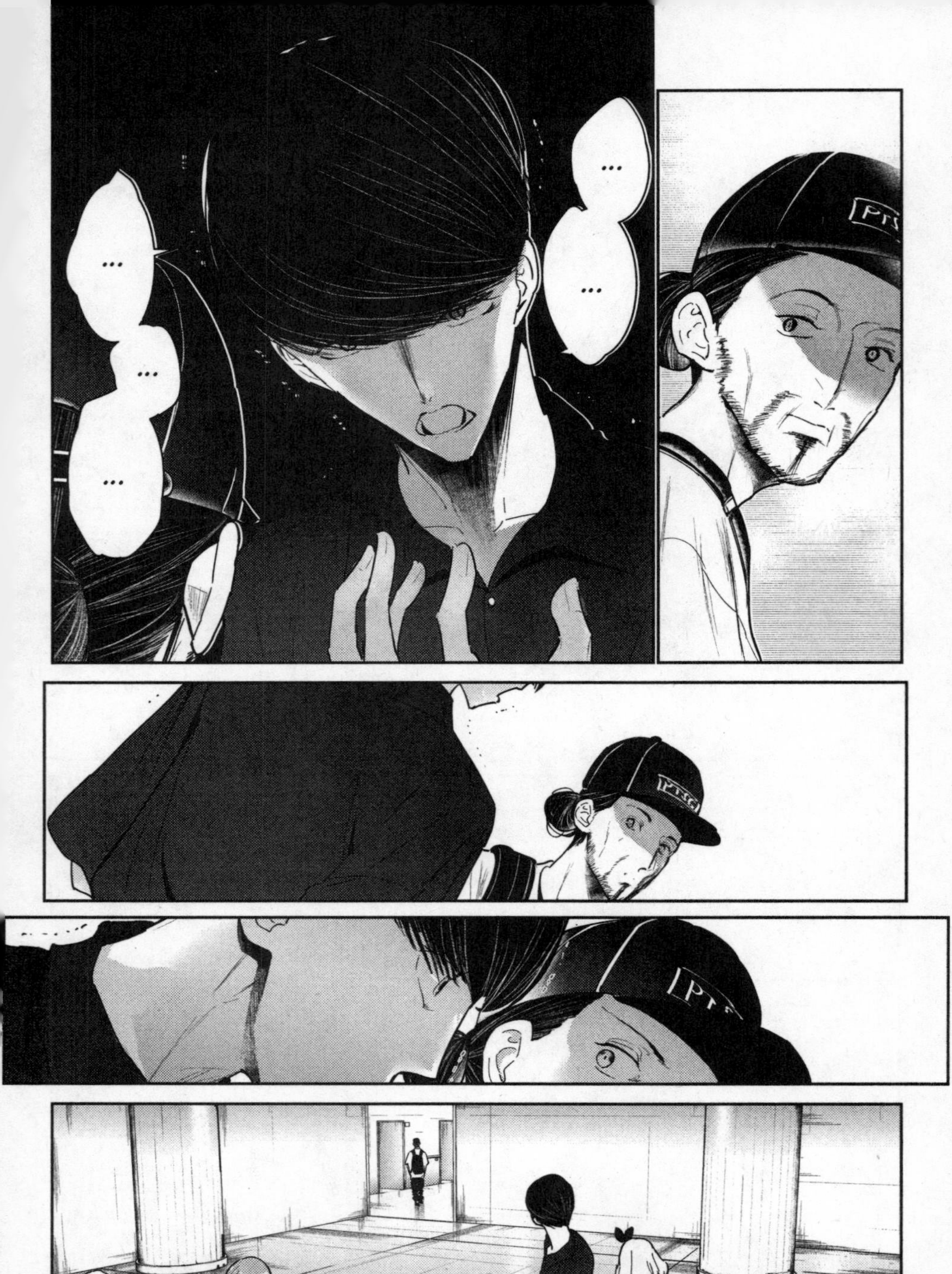
...
...
...
...
...

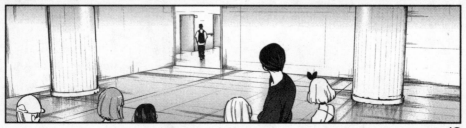

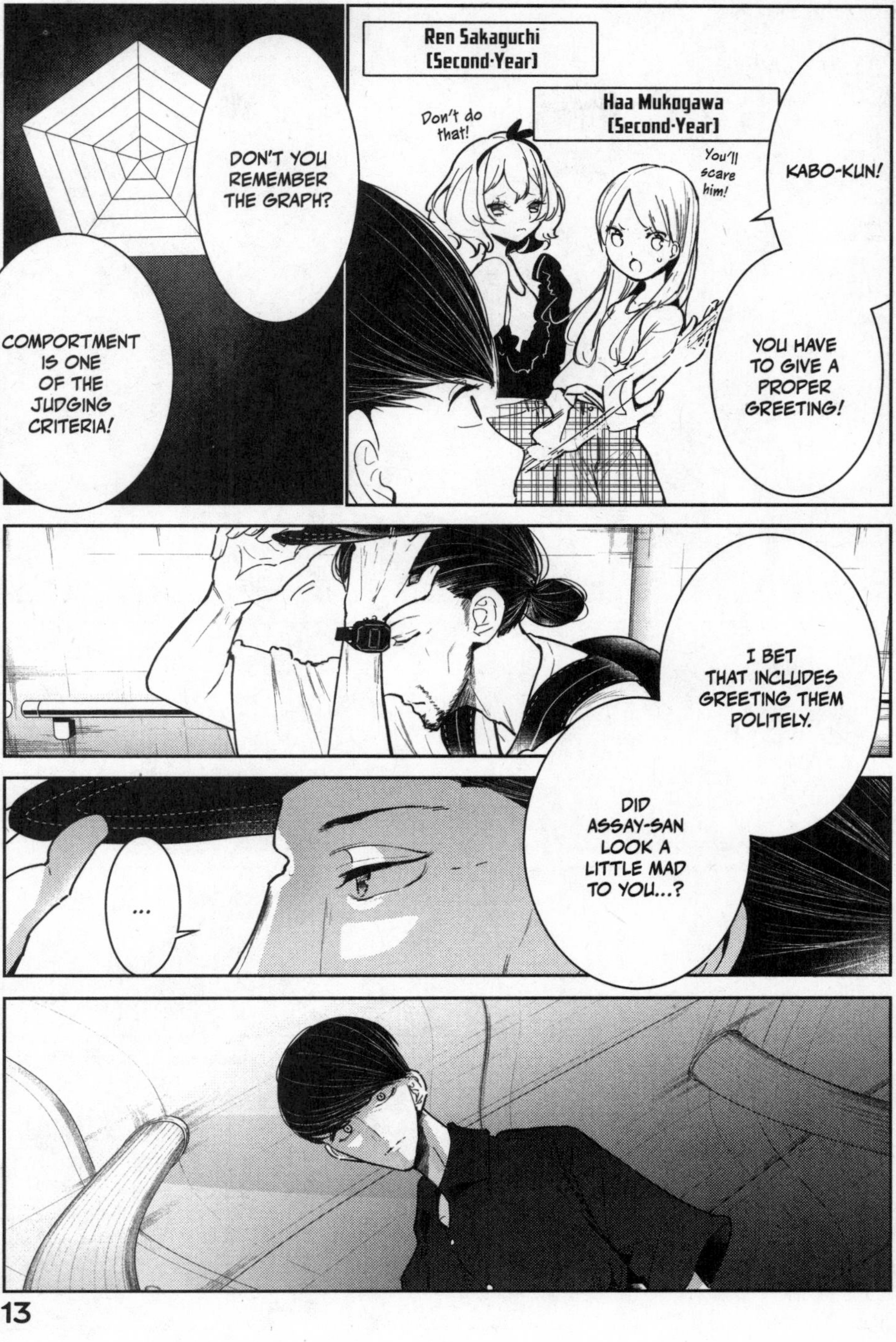
KABO-KUN!
YOU HAVE TO GIVE A PROPER GREETING!
Ren Sakaguchi [Second-Year]
Haa Mukogawa [Second-Year]
You'll scare him!
Don't do that!
DON'T YOU REMEMBER THE GRAPH?
COMPORTMENT IS ONE OF THE JUDGING CRITERIA!
I BET THAT INCLUDES GREETING THEM POLITELY.
DID ASSAY-SAN LOOK A LITTLE MAD TO YOU...?
...

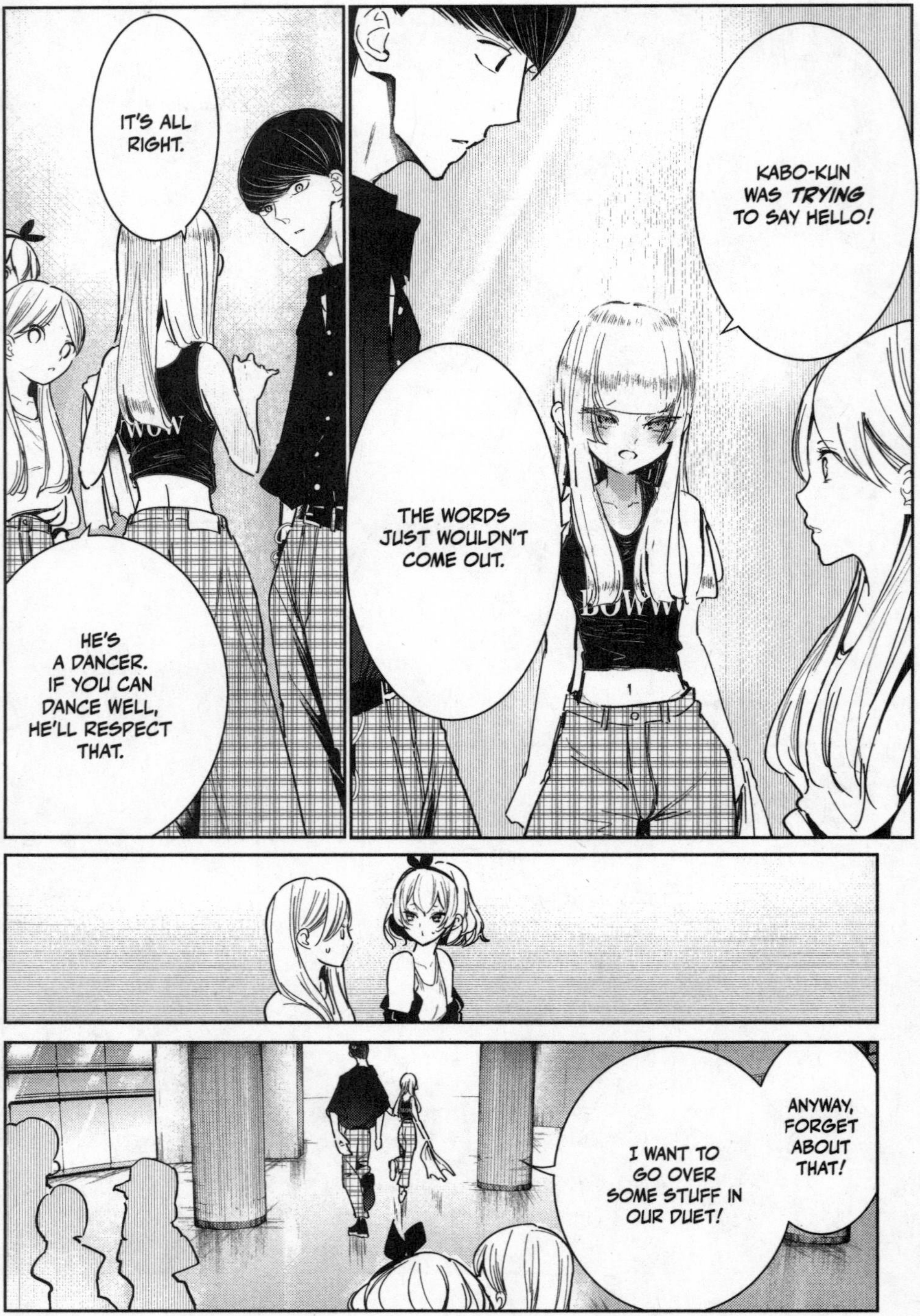
KABO-KUN WAS *TRYING* TO SAY HELLO!
THE WORDS JUST WOULDN'T COME OUT.
IT'S ALL RIGHT.
HE'S A DANCER. IF YOU CAN DANCE WELL, HE'LL RESPECT THAT.
ANYWAY, FORGET ABOUT THAT!
I WANT TO GO OVER SOME STUFF IN OUR DUET!

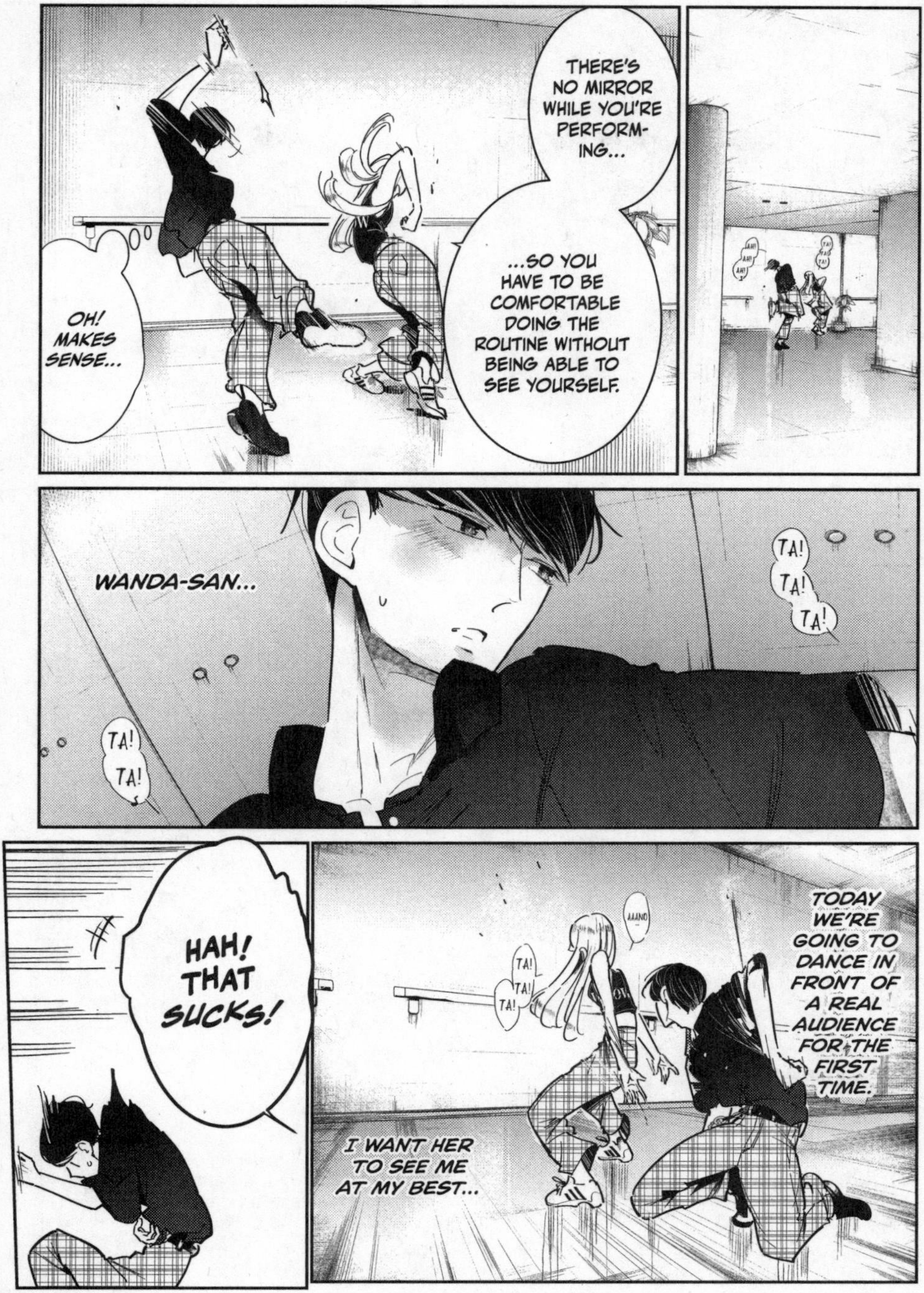
THERE'S NO MIRROR WHILE YOU'RE PERFORM-ING...
...SO YOU HAVE TO BE COMFORTABLE DOING THE ROUTINE WITHOUT BEING ABLE TO SEE YOURSELF.
OH! MAKES SENSE...
TA! TA! TA!
WANDA-SAN...
TA! TA!
TODAY WE'RE GOING TO DANCE IN FRONT OF A REAL AUDIENCE FOR THE FIRST TIME.
AAAND...
TA! TA! TA!
I WANT HER TO SEE ME AT MY BEST...
HAH! THAT SUCKS!

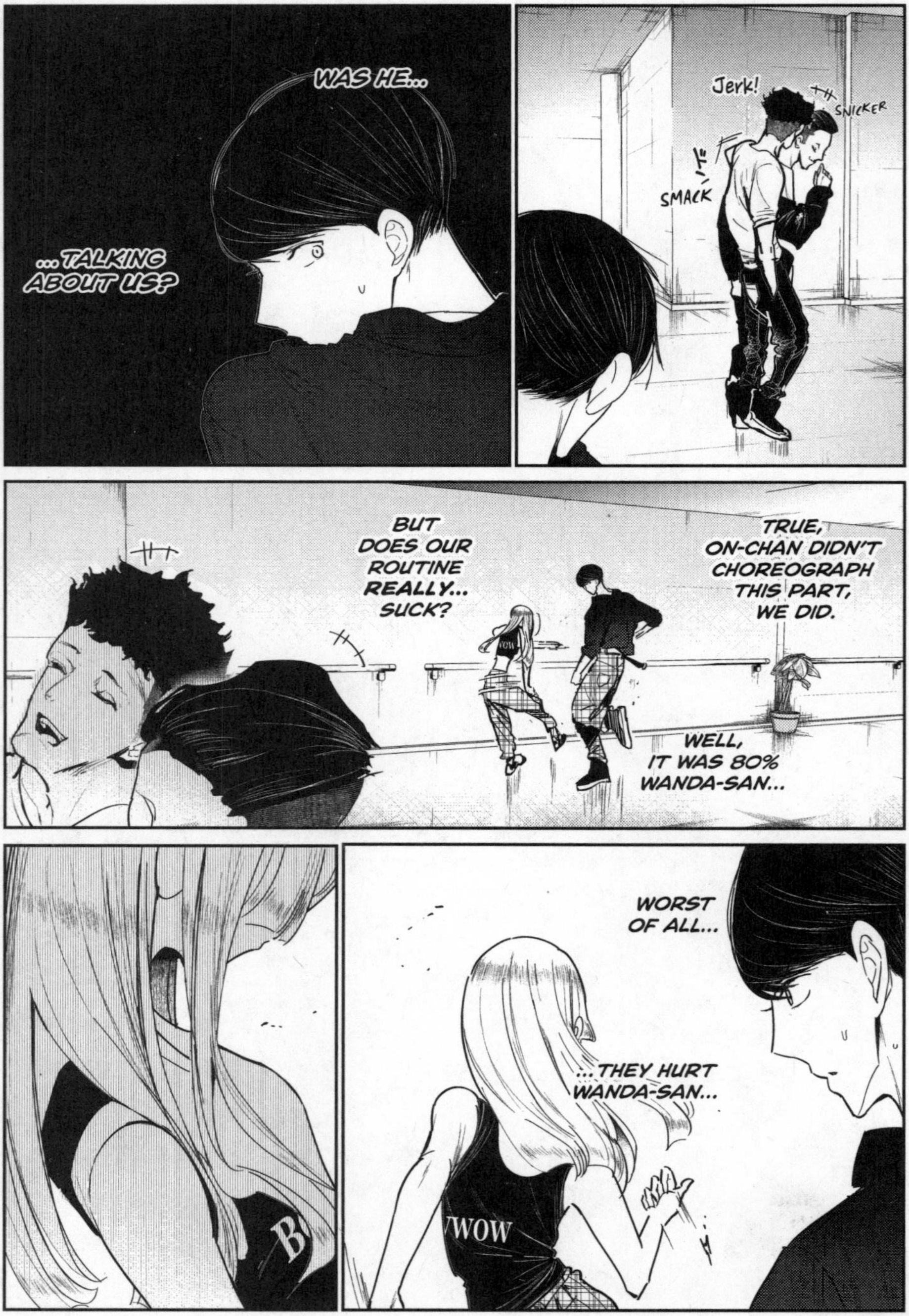
Jerk!
SNICKER
SMACK
WAS HE...
...TALKING ABOUT US?
TRUE, ON-CHAN DIDN'T CHOREOGRAPH THIS PART, WE DID.
BUT DOES OUR ROUTINE REALLY... SUCK?
WELL, IT WAS 80% WANDA-SAN...
WORST OF ALL...
...THEY HURT WANDA-SAN...
WOW
B

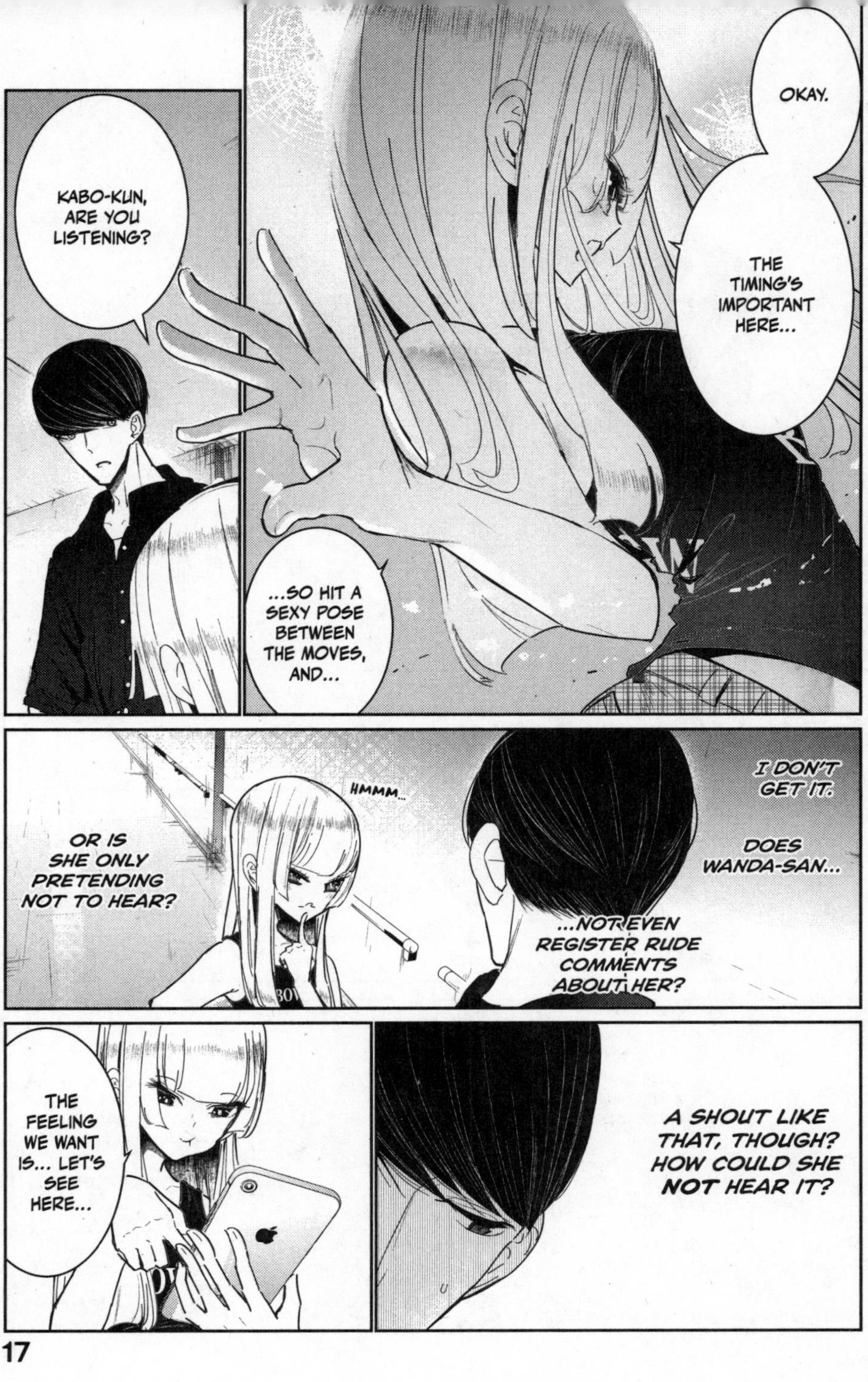
OKAY.
THE TIMING'S IMPORTANT HERE...
...SO HIT A SEXY POSE BETWEEN THE MOVES, AND...
KABO-KUN, ARE YOU LISTENING?
I DON'T GET IT.
DOES WANDA-SAN...
...NOT EVEN REGISTER RUDE COMMENTS ABOUT HER?
HMMM...
OR IS SHE ONLY PRETENDING NOT TO HEAR?
A SHOUT LIKE THAT, THOUGH? HOW COULD SHE NOT HEAR IT?
THE FEELING WE WANT IS... LET'S SEE HERE...

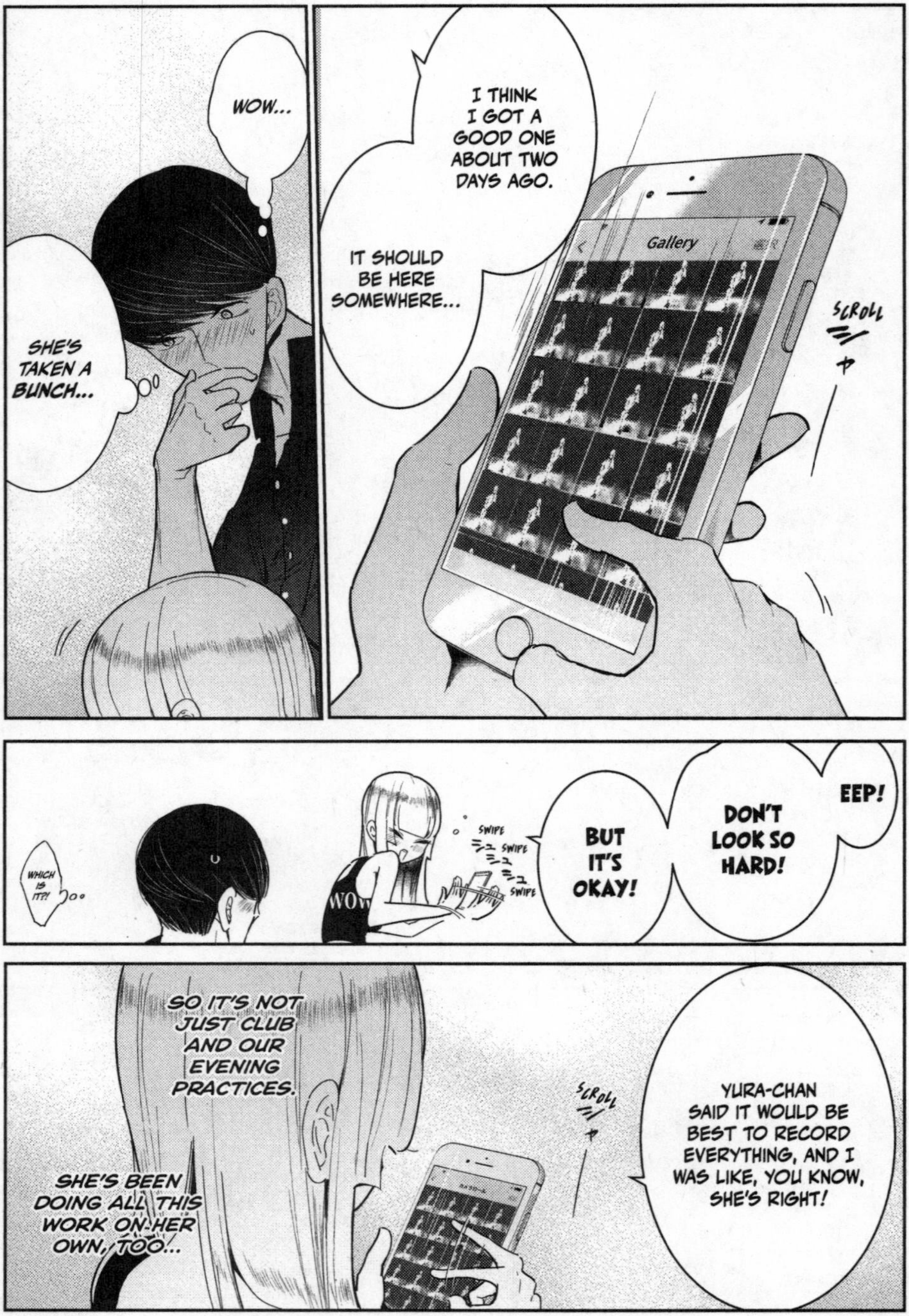
I THINK I GOT A GOOD ONE ABOUT TWO DAYS AGO.
Gallery
IT SHOULD BE HERE SOMEWHERE...
SCROLL
WOW...
SHE'S TAKEN A BUNCH...
EEP!
DON'T LOOK SO HARD!
BUT IT'S OKAY!
SWIPE
SWIPE
SWIPE
WOW
WHICH IS IT?!
YURA-CHAN SAID IT WOULD BE BEST TO RECORD EVERYTHING, AND I WAS LIKE, YOU KNOW, SHE'S RIGHT!
SCROLL
SO IT'S NOT JUST CLUB AND OUR EVENING PRACTICES.
SHE'S BEEN DOING ALL THIS WORK ON HER OWN, TOO...

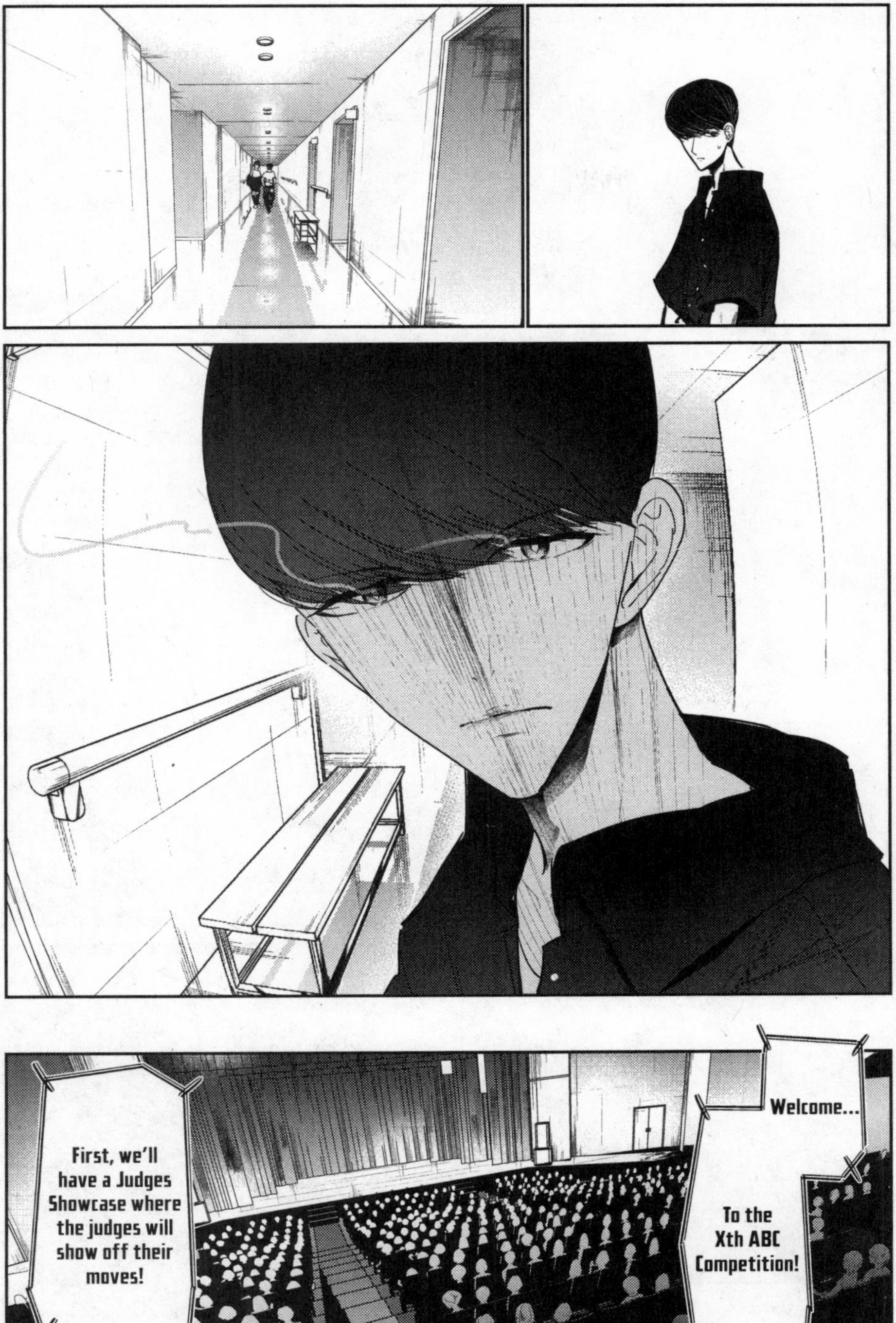
Welcome...
To the Xth ABC Competition!
First, we'll have a Judges Showcase where the judges will show off their moves!

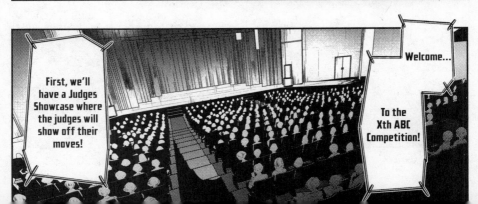

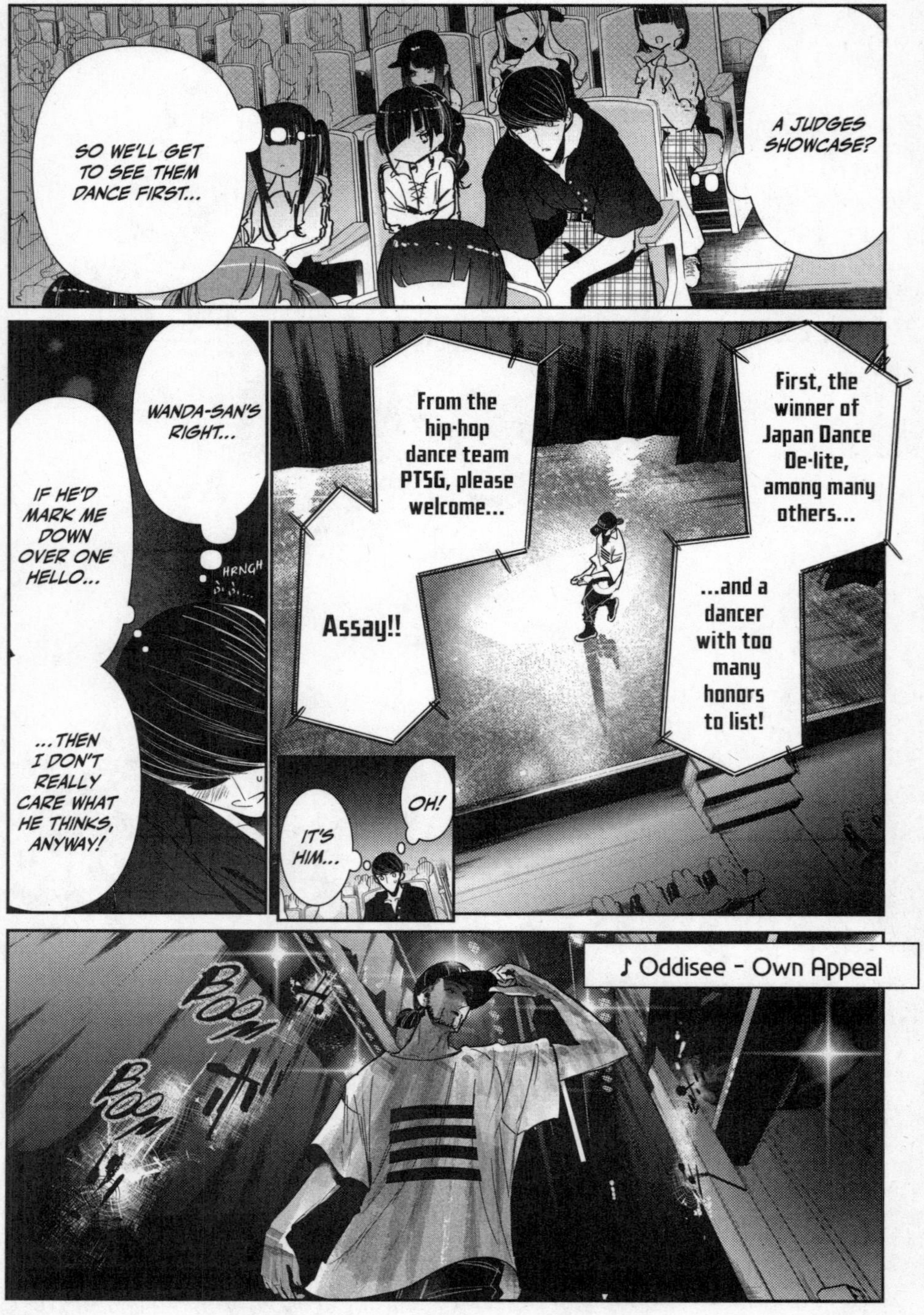
A JUDGES SHOWCASE?
SO WE'LL GET TO SEE THEM DANCE FIRST...
First, the winner of Japan Dance De-lite, among many others...
...and a dancer with too many honors to list!
From the hip-hop dance team PTSG, please welcome...
Assay!!
OH!
IT'S HIM...
WANDA-SAN'S RIGHT...
IF HE'D MARK ME DOWN OVER ONE HELLO...
HRNGH
...THEN I DON'T REALLY CARE WHAT HE THINKS, ANYWAY!
♪ Oddisee - Own Appeal
BOOM
BOOM

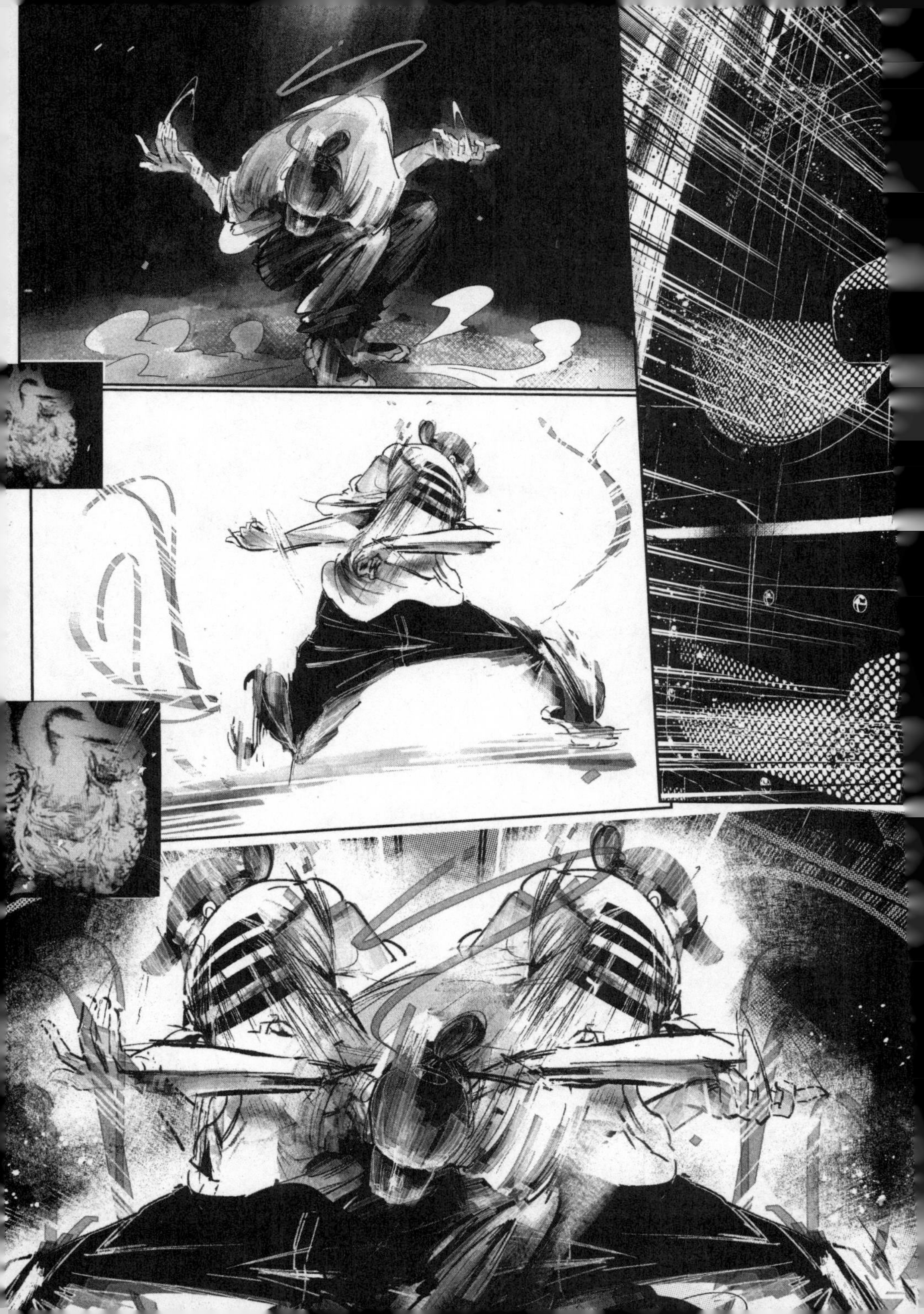

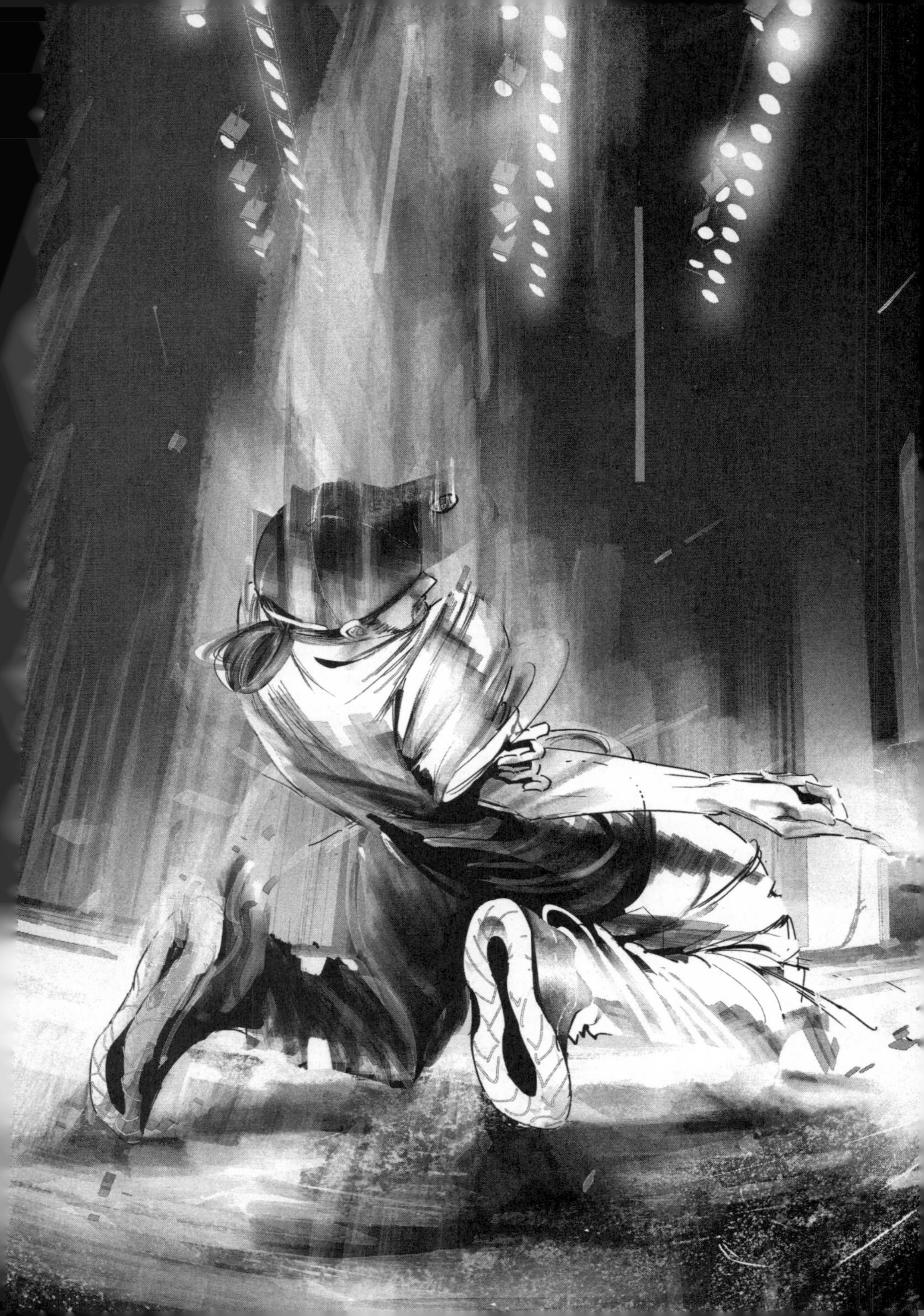

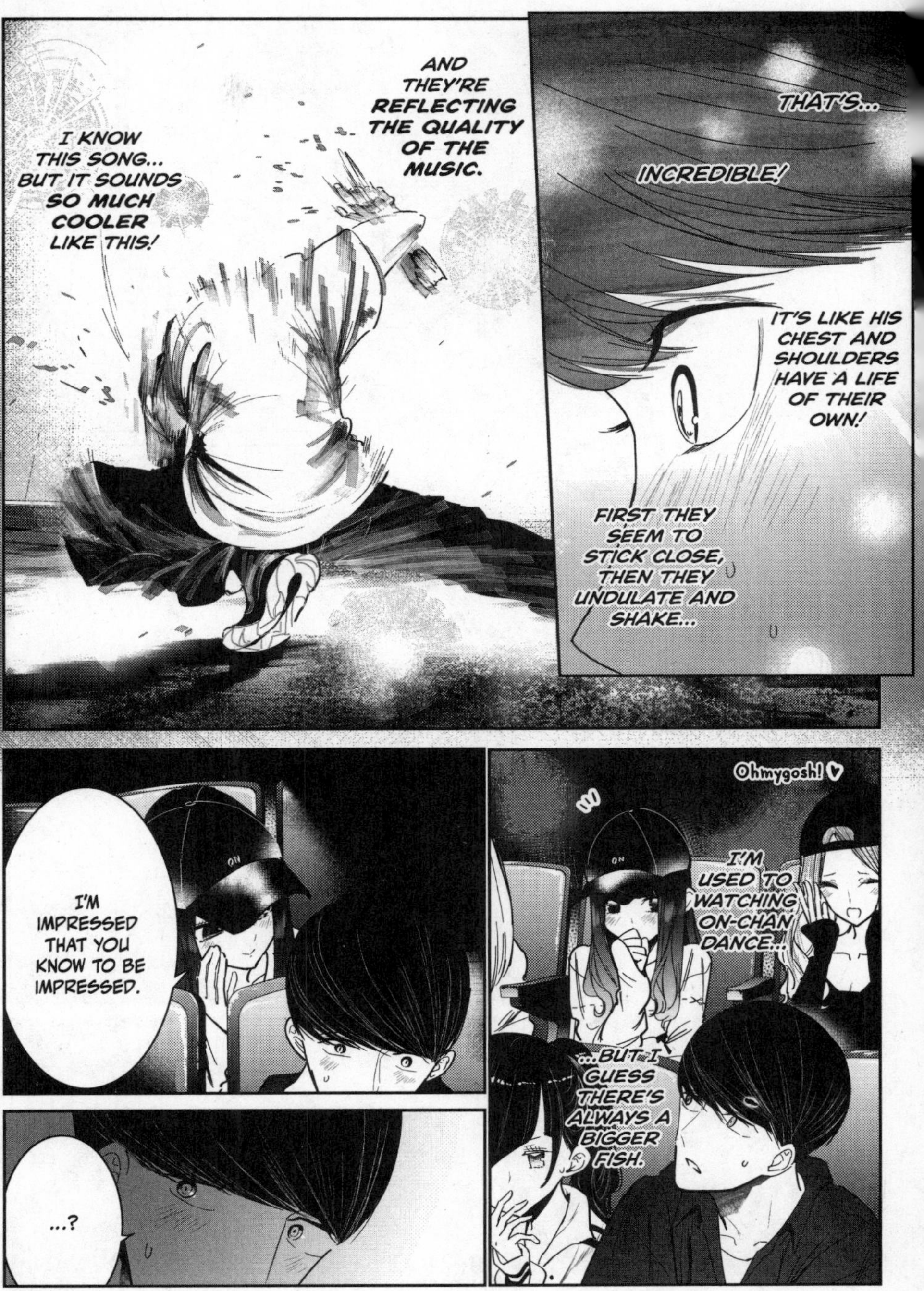
THAT'S...
INCREDIBLE!
IT'S LIKE HIS CHEST AND SHOULDERS HAVE A LIFE OF THEIR OWN!
FIRST THEY SEEM TO STICK CLOSE, THEN THEY UNDULATE AND SHAKE...
AND THEY'RE REFLECTING THE QUALITY OF THE MUSIC.
I KNOW THIS SONG... BUT IT SOUNDS SO MUCH COOLER LIKE THIS!
Ohmygosh! ♥
I'M USED TO WATCHING ON-CHAN DANCE...
...BUT I GUESS THERE'S ALWAYS A BIGGER FISH.
I'M IMPRESSED THAT YOU KNOW TO BE IMPRESSED.
...?

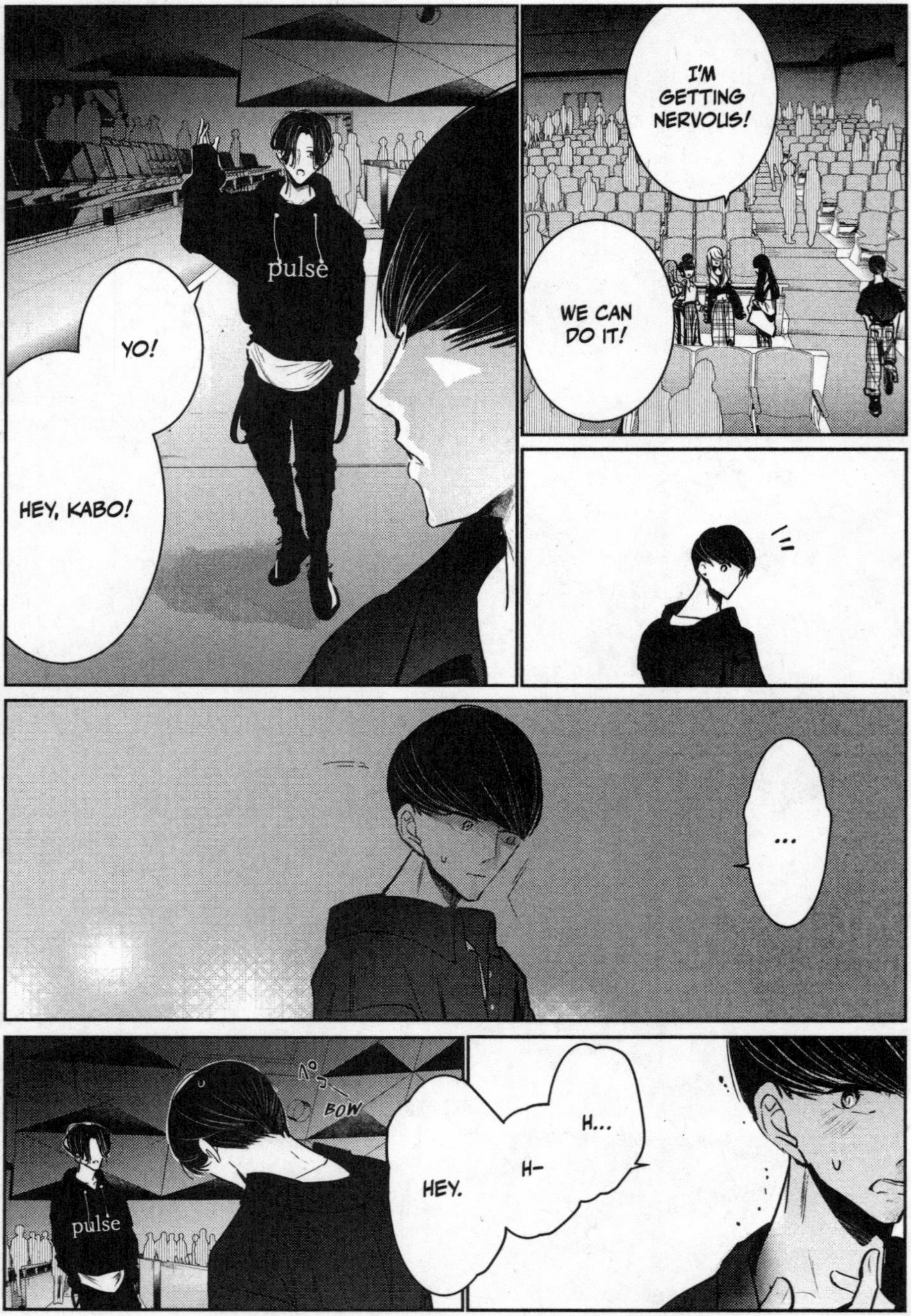
I'M GETTING NERVOUS!
WE CAN DO IT!
pulse
YO!
HEY, KABO!
...
H...
H-
HEY.
BOW
pulse

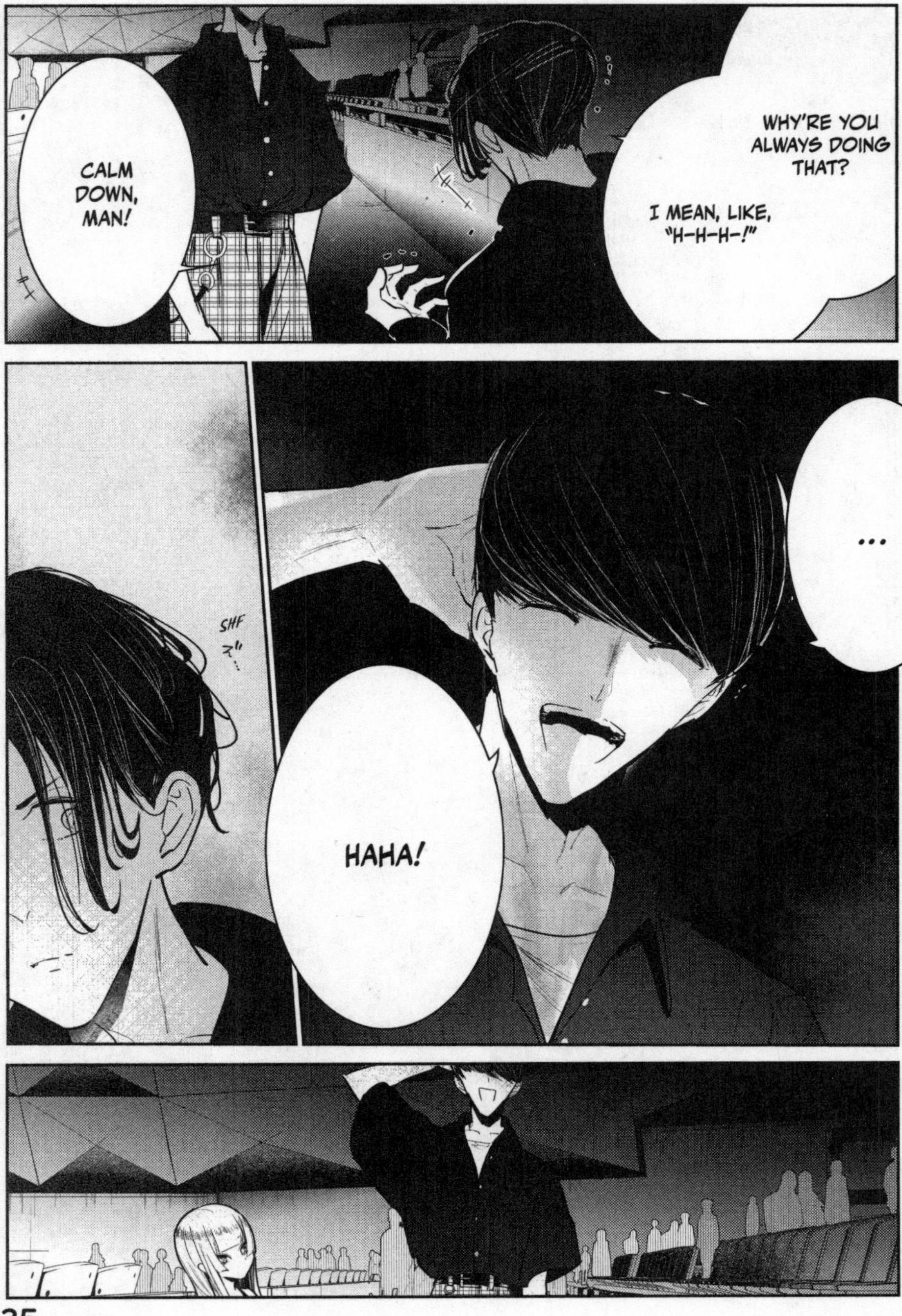
WHY'RE YOU ALWAYS DOING THAT?
I MEAN, LIKE, "H-H-H-!"
CALM DOWN, MAN!
...
HAHA!
SHF

WORDS DON'T ALWAYS COME EASILY FOR KABO-KUN.

AH!

AH HA!

NOW IT ALL MAKES SENSE.

I'VE GOT IT *ALL* FIGURED OUT.

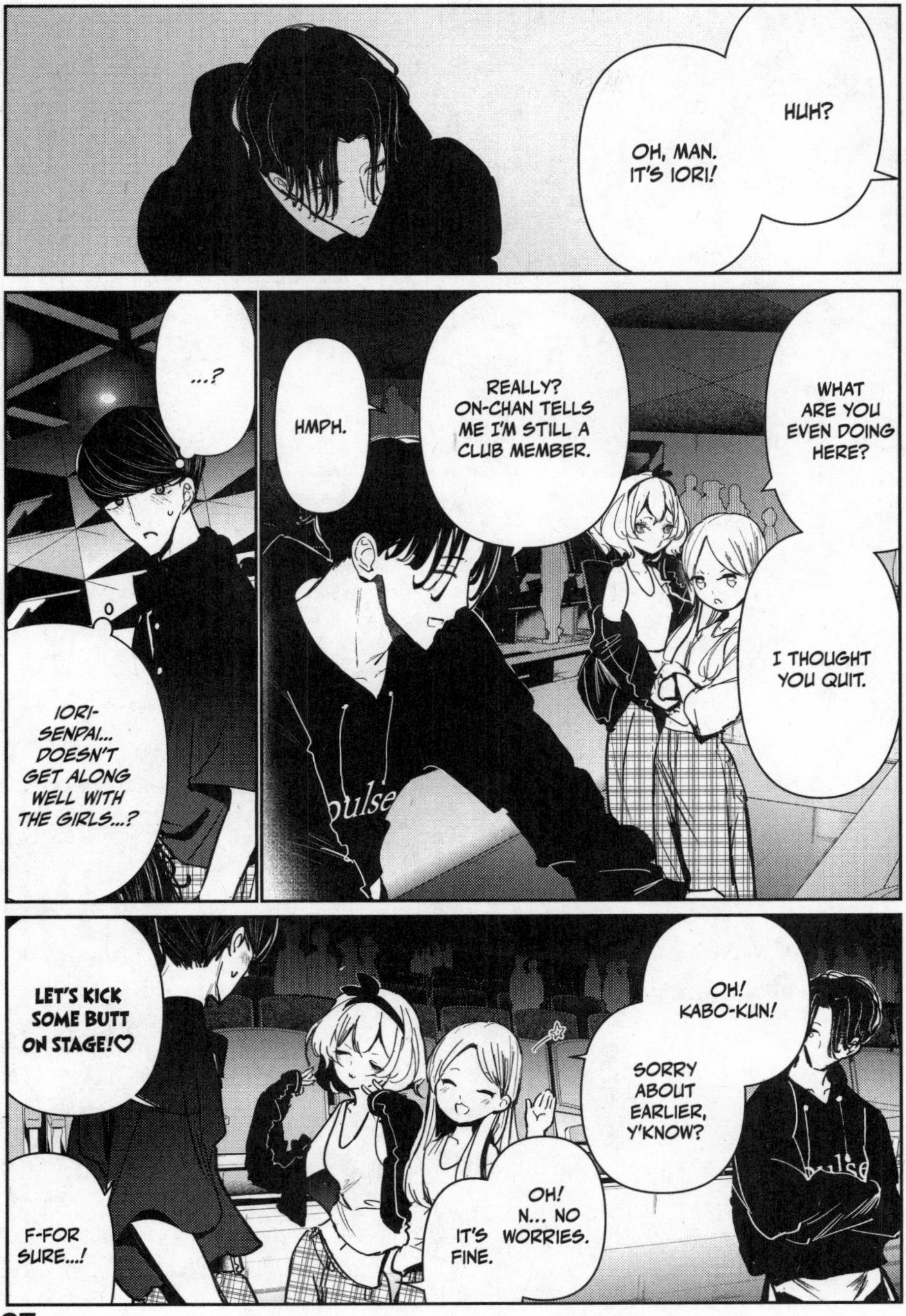
HUH?
OH, MAN. IT'S IORI!
WHAT ARE YOU EVEN DOING HERE?
I THOUGHT YOU QUIT.
REALLY? ON-CHAN TELLS ME I'M STILL A CLUB MEMBER.
HMPH.
...?
IORI-SENPAI... DOESN'T GET ALONG WELL WITH THE GIRLS...?
OH! KABO-KUN!
SORRY ABOUT EARLIER, Y'KNOW?
OH! N... NO WORRIES.
IT'S FINE.
LET'S KICK SOME BUTT ON STAGE!♡
F-FOR SURE...!

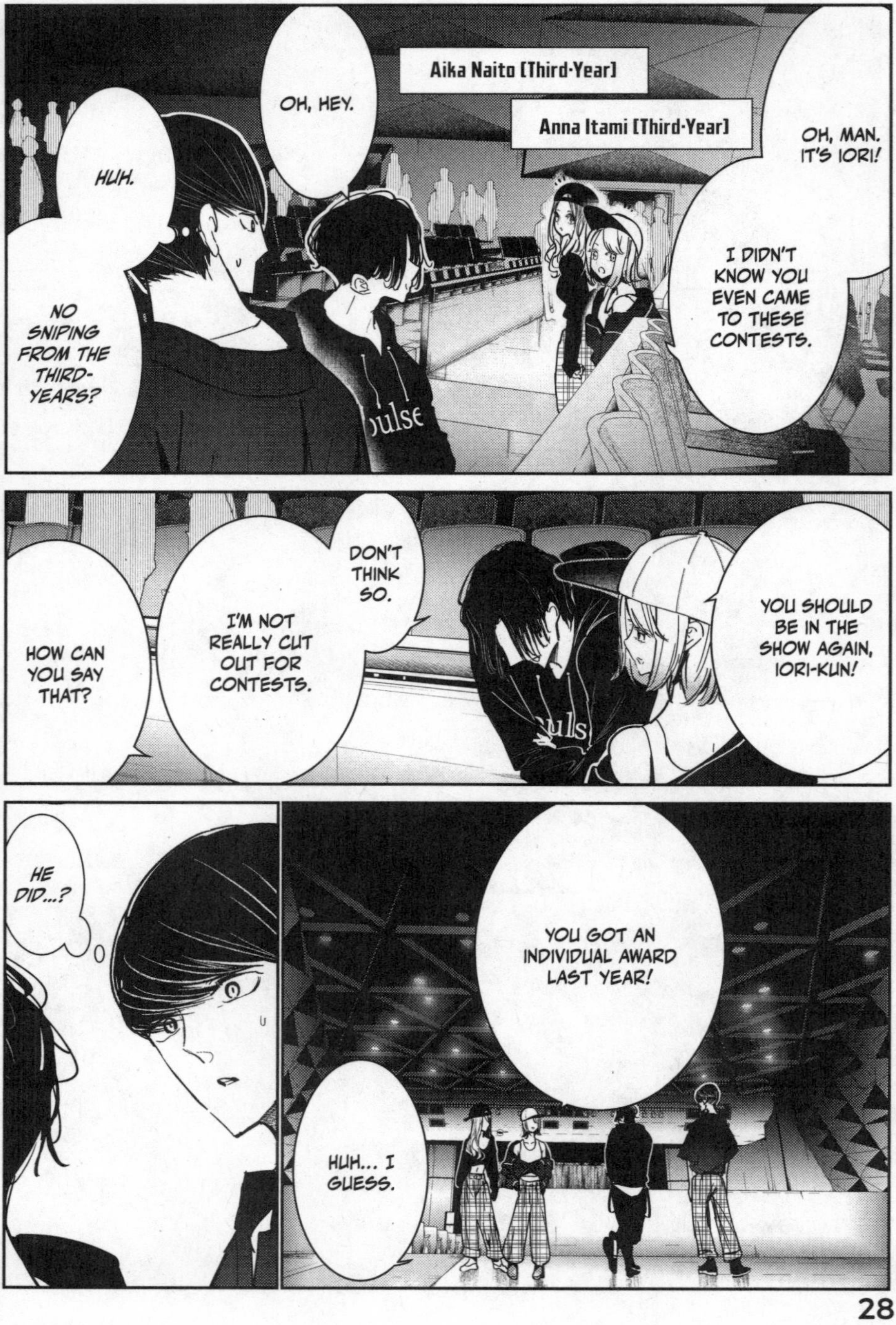
OH, MAN. IT'S IORI!
I DIDN'T KNOW YOU EVEN CAME TO THESE CONTESTS.
Aika Naito [Third-Year]
Anna Itami [Third-Year]
OH, HEY.
HUH.
NO SNIPING FROM THE THIRD-YEARS?
YOU SHOULD BE IN THE SHOW AGAIN, IORI-KUN!
DON'T THINK SO.
I'M NOT REALLY CUT OUT FOR CONTESTS.
HOW CAN YOU SAY THAT?
YOU GOT AN INDIVIDUAL AWARD LAST YEAR!
HUH... I GUESS.
HE DID...?

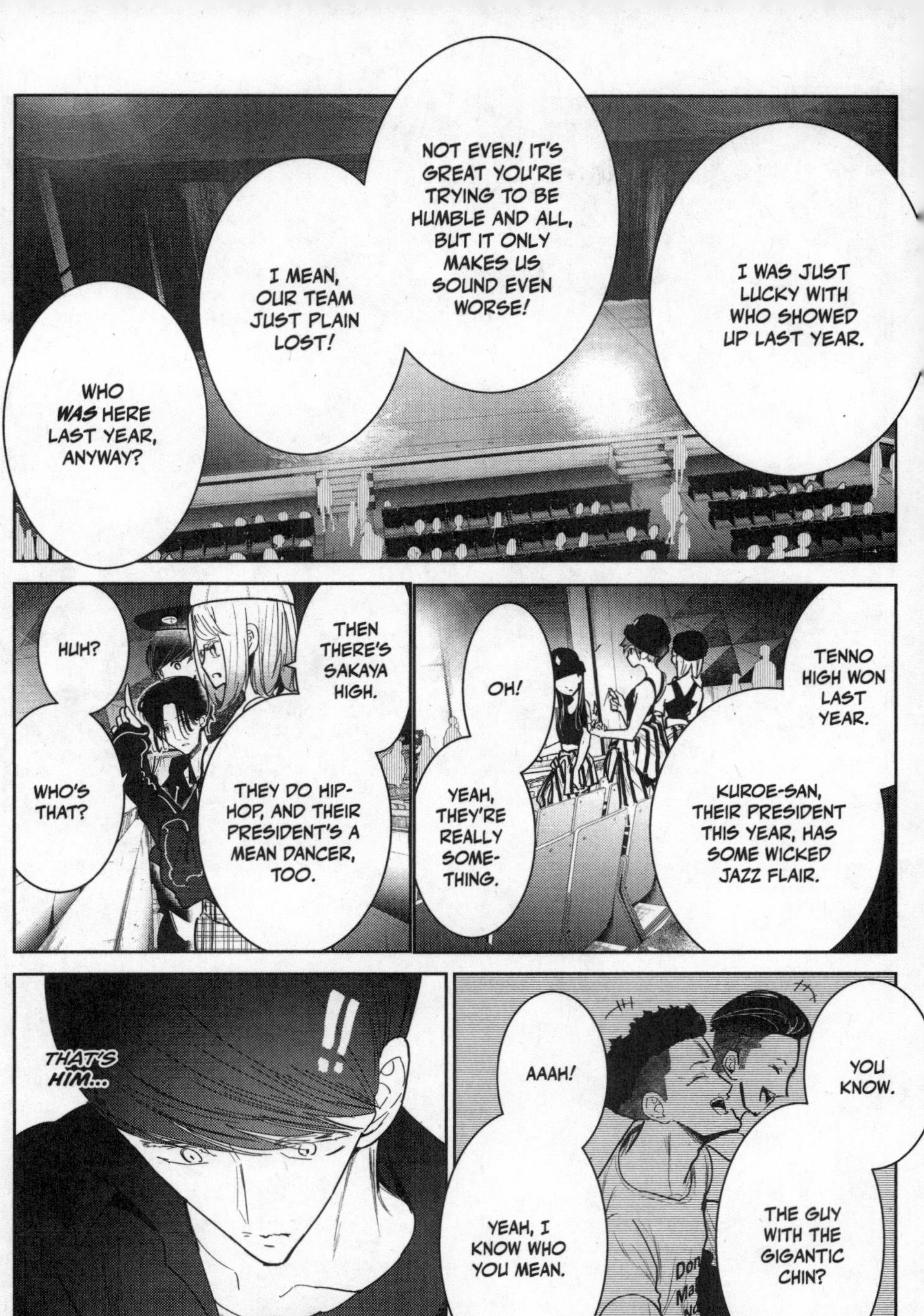
I WAS JUST LUCKY WITH WHO SHOWED UP LAST YEAR.
NOT EVEN! IT'S GREAT YOU'RE TRYING TO BE HUMBLE AND ALL, BUT IT ONLY MAKES US SOUND EVEN WORSE!
I MEAN, OUR TEAM JUST PLAIN LOST!
WHO *WAS* HERE LAST YEAR, ANYWAY?
TENNO HIGH WON LAST YEAR.
KUROE-SAN, THEIR PRESIDENT THIS YEAR, HAS SOME WICKED JAZZ FLAIR.
OH!
YEAH, THEY'RE REALLY SOME-THING.
THEN THERE'S SAKAYA HIGH.
THEY DO HIP-HOP, AND THEIR PRESIDENT'S A MEAN DANCER, TOO.
HUH?
WHO'S THAT?
YOU KNOW.
THE GUY WITH THE GIGANTIC CHIN?
AAAH!
YEAH, I KNOW WHO YOU MEAN.
!!
THAT'S HIM...

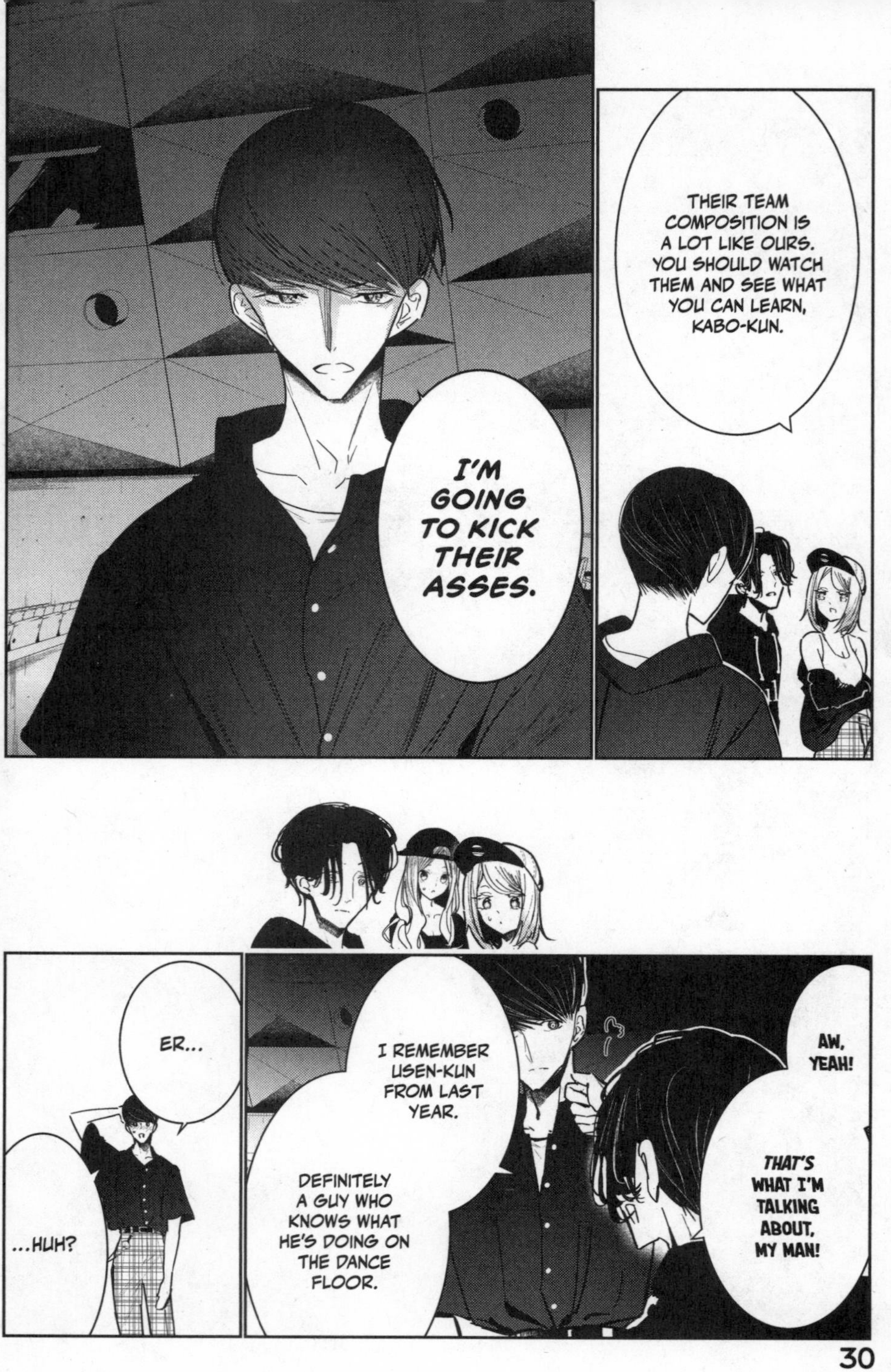
THEIR TEAM COMPOSITION IS A LOT LIKE OURS. YOU SHOULD WATCH THEM AND SEE WHAT YOU CAN LEARN, KABO-KUN.
I'M GOING TO KICK THEIR ASSES.
I REMEMBER USEN-KUN FROM LAST YEAR.
DEFINITELY A GUY WHO KNOWS WHAT HE'S DOING ON THE DANCE FLOOR.
AW, YEAH!
THAT'S WHAT I'M TALKING ABOUT, MY MAN!
ER...
...HUH?

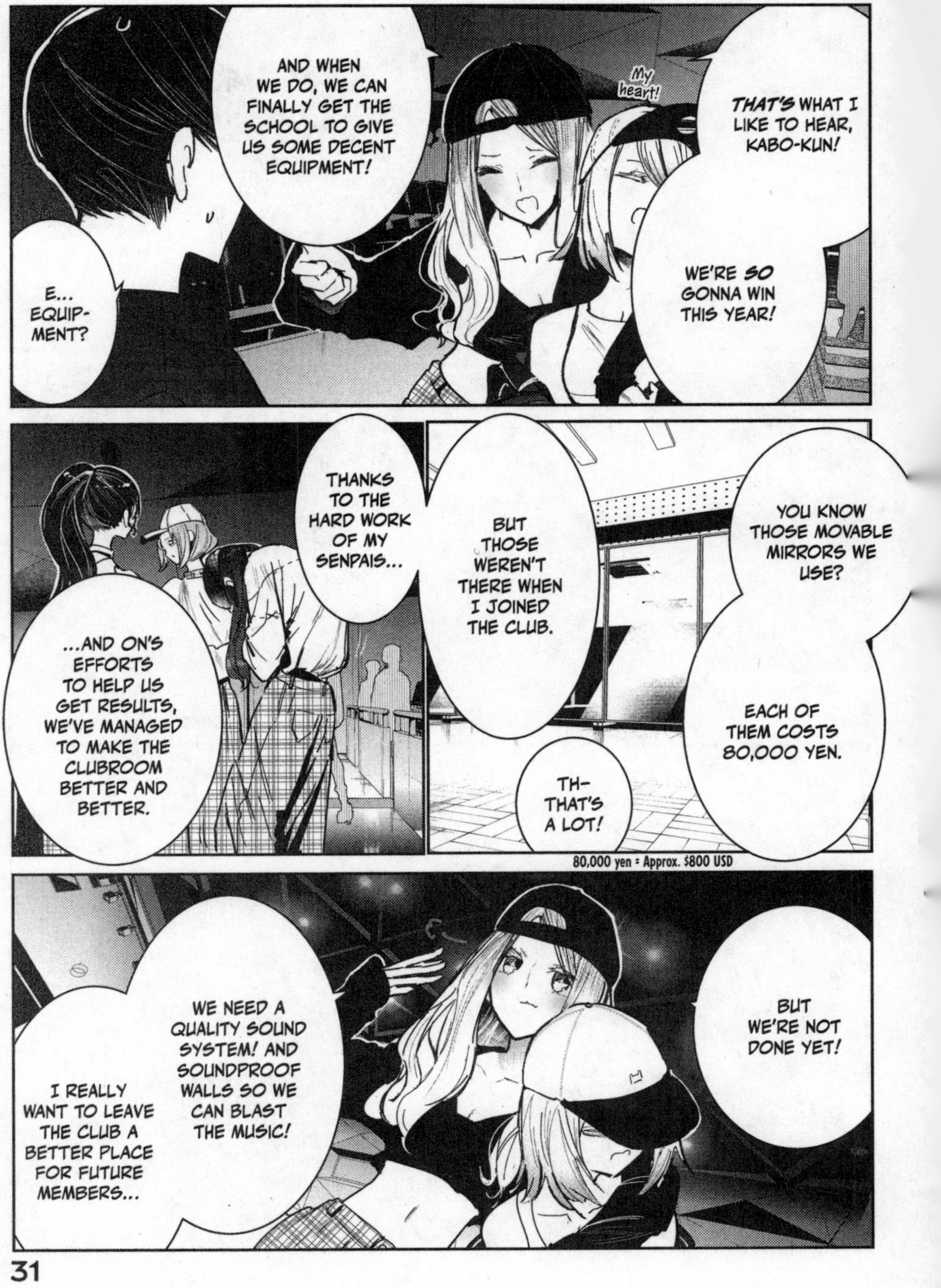
THAT'S WHAT I LIKE TO HEAR, KABO-KUN!
WE'RE SO GONNA WIN THIS YEAR!
My heart!
AND WHEN WE DO, WE CAN FINALLY GET THE SCHOOL TO GIVE US SOME DECENT EQUIPMENT!
E... EQUIPMENT?
YOU KNOW THOSE MOVABLE MIRRORS WE USE?
EACH OF THEM COSTS 80,000 YEN.
BUT THOSE WEREN'T THERE WHEN I JOINED THE CLUB.
TH-THAT'S A LOT!
THANKS TO THE HARD WORK OF MY SENPAIS...
...AND ON'S EFFORTS TO HELP US GET RESULTS, WE'VE MANAGED TO MAKE THE CLUBROOM BETTER AND BETTER.
BUT WE'RE NOT DONE YET!
WE NEED A QUALITY SOUND SYSTEM! AND SOUNDPROOF WALLS SO WE CAN BLAST THE MUSIC!
I REALLY WANT TO LEAVE THE CLUB A BETTER PLACE FOR FUTURE MEMBERS...
80,000 yen = Approx. $800 USD

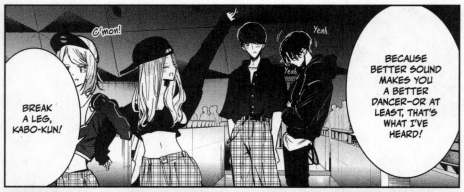

BECAUSE BETTER SOUND MAKES YOU A BETTER DANCER—OR AT LEAST, THAT'S WHAT I'VE HEARD!
Yeah.
Yeah.
C'mon!
BREAK A LEG, KABO-KUN!
THIS IS THEIR LAST YEAR...
...BUT THEY'RE STILL TRYING TO HELP THOSE WHO WILL COME AFTER THEM?
WOW...
I THINK I'M...
...FREAKING OUT A LITTLE...
I CAN'T FEEL THE BOTTOMS OF MY FEET...

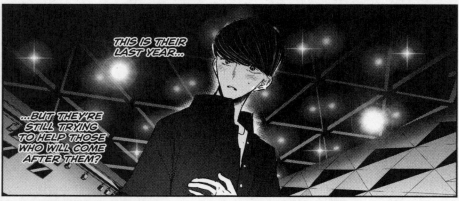

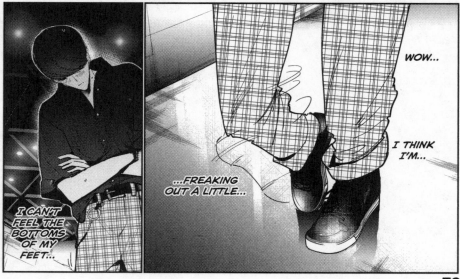

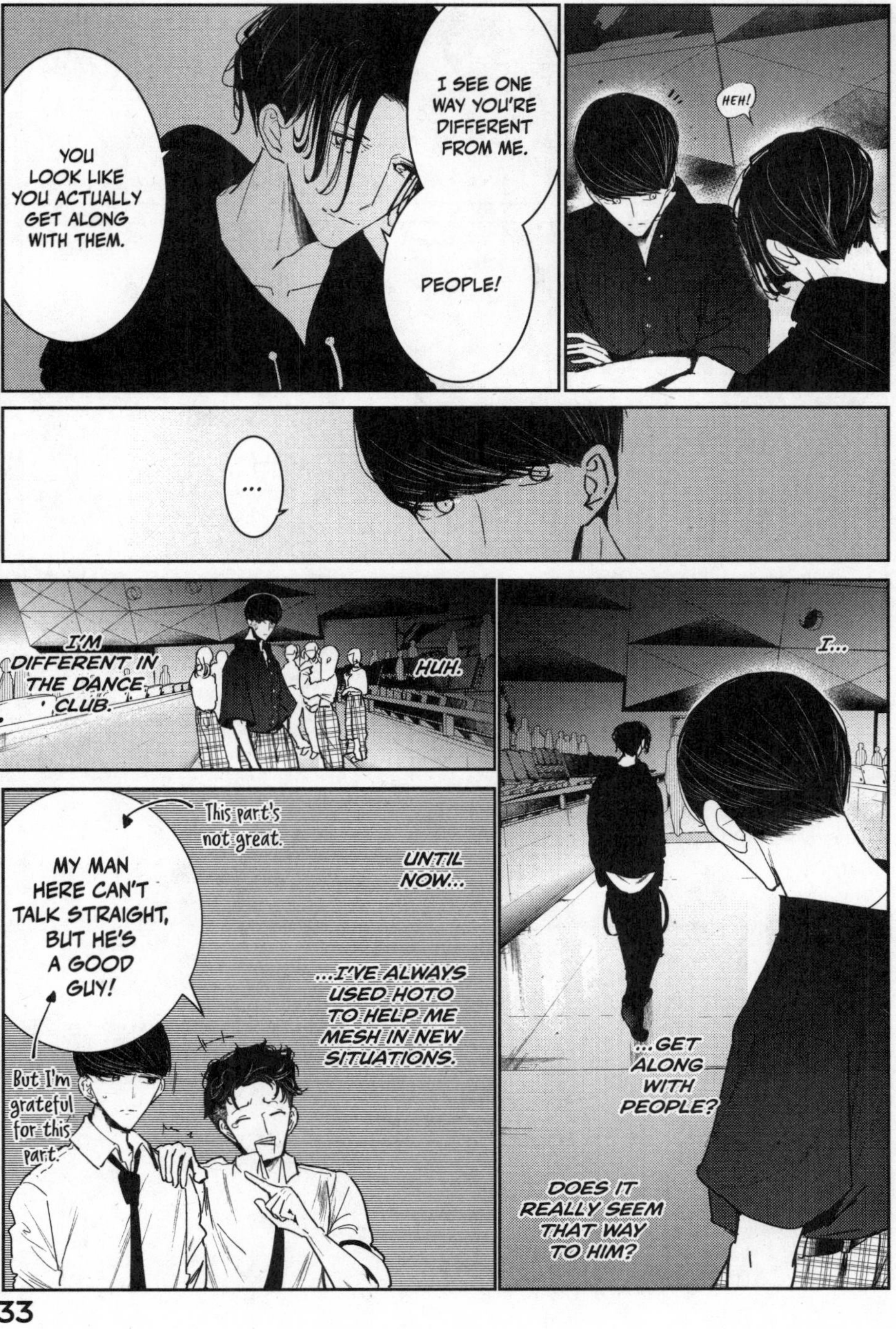
HEH!
I SEE ONE WAY YOU'RE DIFFERENT FROM ME.
PEOPLE!
YOU LOOK LIKE YOU ACTUALLY GET ALONG WITH THEM.
...
I...
...GET ALONG WITH PEOPLE?
DOES IT REALLY SEEM THAT WAY TO HIM?
HUH.
I'M DIFFERENT IN THE DANCE CLUB.
This part's not great.
UNTIL NOW...
...I'VE ALWAYS USED HOTO TO HELP ME MESH IN NEW SITUATIONS.
MY MAN HERE CAN'T TALK STRAIGHT, BUT HE'S A GOOD GUY!
But I'm grateful for this part.

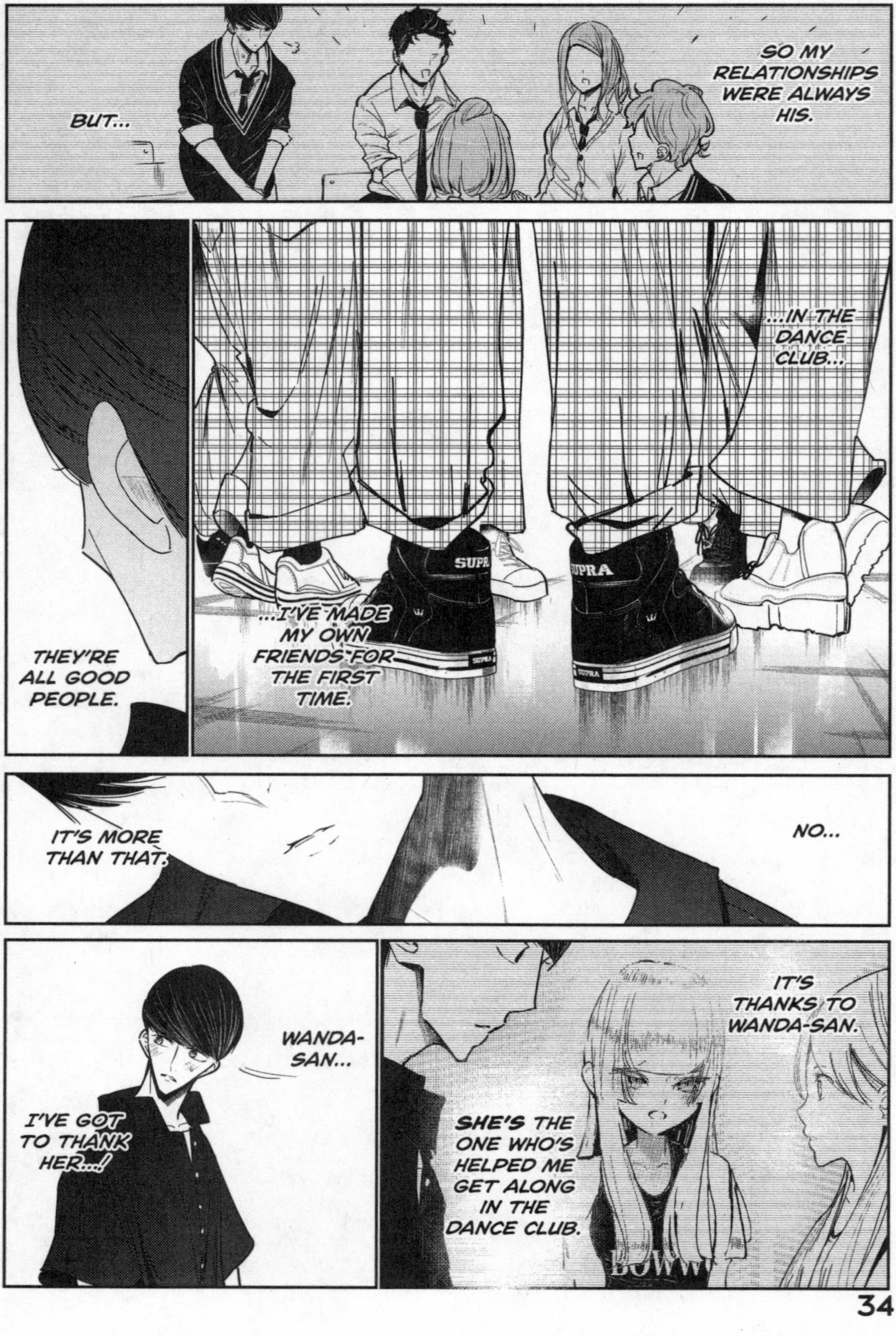
SO MY RELATIONSHIPS WERE ALWAYS HIS.
BUT...
...IN THE DANCE CLUB...
SUPRA
SUPRA
...I'VE MADE MY OWN FRIENDS FOR THE FIRST TIME.
THEY'RE ALL GOOD PEOPLE.
NO...
IT'S MORE THAN THAT.
IT'S THANKS TO WANDA-SAN.
SHE'S THE ONE WHO'S HELPED ME GET ALONG IN THE DANCE CLUB.
WANDA-SAN...
I'VE GOT TO THANK HER...!

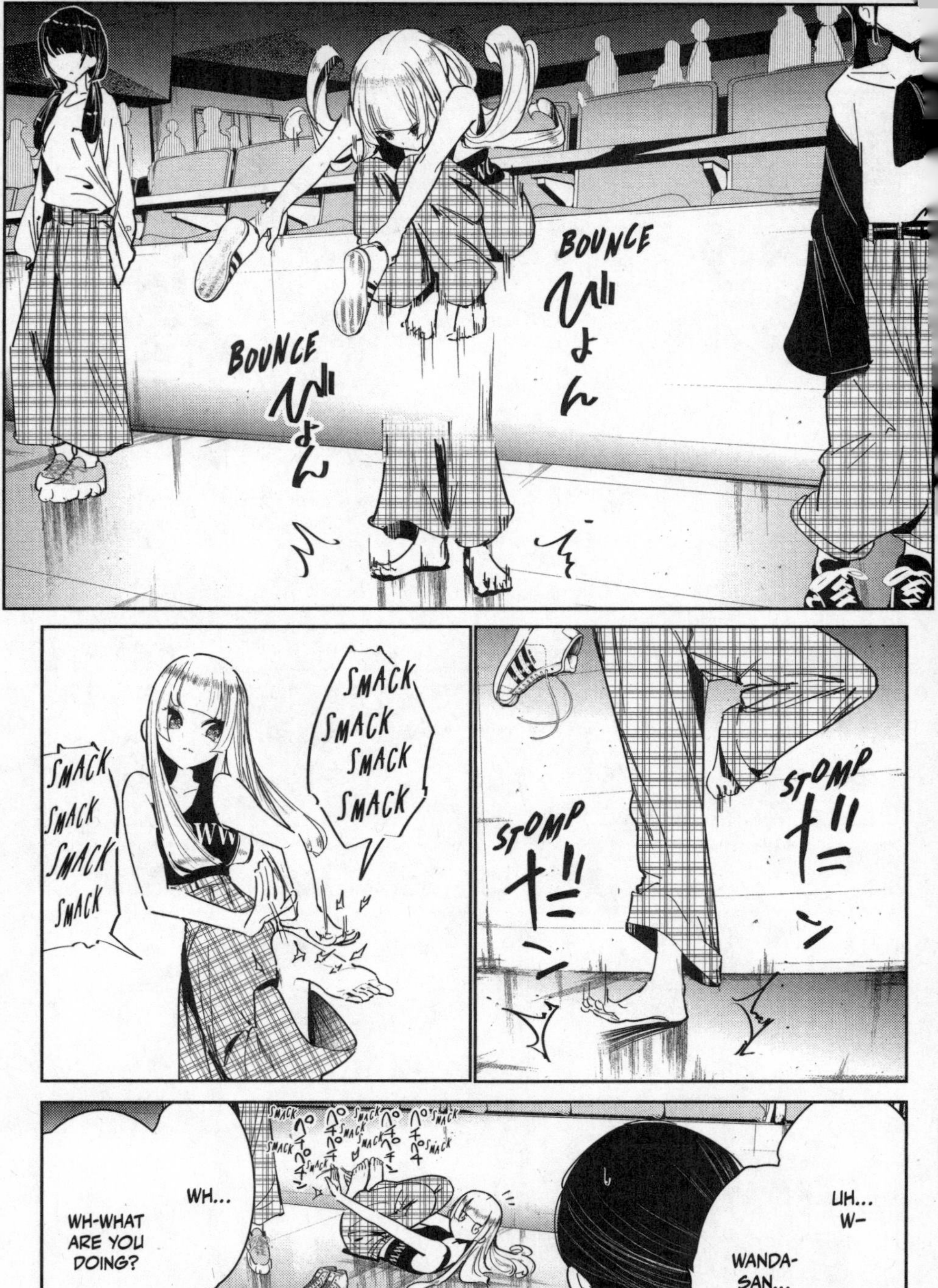
BOUNCE
びよん
BOUNCE
びよん
STOMP
ダン
STOMP
ダン
SMACK SMACK SMACK SMACK
SMACK SMACK SMACK SMACK
UH... W-
WANDA-SAN...
WH...
WH-WHAT ARE YOU DOING?

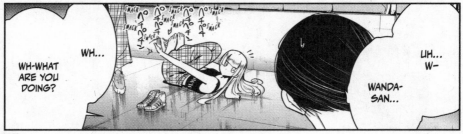

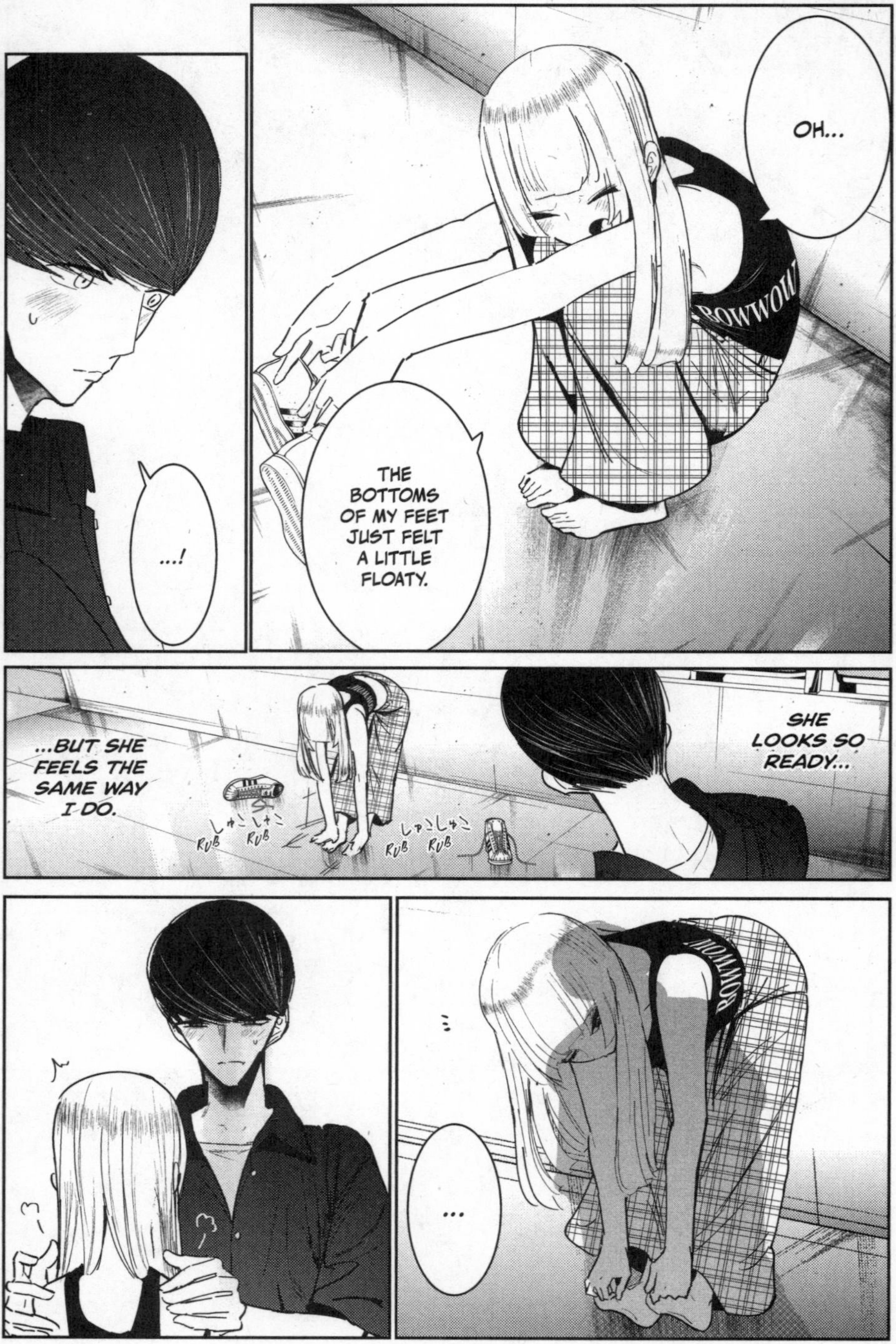
OH...
THE BOTTOMS OF MY FEET JUST FELT A LITTLE FLOATY.
...!
SHE LOOKS SO READY...
...BUT SHE FEELS THE SAME WAY I DO.
しゃこしゃこ RUB RUB
しゃこしゃこ RUB RUB
...

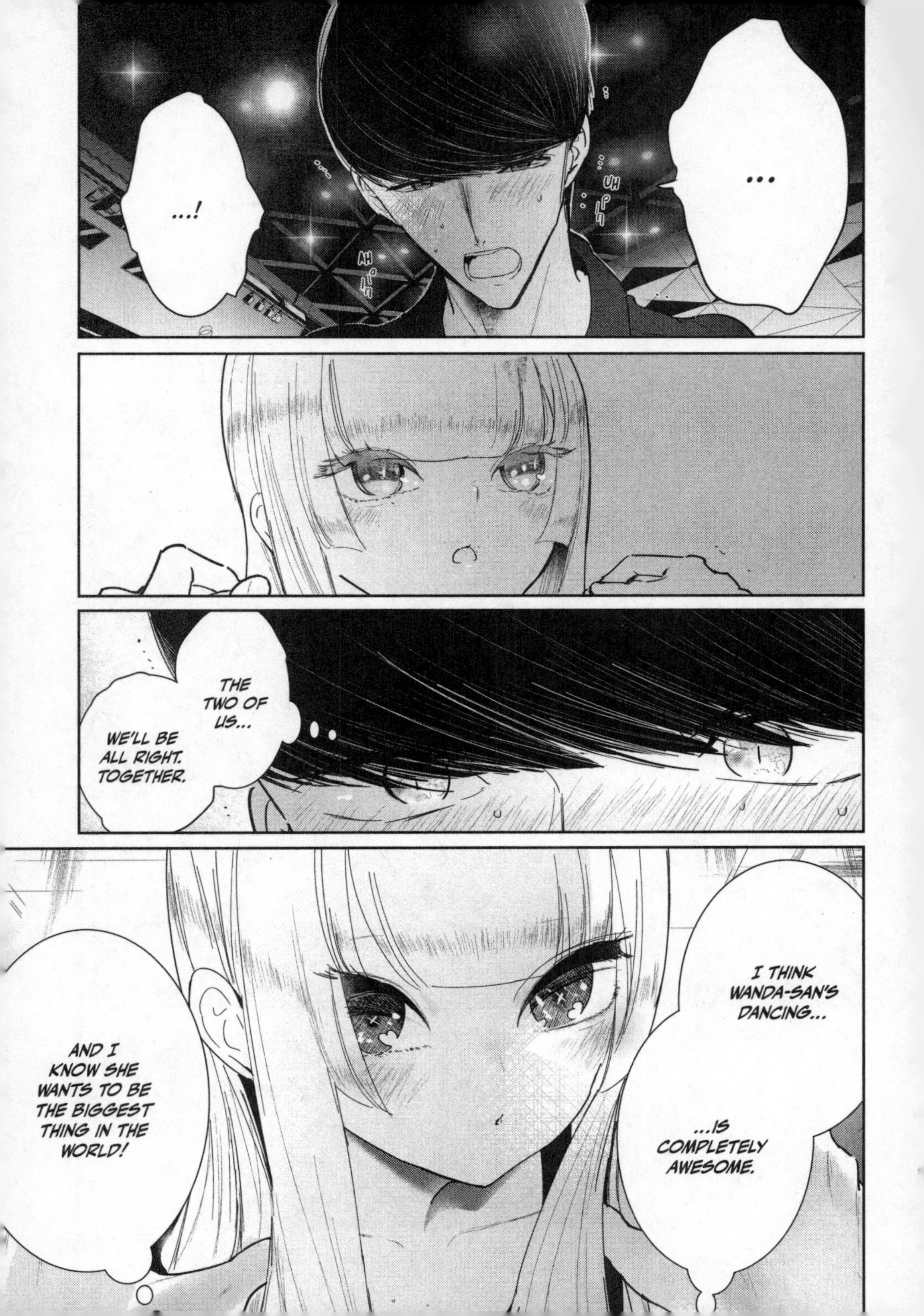
...
UH
AH
...!
THE TWO OF US...
WE'LL BE ALL RIGHT. TOGETHER.
I THINK WANDA-SAN'S DANCING...
...IS COMPLETELY AWESOME.
AND I KNOW SHE WANTS TO BE THE BIGGEST THING IN THE WORLD!

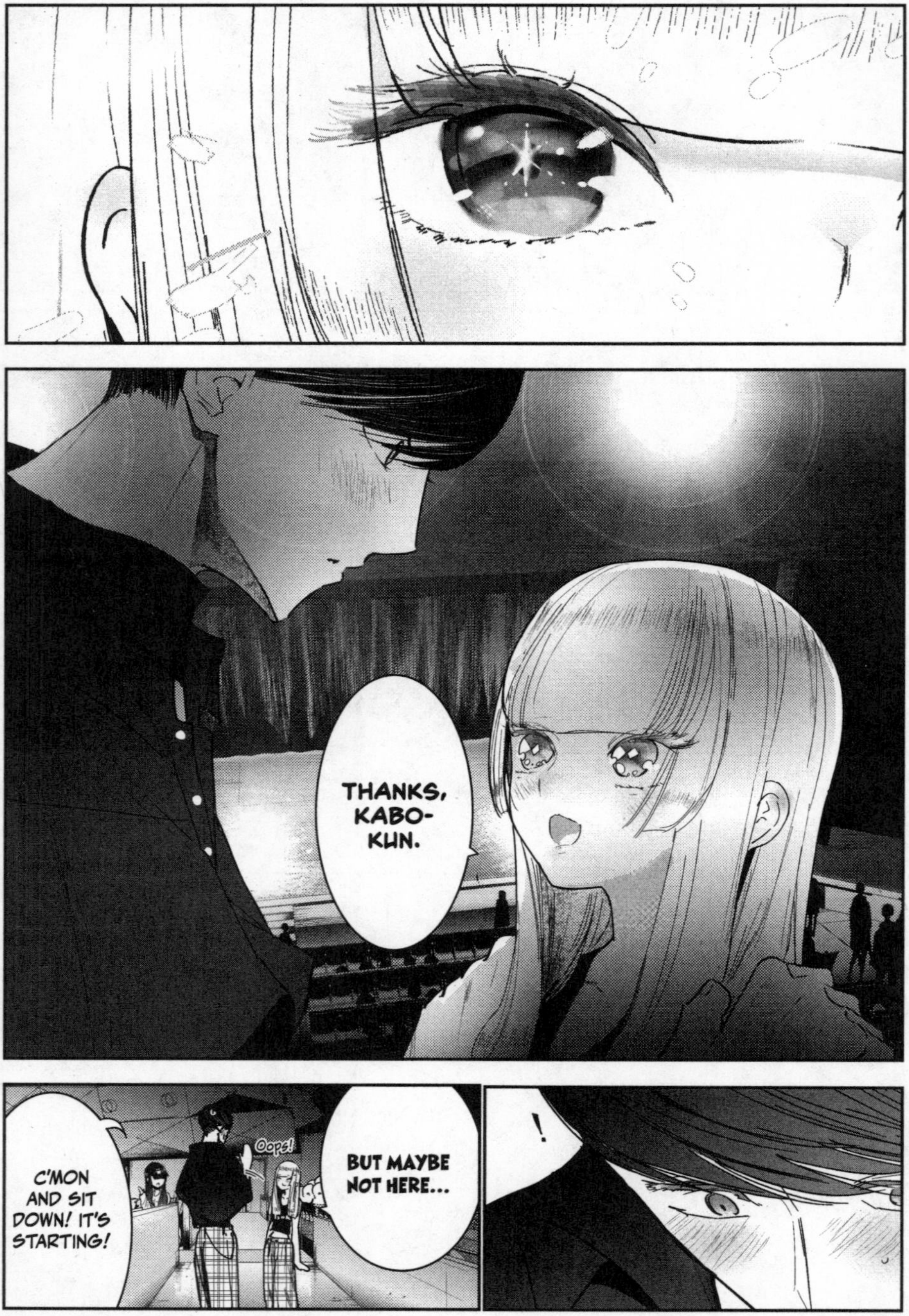
THANKS, KABO-KUN.
!
BUT MAYBE NOT HERE...
Oops!
C'MON AND SIT DOWN! IT'S STARTING!

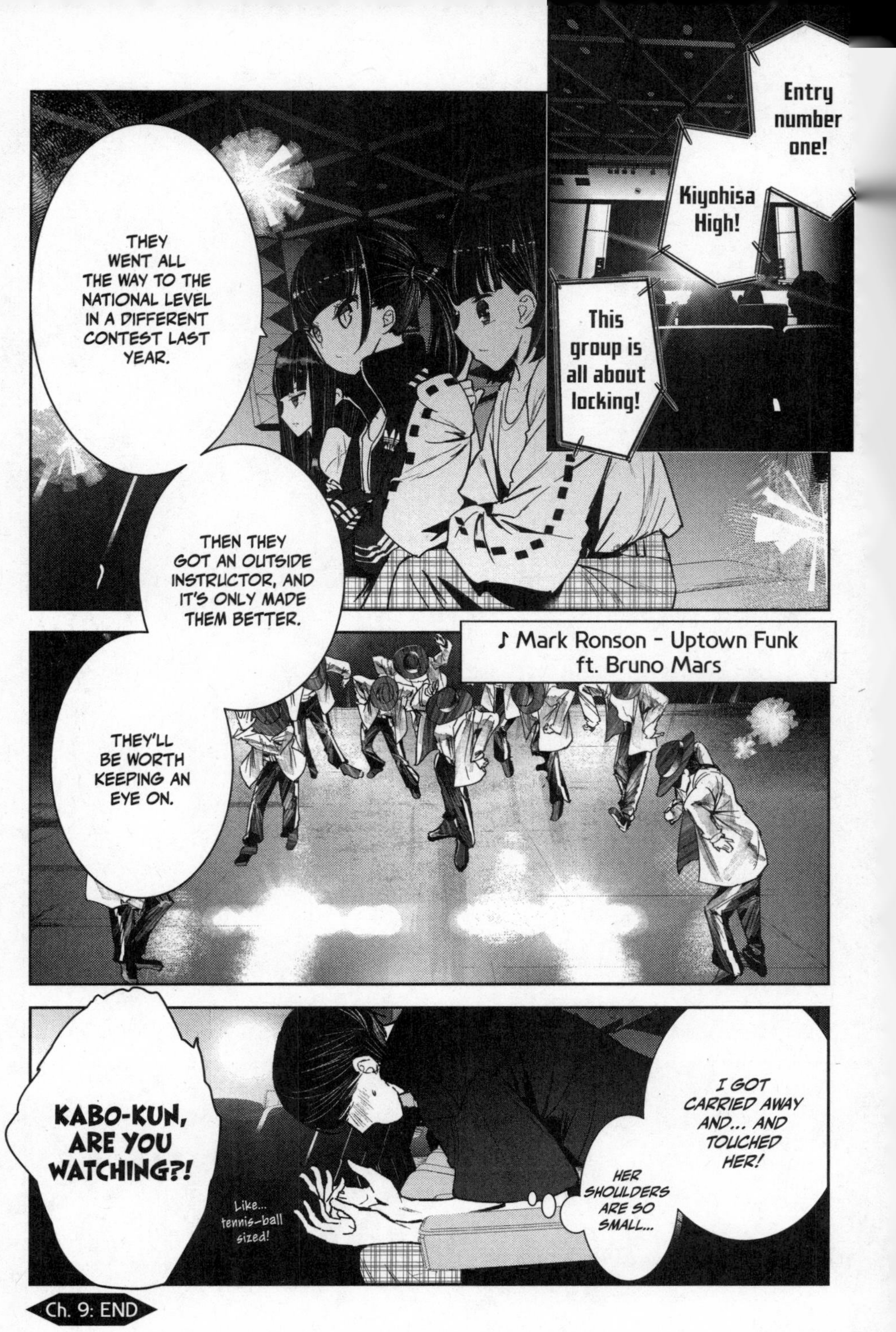
Entry number one!
Kiyohisa High!
This group is all about locking!
THEY WENT ALL THE WAY TO THE NATIONAL LEVEL IN A DIFFERENT CONTEST LAST YEAR.
THEN THEY GOT AN OUTSIDE INSTRUCTOR, AND IT'S ONLY MADE THEM BETTER.
♪ Mark Ronson - Uptown Funk ft. Bruno Mars
THEY'LL BE WORTH KEEPING AN EYE ON.
I GOT CARRIED AWAY AND... AND TOUCHED HER!
HER SHOULDERS ARE SO SMALL...
Like... tennis-ball sized!
KABO-KUN, ARE YOU WATCHING?!

Ch. 9: END

WANDANCE

Ch. 10: First Contest (Pt. 2)

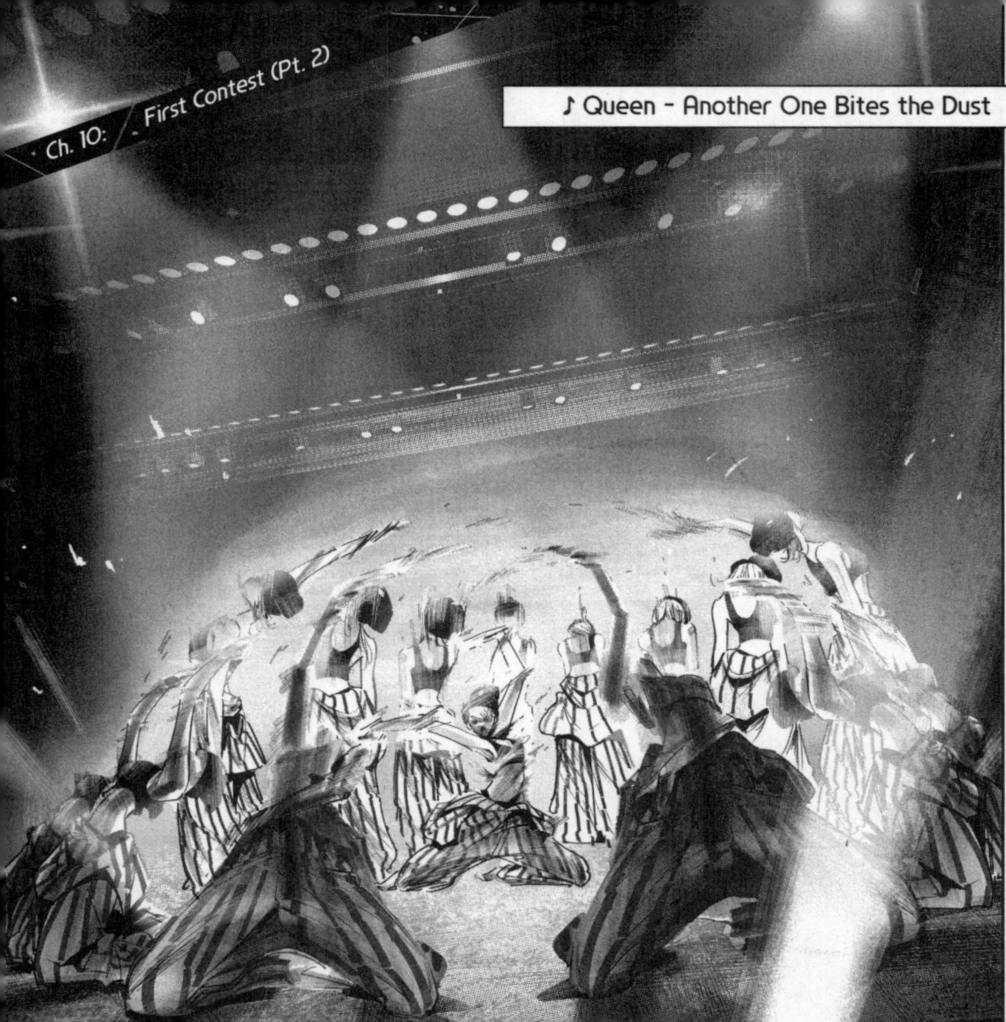
♪ Queen - Another One Bites the Dust

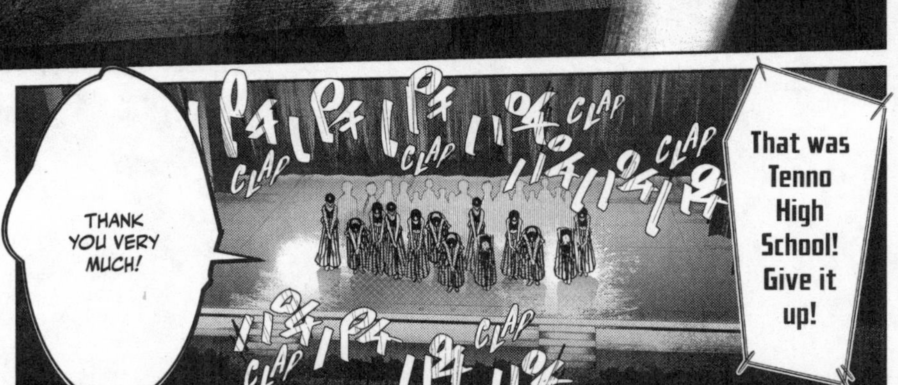
That was Tenno High School! Give it up!
CLAP
CLAP
CLAP
CLAP
CLAP
CLAP
THANK YOU VERY MUCH!

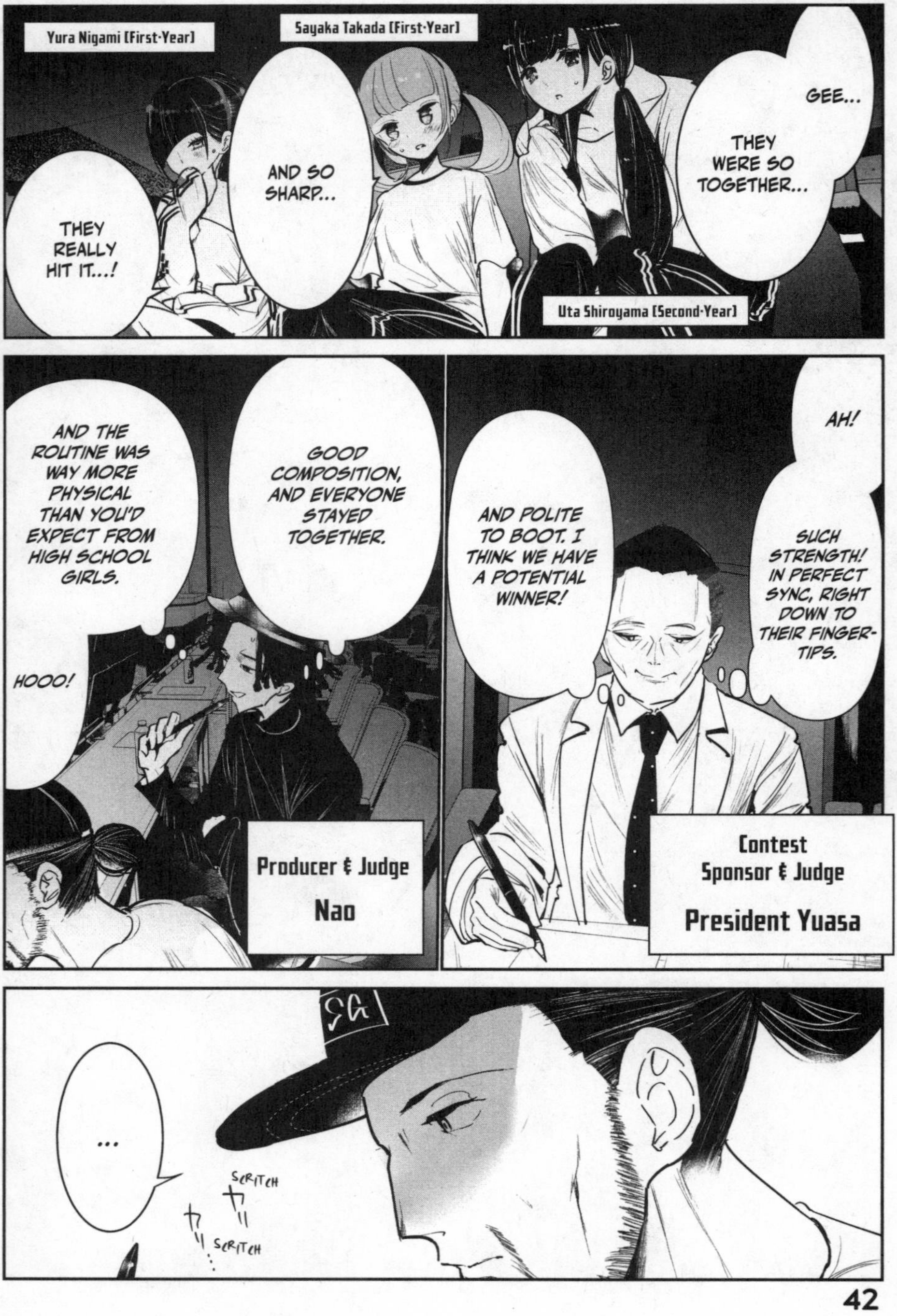
Uta Shiroyama [Second-Year]
GEE...
THEY WERE SO TOGETHER...
Sayaka Takada [First-Year]
AND SO SHARP...
Yura Nigami [First-Year]
THEY REALLY HIT IT...!
AH!
SUCH STRENGTH! IN PERFECT SYNC, RIGHT DOWN TO THEIR FINGER-TIPS.
AND POLITE TO BOOT. I THINK WE HAVE A POTENTIAL WINNER!
Contest Sponsor & Judge
President Yuasa
GOOD COMPOSITION, AND EVERYONE STAYED TOGETHER.
AND THE ROUTINE WAS WAY MORE PHYSICAL THAN YOU'D EXPECT FROM HIGH SCHOOL GIRLS.
HOOO!
Producer & Judge
Nao
...
SCRITCH
SCRITCH

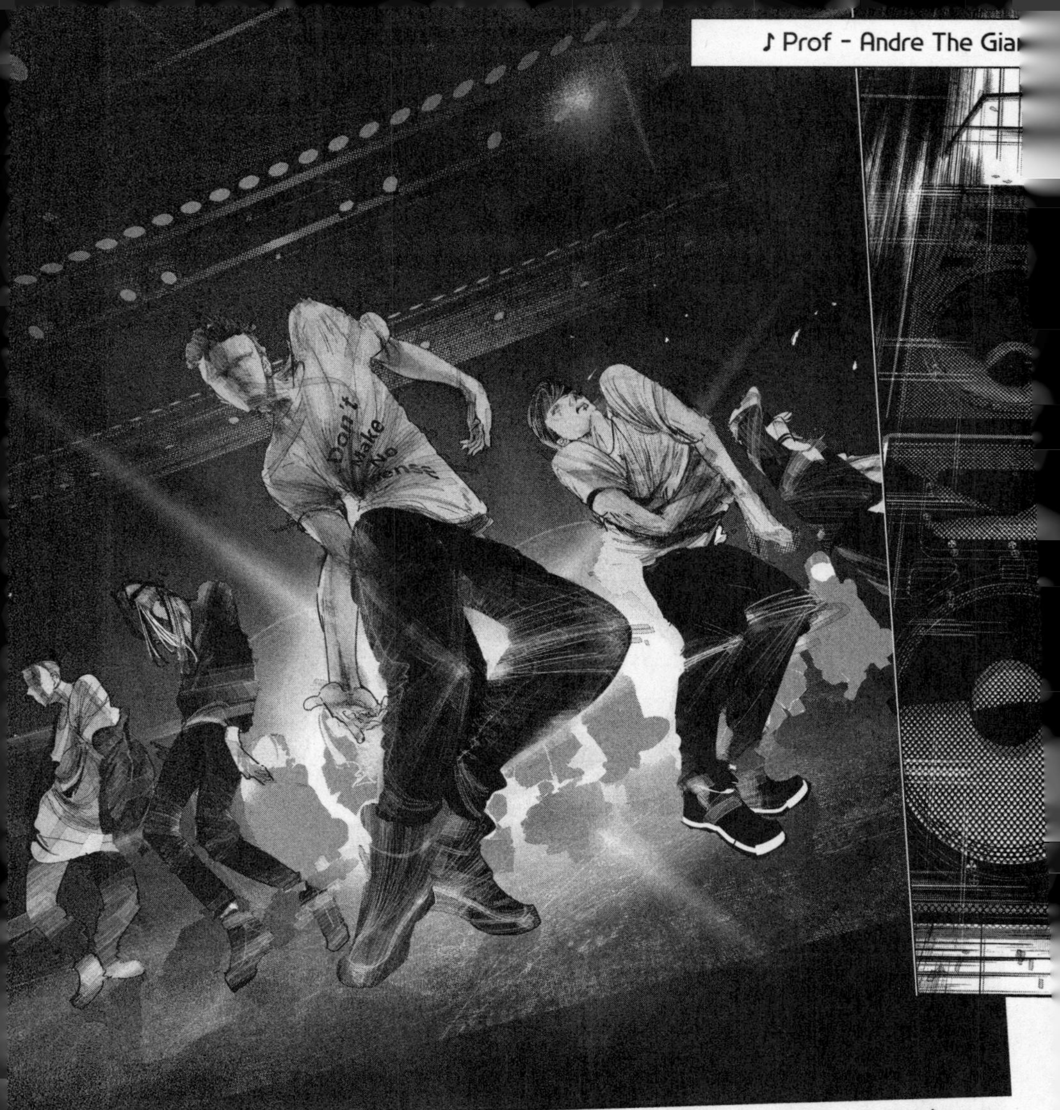
♪ Prof - Andre The Gia
Don't Make No
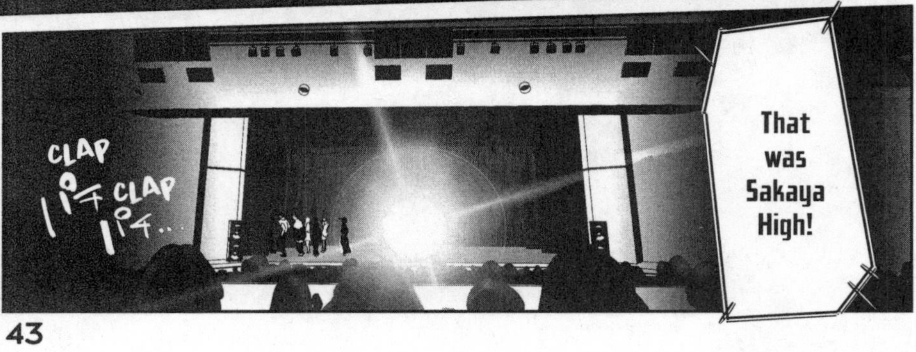
That was Sakaya High!
CLAP パチ
CLAP パチ...

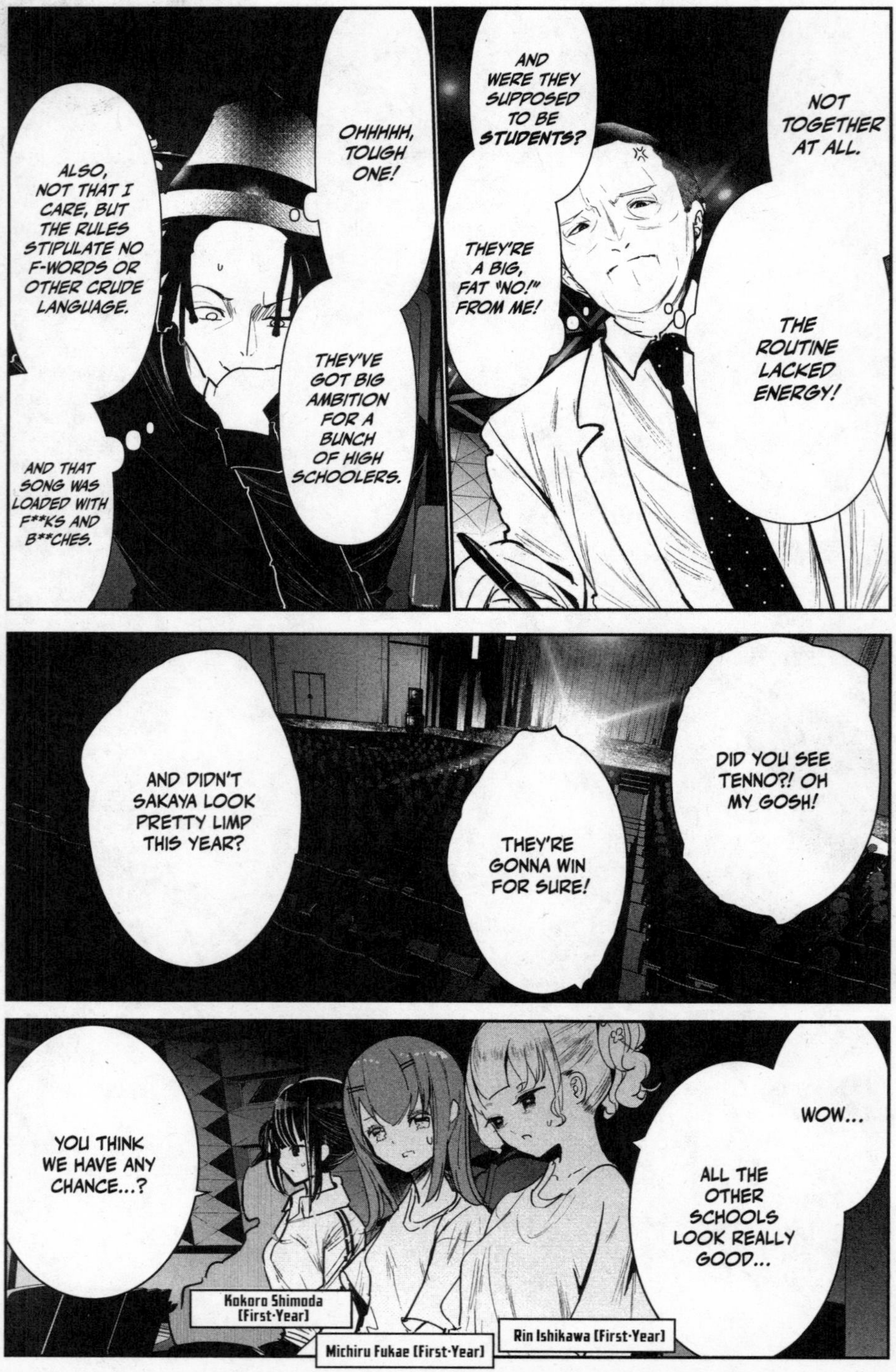
NOT TOGETHER AT ALL.
THE ROUTINE LACKED ENERGY!
AND WERE THEY SUPPOSED TO BE STUDENTS?
THEY'RE A BIG, FAT "NO!" FROM ME!
OHHHHH, TOUGH ONE!
THEY'VE GOT BIG AMBITION FOR A BUNCH OF HIGH SCHOOLERS.
ALSO, NOT THAT I CARE, BUT THE RULES STIPULATE NO F-WORDS OR OTHER CRUDE LANGUAGE.
AND THAT SONG WAS LOADED WITH F**KS AND B**CHES.
DID YOU SEE TENNO?! OH MY GOSH!
THEY'RE GONNA WIN FOR SURE!
AND DIDN'T SAKAYA LOOK PRETTY LIMP THIS YEAR?
WOW...
ALL THE OTHER SCHOOLS LOOK REALLY GOOD...
Rin Ishikawa (First-Year)
Michiru Fukae (First-Year)
Kokoro Shimoda (First-Year)
YOU THINK WE HAVE ANY CHANCE...?

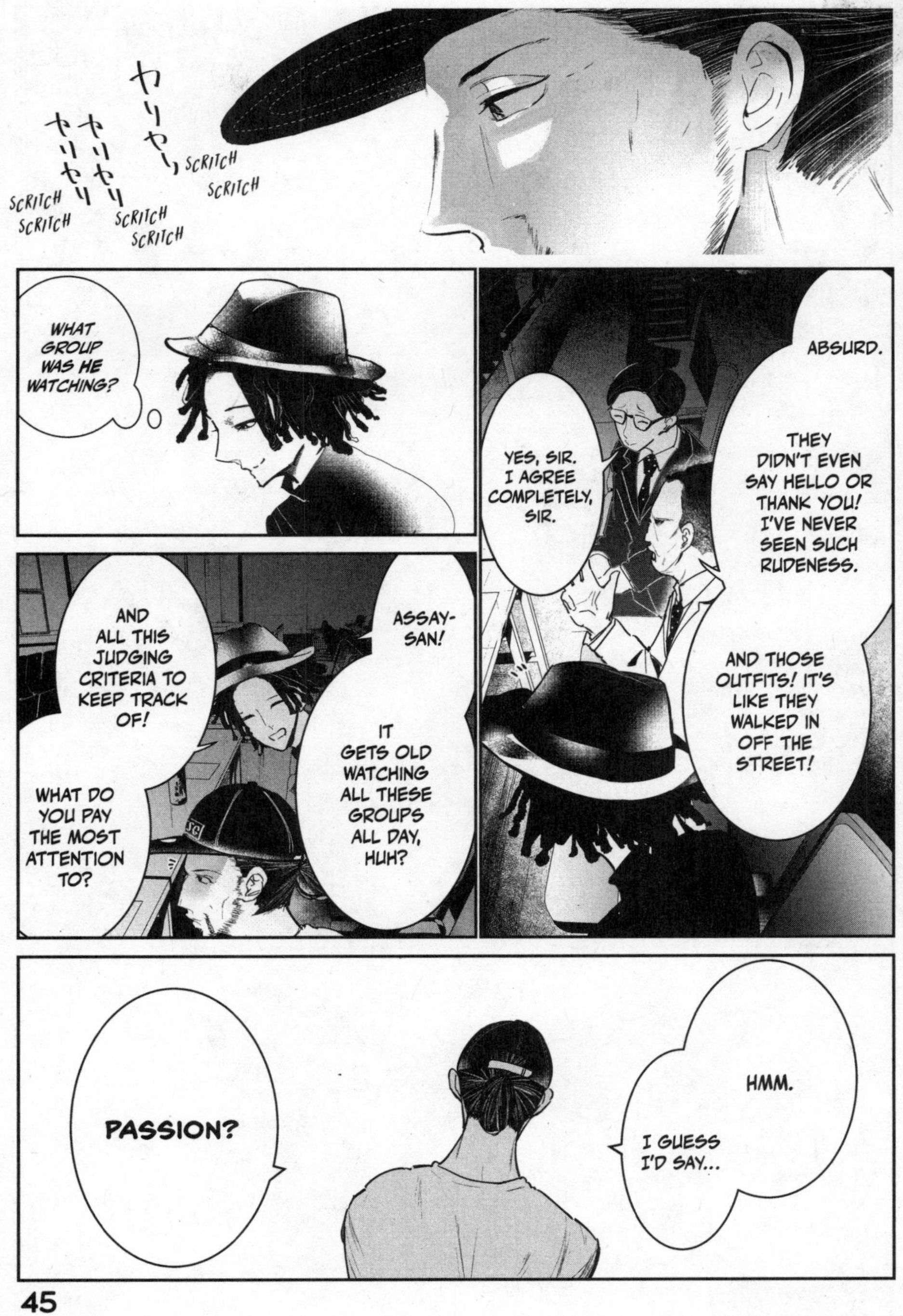
ヤリヤリ SCRITCH SCRITCH
ヤリヤリ SCRITCH SCRITCH
ヤリヤリ SCRITCH SCRITCH
ABSURD.
THEY DIDN'T EVEN SAY HELLO OR THANK YOU! I'VE NEVER SEEN SUCH RUDENESS.
YES, SIR. I AGREE COMPLETELY, SIR.
AND THOSE OUTFITS! IT'S LIKE THEY WALKED IN OFF THE STREET!
WHAT GROUP WAS HE WATCHING?
ASSAY-SAN!
IT GETS OLD WATCHING ALL THESE GROUPS ALL DAY, HUH?
AND ALL THIS JUDGING CRITERIA TO KEEP TRACK OF!
WHAT DO YOU PAY THE MOST ATTENTION TO?
HMM.
I GUESS I'D SAY...
PASSION?

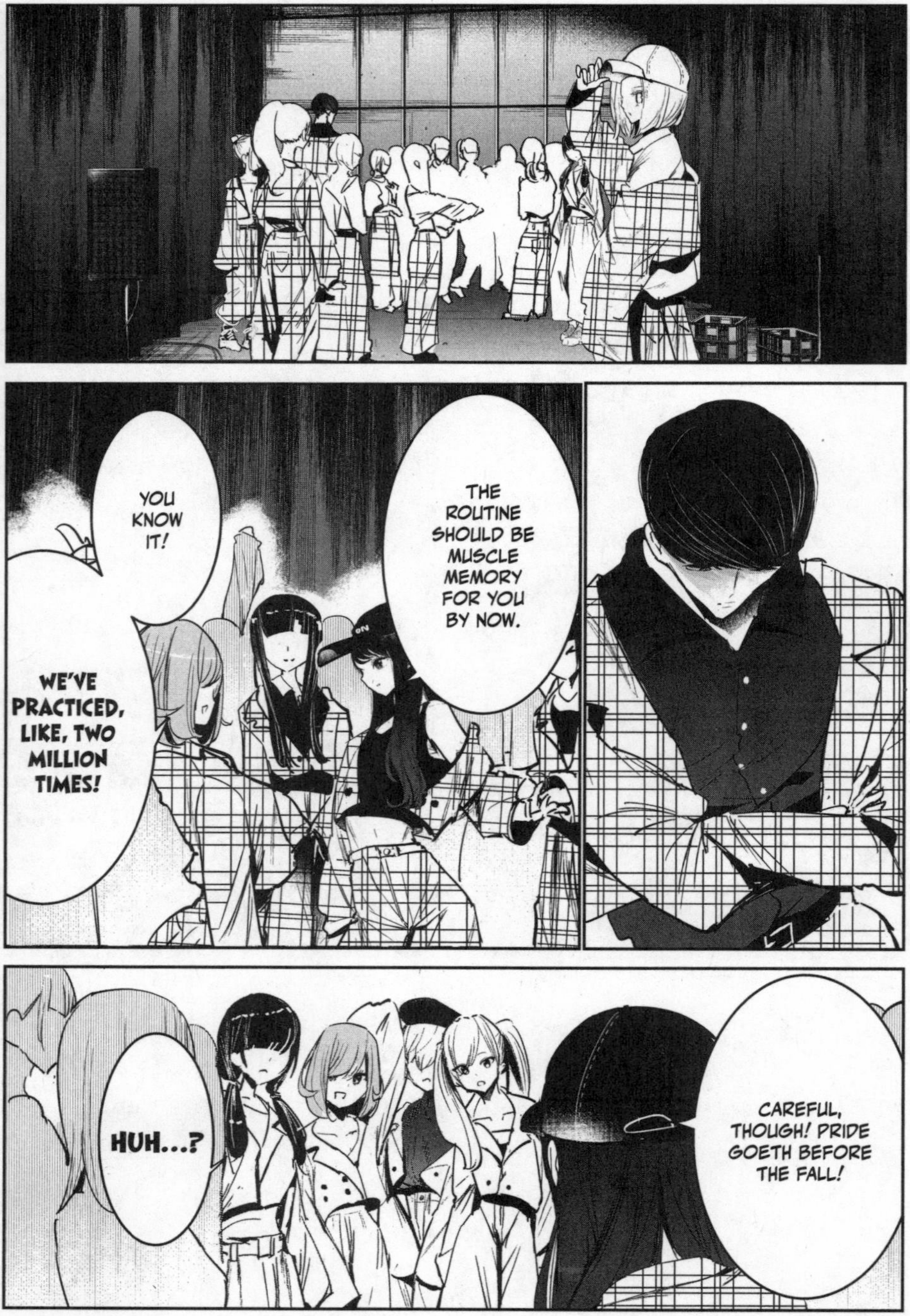
THE ROUTINE SHOULD BE MUSCLE MEMORY FOR YOU BY NOW.
YOU KNOW IT!
WE'VE PRACTICED, LIKE, TWO MILLION TIMES!
CAREFUL, THOUGH! PRIDE GOETH BEFORE THE FALL!
HUH...?

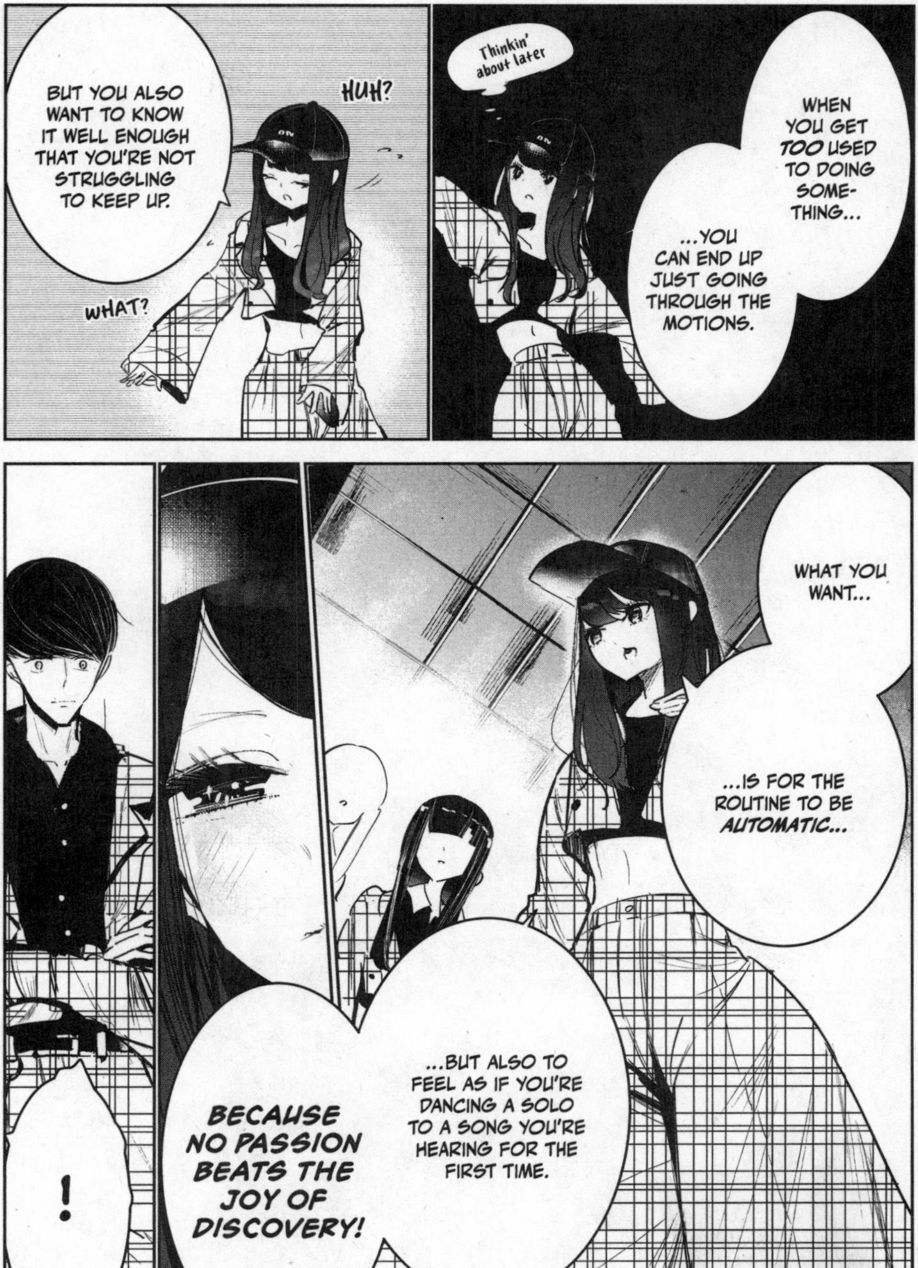
Thinkin' about later
WHEN YOU GET *TOO* USED TO DOING SOME-THING...
...YOU CAN END UP JUST GOING THROUGH THE MOTIONS.
BUT YOU ALSO WANT TO KNOW IT WELL ENOUGH THAT YOU'RE NOT STRUGGLING TO KEEP UP.
HUH?
WHAT?
WHAT YOU WANT...
...IS FOR THE ROUTINE TO BE *AUTOMATIC*...
...BUT ALSO TO FEEL AS IF YOU'RE DANCING A SOLO TO A SONG YOU'RE HEARING FOR THE FIRST TIME.
BECAUSE NO PASSION BEATS THE JOY OF DISCOVERY!
!

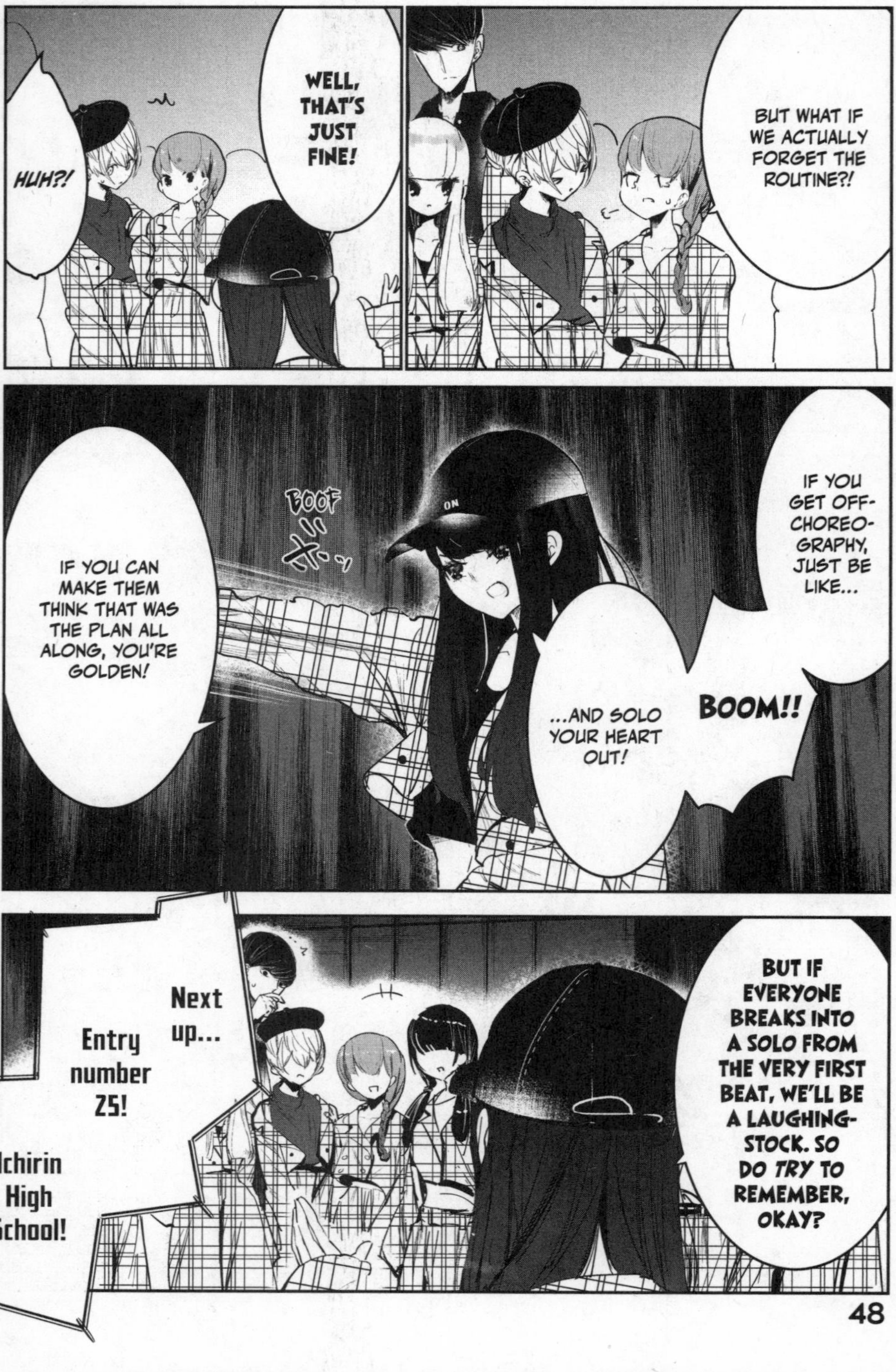
BUT WHAT IF WE ACTUALLY FORGET THE ROUTINE?!
WELL, THAT'S JUST FINE!
HUH?!
IF YOU GET OFF-CHOREOGRAPHY, JUST BE LIKE...
BOOM!!
...AND SOLO YOUR HEART OUT!
BOOF
IF YOU CAN MAKE THEM THINK THAT WAS THE PLAN ALL ALONG, YOU'RE GOLDEN!
BUT IF EVERYONE BREAKS INTO A SOLO FROM THE VERY FIRST BEAT, WE'LL BE A LAUGHING-STOCK. SO DO *TRY* TO REMEMBER, OKAY?
Next up...
Entry number 25!
Ichirin High School!

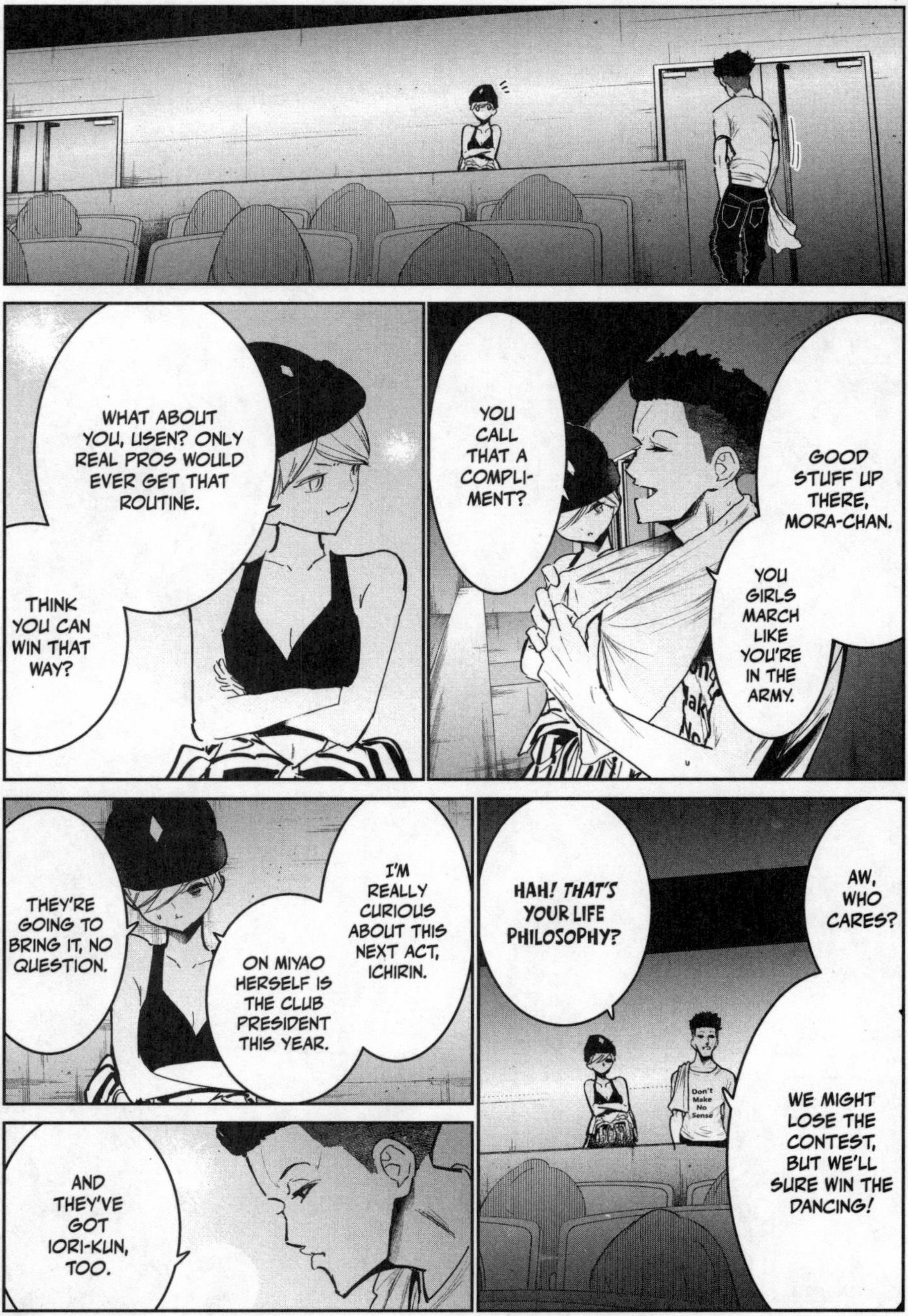
GOOD STUFF UP THERE, MORA-CHAN.
YOU GIRLS MARCH LIKE YOU'RE IN THE ARMY.
YOU CALL THAT A COMPLI-MENT?
WHAT ABOUT YOU, USEN? ONLY REAL PROS WOULD EVER GET THAT ROUTINE.
THINK YOU CAN WIN THAT WAY?
AW, WHO CARES?
HAH! *THAT'S* YOUR LIFE PHILOSOPHY?
Don't Make No Sense
WE MIGHT LOSE THE CONTEST, BUT WE'LL SURE WIN THE DANCING!
I'M REALLY CURIOUS ABOUT THIS NEXT ACT, ICHIRIN.
ON MIYAO HERSELF IS THE CLUB PRESIDENT THIS YEAR.
THEY'RE GOING TO BRING IT, NO QUESTION.
AND THEY'VE GOT IORI-KUN, TOO.

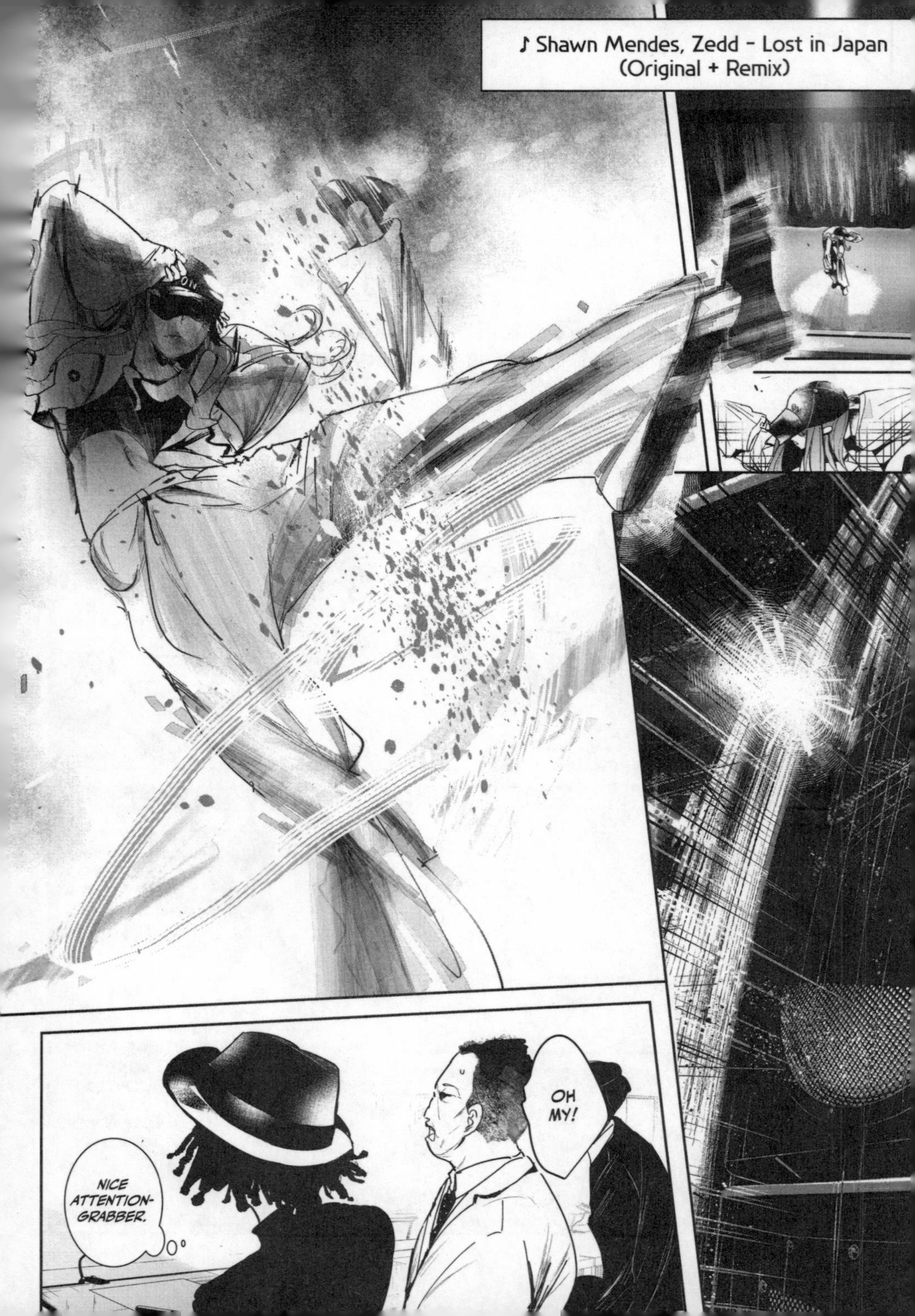
♪ Shawn Mendes, Zedd - Lost in Japan (Original + Remix)
OH MY!
NICE ATTENTION-GRABBER.

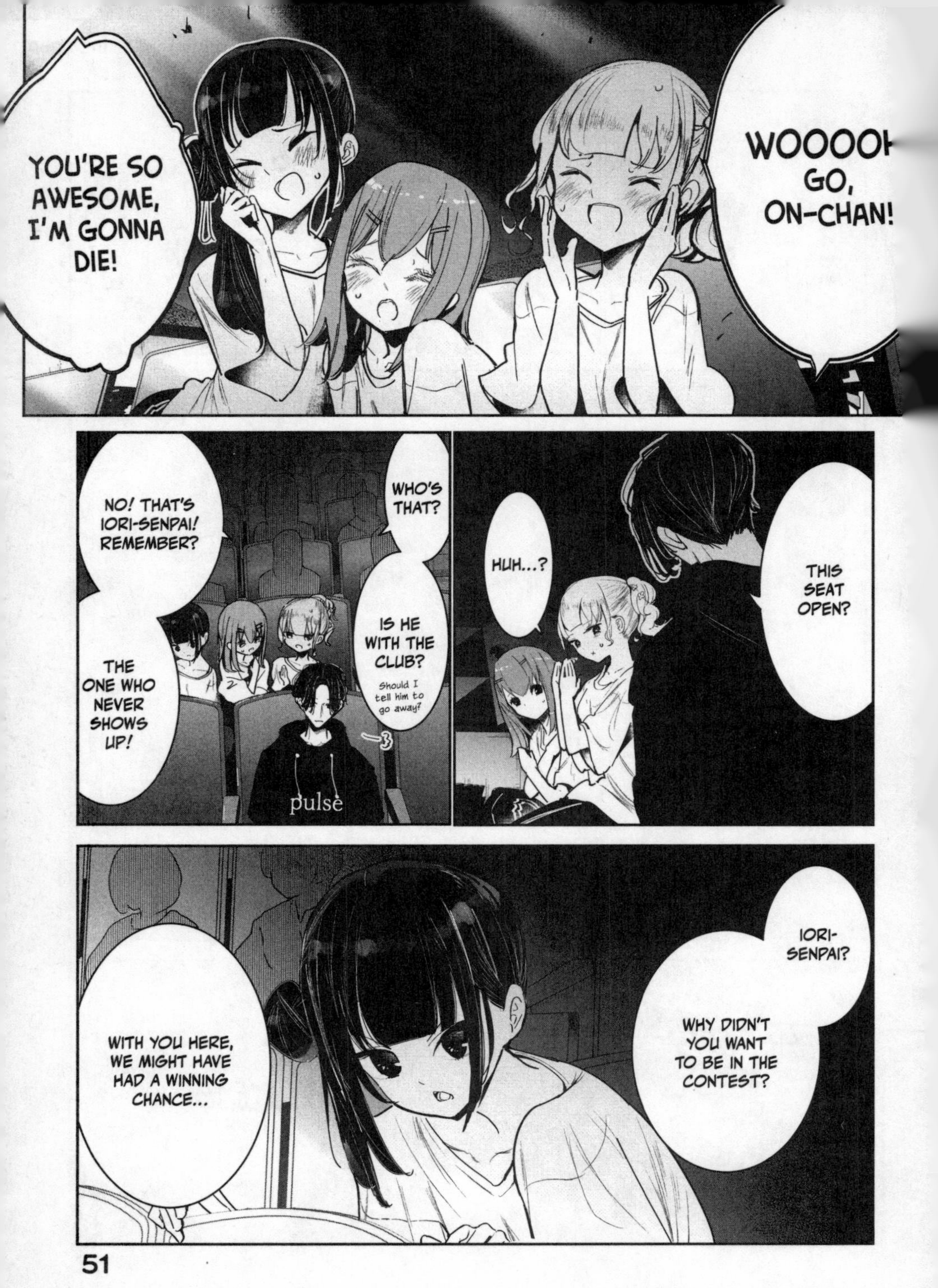
WOOOOH GO, ON-CHAN!
YOU'RE SO AWESOME, I'M GONNA DIE!
THIS SEAT OPEN?
HUH...?
WHO'S THAT?
IS HE WITH THE CLUB?
Should I tell him to go away?
NO! THAT'S IORI-SENPAI! REMEMBER?
THE ONE WHO NEVER SHOWS UP!
pulse
IORI-SENPAI?
WHY DIDN'T YOU WANT TO BE IN THE CONTEST?
WITH YOU HERE, WE MIGHT HAVE HAD A WINNING CHANCE...

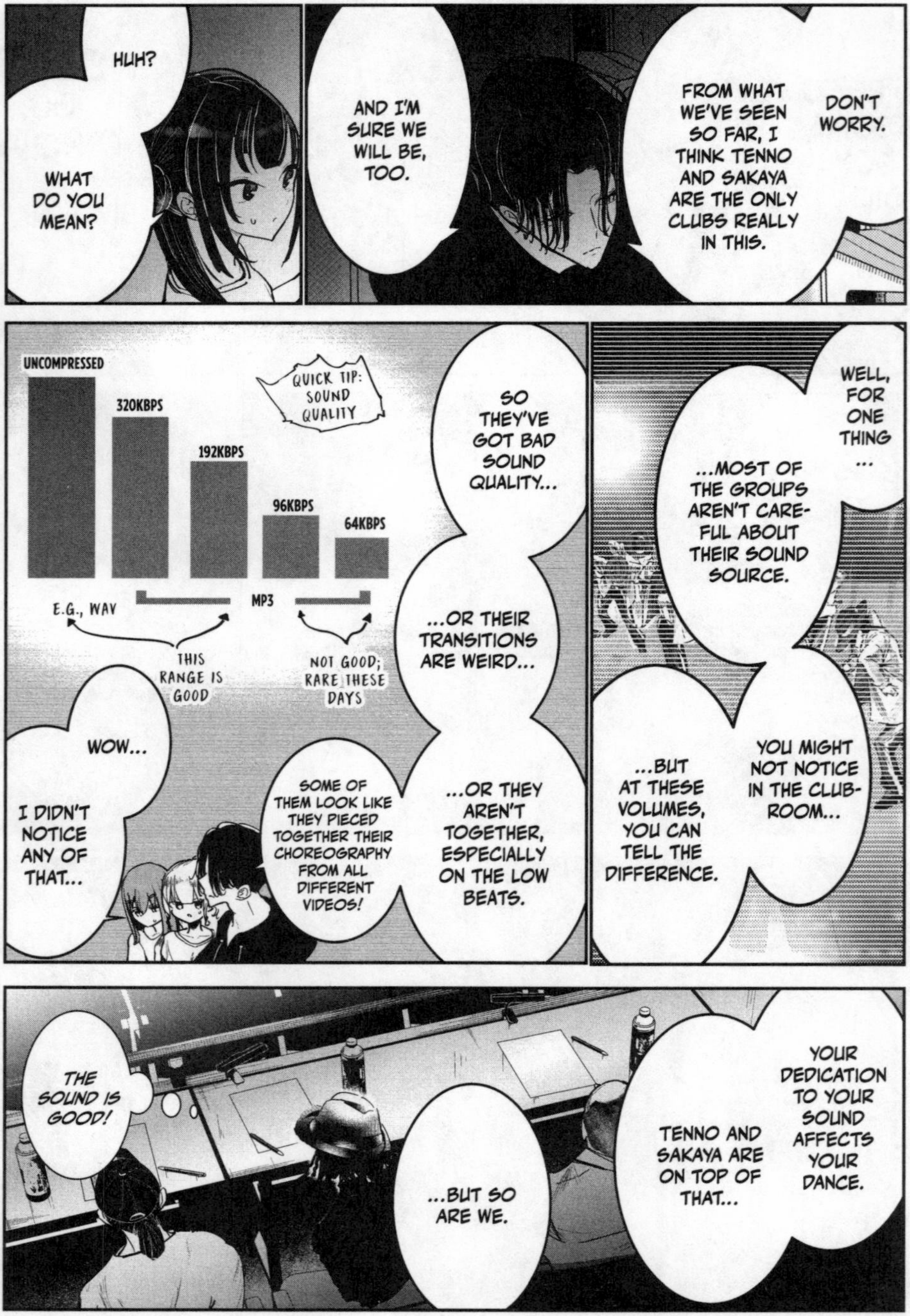
DON'T WORRY.
FROM WHAT WE'VE SEEN SO FAR, I THINK TENNO AND SAKAYA ARE THE ONLY CLUBS REALLY IN THIS.
AND I'M SURE WE WILL BE, TOO.
HUH?
WHAT DO YOU MEAN?
WELL, FOR ONE THING...
...MOST OF THE GROUPS AREN'T CARE-FUL ABOUT THEIR SOUND SOURCE.
YOU MIGHT NOT NOTICE IN THE CLUB-ROOM...
...BUT AT THESE VOLUMES, YOU CAN TELL THE DIFFERENCE.
SO THEY'VE GOT BAD SOUND QUALITY...
...OR THEIR TRANSITIONS ARE WEIRD...
...OR THEY AREN'T TOGETHER, ESPECIALLY ON THE LOW BEATS.
QUICK TIP: SOUND QUALITY
UNCOMPRESSED
320KBPS
192KBPS
96KBPS
64KBPS
E.G., WAV
MP3
THIS RANGE IS GOOD
NOT GOOD; RARE THESE DAYS
SOME OF THEM LOOK LIKE THEY PIECED TOGETHER THEIR CHOREOGRAPHY FROM ALL DIFFERENT VIDEOS!
WOW...
I DIDN'T NOTICE ANY OF THAT...
YOUR DEDICATION TO YOUR SOUND AFFECTS YOUR DANCE.
TENNO AND SAKAYA ARE ON TOP OF THAT...
...BUT SO ARE WE.
THE SOUND IS GOOD!

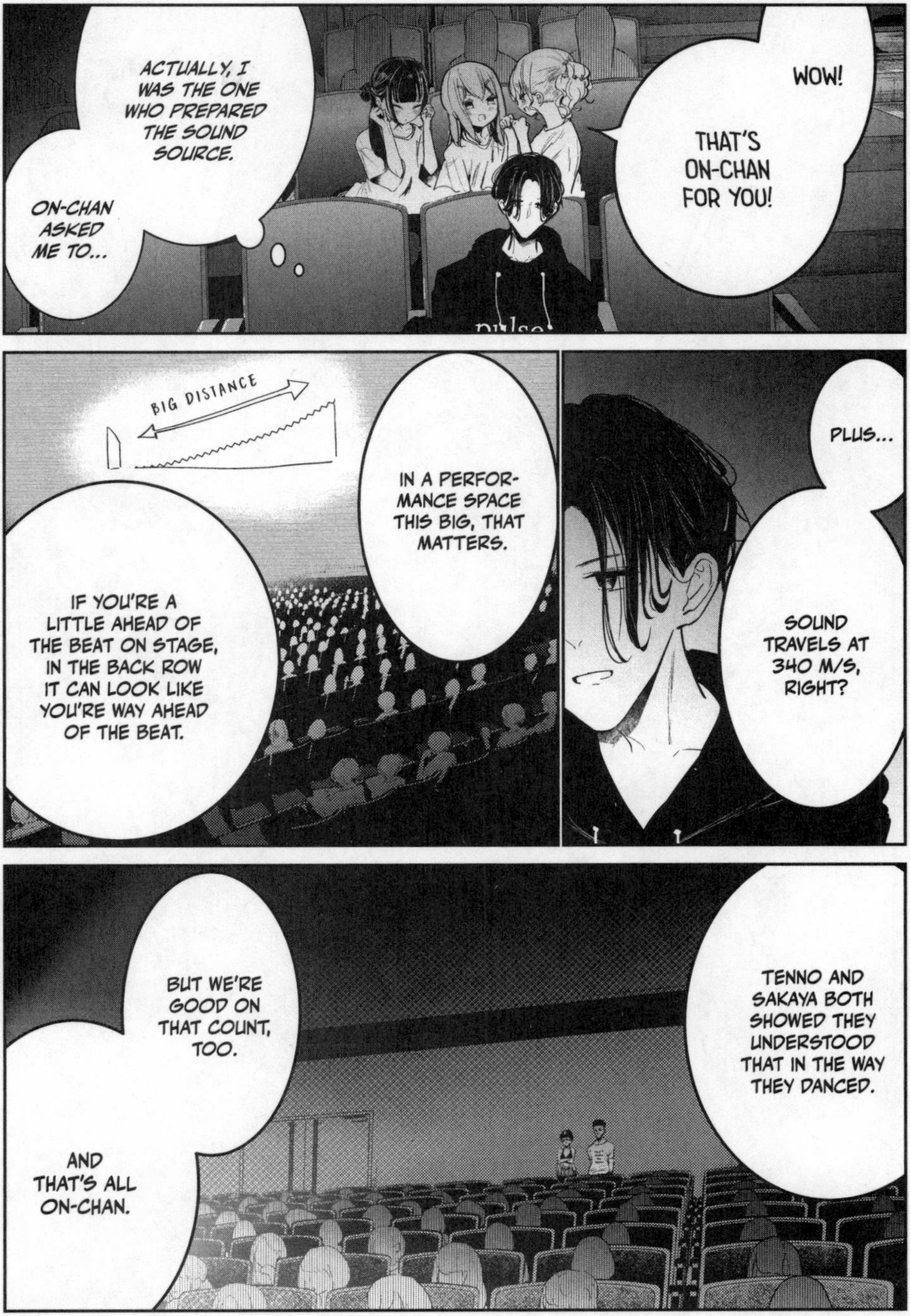
WOW!
THAT'S ON-CHAN FOR YOU!
ACTUALLY, I WAS THE ONE WHO PREPARED THE SOUND SOURCE.
ON-CHAN ASKED ME TO...
PLUS...
SOUND TRAVELS AT 340 M/S, RIGHT?
IN A PERFORMANCE SPACE THIS BIG, THAT MATTERS.
BIG DISTANCE
IF YOU'RE A LITTLE AHEAD OF THE BEAT ON STAGE, IN THE BACK ROW IT CAN LOOK LIKE YOU'RE WAY AHEAD OF THE BEAT.
TENNO AND SAKAYA BOTH SHOWED THEY UNDERSTOOD THAT IN THE WAY THEY DANCED.
BUT WE'RE GOOD ON THAT COUNT, TOO.
AND THAT'S ALL ON-CHAN.

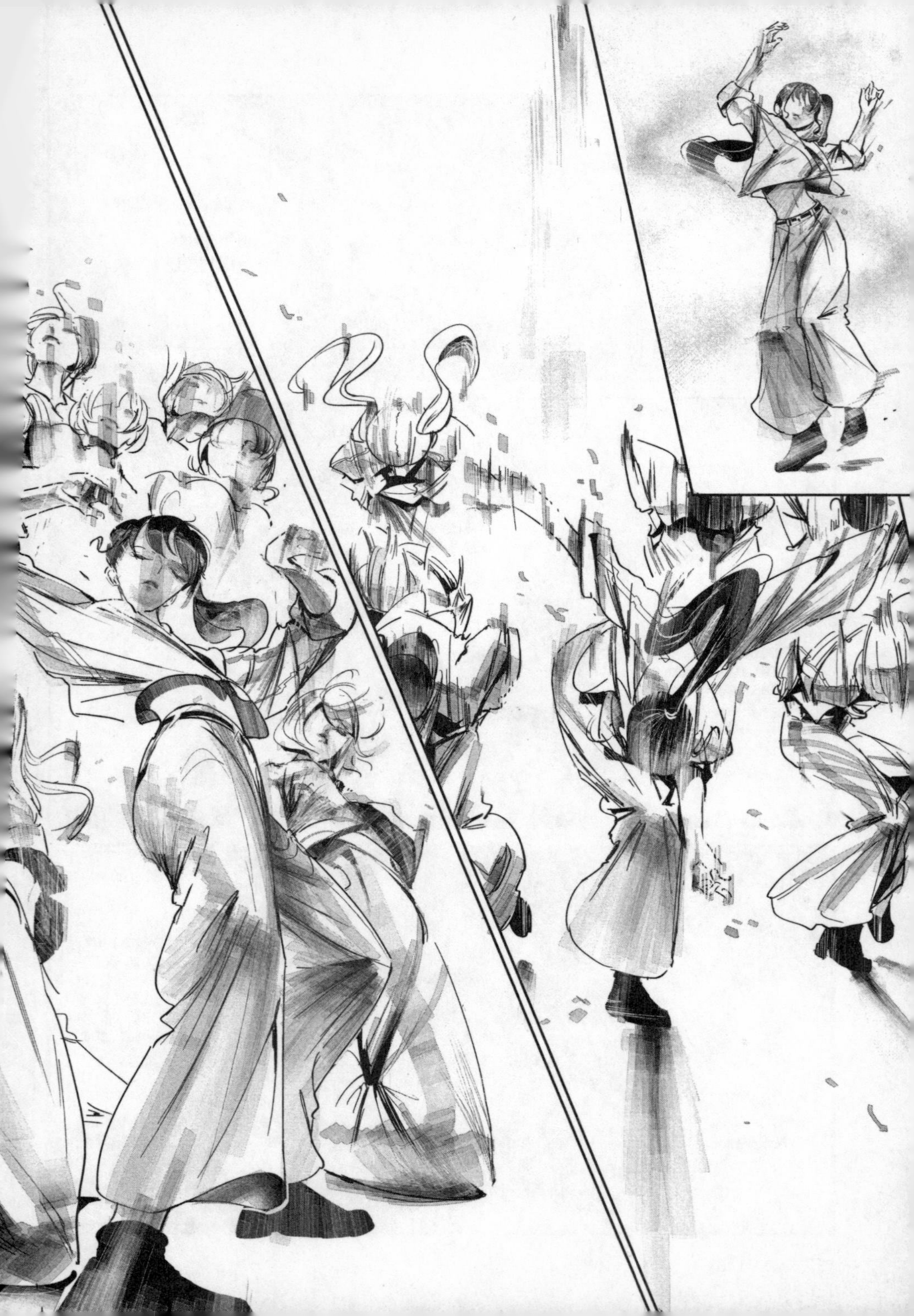

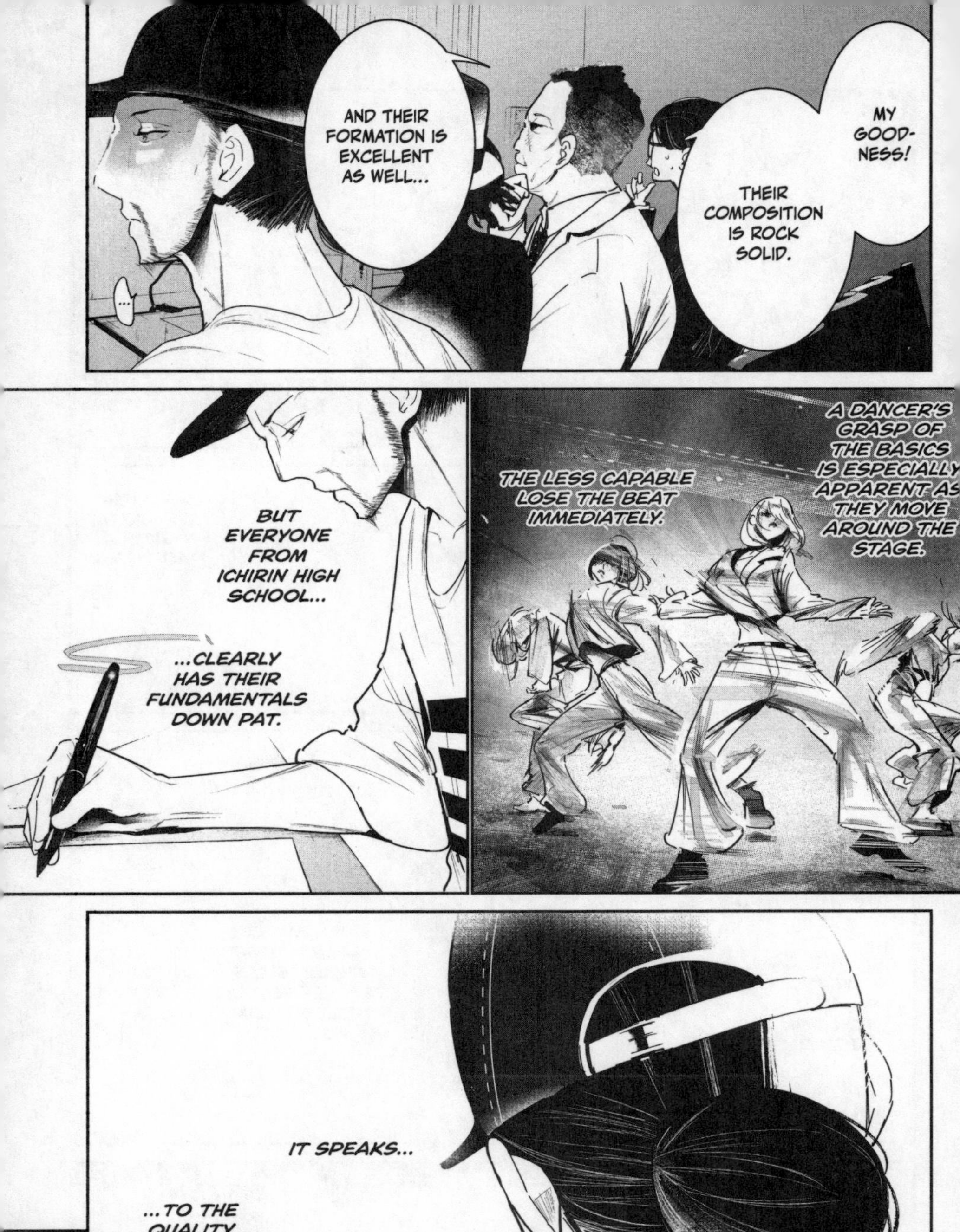
MY GOODNESS!
THEIR COMPOSITION IS ROCK SOLID.
AND THEIR FORMATION IS EXCELLENT AS WELL...
...
A DANCER'S GRASP OF THE BASICS IS ESPECIALLY APPARENT AS THEY MOVE AROUND THE STAGE.
THE LESS CAPABLE LOSE THE BEAT IMMEDIATELY.
BUT EVERYONE FROM ICHIRIN HIGH SCHOOL...
...CLEARLY HAS THEIR FUNDAMENTALS DOWN PAT.
IT SPEAKS...
...TO THE QUALITY OF THEIR PRACTICE.

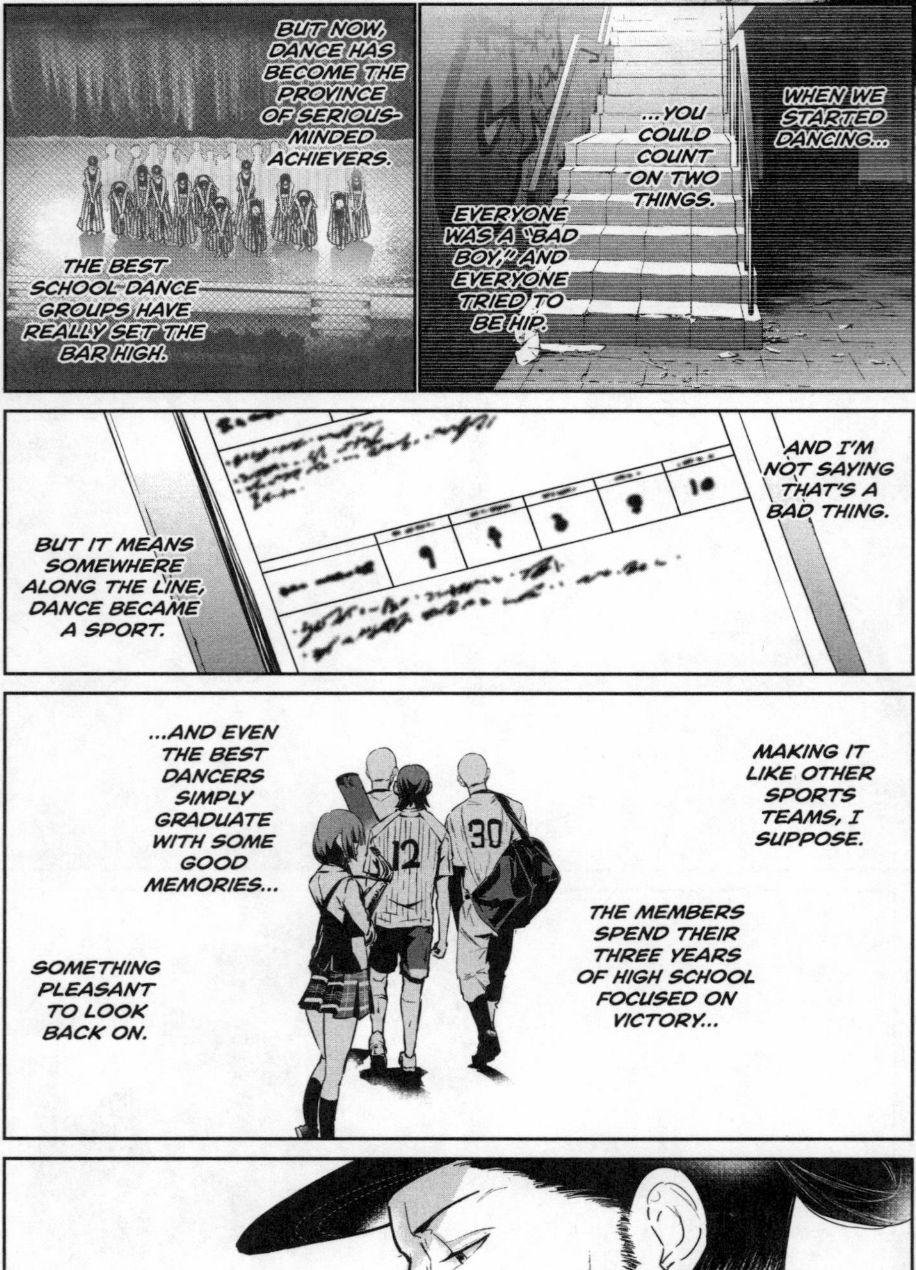
WHEN WE STARTED DANCING...
...YOU COULD COUNT ON TWO THINGS.
EVERYONE WAS A "BAD BOY," AND EVERYONE TRIED TO BE HIP.
BUT NOW, DANCE HAS BECOME THE PROVINCE OF SERIOUS-MINDED ACHIEVERS.
THE BEST SCHOOL DANCE GROUPS HAVE REALLY SET THE BAR HIGH.
AND I'M NOT SAYING THAT'S A BAD THING.
BUT IT MEANS SOMEWHERE ALONG THE LINE, DANCE BECAME A SPORT.
MAKING IT LIKE OTHER SPORTS TEAMS, I SUPPOSE.
THE MEMBERS SPEND THEIR THREE YEARS OF HIGH SCHOOL FOCUSED ON VICTORY...
...AND EVEN THE BEST DANCERS SIMPLY GRADUATE WITH SOME GOOD MEMORIES...
SOMETHING PLEASANT TO LOOK BACK ON.

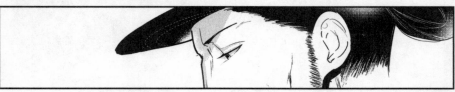

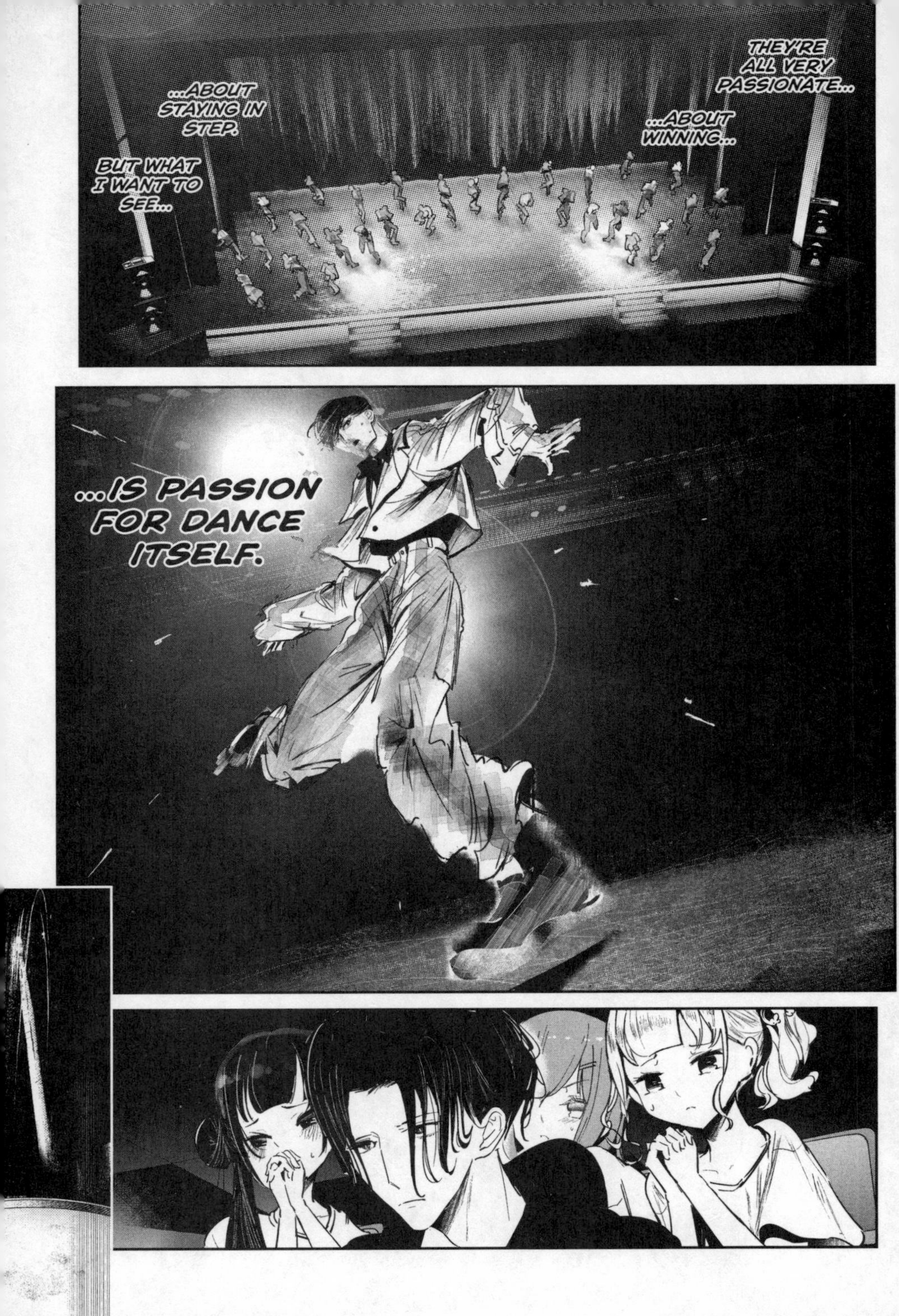
THEY'RE ALL VERY PASSIONATE...
...ABOUT WINNING...
...ABOUT STAYING IN STEP.
BUT WHAT I WANT TO SEE...
...IS PASSION FOR DANCE ITSELF.

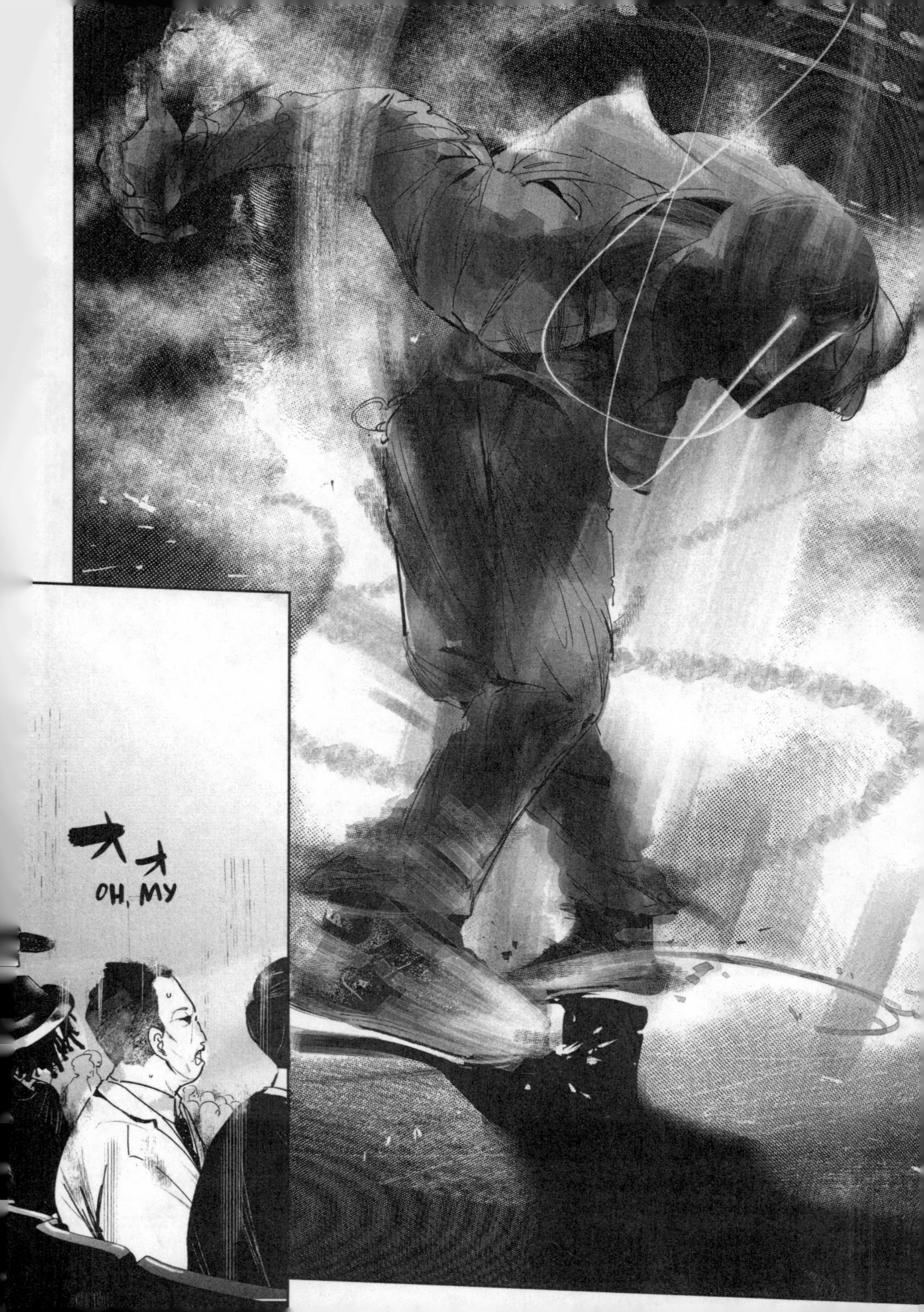
オォ
OH, MY

*A basic hip-hop move that involves crossing the heels.

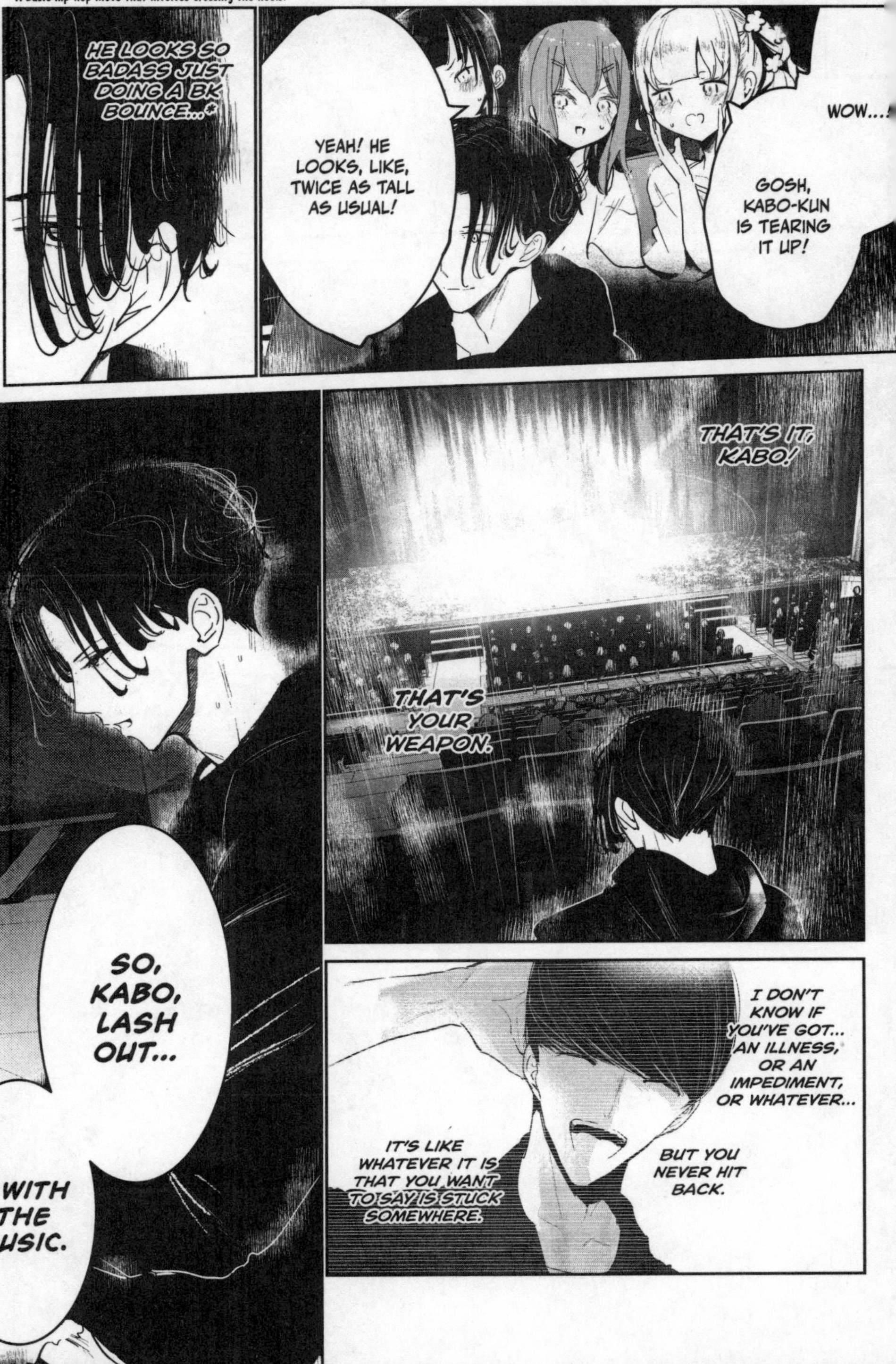

WOW...!
GOSH, KABO-KUN IS TEARING IT UP!
YEAH! HE LOOKS, LIKE, TWICE AS TALL AS USUAL!
HE LOOKS SO BADASS JUST DOING A BK BOUNCE...*
THAT'S IT, KABO!
THAT'S YOUR WEAPON.
I DON'T KNOW IF YOU'VE GOT... AN ILLNESS, OR AN IMPEDIMENT, OR WHATEVER...
BUT YOU NEVER HIT BACK.
IT'S LIKE WHATEVER IT IS THAT YOU WANT TO SAY IS STUCK SOMEWHERE.
SO, KABO, LASH OUT...
...WITH THE MUSIC.

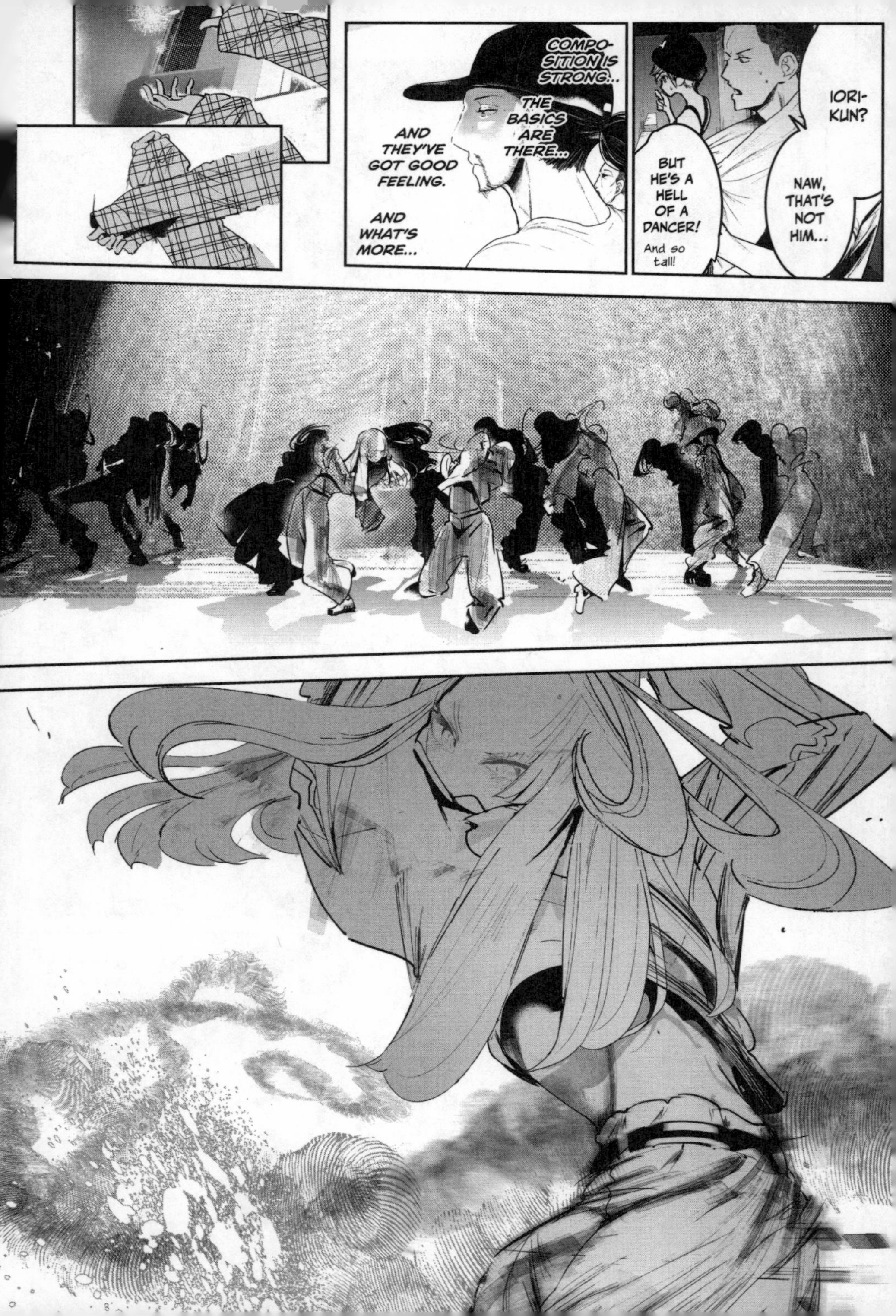
IORI-KUN?
NAW, THAT'S NOT HIM...
BUT HE'S A HELL OF A DANCER!
And so tall!
COMPOSITION IS STRONG...
THE BASICS ARE THERE...
AND THEY'VE GOT GOOD FEELING.
AND WHAT'S MORE...

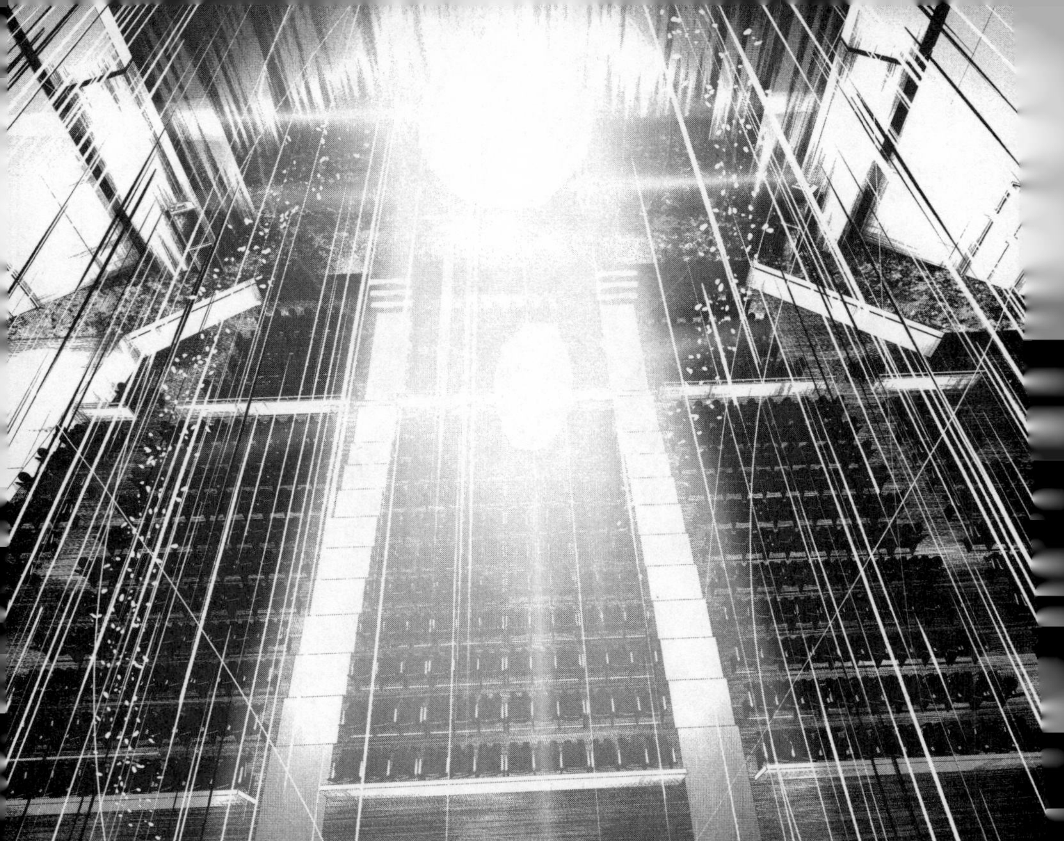
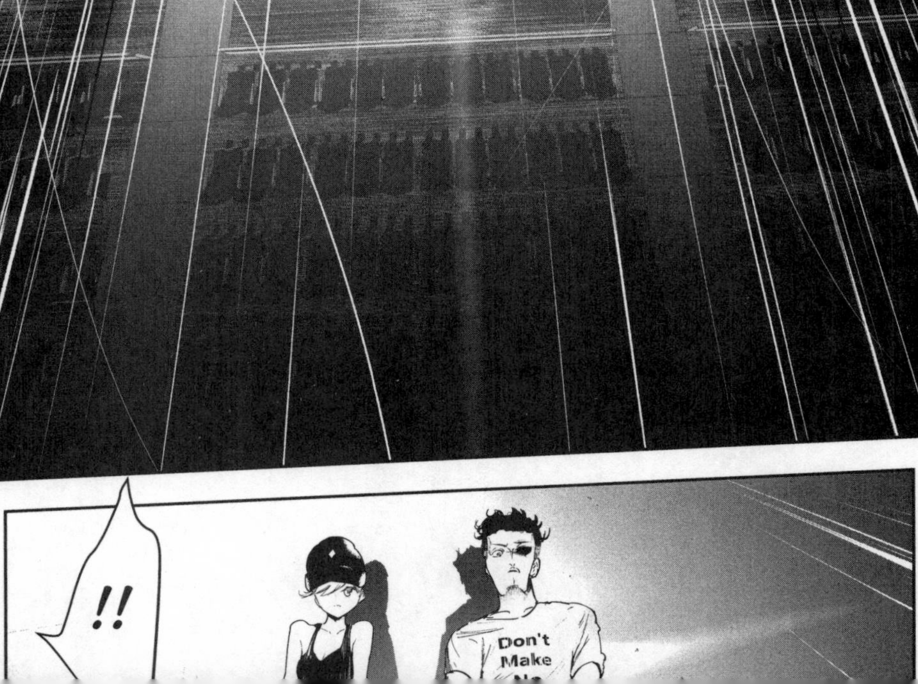
!!
Don't
Make

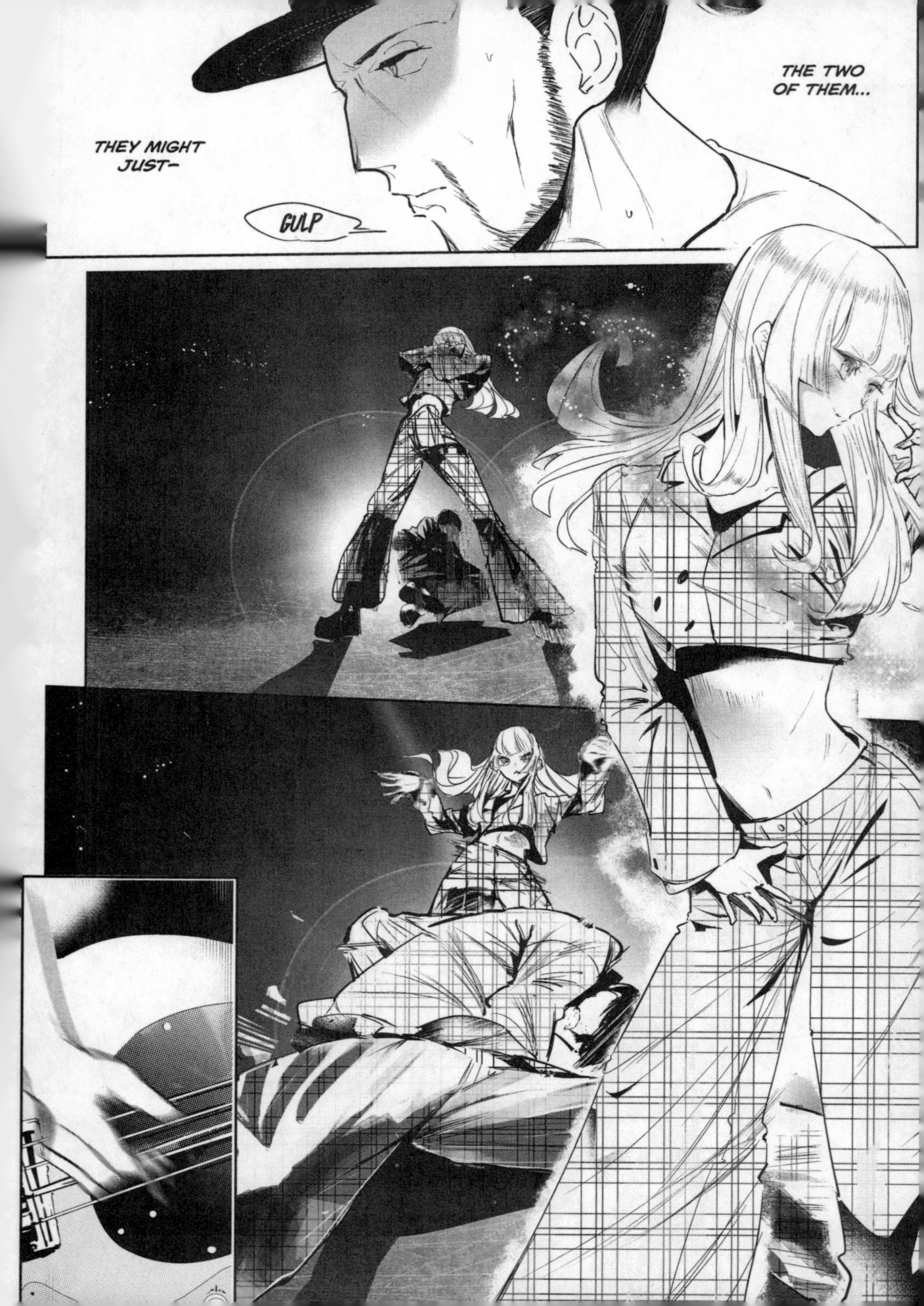
THE TWO OF THEM...
THEY MIGHT JUST-
GULP

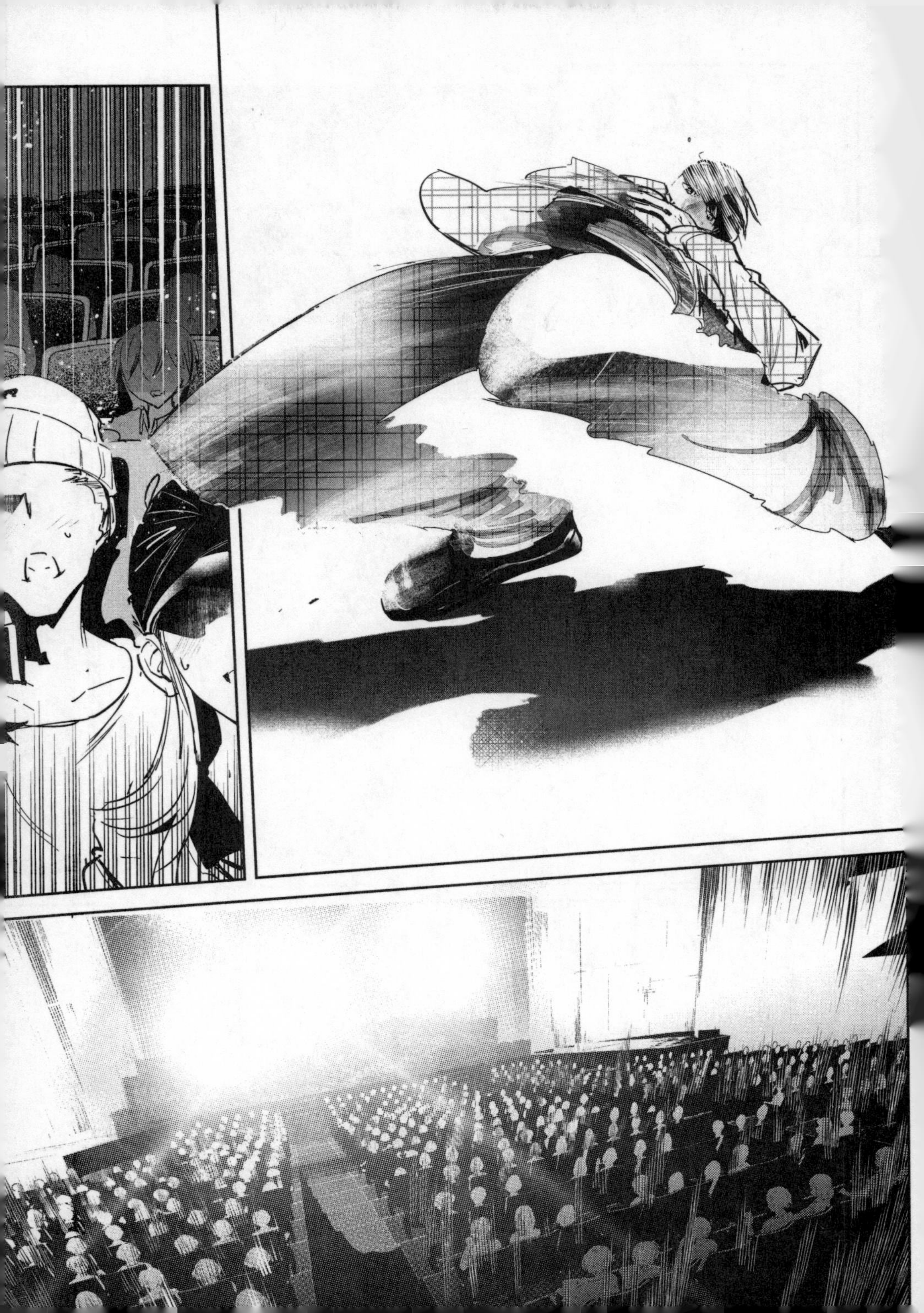

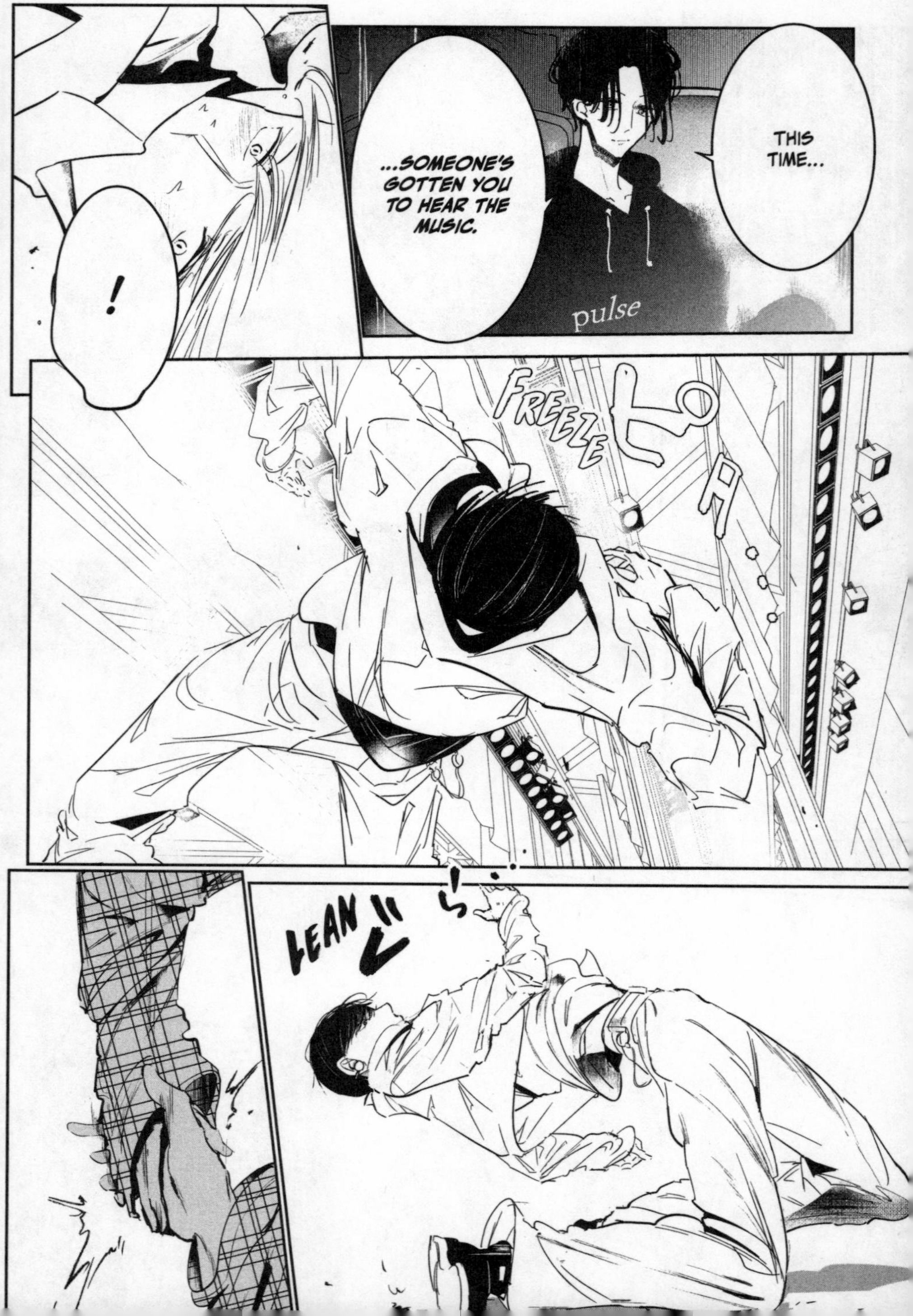
THIS TIME...
...SOMEONE'S GOTTEN YOU TO HEAR THE MUSIC.
pulse
!
FREEZE
LEAN

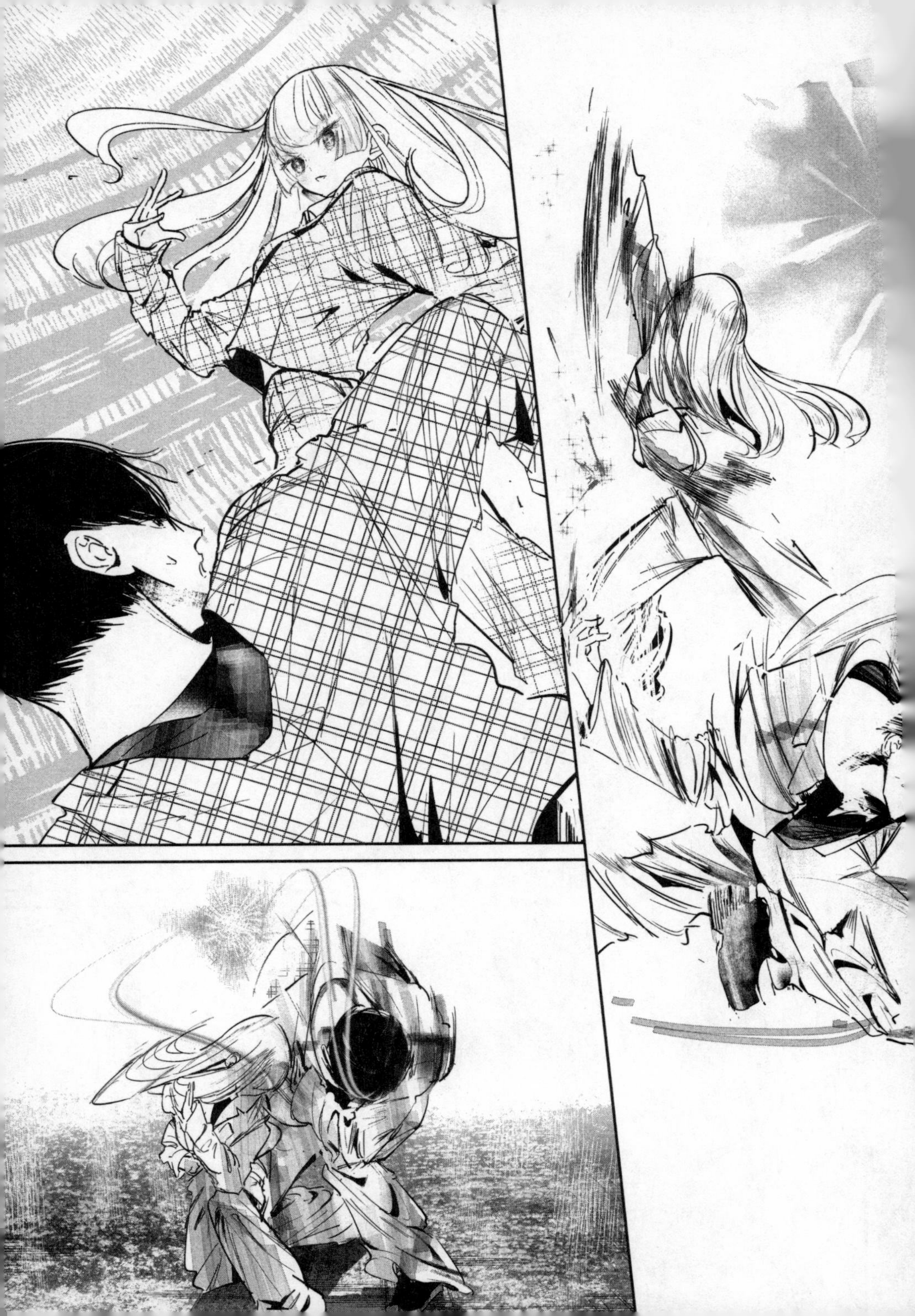

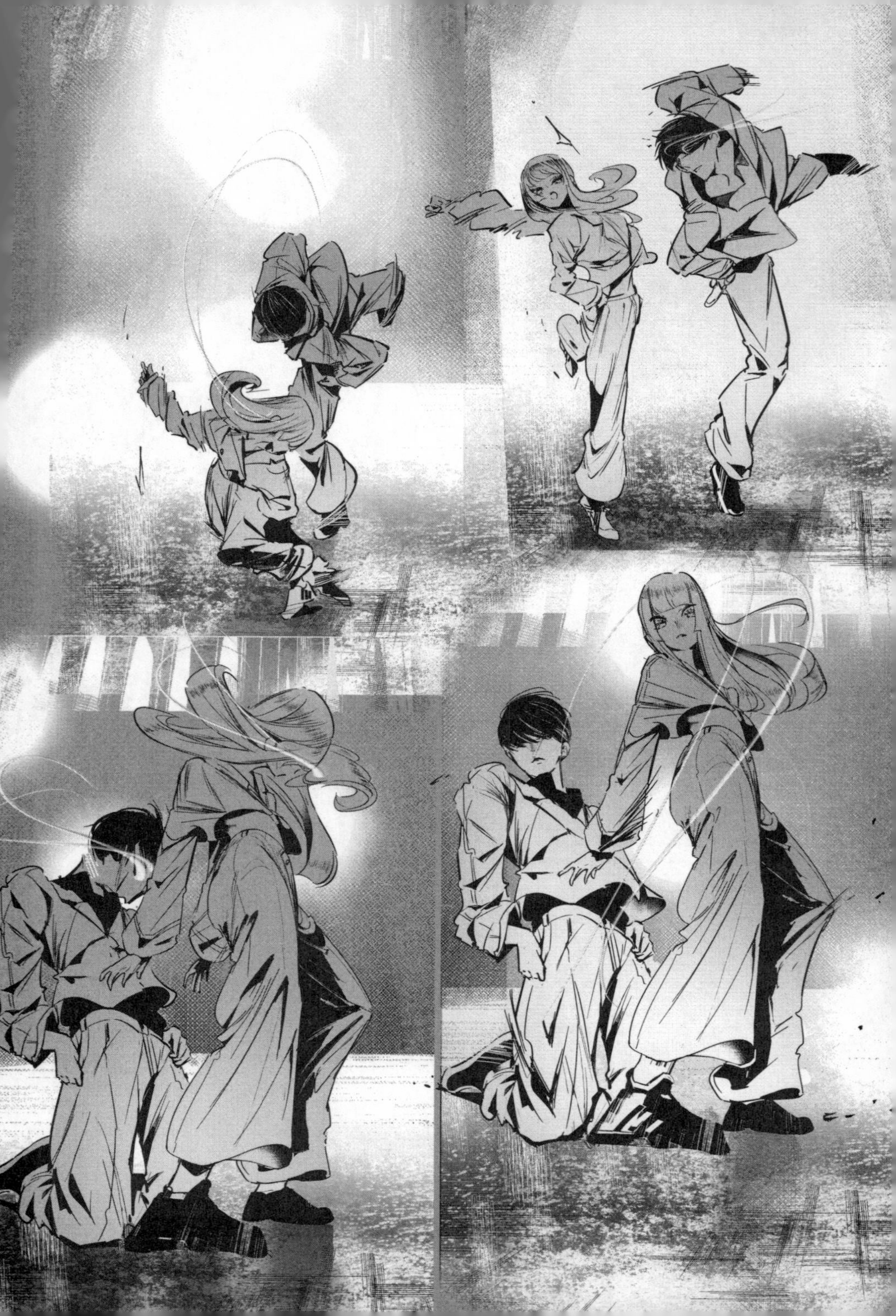

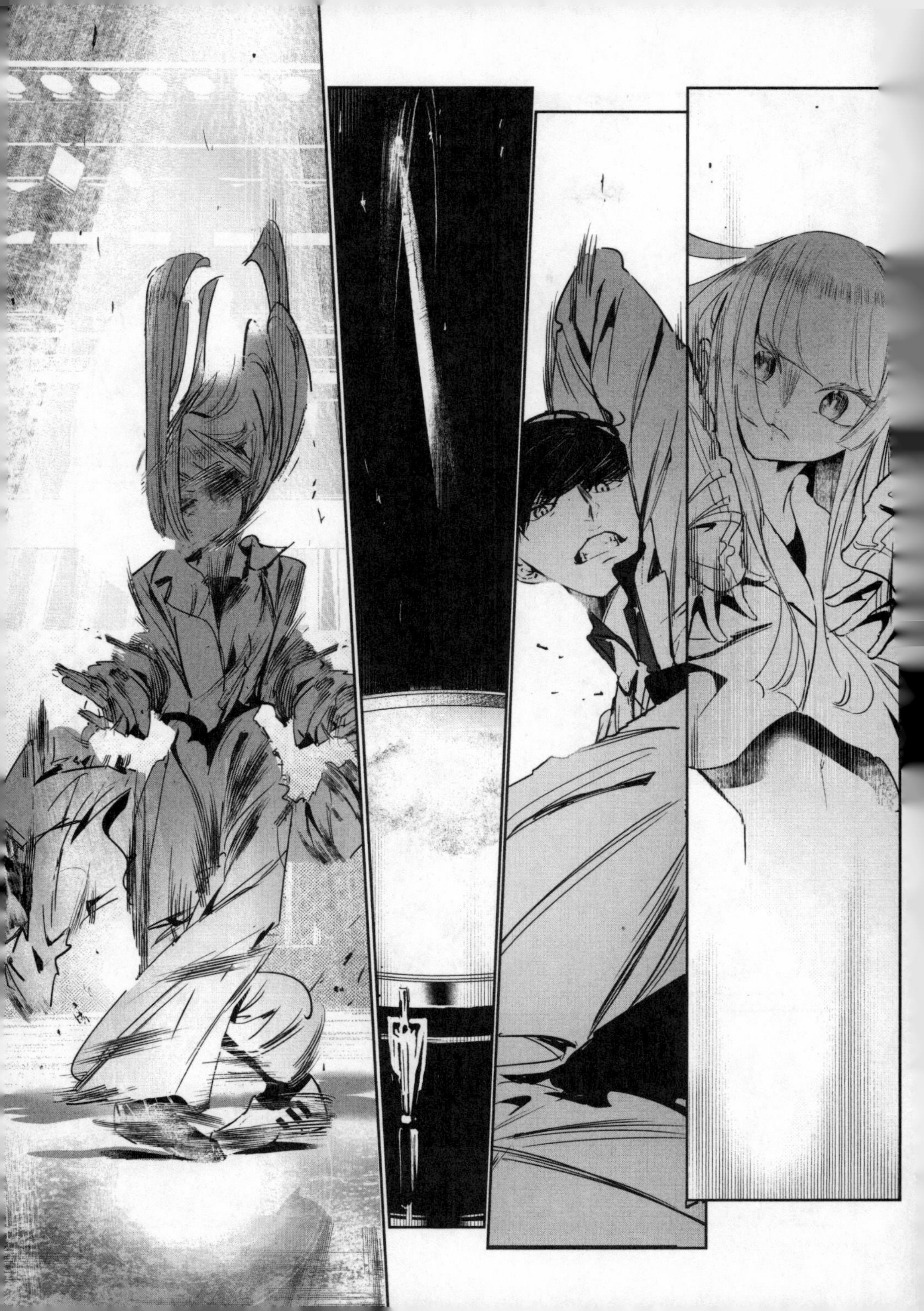

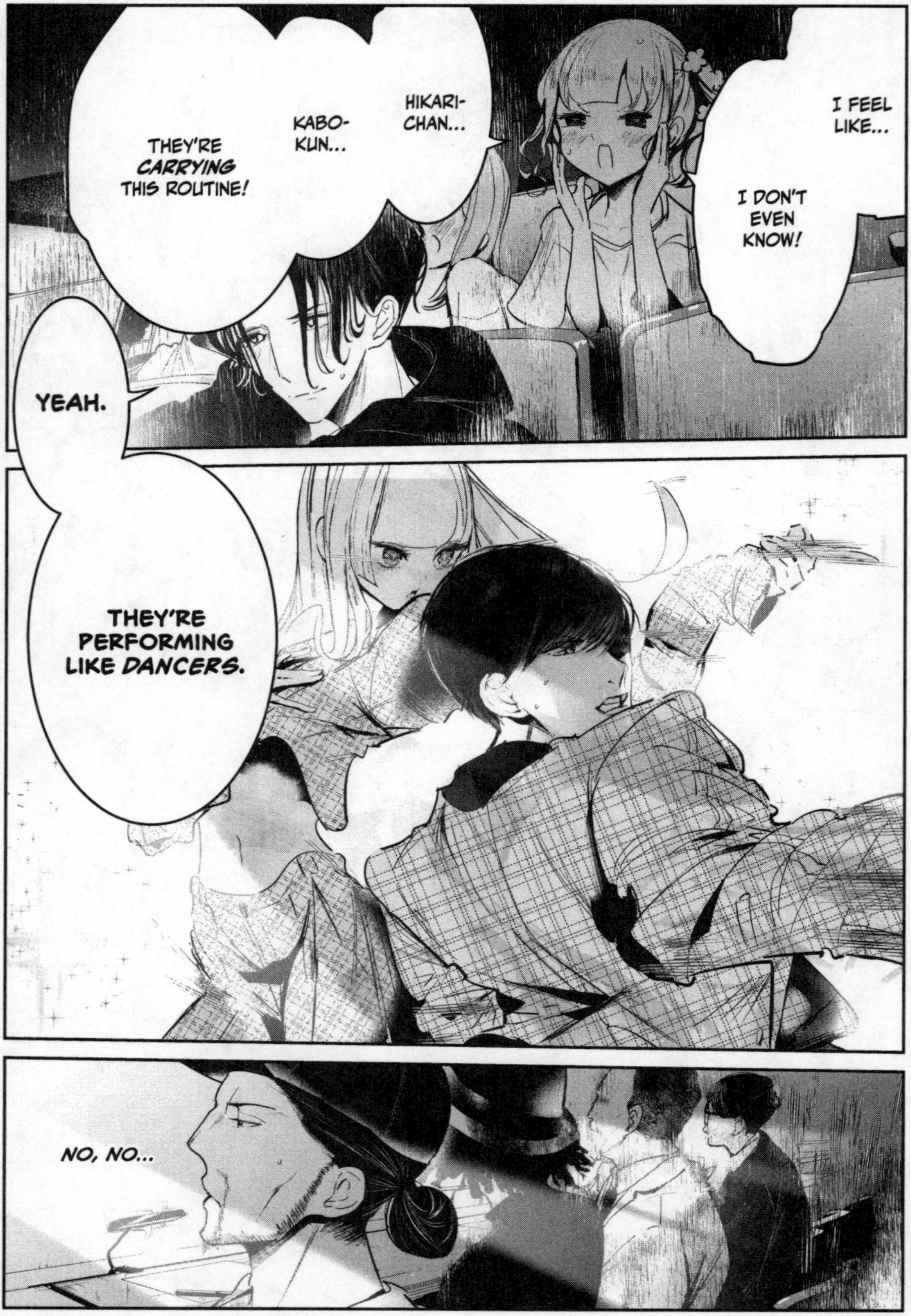
I FEEL LIKE...
I DON'T EVEN KNOW!
HIKARI-CHAN...
KABO-KUN...
THEY'RE CARRYING THIS ROUTINE!
YEAH.
THEY'RE PERFORMING LIKE DANCERS.
NO, NO...

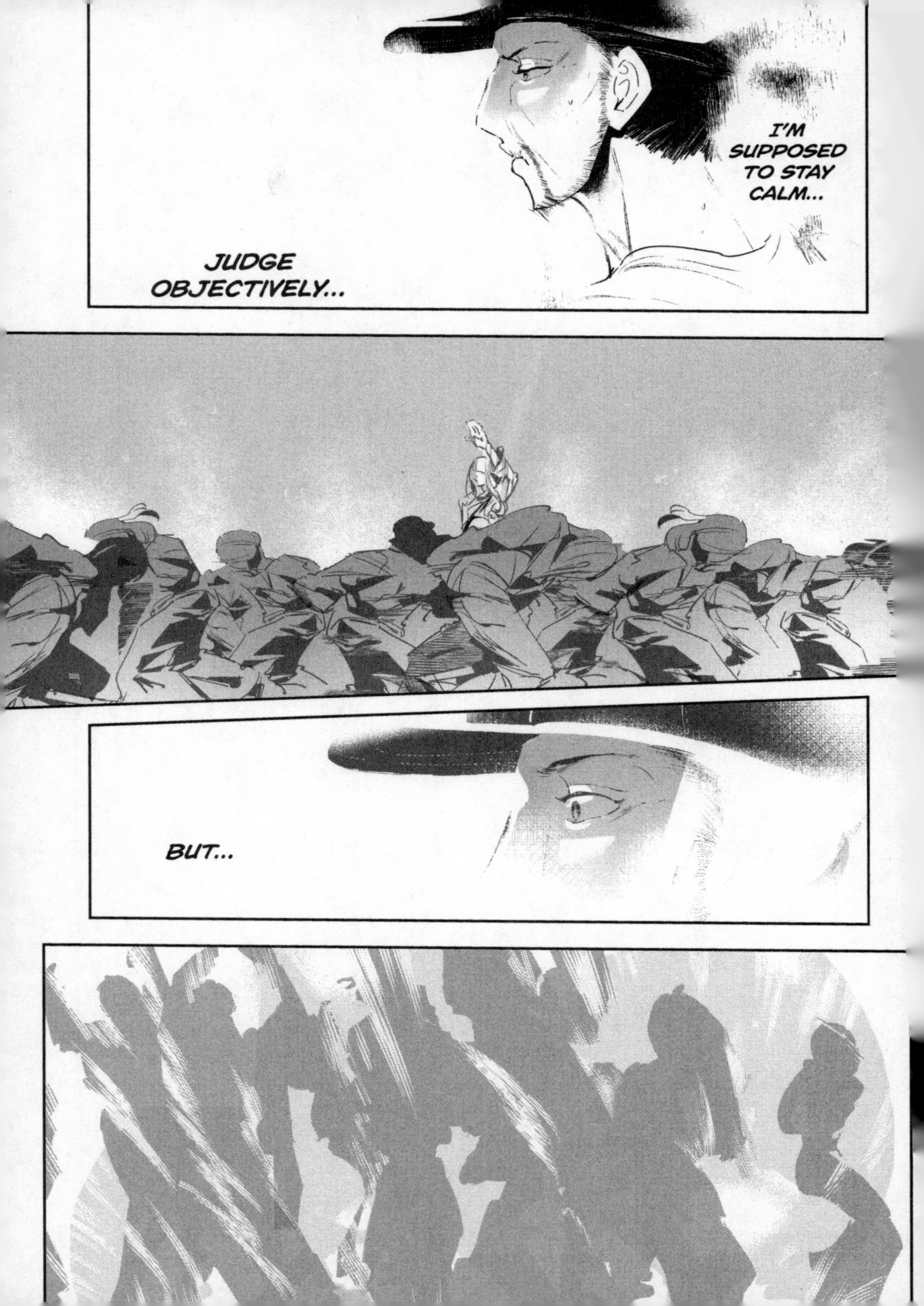
I'M SUPPOSED TO STAY CALM...
JUDGE OBJECTIVELY...
BUT...

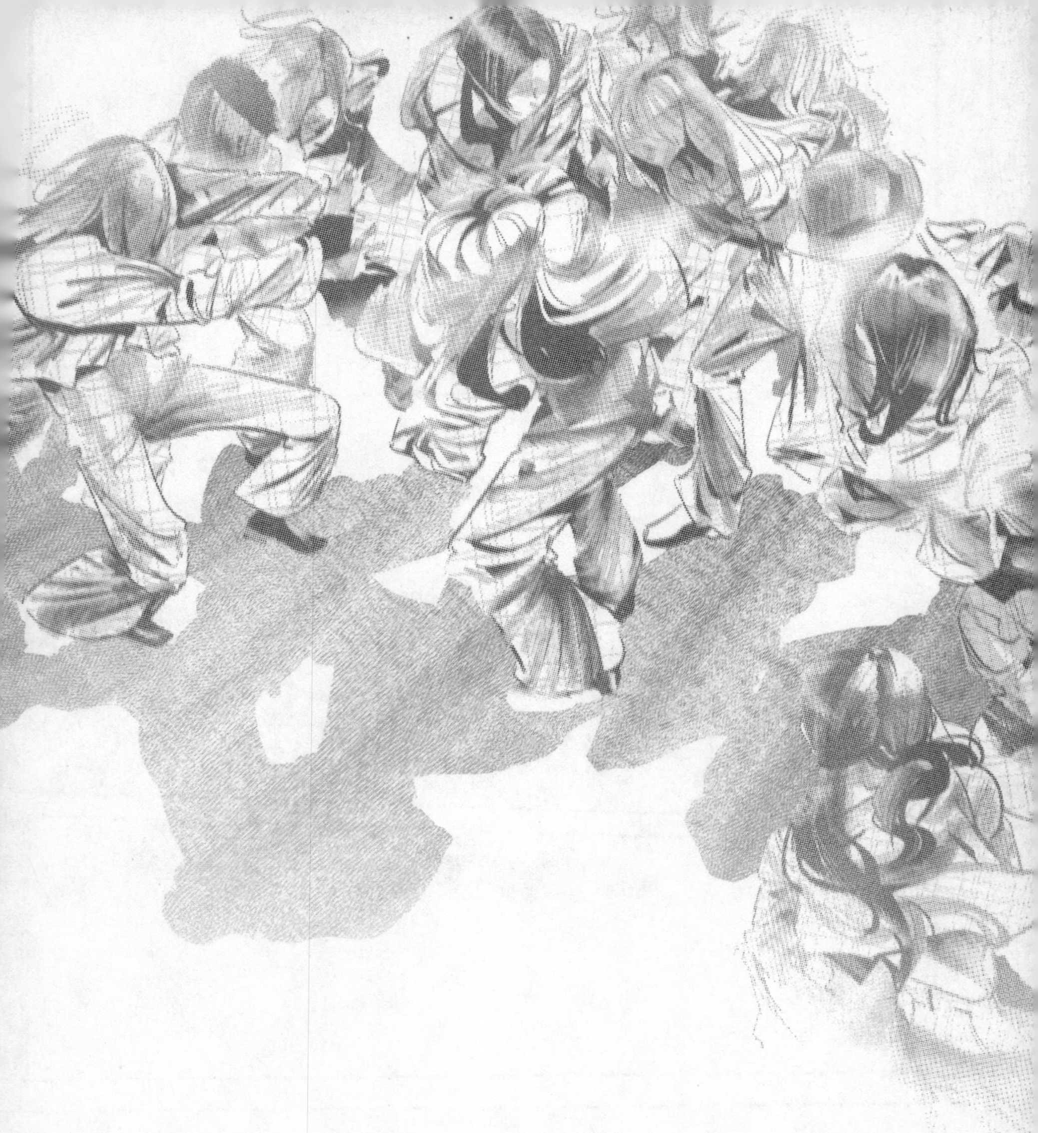

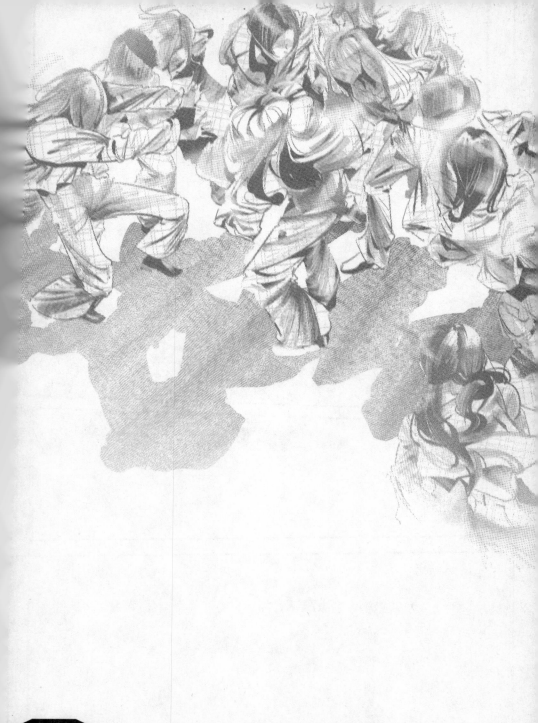

Ch. 10: END

WANDANCE

Ch. 11: First Contest (Pt. 3)

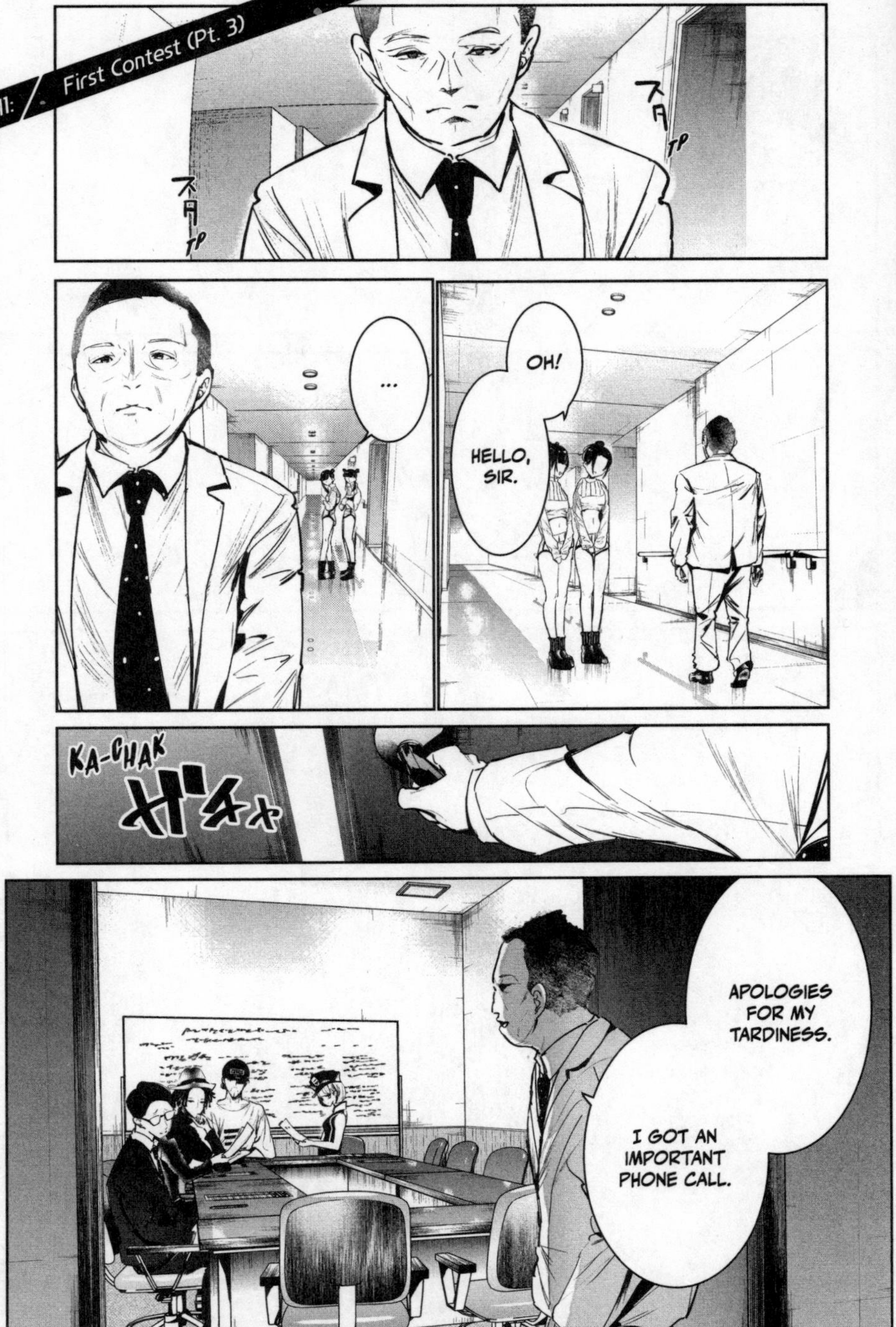
TP
TP
OH!
HELLO, SIR.
...
KA-CHAK
APOLOGIES FOR MY TARDINESS.
I GOT AN IMPORTANT PHONE CALL.

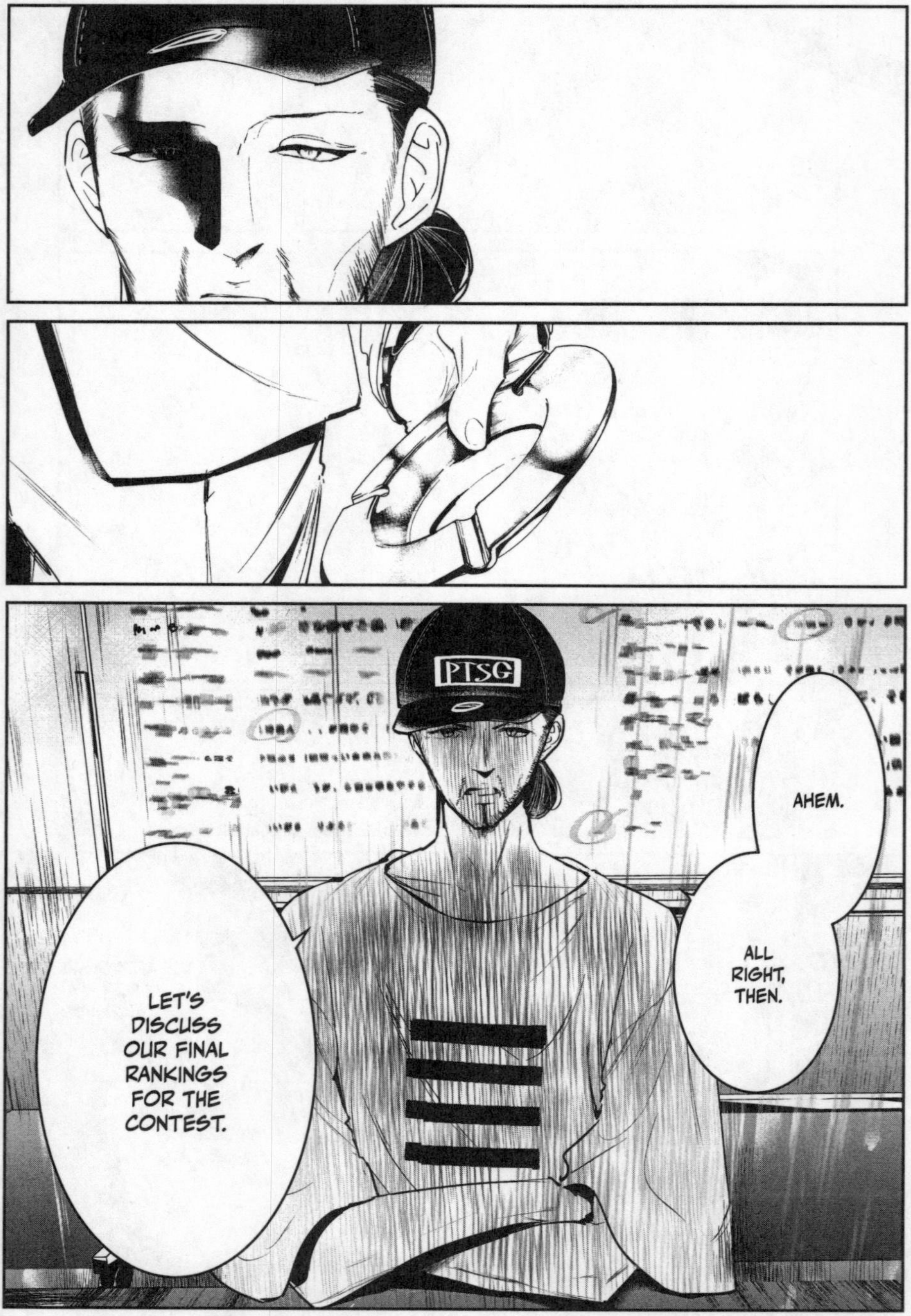
PTSG
AHEM.
ALL RIGHT, THEN.
LET'S DISCUSS OUR FINAL RANKINGS FOR THE CONTEST.

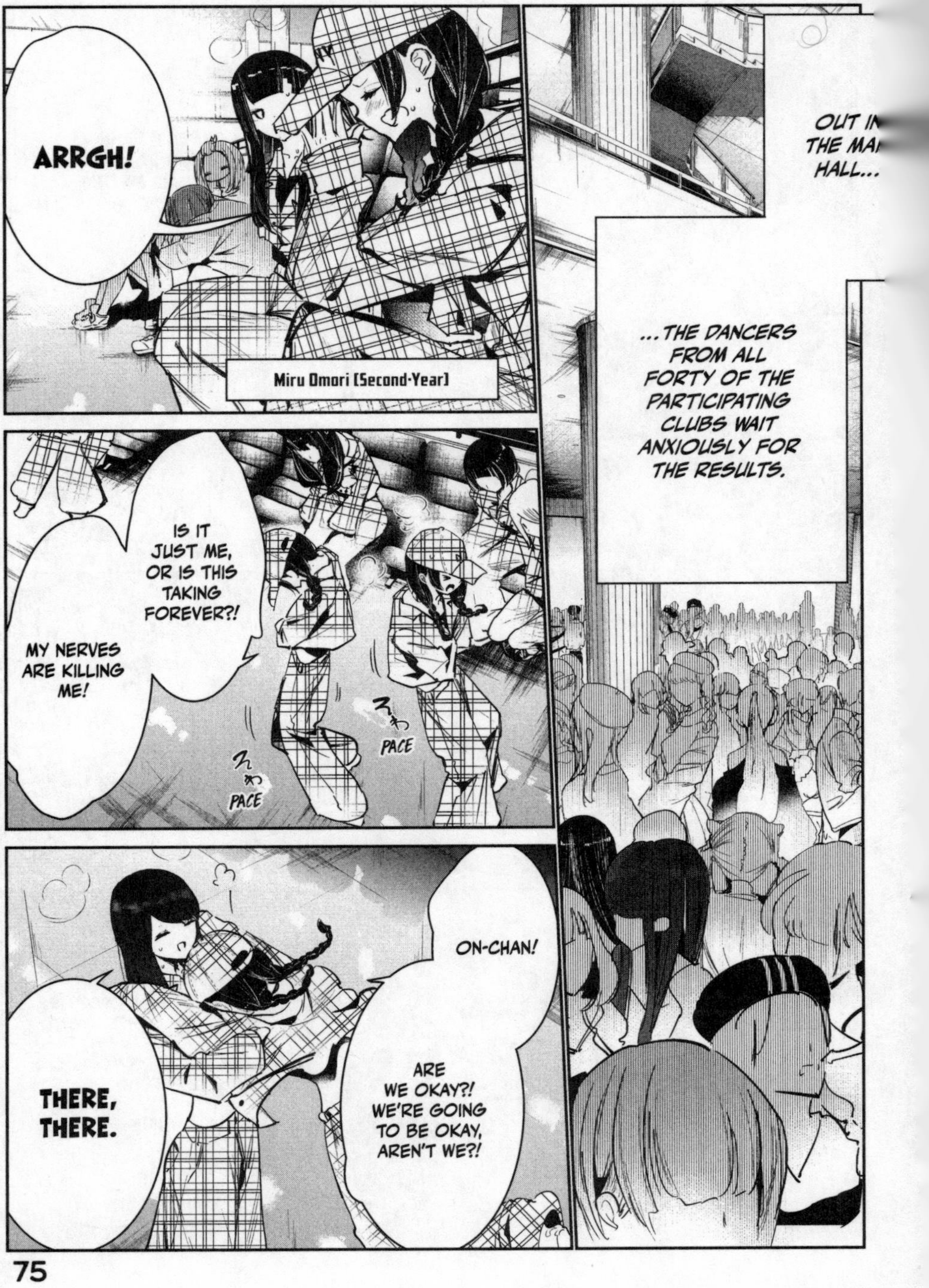
OUT IN THE MA HALL...
...THE DANCERS FROM ALL FORTY OF THE PARTICIPATING CLUBS WAIT ANXIOUSLY FOR THE RESULTS.
ARRGH!
Miru Omori [Second-Year]
IS IT JUST ME, OR IS THIS TAKING FOREVER?!
MY NERVES ARE KILLING ME!
PACE
PACE
ON-CHAN!
ARE WE OKAY?! WE'RE GOING TO BE OKAY, AREN'T WE?!
THERE, THERE.

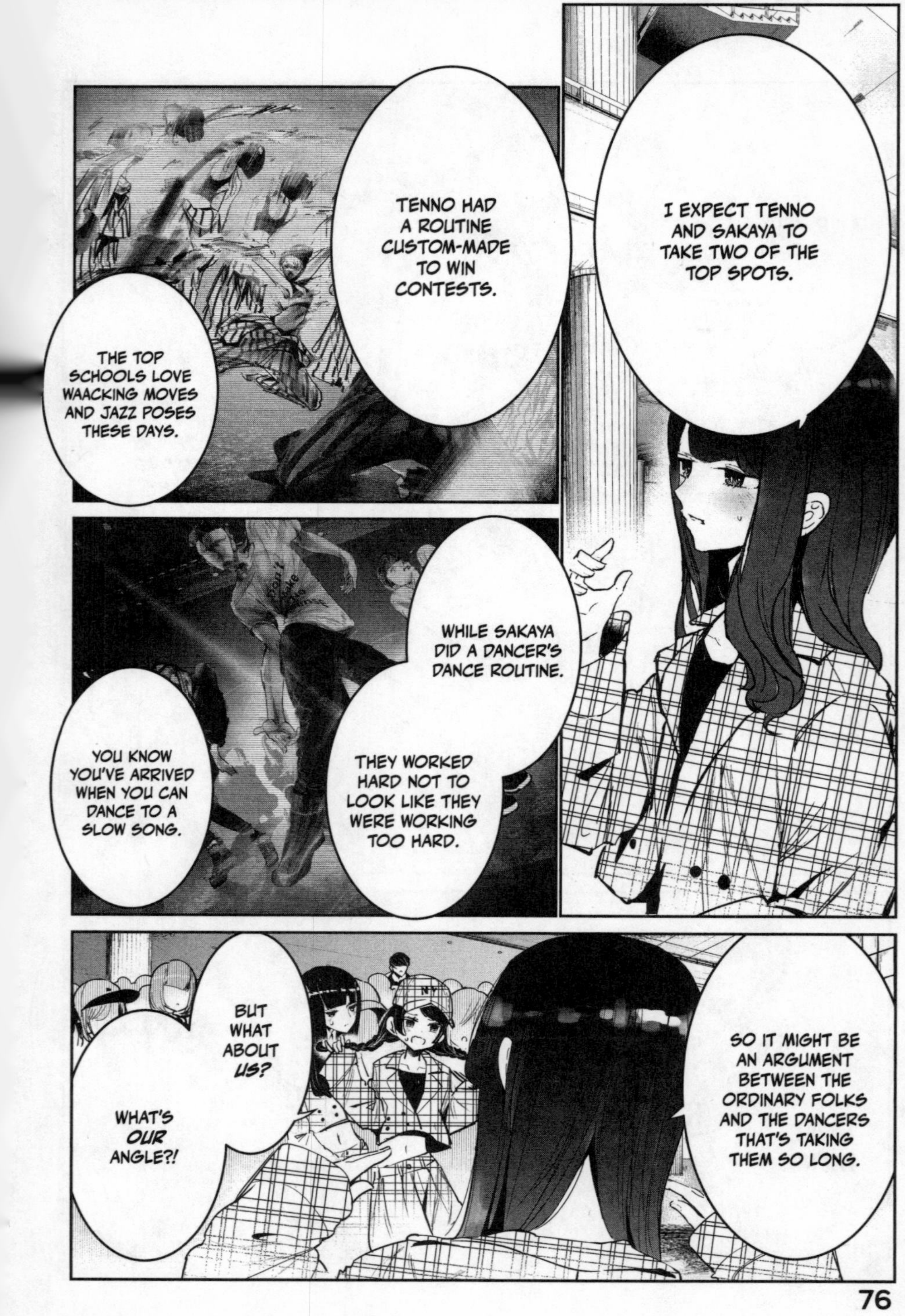
I EXPECT TENNO AND SAKAYA TO TAKE TWO OF THE TOP SPOTS.
TENNO HAD A ROUTINE CUSTOM-MADE TO WIN CONTESTS.
THE TOP SCHOOLS LOVE WAACKING MOVES AND JAZZ POSES THESE DAYS.
WHILE SAKAYA DID A DANCER'S DANCE ROUTINE.
THEY WORKED HARD NOT TO LOOK LIKE THEY WERE WORKING TOO HARD.
YOU KNOW YOU'VE ARRIVED WHEN YOU CAN DANCE TO A SLOW SONG.
SO IT MIGHT BE AN ARGUMENT BETWEEN THE ORDINARY FOLKS AND THE DANCERS THAT'S TAKING THEM SO LONG.
BUT WHAT ABOUT *US*?
WHAT'S *OUR* ANGLE?!

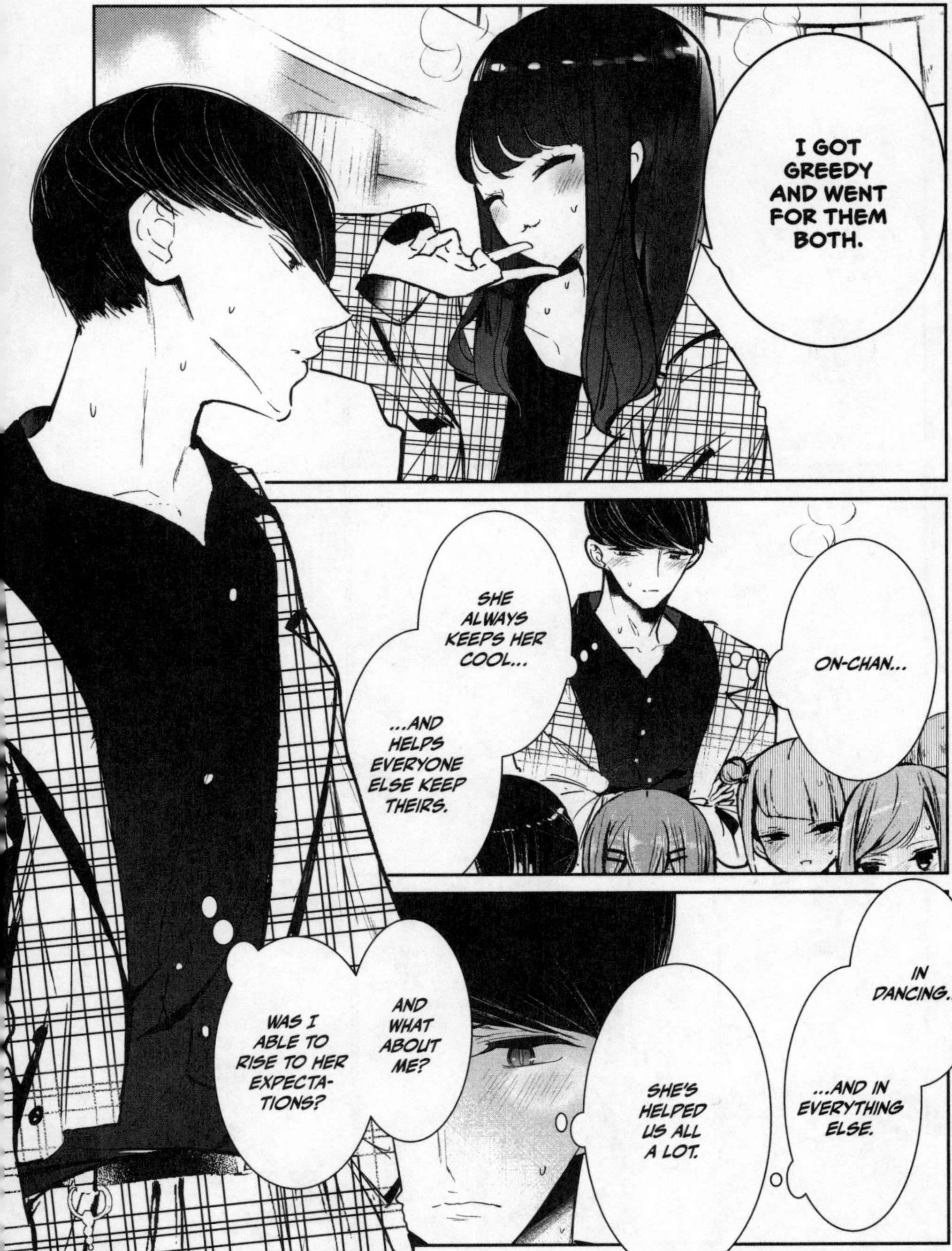
I GOT GREEDY AND WENT FOR THEM BOTH.
ON-CHAN...
SHE ALWAYS KEEPS HER COOL...
...AND HELPS EVERYONE ELSE KEEP THEIRS.
IN DANCING...
...AND IN EVERYTHING ELSE.
SHE'S HELPED US ALL A LOT.
AND WHAT ABOUT ME?
WAS I ABLE TO RISE TO HER EXPECTA-TIONS?

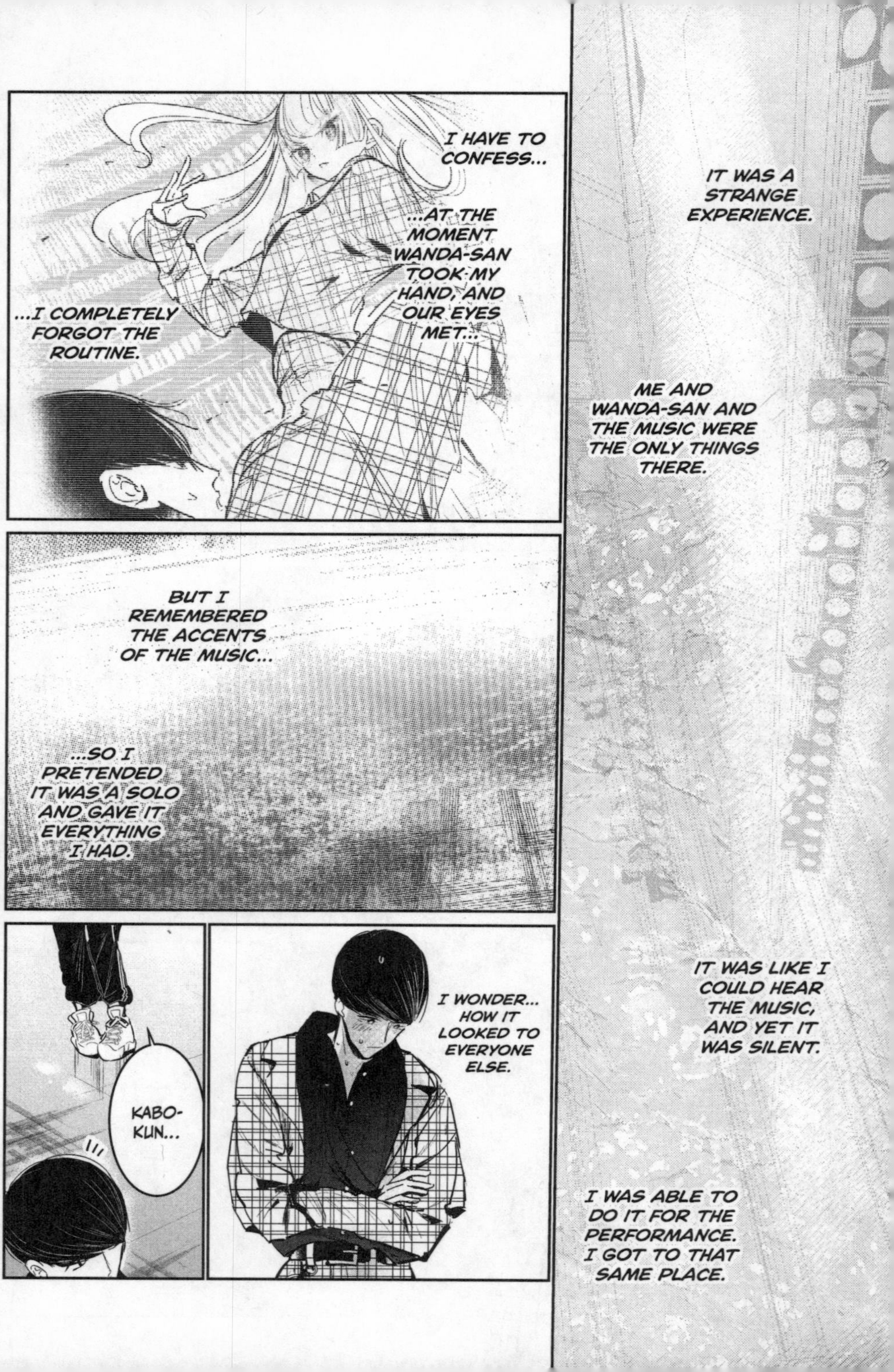
IT WAS A STRANGE EXPERIENCE.
ME AND WANDA-SAN AND THE MUSIC WERE THE ONLY THINGS THERE.
IT WAS LIKE I COULD HEAR THE MUSIC, AND YET IT WAS SILENT.
I WAS ABLE TO DO IT FOR THE PERFORMANCE. I GOT TO THAT SAME PLACE.
I HAVE TO CONFESS...
...AT THE MOMENT WANDA-SAN TOOK MY HAND, AND OUR EYES MET...
...I COMPLETELY FORGOT THE ROUTINE.
BUT I REMEMBERED THE ACCENTS OF THE MUSIC...
...SO I PRETENDED IT WAS A SOLO AND GAVE IT EVERYTHING I HAD.
I WONDER... HOW IT LOOKED TO EVERYONE ELSE.
KABO-KUN...

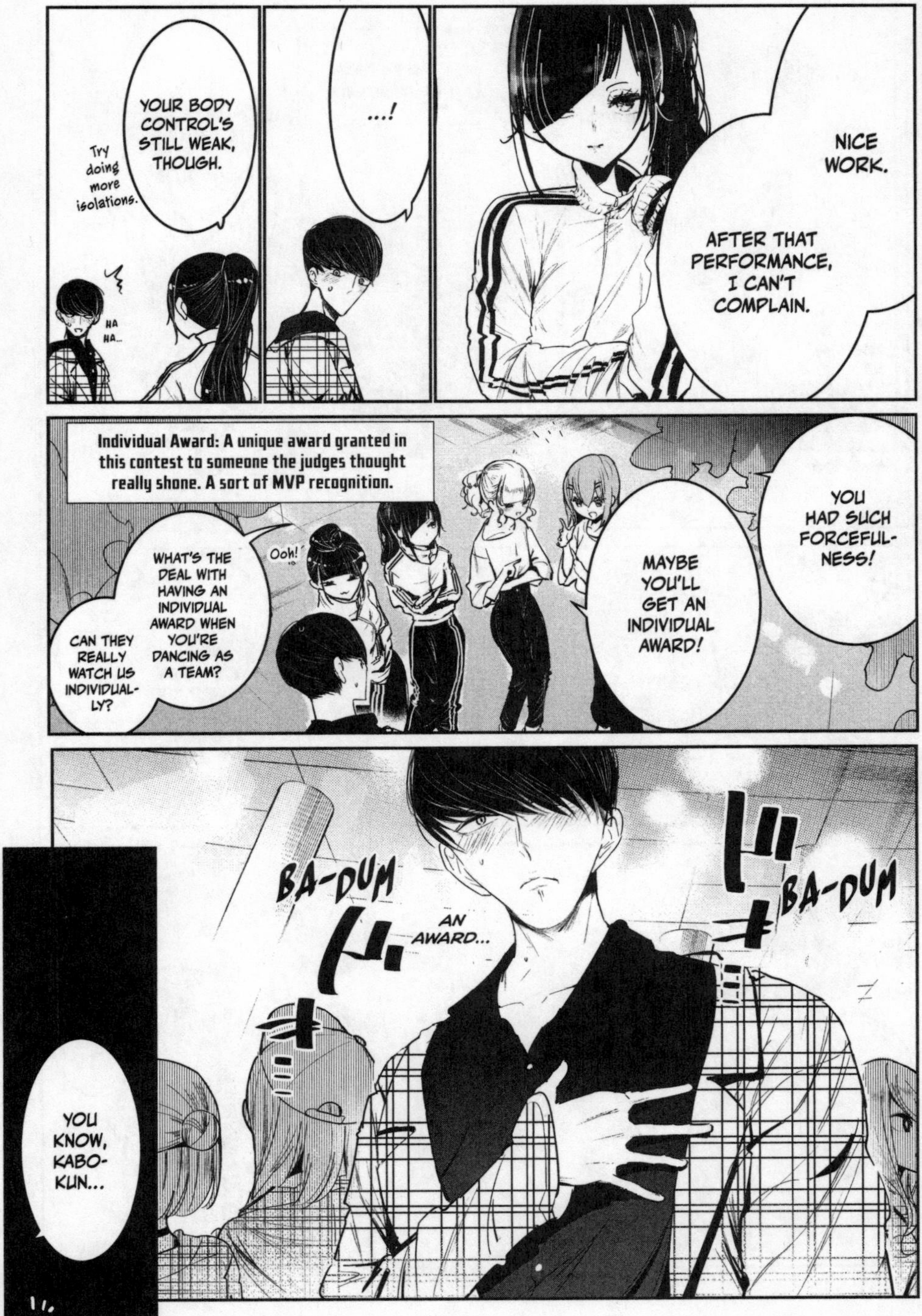
NICE WORK.
AFTER THAT PERFORMANCE, I CAN'T COMPLAIN.
...!
YOUR BODY CONTROL'S STILL WEAK, THOUGH.
Try doing more isolations.
HA HA...
YOU HAD SUCH FORCEFUL-NESS!
MAYBE YOU'LL GET AN INDIVIDUAL AWARD!
Individual Award: A unique award granted in this contest to someone the judges thought really shone. A sort of MVP recognition.
Ooh!
WHAT'S THE DEAL WITH HAVING AN INDIVIDUAL AWARD WHEN YOU'RE DANCING AS A TEAM?
CAN THEY REALLY WATCH US INDIVIDUAL-LY?
BA-DUM
BA-DUM
AN AWARD...
YOU KNOW, KABO-KUN...

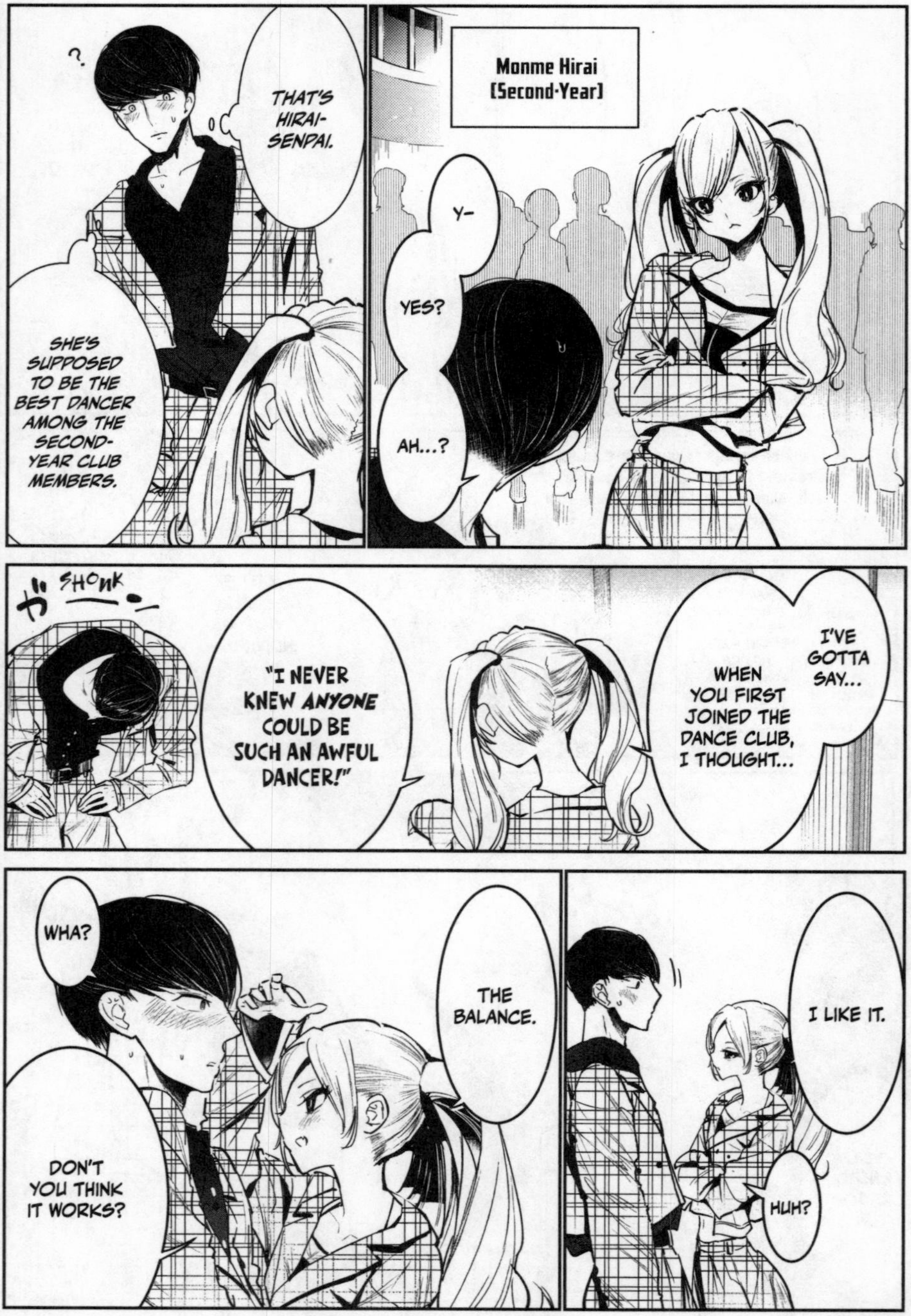
Monme Hirai
[Second-Year]
Y-
YES?
AH...?
?
THAT'S HIRAI-SENPAI.
SHE'S SUPPOSED TO BE THE BEST DANCER AMONG THE SECOND-YEAR CLUB MEMBERS.
I'VE GOTTA SAY...
WHEN YOU FIRST JOINED THE DANCE CLUB, I THOUGHT...
"I NEVER KNEW *ANYONE* COULD BE SUCH AN AWFUL DANCER!"
ガ SHONK
I LIKE IT.
HUH?
THE BALANCE.
WHA?
DON'T YOU THINK IT WORKS?

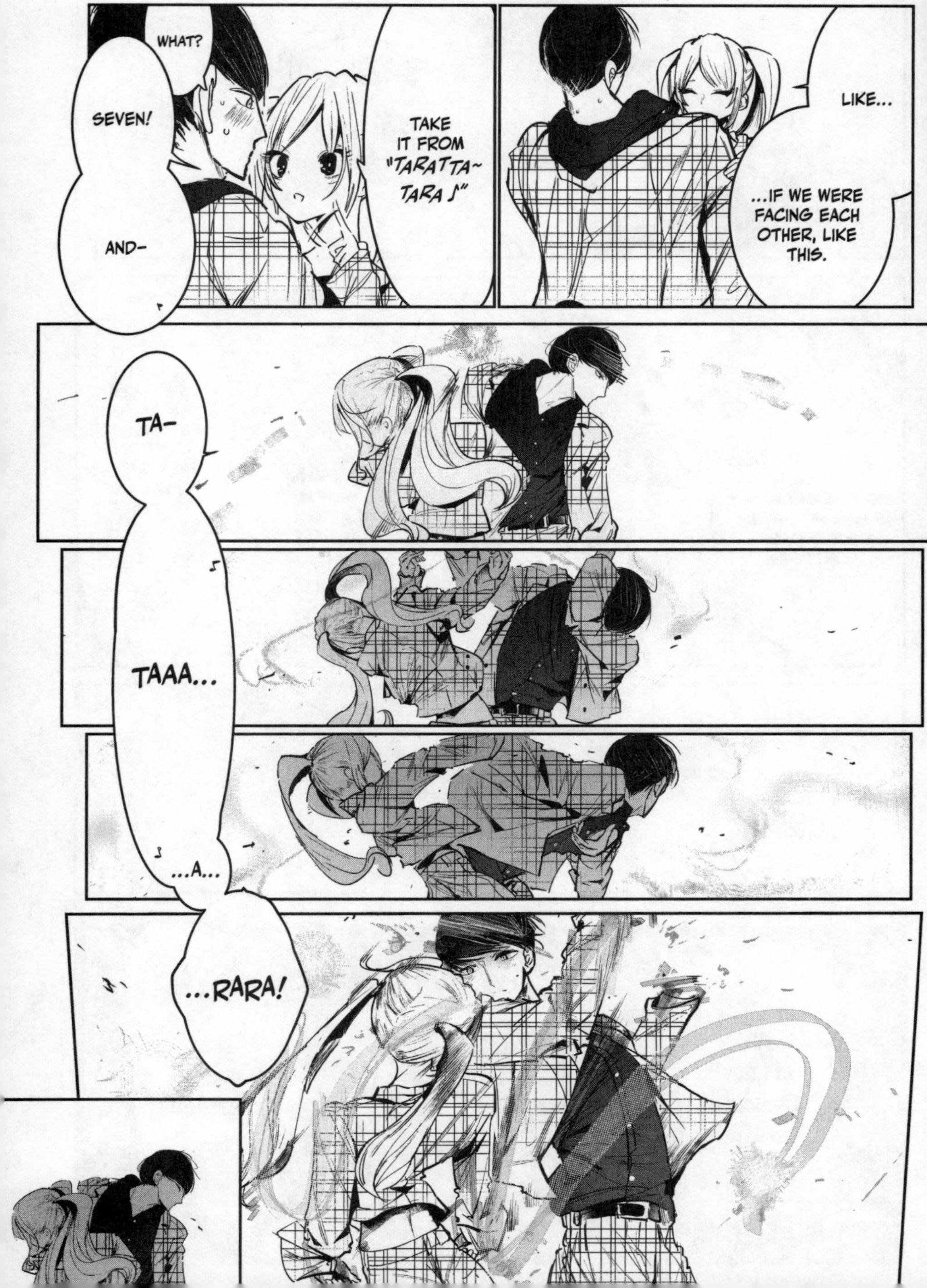
LIKE...
...IF WE WERE FACING EACH OTHER, LIKE THIS.
TAKE IT FROM "TARATTA~ TARA ♪"
WHAT?
SEVEN!
AND-
TA-
TAAA...
...A...
...RARA!

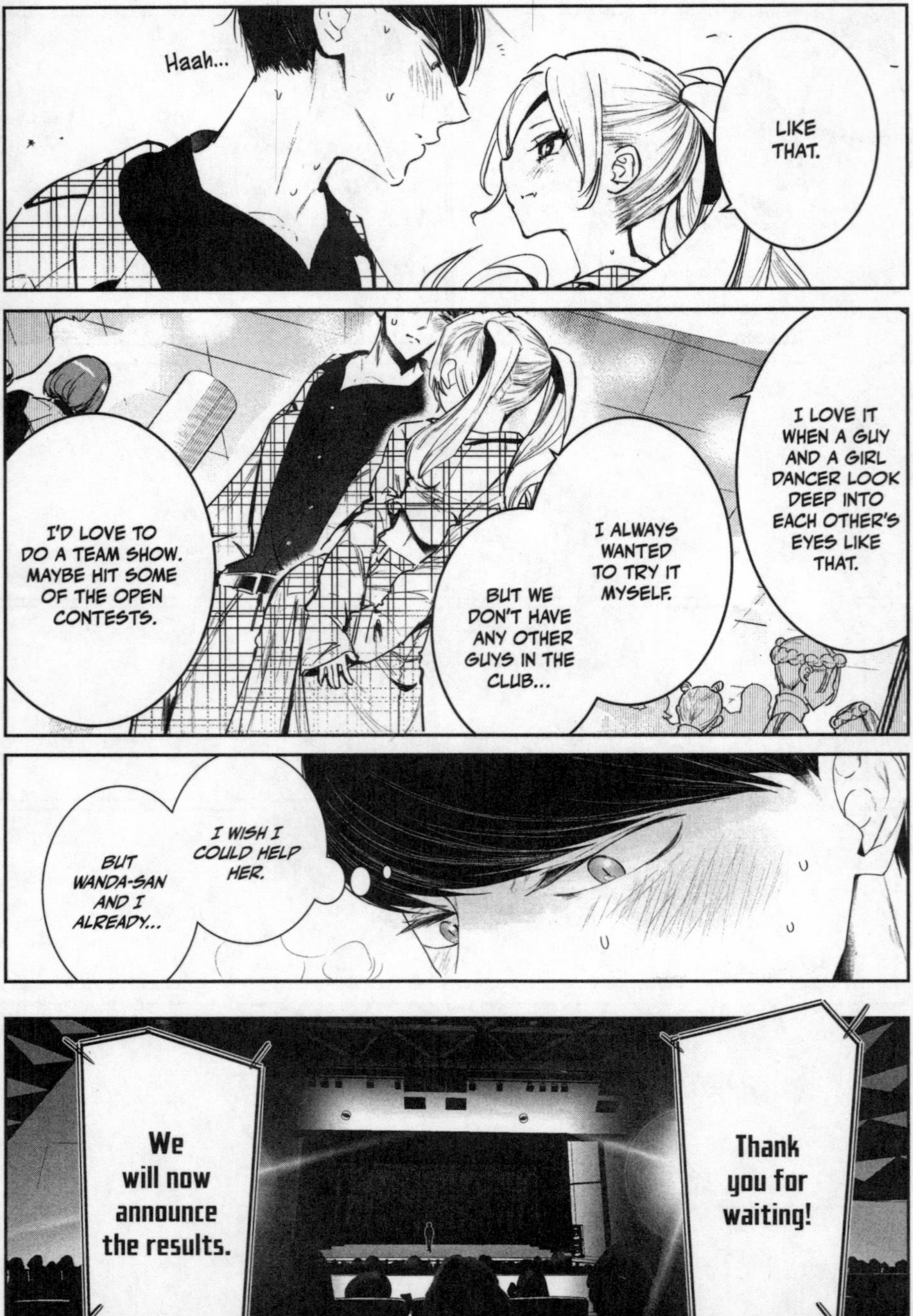
LIKE THAT.
Haaah...
I LOVE IT WHEN A GUY AND A GIRL DANCER LOOK DEEP INTO EACH OTHER'S EYES LIKE THAT.
I ALWAYS WANTED TO TRY IT MYSELF.
BUT WE DON'T HAVE ANY OTHER GUYS IN THE CLUB...
I'D LOVE TO DO A TEAM SHOW. MAYBE HIT SOME OF THE OPEN CONTESTS.
I WISH I COULD HELP HER.
BUT WANDA-SAN AND I ALREADY...
Thank you for waiting!
We will now announce the results.

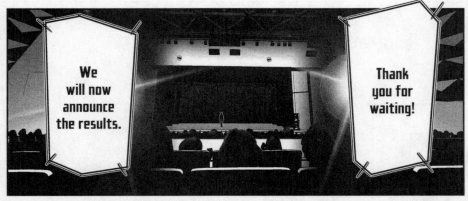

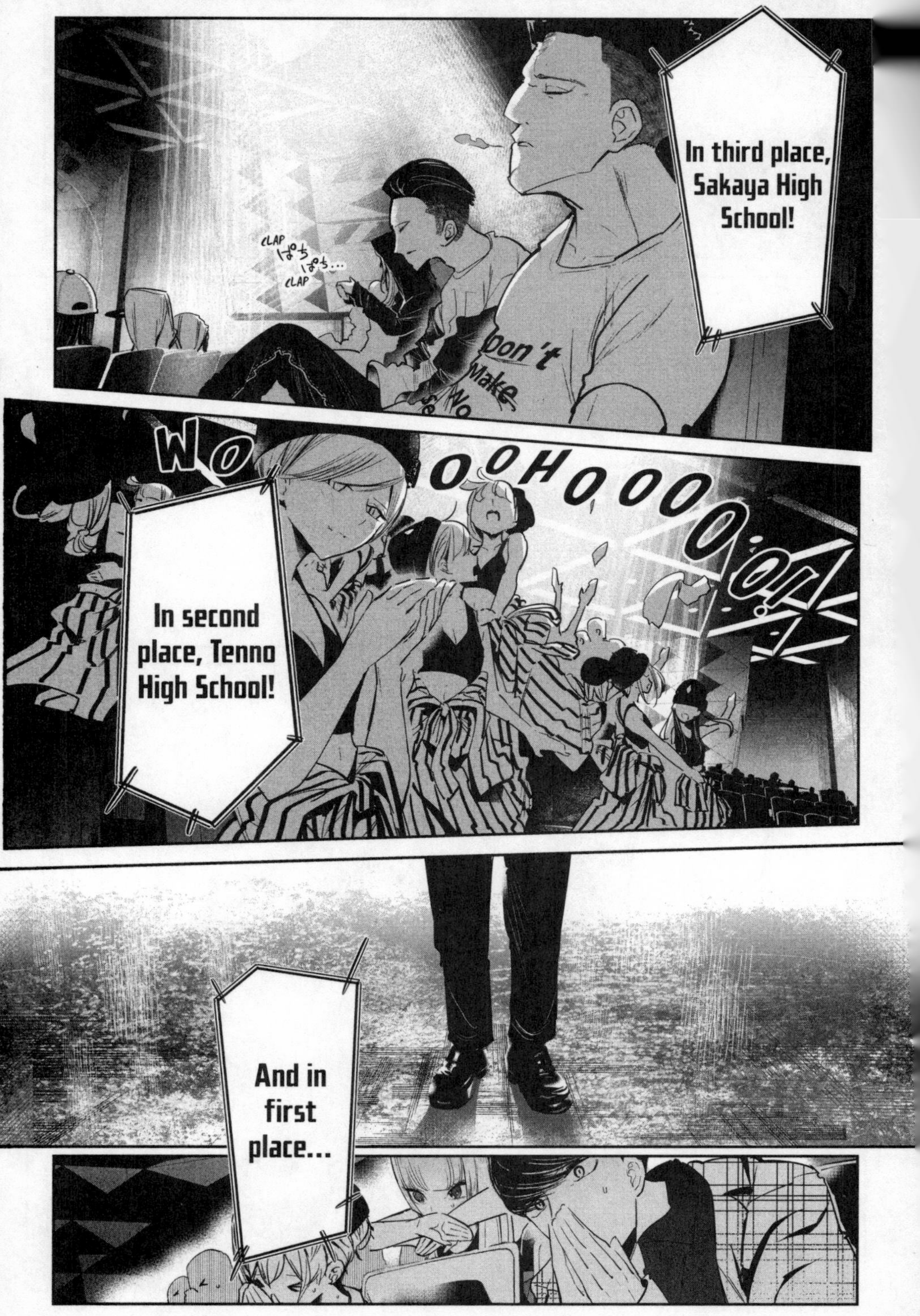
In third place, Sakaya High School!
CLAP ぱち ぱち… CLAP
WOOOHOOOOOO!!
In second place, Tenno High School!
And in first place...

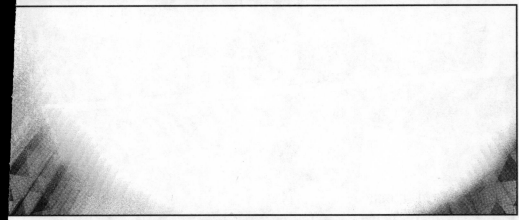

Ichirin
High
School!

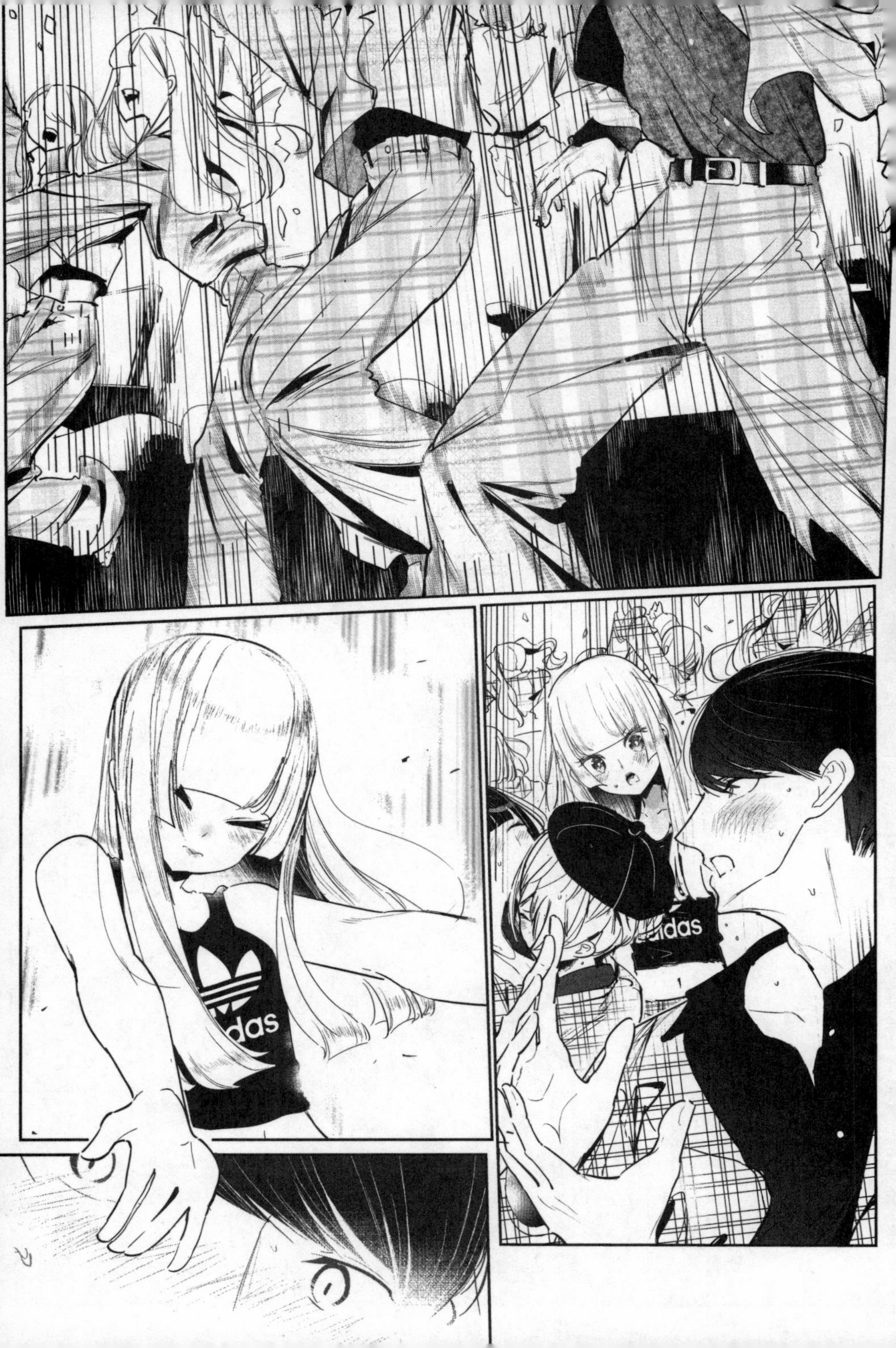

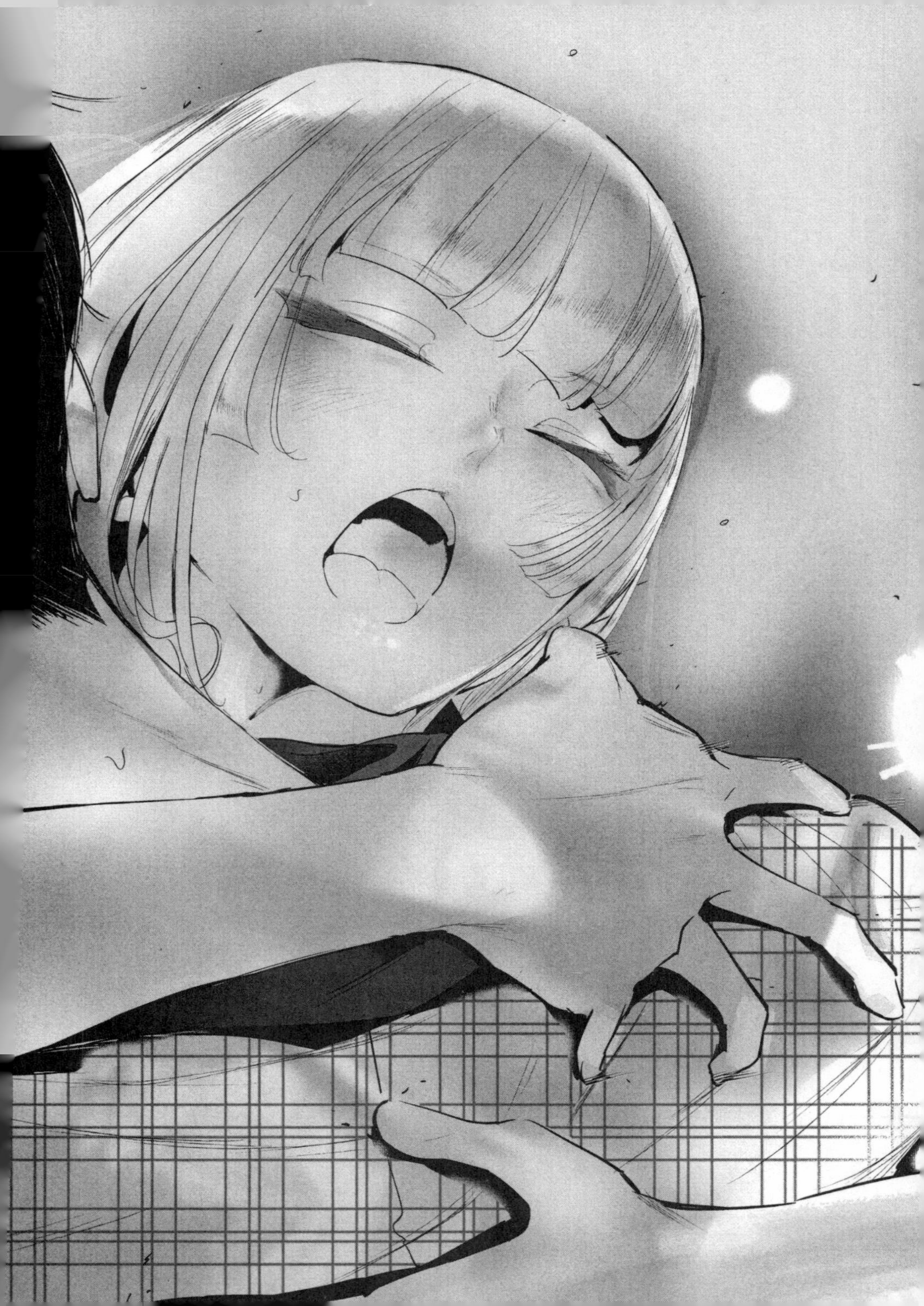

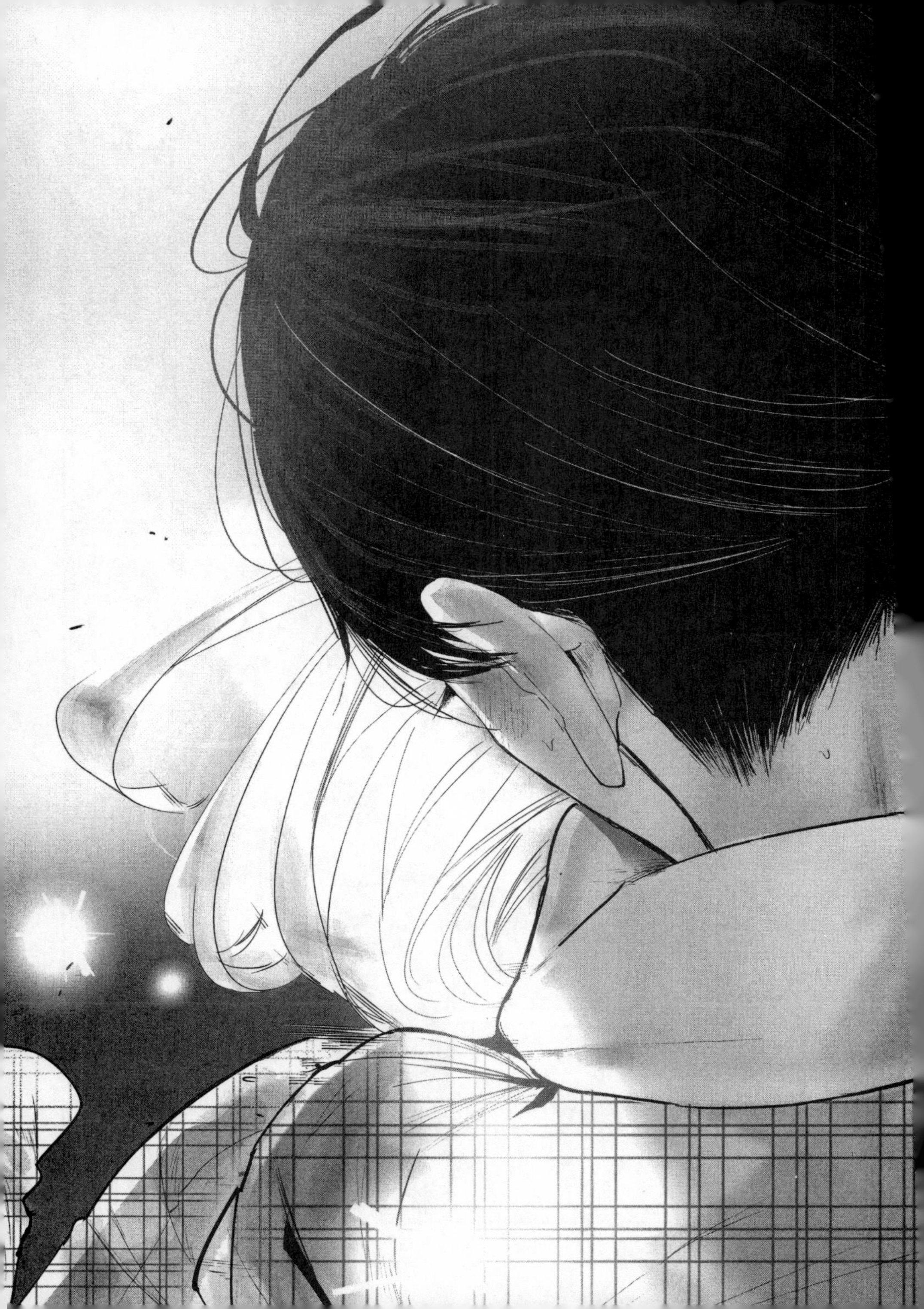

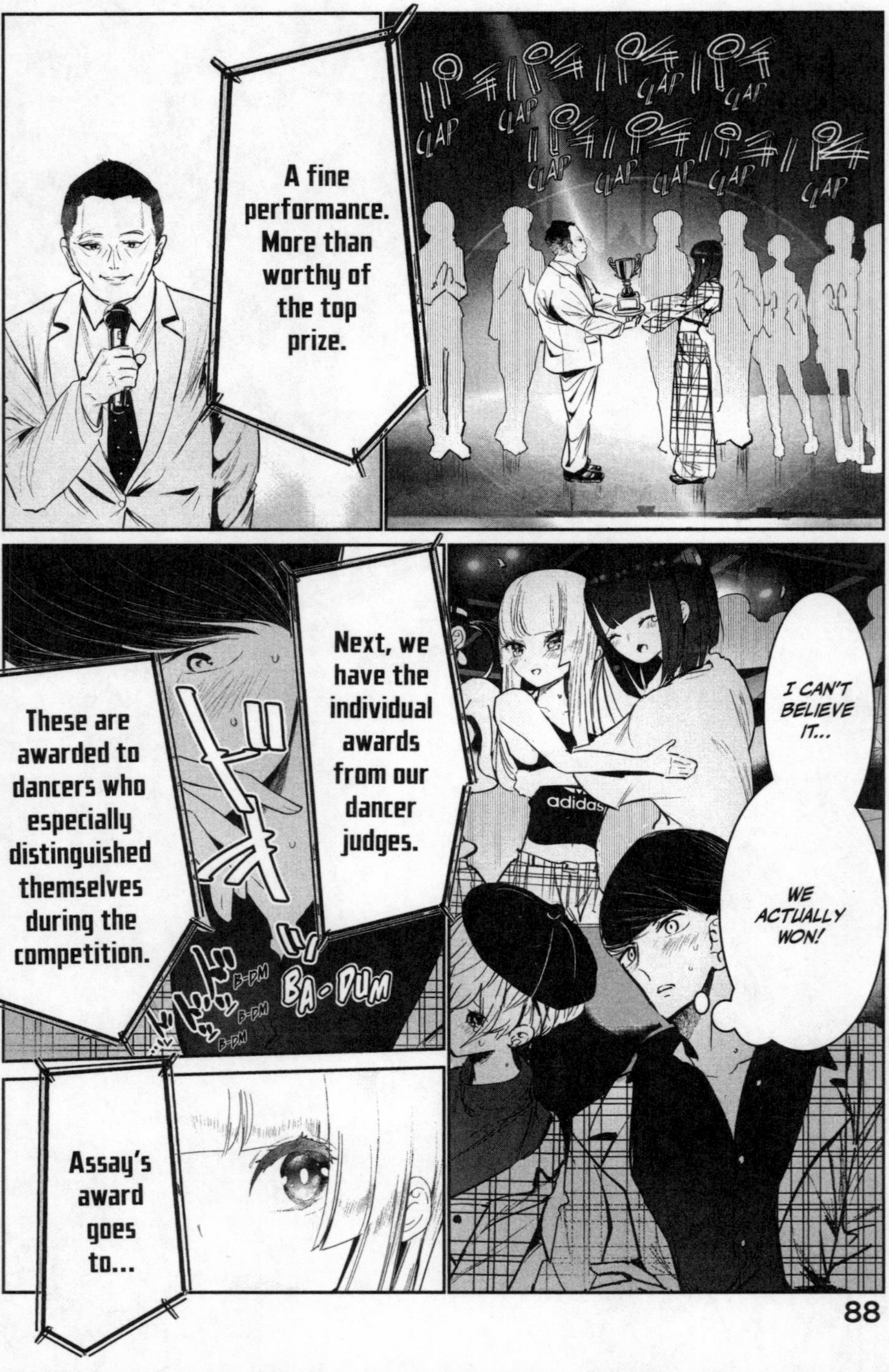
CLAP CLAP CLAP CLAP CLAP CLAP CLAP CLAP CLAP
A fine performance. More than worthy of the top prize.
I CAN'T BELIEVE IT...
WE ACTUALLY WON!
Next, we have the individual awards from our dancer judges.
These are awarded to dancers who especially distinguished themselves during the competition.
BA-DUM
B-DM B-DM B-DM
Assay's award goes to...

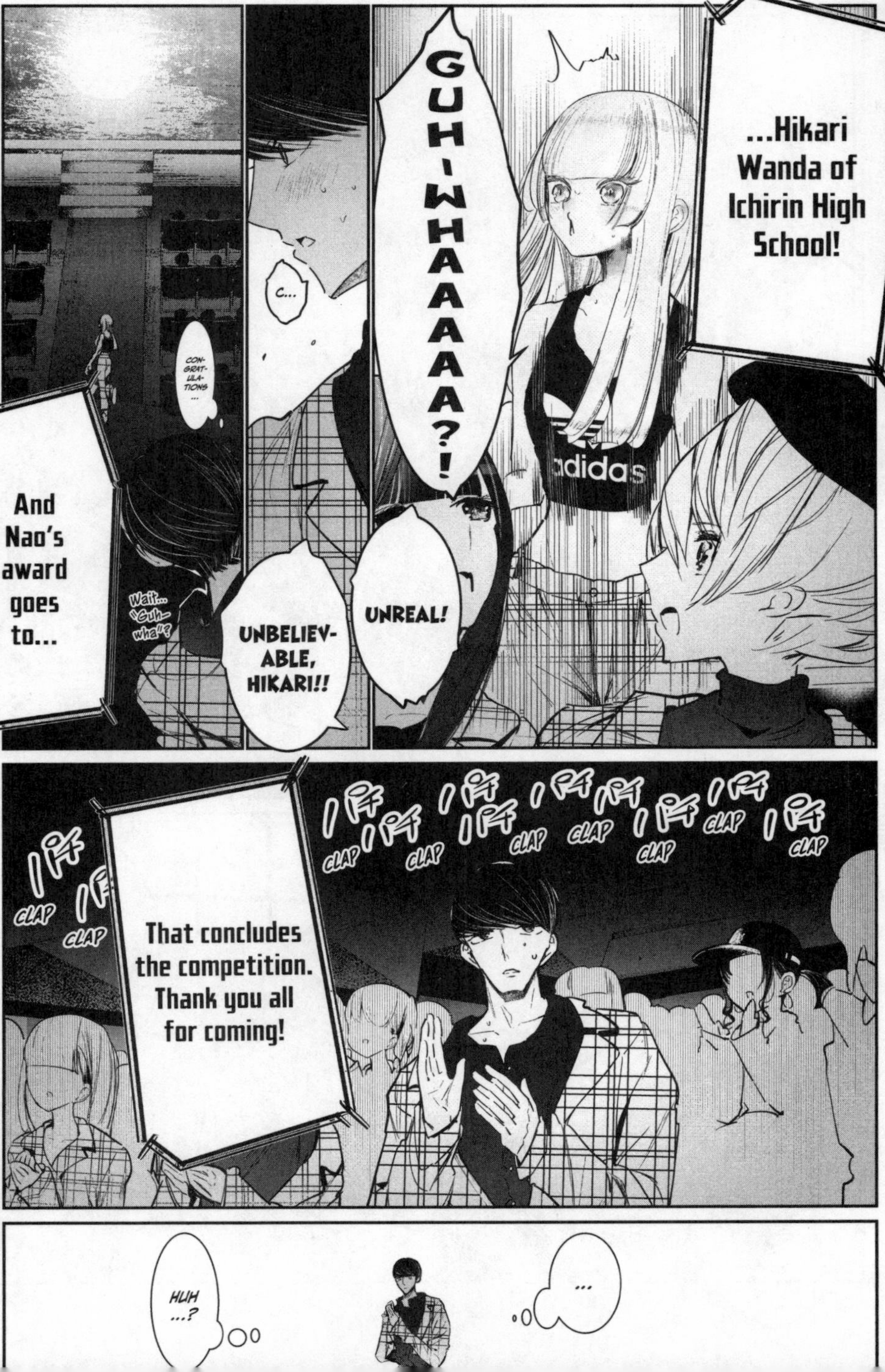
...Hikari Wanda of Ichirin High School!
GUH-WHAAAAAAA?!
UNREAL!
UNBELIEVABLE, HIKARI!!
C...
CONGRATULATIONS...
And Nao's award goes to...
Wait... "Guh-wha"?
CLAP CLAP CLAP CLAP CLAP CLAP CLAP CLAP CLAP
That concludes the competition. Thank you all for coming!
...
HUH...?

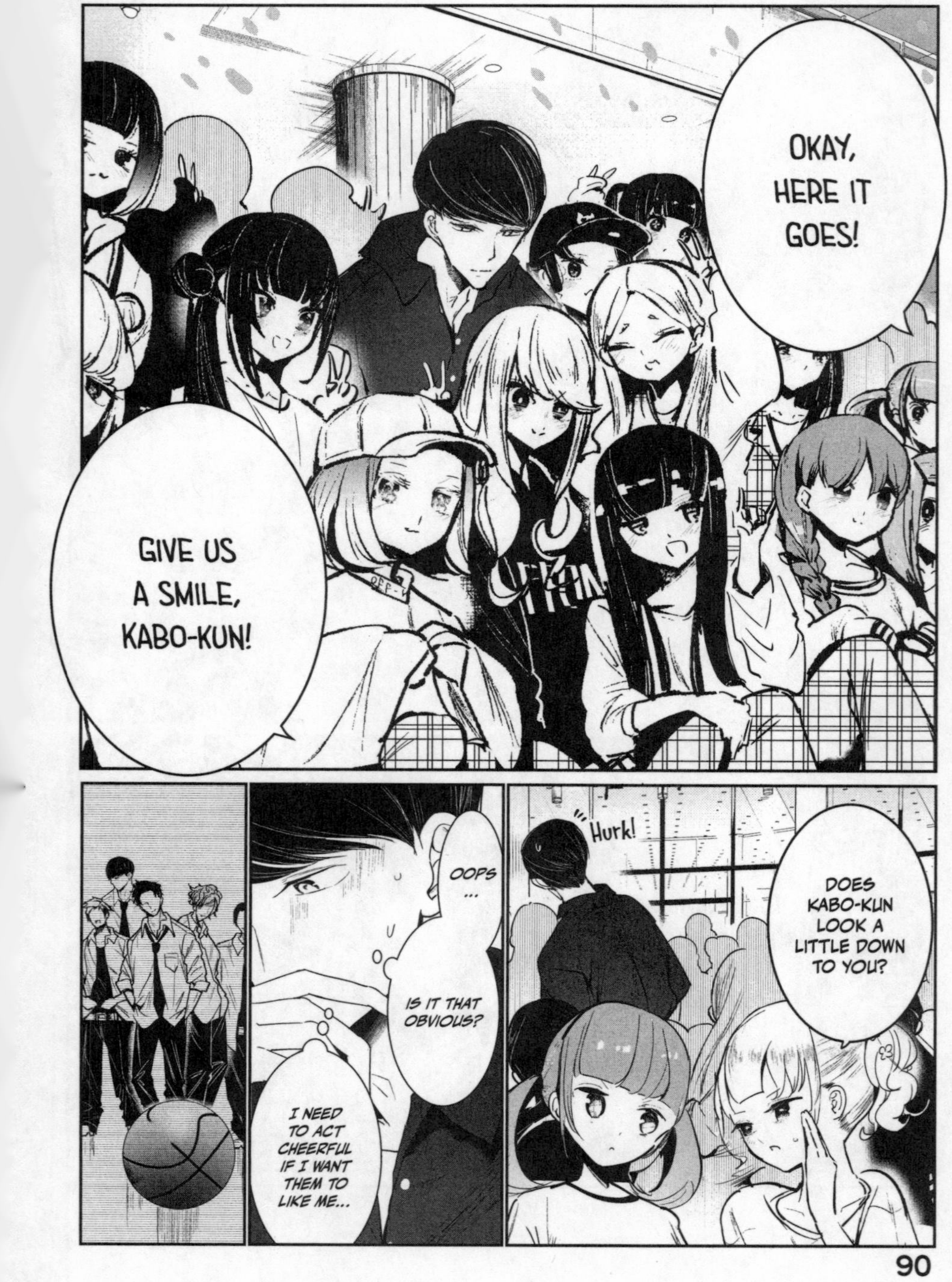
OKAY, HERE IT GOES!
GIVE US A SMILE, KABO-KUN!
DOES KABO-KUN LOOK A LITTLE DOWN TO YOU?
Hurk!
OOPS ...
IS IT THAT OBVIOUS?
I NEED TO ACT CHEERFUL IF I WANT THEM TO LIKE ME...

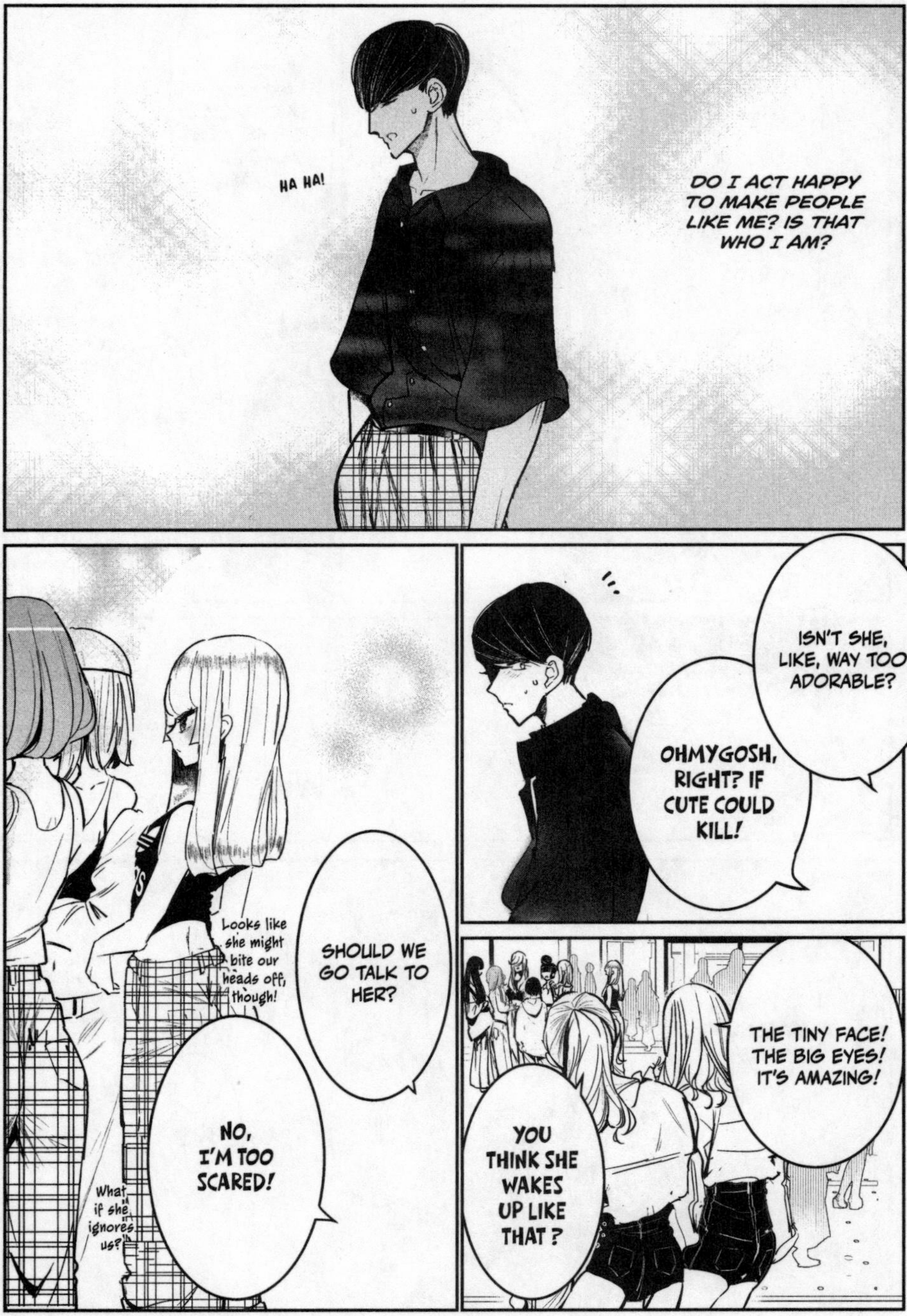
DO I ACT HAPPY TO MAKE PEOPLE LIKE ME? IS THAT WHO I AM?
HA HA!
ISN'T SHE, LIKE, WAY TOO ADORABLE?
OHMYGOSH, RIGHT? IF CUTE COULD KILL!
THE TINY FACE! THE BIG EYES! IT'S AMAZING!
YOU THINK SHE WAKES UP LIKE THAT ?
SHOULD WE GO TALK TO HER?
Looks like she might bite our heads off, though!
NO, I'M TOO SCARED!
What if she ignores us?

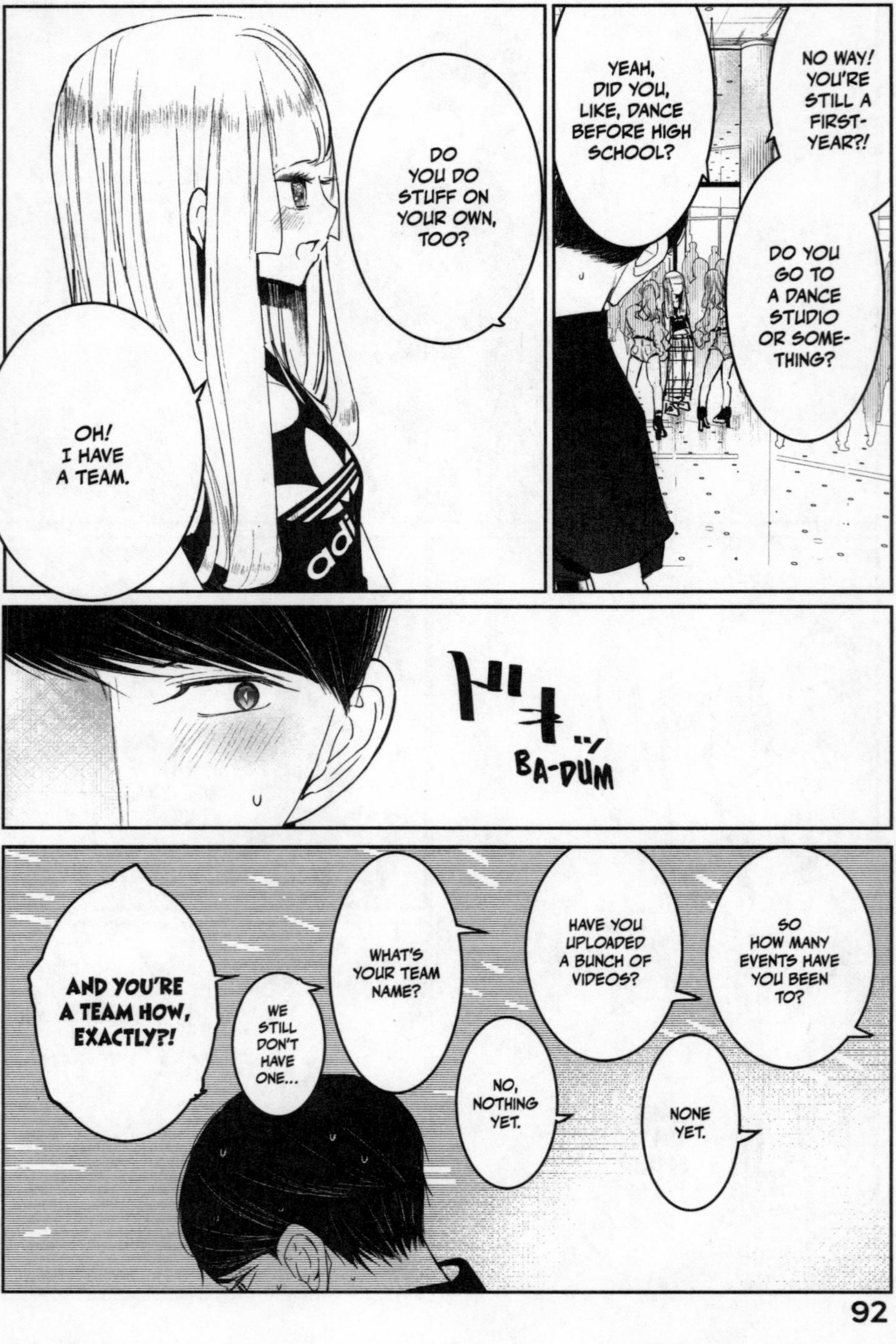
NO WAY! YOU'RE STILL A FIRST-YEAR?!
YEAH, DID YOU, LIKE, DANCE BEFORE HIGH SCHOOL?
DO YOU GO TO A DANCE STUDIO OR SOMETHING?
DO YOU DO STUFF ON YOUR OWN, TOO?
OH! I HAVE A TEAM.
ドキッ
BA-DUM
SO HOW MANY EVENTS HAVE YOU BEEN TO?
NONE YET.
HAVE YOU UPLOADED A BUNCH OF VIDEOS?
NO, NOTHING YET.
WHAT'S YOUR TEAM NAME?
WE STILL DON'T HAVE ONE...
AND YOU'RE A TEAM HOW, EXACTLY?!

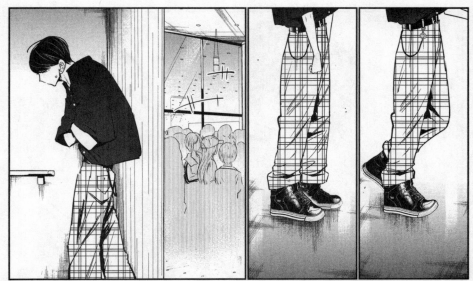

HEY, MAN!

GRAB

NOW WANDA-SAN'S BEEN IN FRONT OF AN AUDIENCE...

...AND THEY KNEW SHE WAS THE REAL DEAL. I KNEW THEY WOULD.

I SAW YOU.

OH, HEY...!

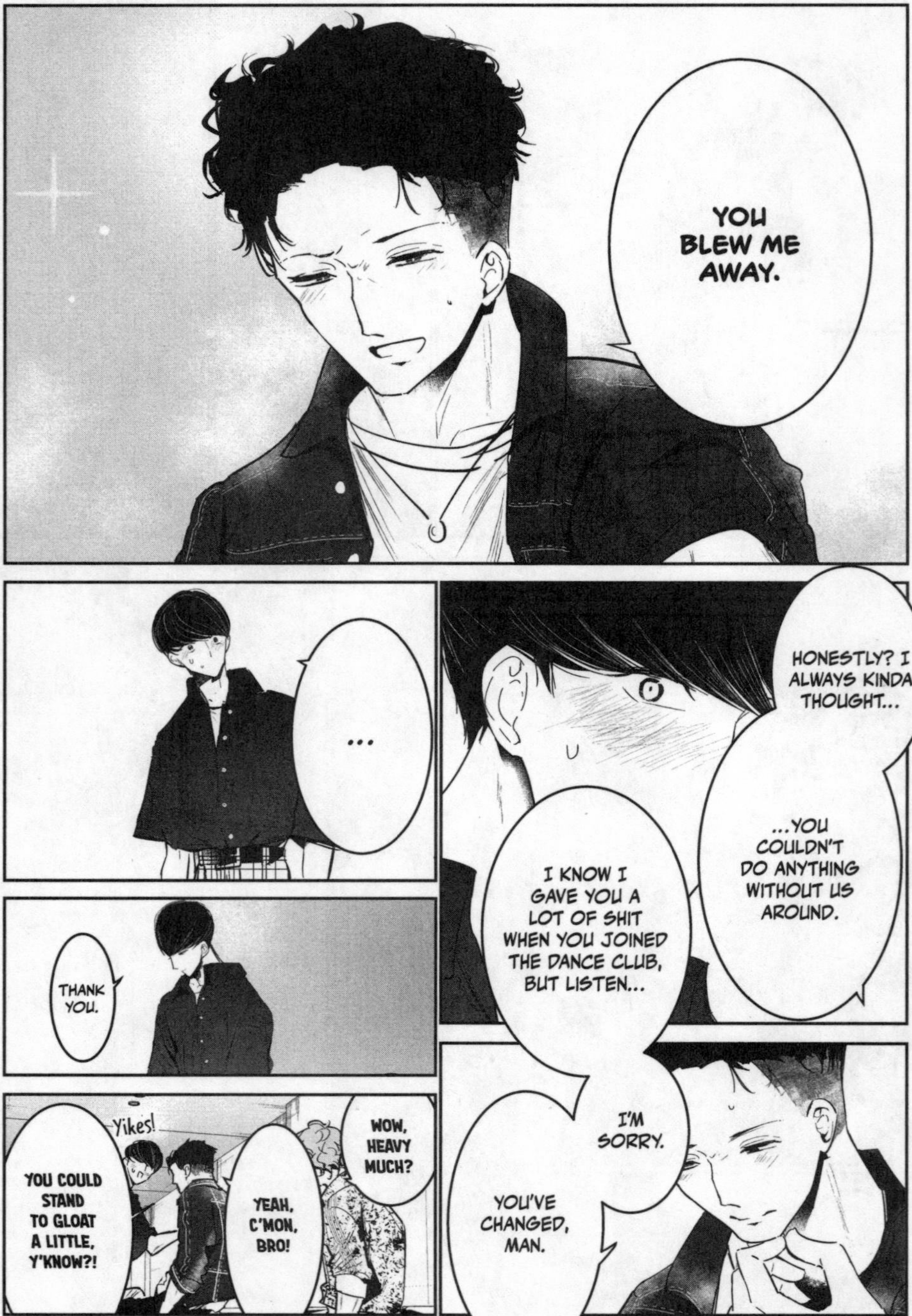
YOU BLEW ME AWAY.
HONESTLY? I ALWAYS KINDA THOUGHT...
...YOU COULDN'T DO ANYTHING WITHOUT US AROUND.
I KNOW I GAVE YOU A LOT OF SHIT WHEN YOU JOINED THE DANCE CLUB, BUT LISTEN...
I'M SORRY.
YOU'VE CHANGED, MAN.
...
THANK YOU.
WOW, HEAVY MUCH?
YEAH, C'MON, BRO!
Yikes!
YOU COULD STAND TO GLOAT A LITTLE, Y'KNOW?!

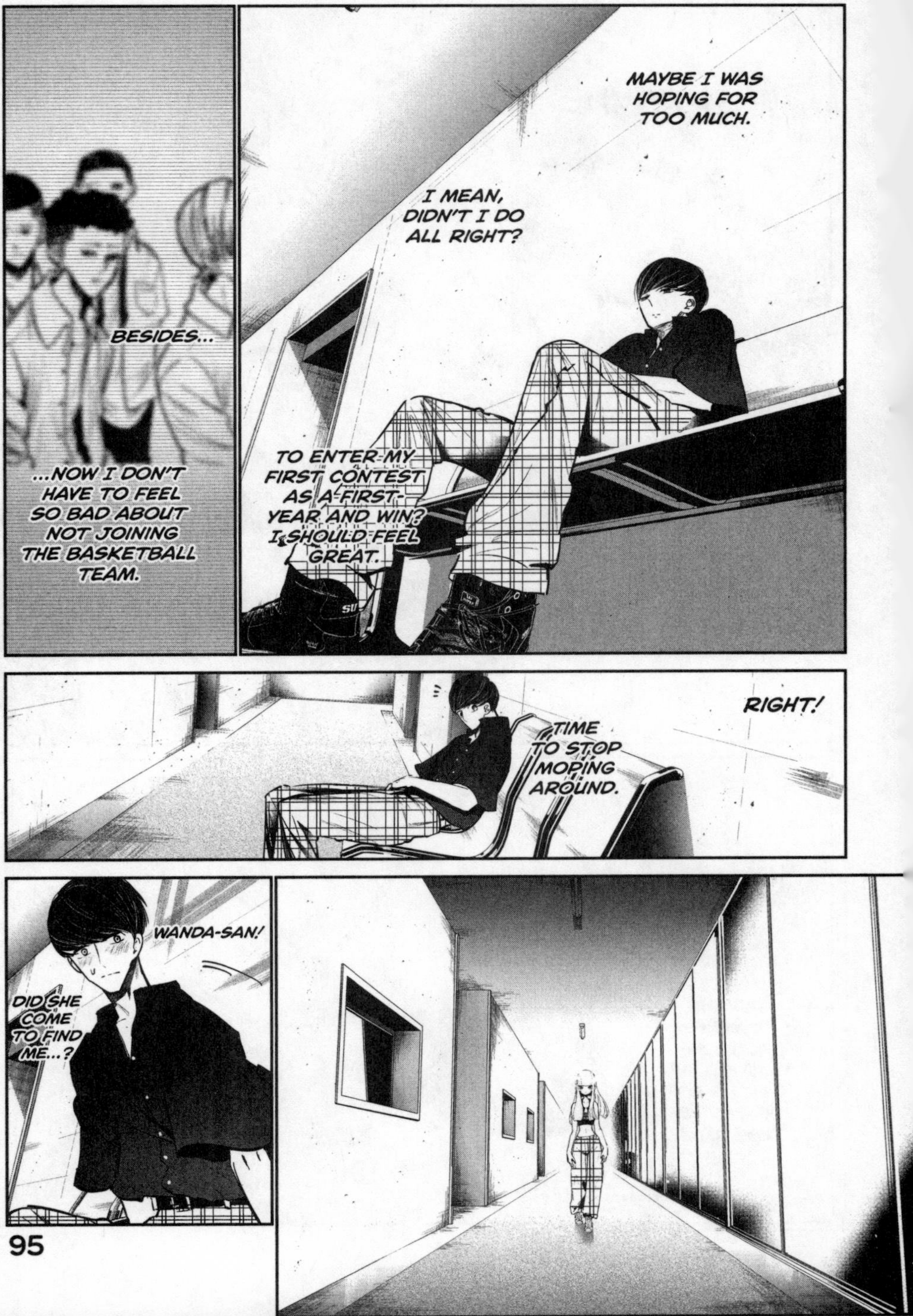
MAYBE I WAS HOPING FOR TOO MUCH.
I MEAN, DIDN'T I DO ALL RIGHT?
TO ENTER MY FIRST CONTEST AS A FIRST-YEAR AND WIN? I SHOULD FEEL GREAT.
BESIDES...
...NOW I DON'T HAVE TO FEEL SO BAD ABOUT NOT JOINING THE BASKETBALL TEAM.
RIGHT!
TIME TO STOP MOPING AROUND.
WANDA-SAN!
DID SHE COME TO FIND ME...?

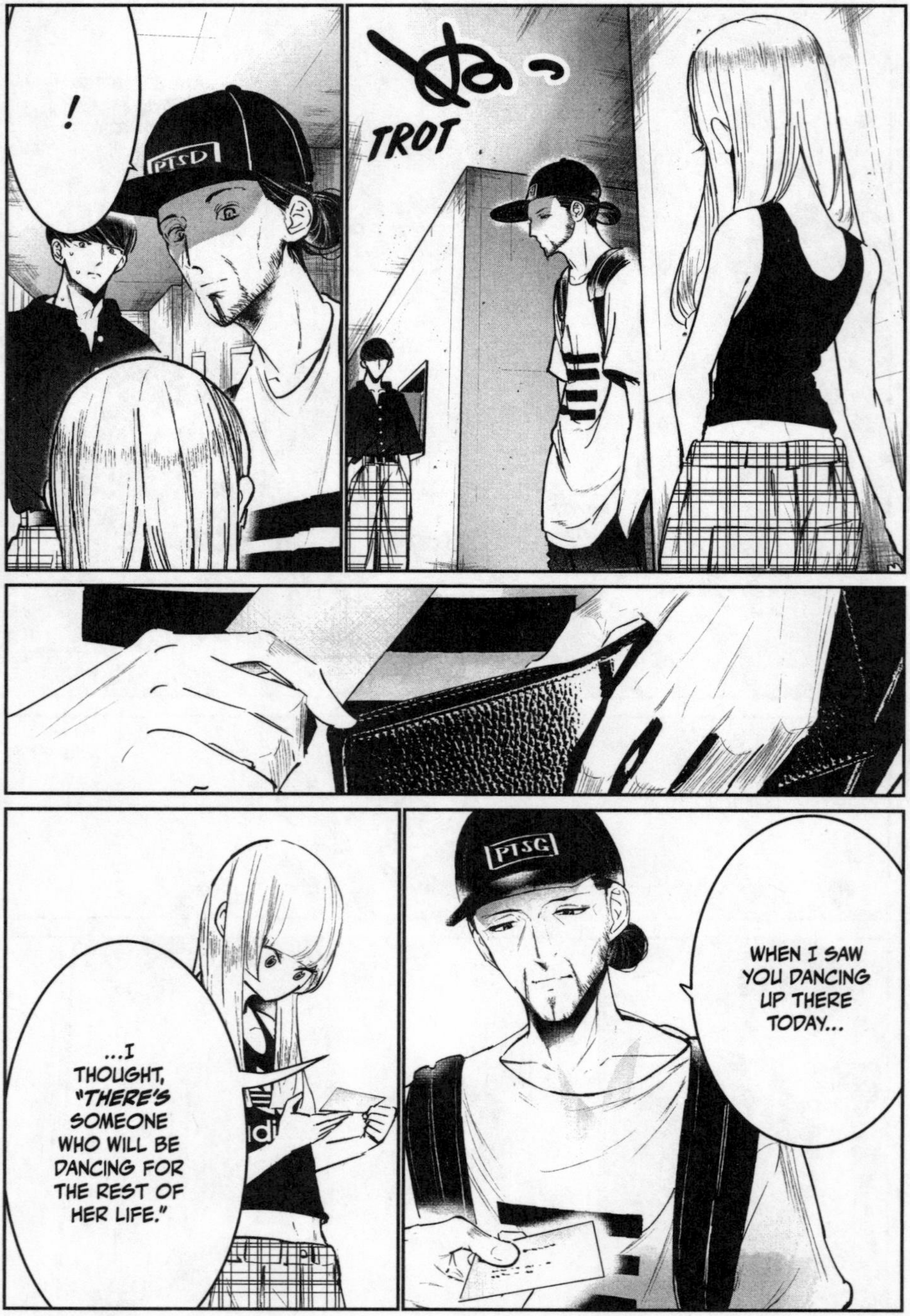
ぬっ
TROT
!
WHEN I SAW YOU DANCING UP THERE TODAY...
...I THOUGHT, "*THERE'S* SOMEONE WHO WILL BE DANCING FOR THE REST OF HER LIFE."

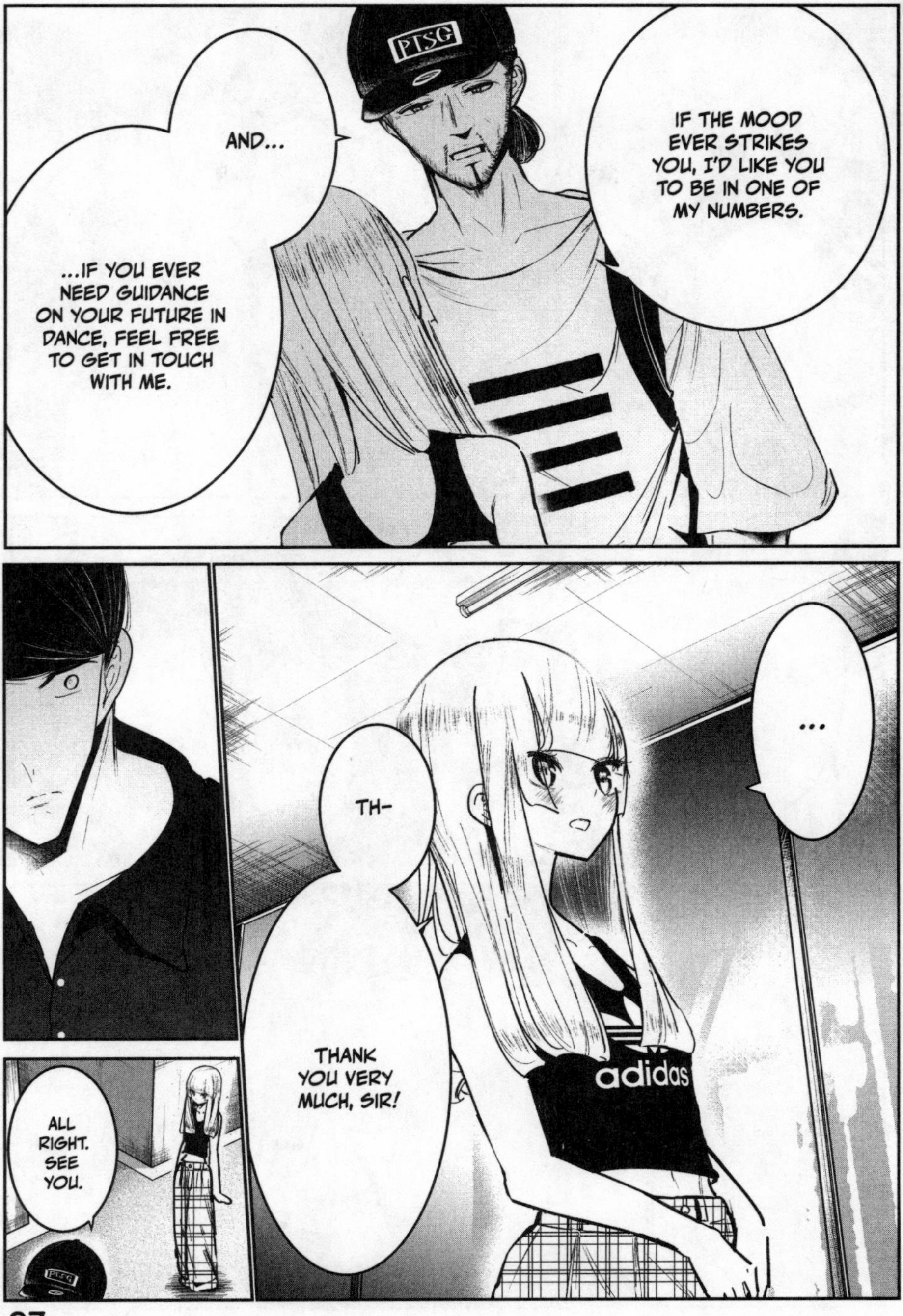
IF THE MOOD EVER STRIKES YOU, I'D LIKE YOU TO BE IN ONE OF MY NUMBERS.
AND...
...IF YOU EVER NEED GUIDANCE ON YOUR FUTURE IN DANCE, FEEL FREE TO GET IN TOUCH WITH ME.
PTSG
...
TH-
THANK YOU VERY MUCH, SIR!
adidas
ALL RIGHT. SEE YOU.

IF—
IF YOU...

HM?

UH—

UM!

ADVICE?

OR ANYTHING...

OR...

...HAVE ANY ADVICE FOR ME...

H—

...

GULP

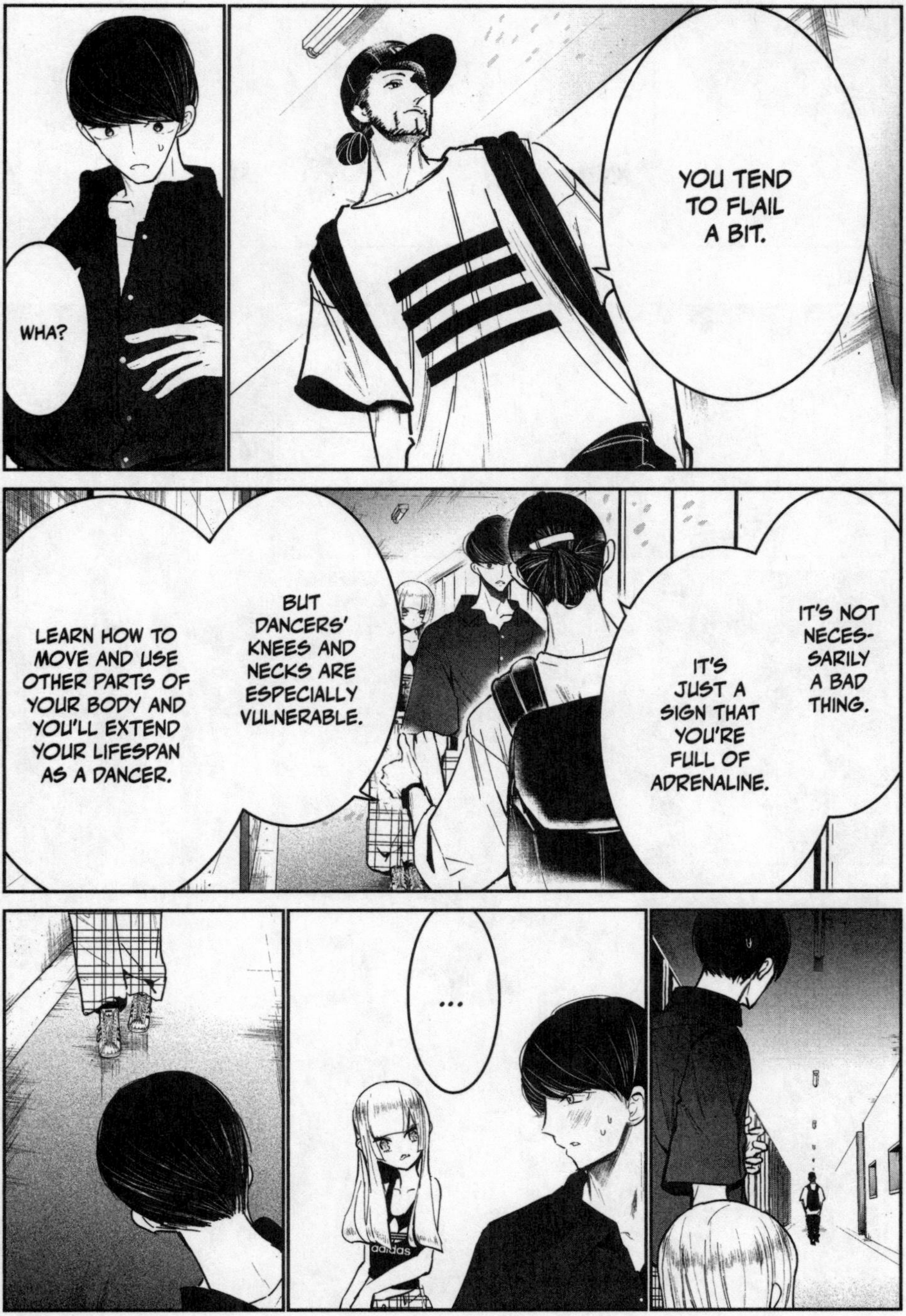
YOU TEND TO FLAIL A BIT.
WHA?
IT'S NOT NECES-SARILY A BAD THING.
IT'S JUST A SIGN THAT YOU'RE FULL OF ADRENALINE.
BUT DANCERS' KNEES AND NECKS ARE ESPECIALLY VULNERABLE.
LEARN HOW TO MOVE AND USE OTHER PARTS OF YOUR BODY AND YOU'LL EXTEND YOUR LIFESPAN AS A DANCER.
...

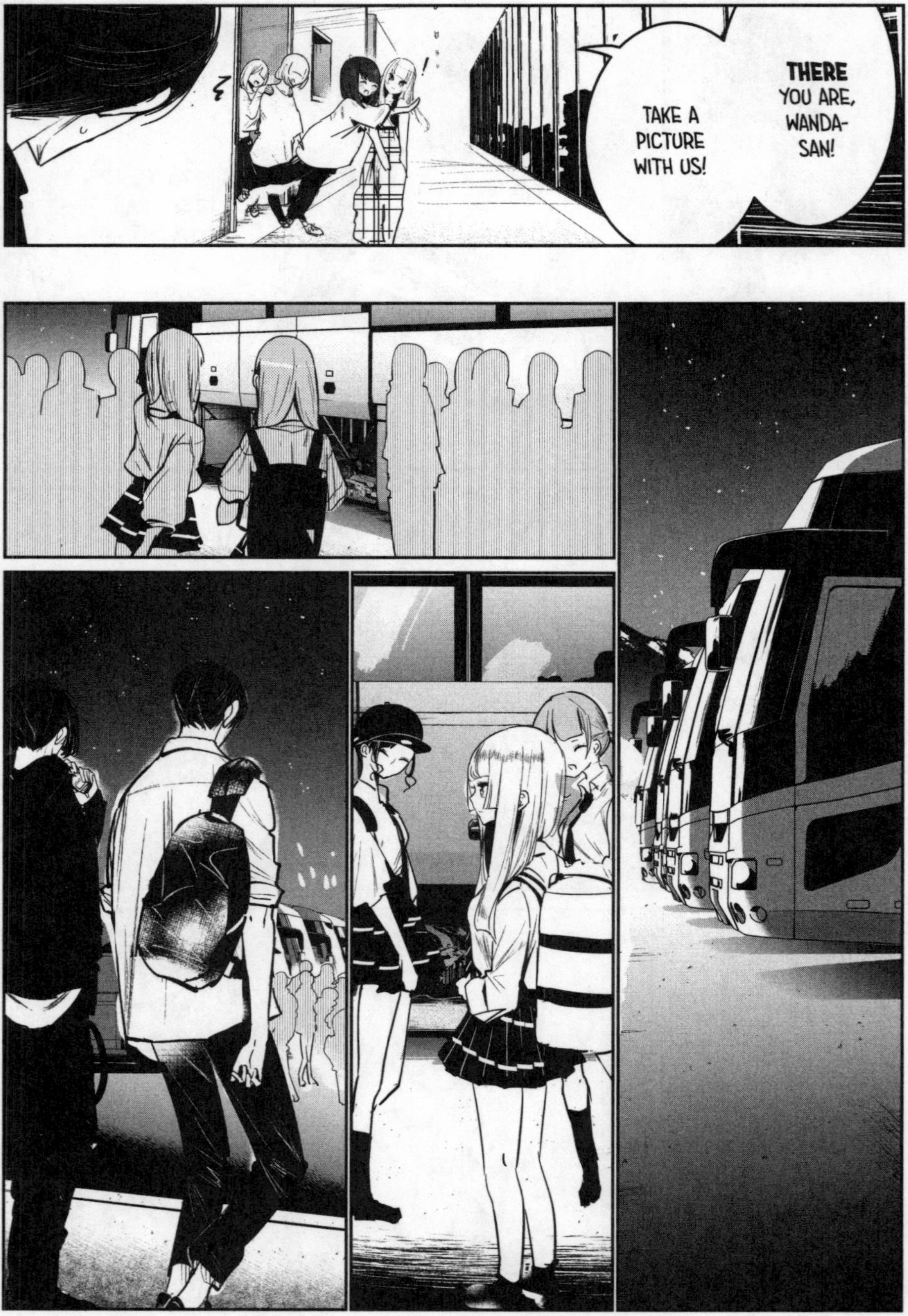
THERE YOU ARE, WANDA-SAN!
TAKE A PICTURE WITH US!

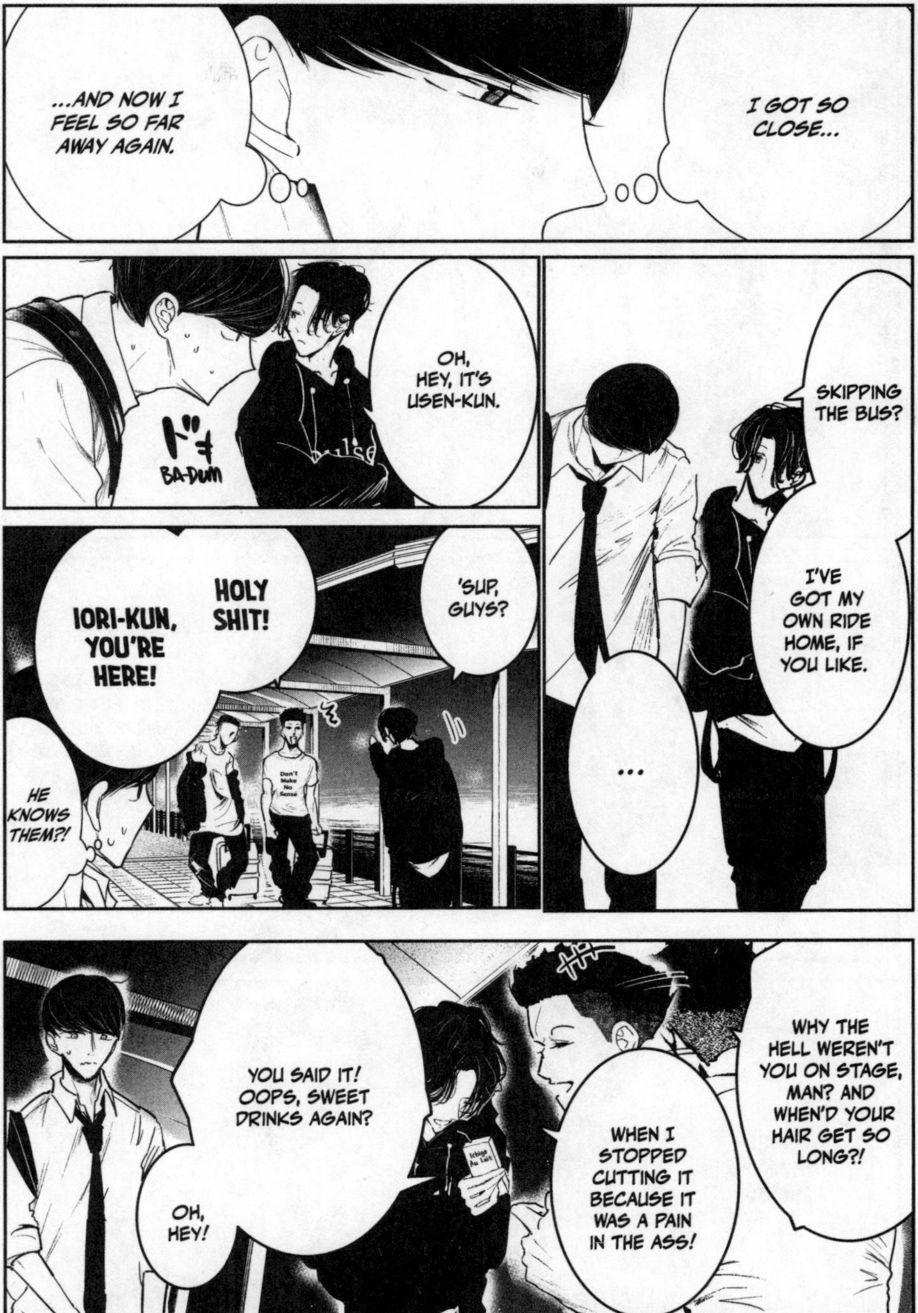
I GOT SO CLOSE...
...AND NOW I FEEL SO FAR AWAY AGAIN.
SKIPPING THE BUS?
I'VE GOT MY OWN RIDE HOME, IF YOU LIKE.
...
OH, HEY, IT'S USEN-KUN.
ドキ
BA-DUM
'SUP, GUYS?
HOLY SHIT!
IORI-KUN, YOU'RE HERE!
Don't Make No Sense
HE KNOWS THEM?!
WHY THE HELL WEREN'T YOU ON STAGE, MAN? AND WHEN'D YOUR HAIR GET SO LONG?!
WHEN I STOPPED CUTTING IT BECAUSE IT WAS A PAIN IN THE ASS!
YOU SAID IT! OOPS, SWEET DRINKS AGAIN?
Ichigo Au Lait
OH, HEY!

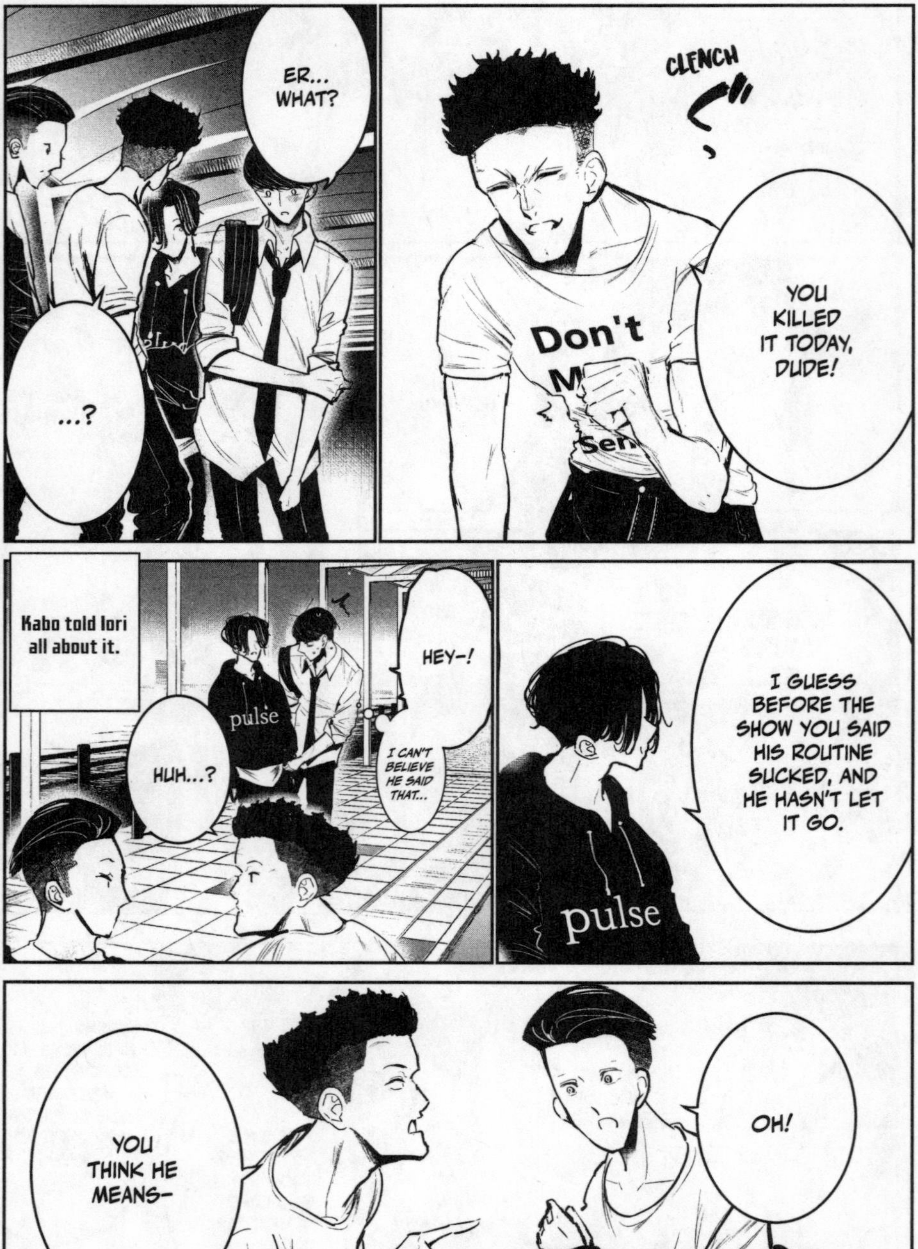
CLENCH
YOU KILLED IT TODAY, DUDE!
ER... WHAT?
...?
I GUESS BEFORE THE SHOW YOU SAID HIS ROUTINE SUCKED, AND HE HASN'T LET IT GO.
HEY–!
Kabo told Iori all about it.
I CAN'T BELIEVE HE SAID THAT...
HUH...?
OH!
YOU THINK HE MEANS–

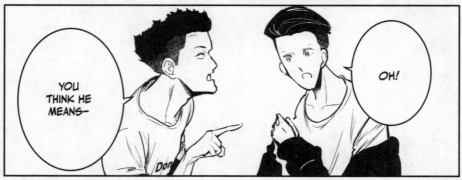

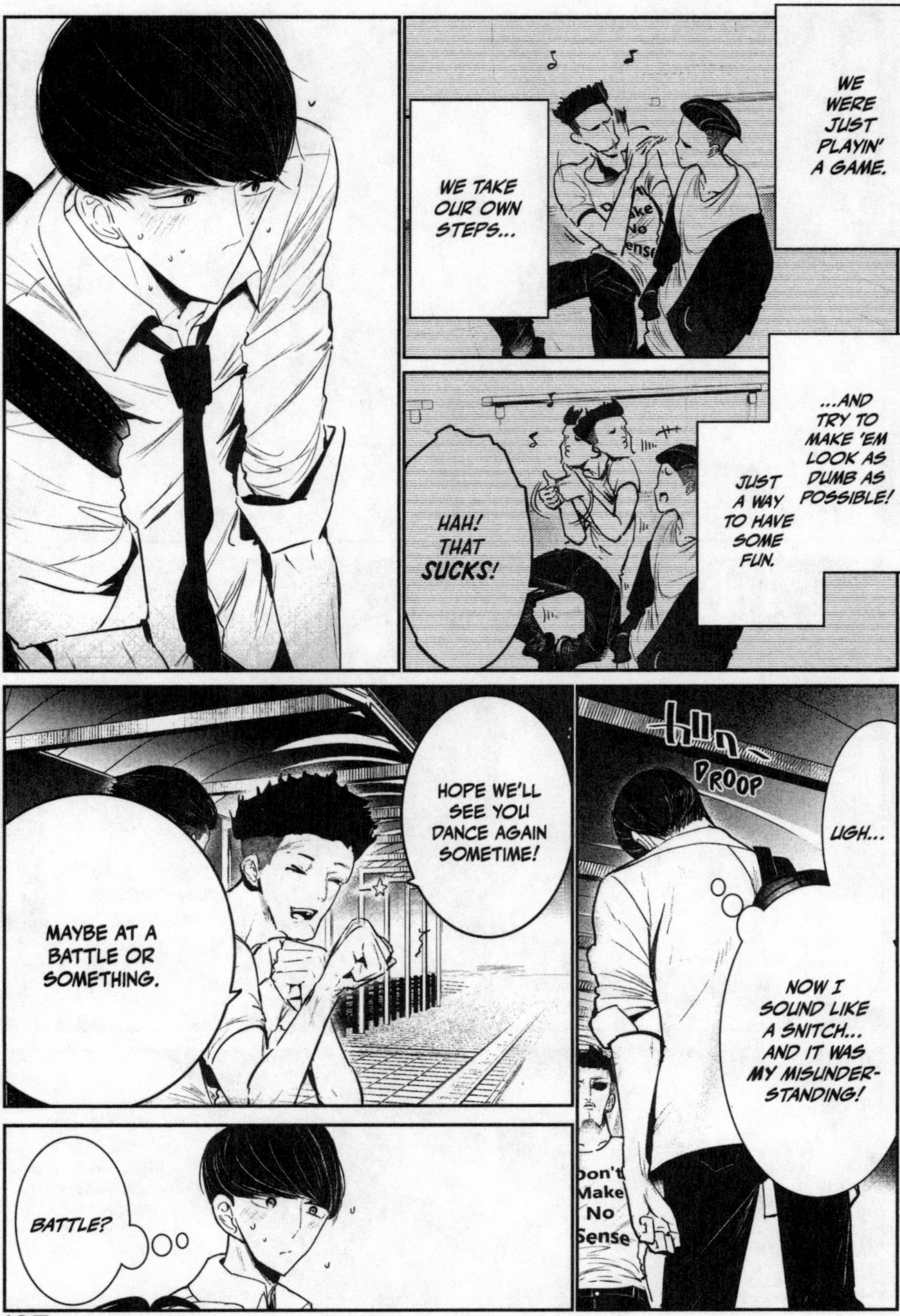
WE WERE JUST PLAYIN' A GAME.
WE TAKE OUR OWN STEPS...
...AND TRY TO MAKE 'EM LOOK AS DUMB AS POSSIBLE!
JUST A WAY TO HAVE SOME FUN.
HAH! THAT SUCKS!
DROOP
UGH...
NOW I SOUND LIKE A SNITCH... AND IT WAS MY MISUNDER-STANDING!
Don't Make No Sense
HOPE WE'LL SEE YOU DANCE AGAIN SOMETIME!
MAYBE AT A BATTLE OR SOMETHING.
BATTLE?

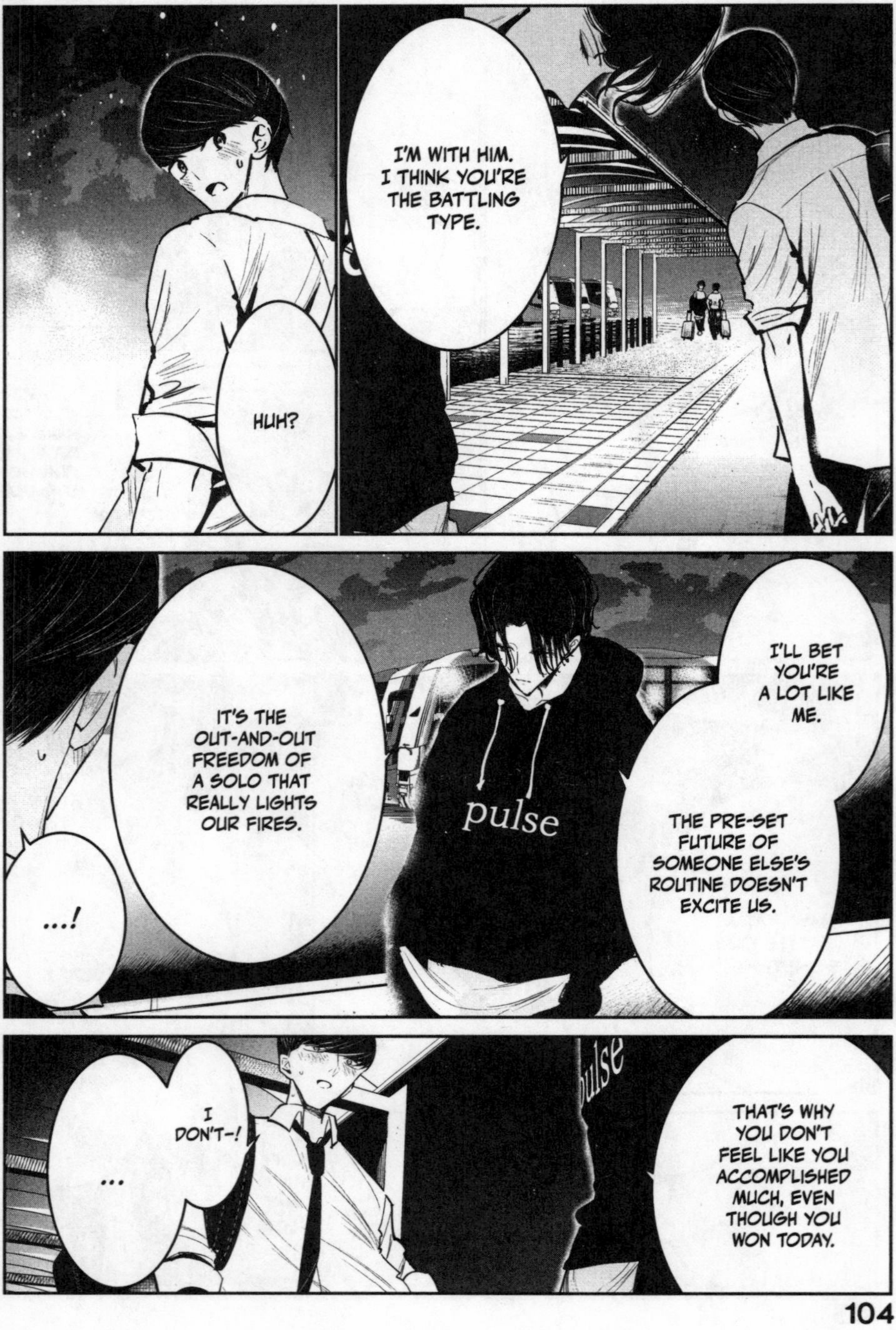
I'M WITH HIM. I THINK YOU'RE THE BATTLING TYPE.
HUH?
I'LL BET YOU'RE A LOT LIKE ME.
THE PRE-SET FUTURE OF SOMEONE ELSE'S ROUTINE DOESN'T EXCITE US.
IT'S THE OUT-AND-OUT FREEDOM OF A SOLO THAT REALLY LIGHTS OUR FIRES.
...!
pulse
THAT'S WHY YOU DON'T FEEL LIKE YOU ACCOMPLISHED MUCH, EVEN THOUGH YOU WON TODAY.
I DON'T-!
...

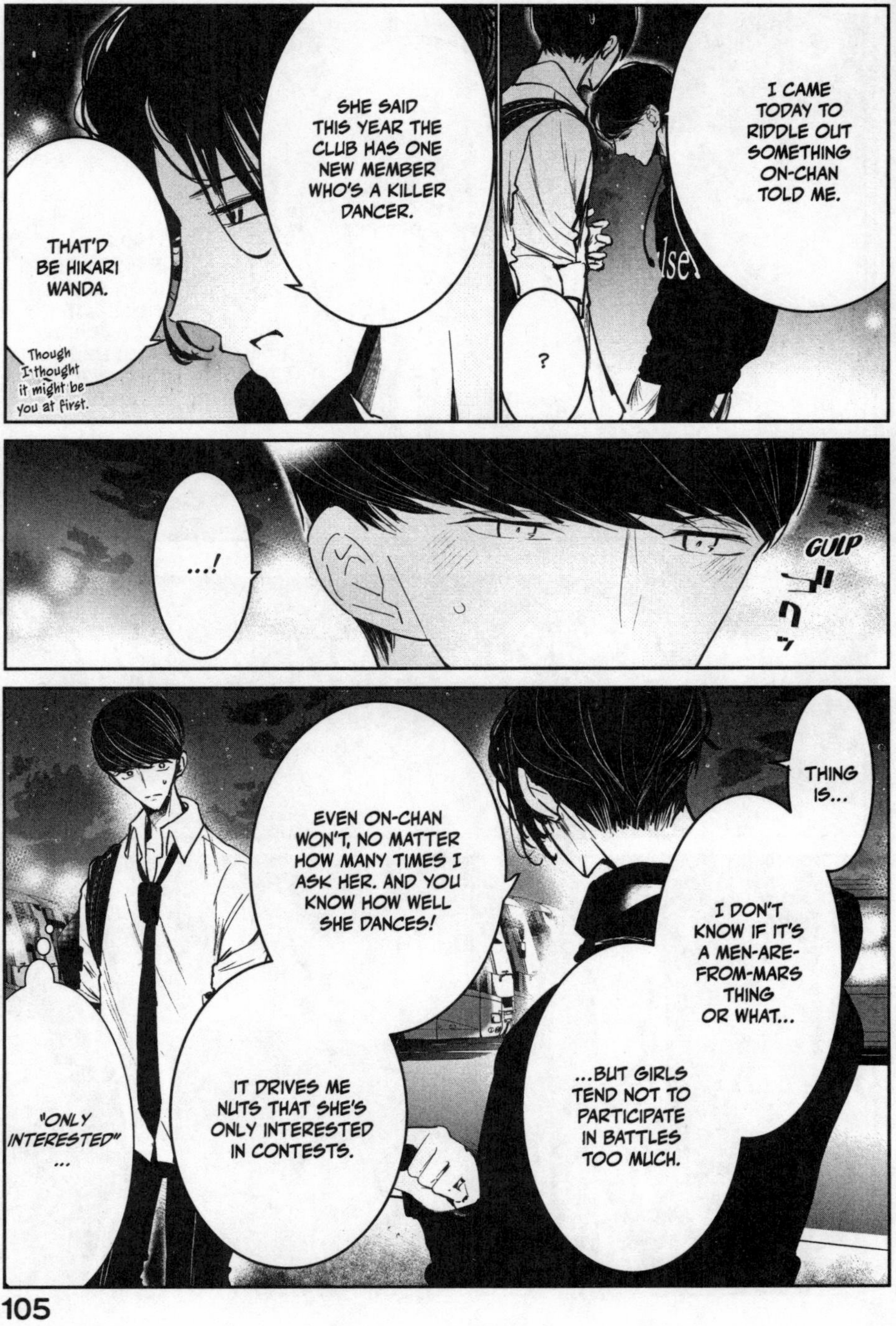
I CAME TODAY TO RIDDLE OUT SOMETHING ON-CHAN TOLD ME.
?
SHE SAID THIS YEAR THE CLUB HAS ONE NEW MEMBER WHO'S A KILLER DANCER.
THAT'D BE HIKARI WANDA.
Though I thought it might be you at first.
GULP
ゴクッ
...!
THING IS...
I DON'T KNOW IF IT'S A MEN-ARE-FROM-MARS THING OR WHAT...
...BUT GIRLS TEND NOT TO PARTICIPATE IN BATTLES TOO MUCH.
EVEN ON-CHAN WON'T, NO MATTER HOW MANY TIMES I ASK HER. AND YOU KNOW HOW WELL SHE DANCES!
IT DRIVES ME NUTS THAT SHE'S ONLY INTERESTED IN CONTESTS.
"ONLY INTERESTED" ...

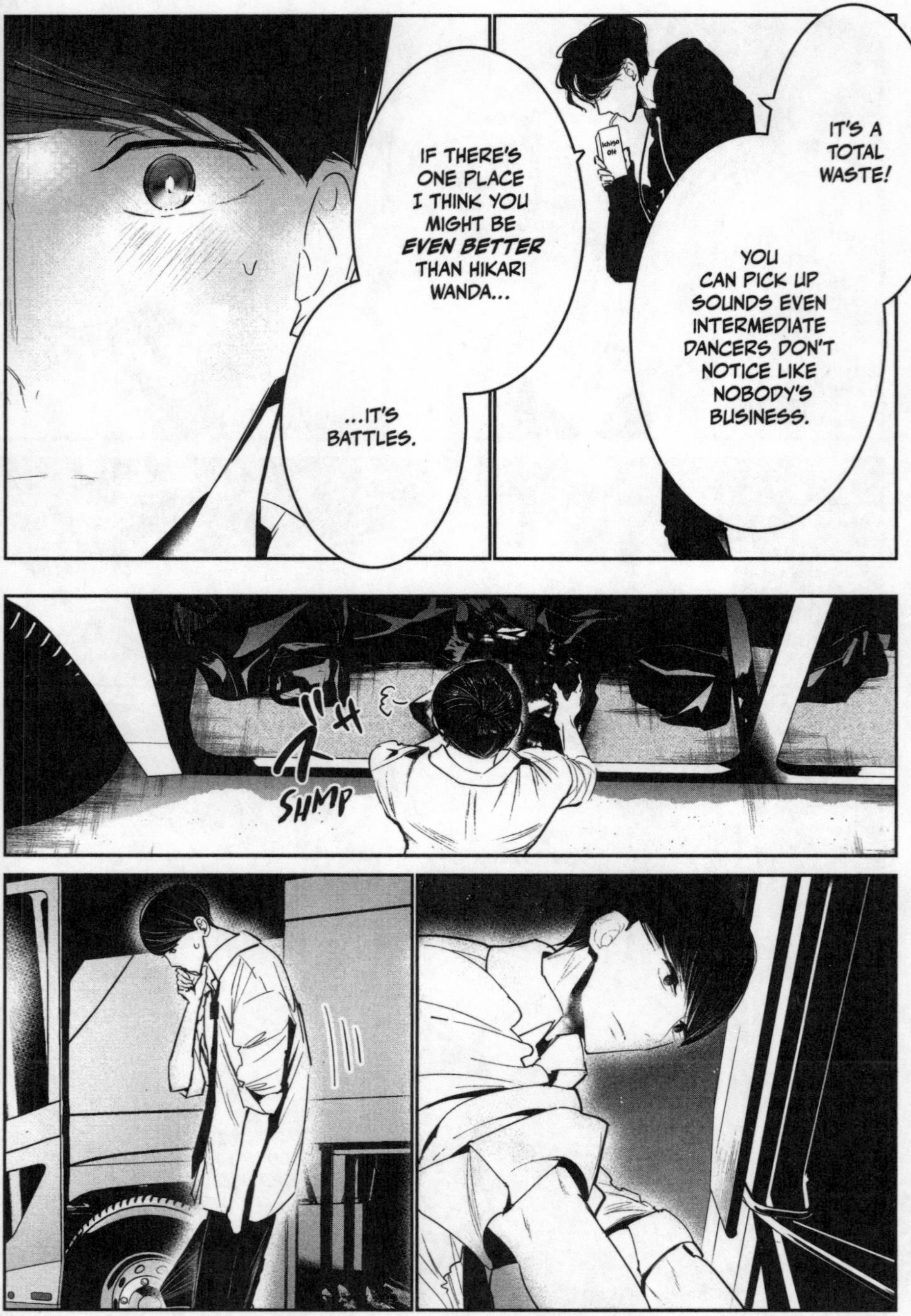
IT'S A TOTAL WASTE!
YOU CAN PICK UP SOUNDS EVEN INTERMEDIATE DANCERS DON'T NOTICE LIKE NOBODY'S BUSINESS.
IF THERE'S ONE PLACE I THINK YOU MIGHT BE *EVEN BETTER* THAN HIKARI WANDA...
...IT'S BATTLES.
SHMP

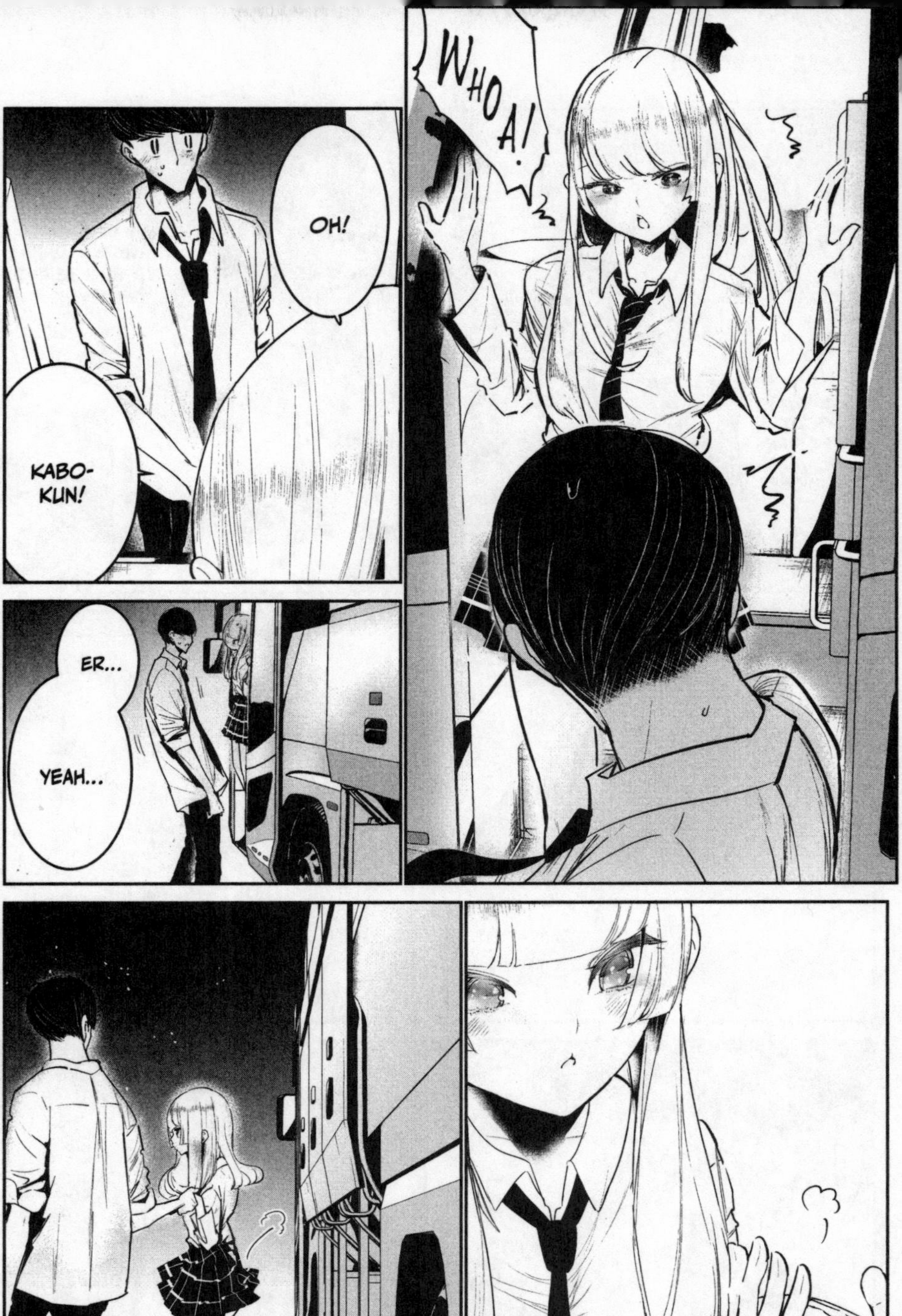
WHOA!
OH!
KABO-KUN!
ER...
YEAH...

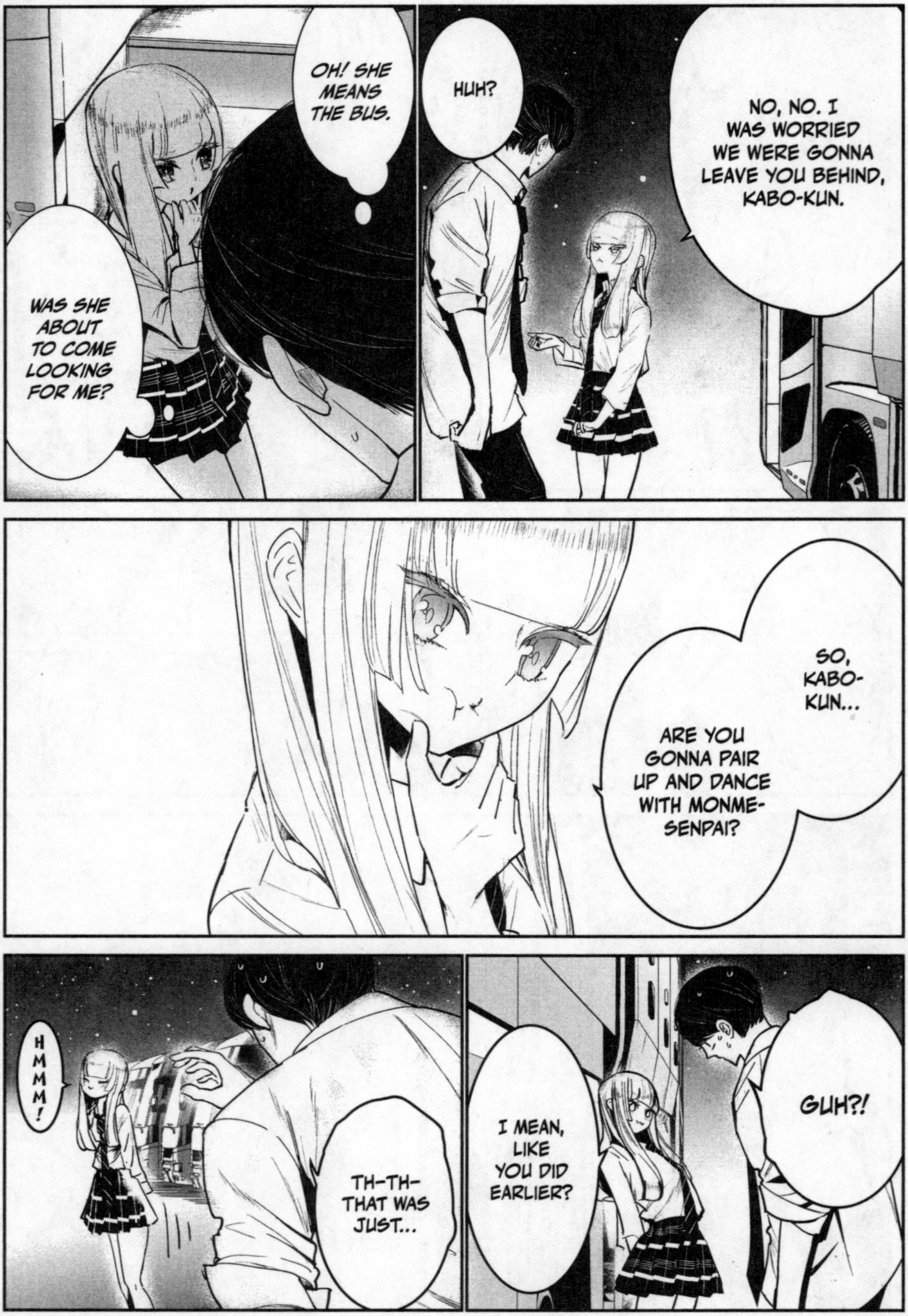
NO, NO. I WAS WORRIED WE WERE GONNA LEAVE YOU BEHIND, KABO-KUN.
HUH?
OH! SHE MEANS THE BUS.
WAS SHE ABOUT TO COME LOOKING FOR ME?
SO, KABO-KUN...
ARE YOU GONNA PAIR UP AND DANCE WITH MONME-SENPAI?
GUH?!
I MEAN, LIKE YOU DID EARLIER?
HMMM!
TH-TH-THAT WAS JUST...

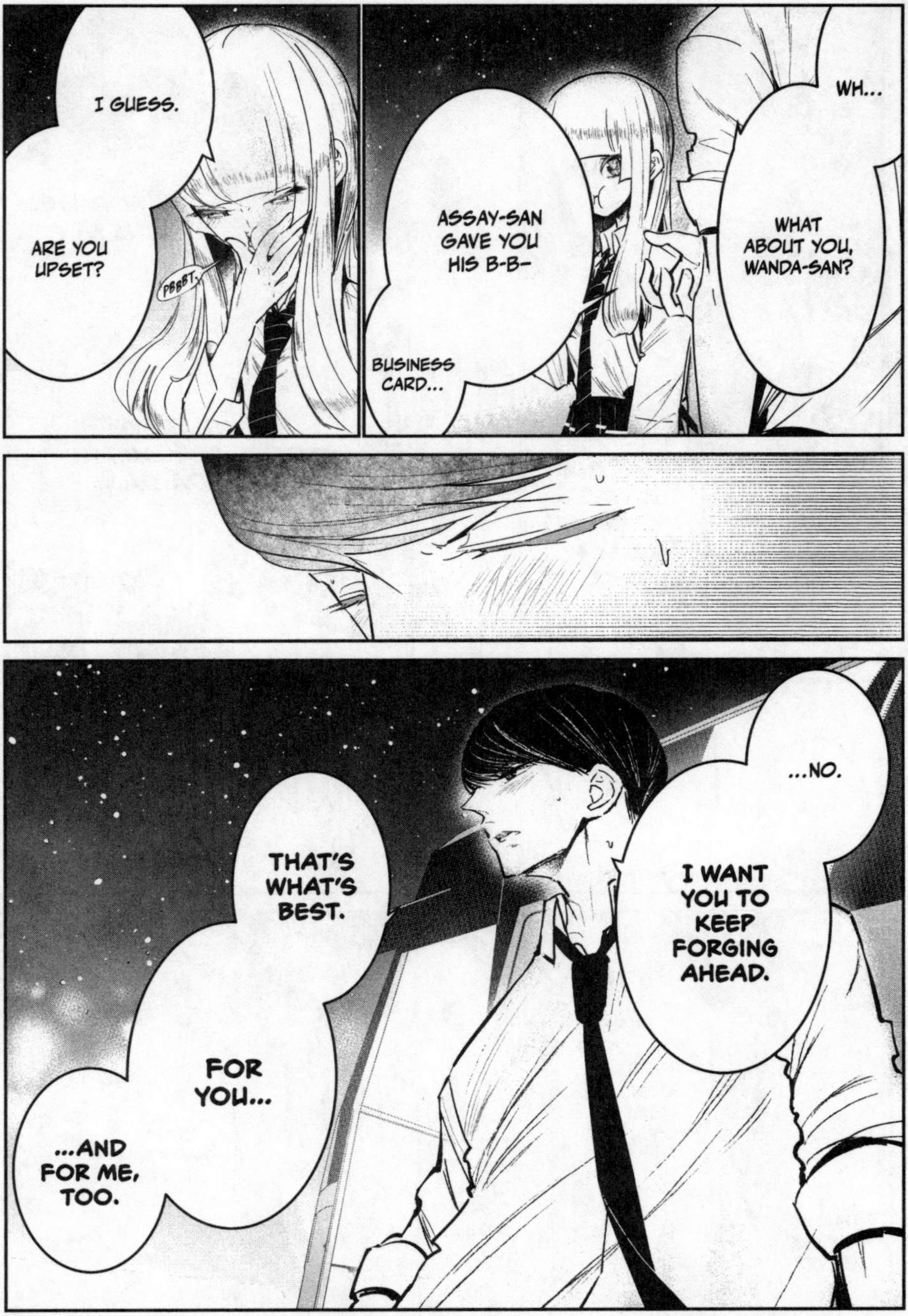
WH...
WHAT ABOUT YOU, WANDA-SAN?
ASSAY-SAN GAVE YOU HIS B-B-
BUSINESS CARD...
I GUESS.
PBBBT.
ARE YOU UPSET?
...NO.
I WANT YOU TO KEEP FORGING AHEAD.
THAT'S WHAT'S BEST.
FOR YOU...
...AND FOR ME, TOO.

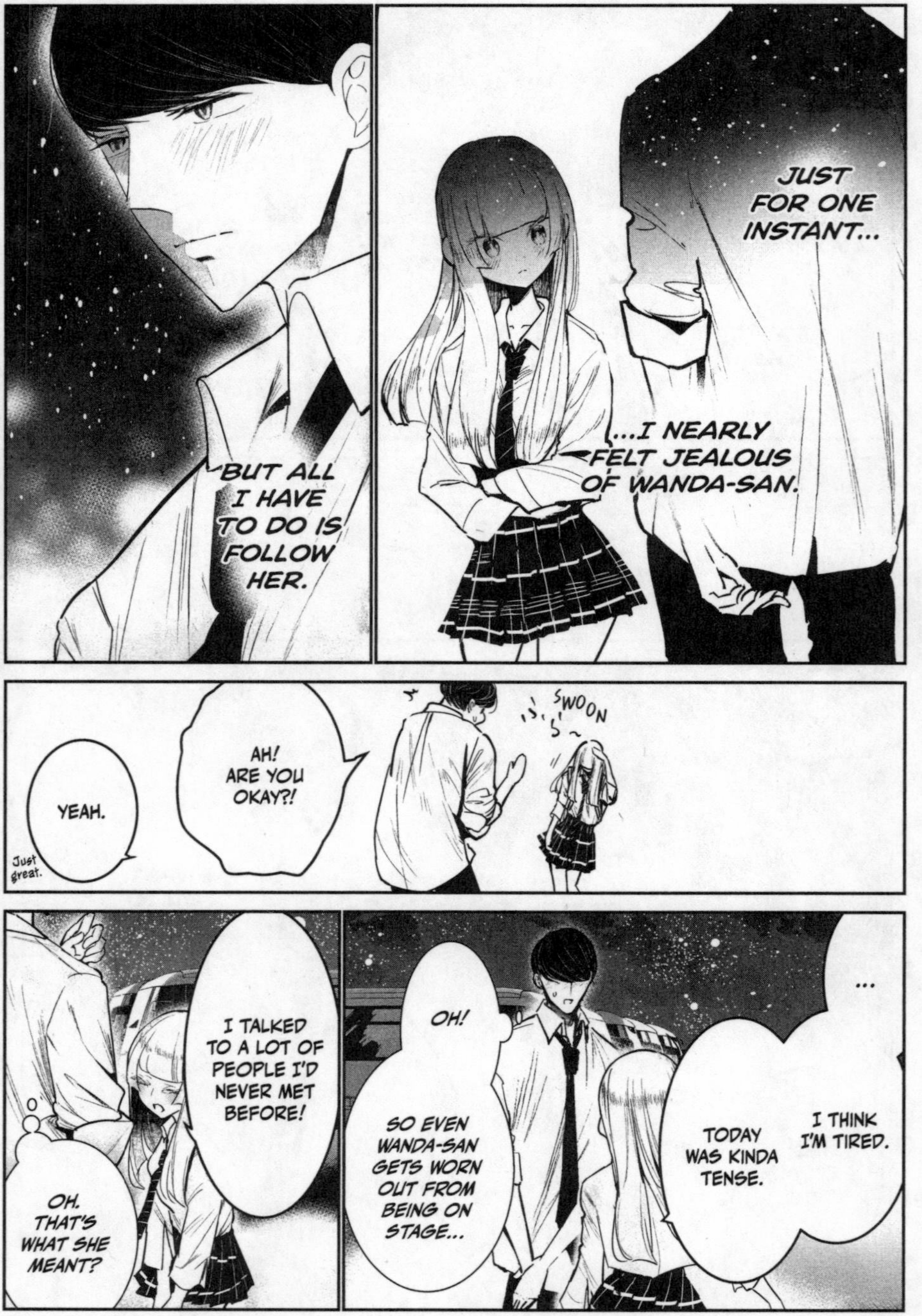
JUST FOR ONE INSTANT...
...I NEARLY FELT JEALOUS OF WANDA-SAN.
BUT ALL I HAVE TO DO IS FOLLOW HER.
SWOON
AH! ARE YOU OKAY?!
YEAH.
Just great.
...
I THINK I'M TIRED.
TODAY WAS KINDA TENSE.
OH!
SO EVEN WANDA-SAN GETS WORN OUT FROM BEING ON STAGE...
I TALKED TO A LOT OF PEOPLE I'D NEVER MET BEFORE!
OH. THAT'S WHAT SHE MEANT?

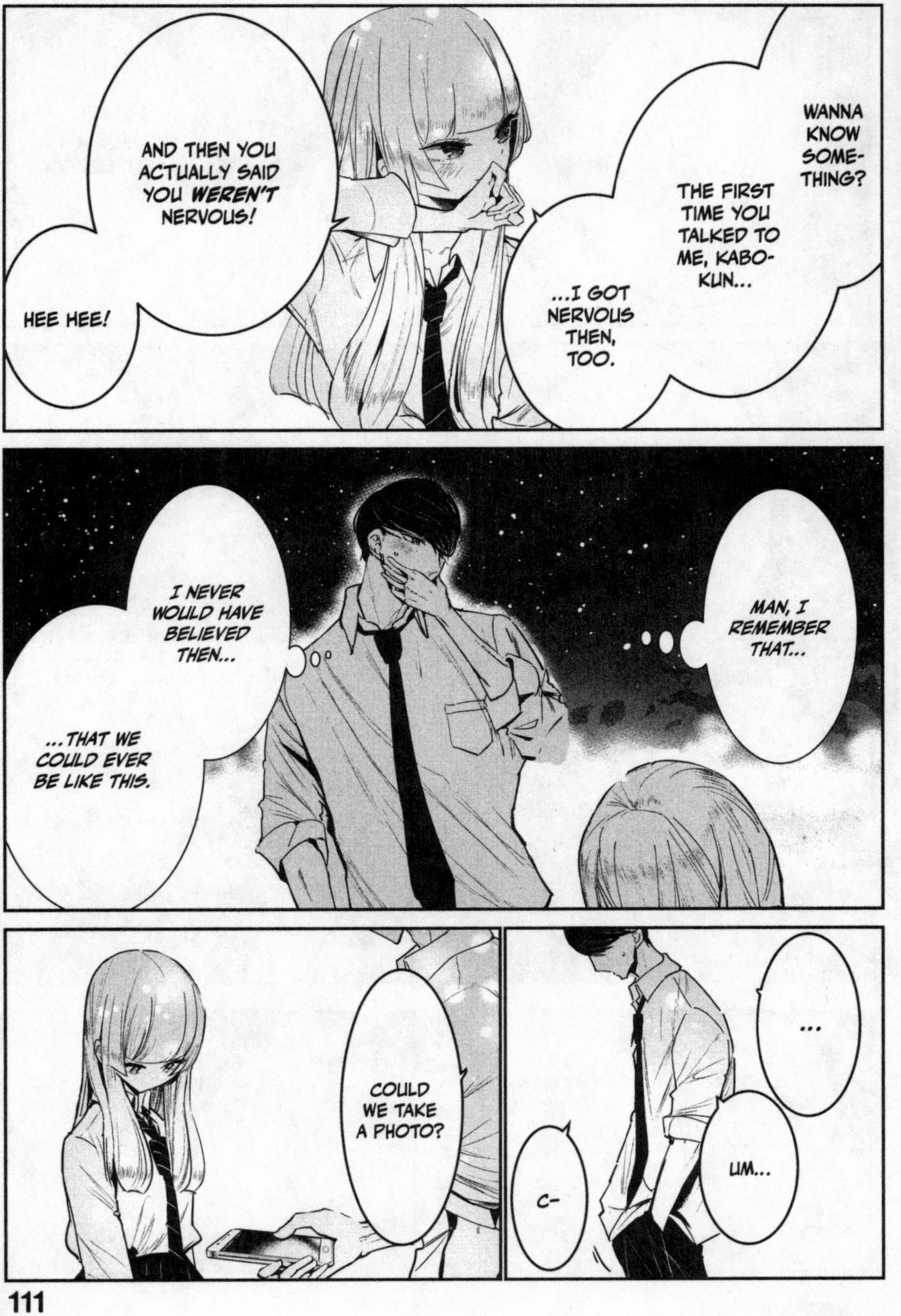
WANNA KNOW SOME-THING?
THE FIRST TIME YOU TALKED TO ME, KABO-KUN...
...I GOT NERVOUS THEN, TOO.
AND THEN YOU ACTUALLY SAID YOU *WEREN'T* NERVOUS!
HEE HEE!
MAN, I REMEMBER THAT...
I NEVER WOULD HAVE BELIEVED THEN...
...THAT WE COULD EVER BE LIKE THIS.
...
UM...
C–
COULD WE TAKE A PHOTO?

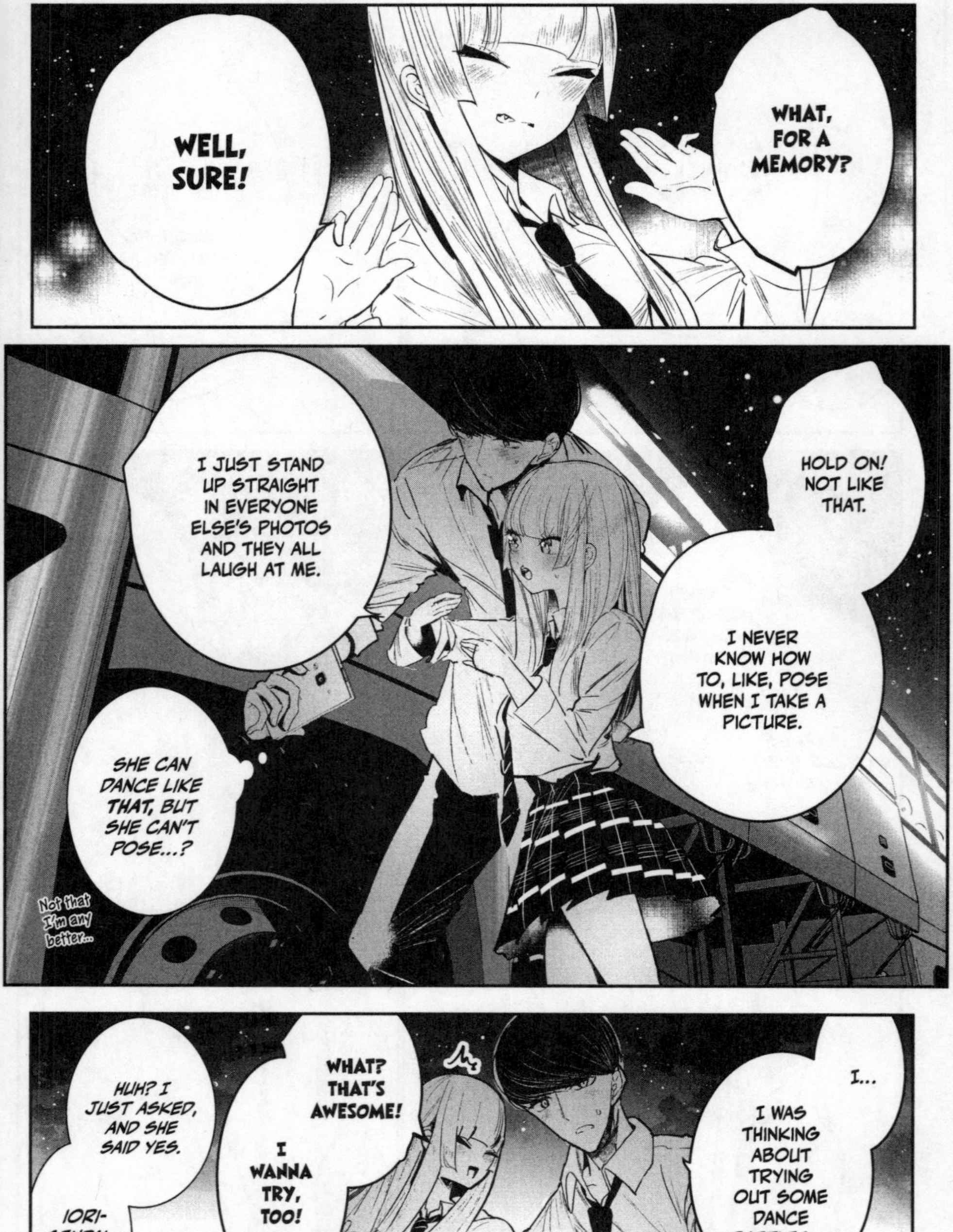
WHAT, FOR A MEMORY?
WELL, SURE!
HOLD ON! NOT LIKE THAT.
I NEVER KNOW HOW TO, LIKE, POSE WHEN I TAKE A PICTURE.
I JUST STAND UP STRAIGHT IN EVERYONE ELSE'S PHOTOS AND THEY ALL LAUGH AT ME.
SHE CAN DANCE LIKE THAT, BUT SHE CAN'T POSE...?
Not that I'm any better...
I...
I WAS THINKING ABOUT TRYING OUT SOME DANCE BATTLES...
WHAT? THAT'S AWESOME!
I WANNA TRY, TOO!
HUH? I JUST ASKED, AND SHE SAID YES.
IORI-SENPAI...

Ch. 11: END

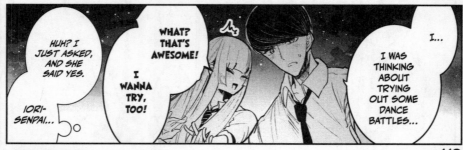

WANDANCE

Ch. 12: On vs. Iori

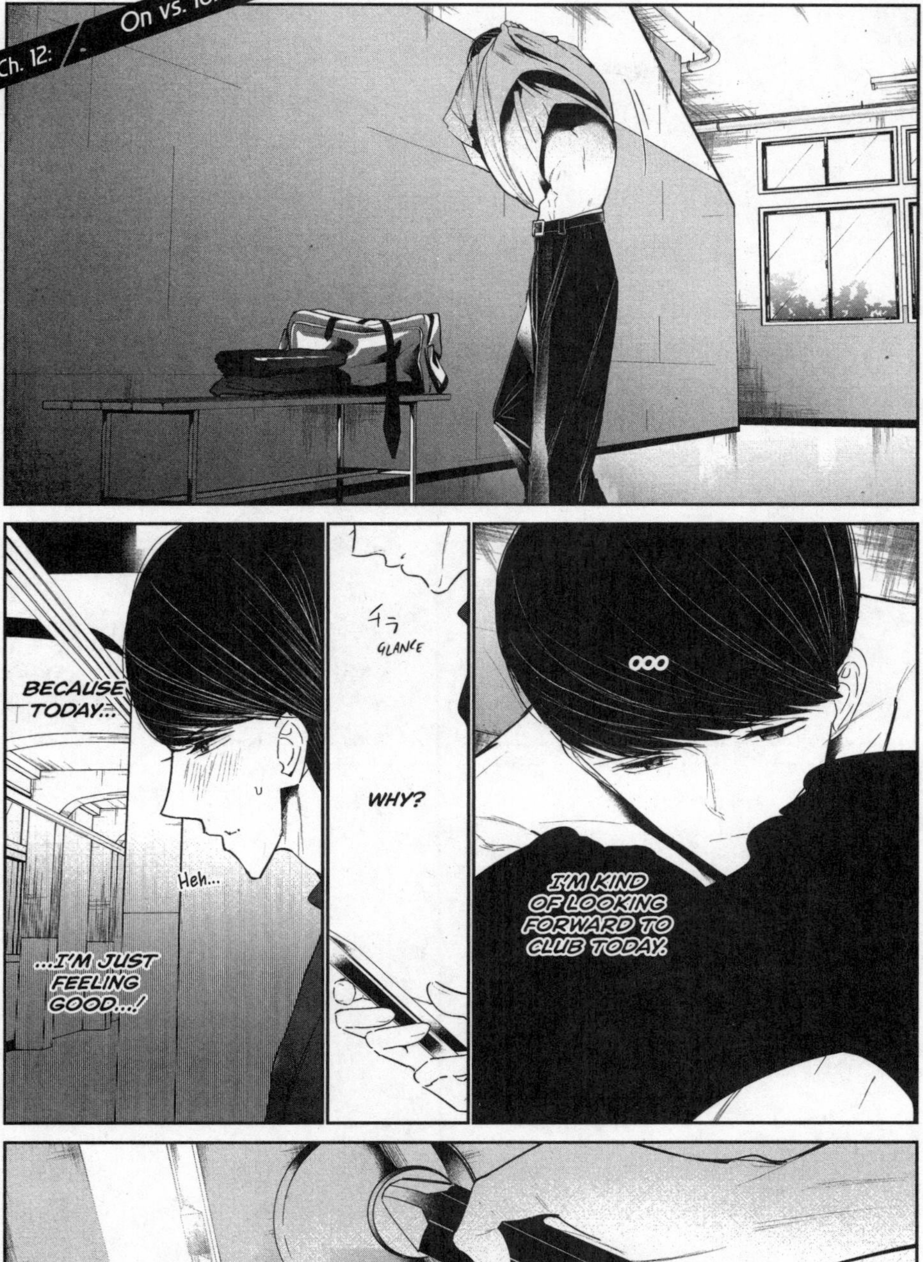
I'M KIND OF LOOKING FORWARD TO CLUB TODAY.
チラ
GLANCE
WHY?
BECAUSE TODAY...
Heh...
...I'M JUST FEELING GOOD...!

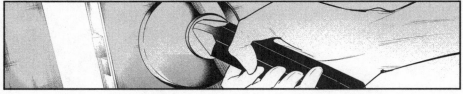

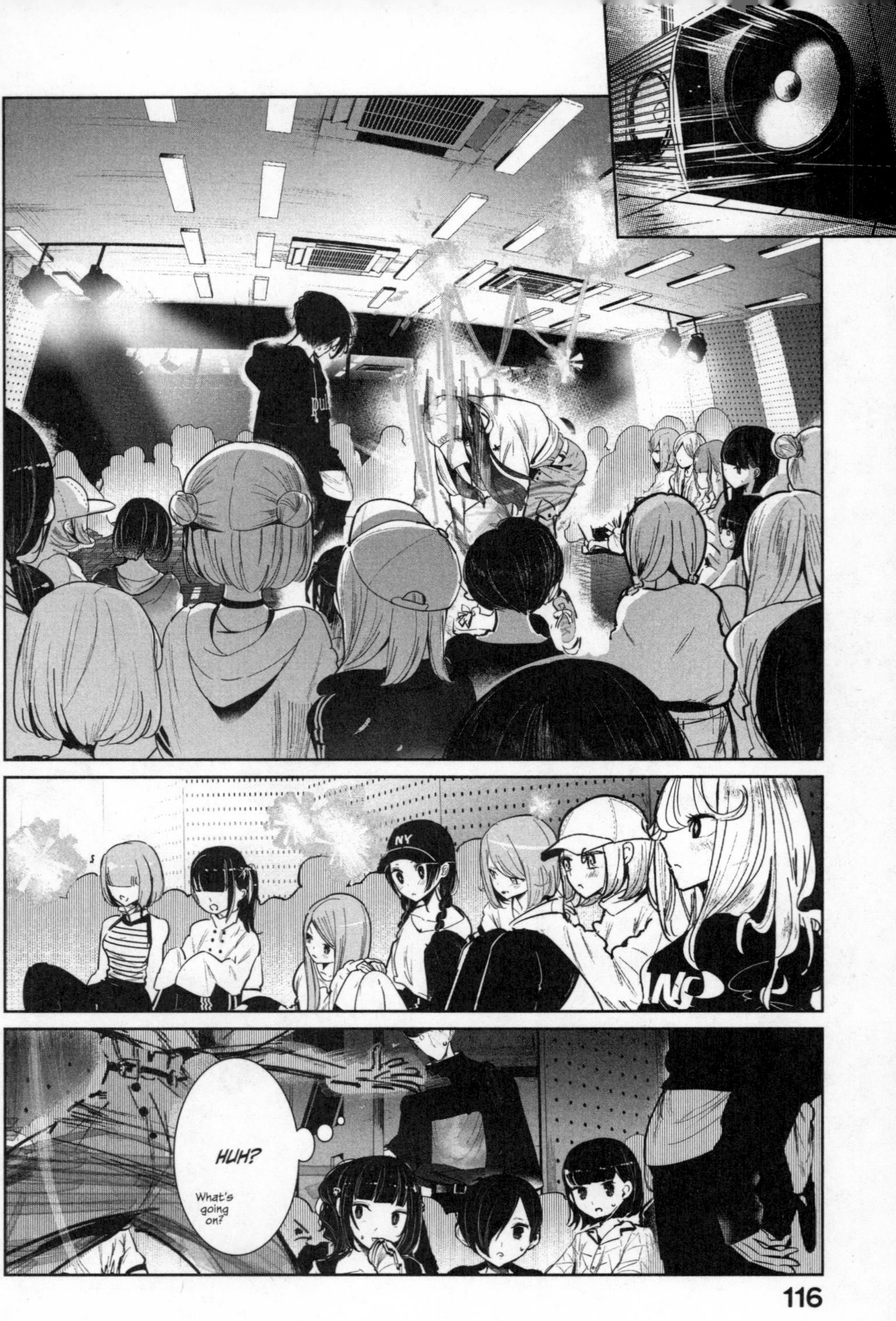
HUH?
What's going on?

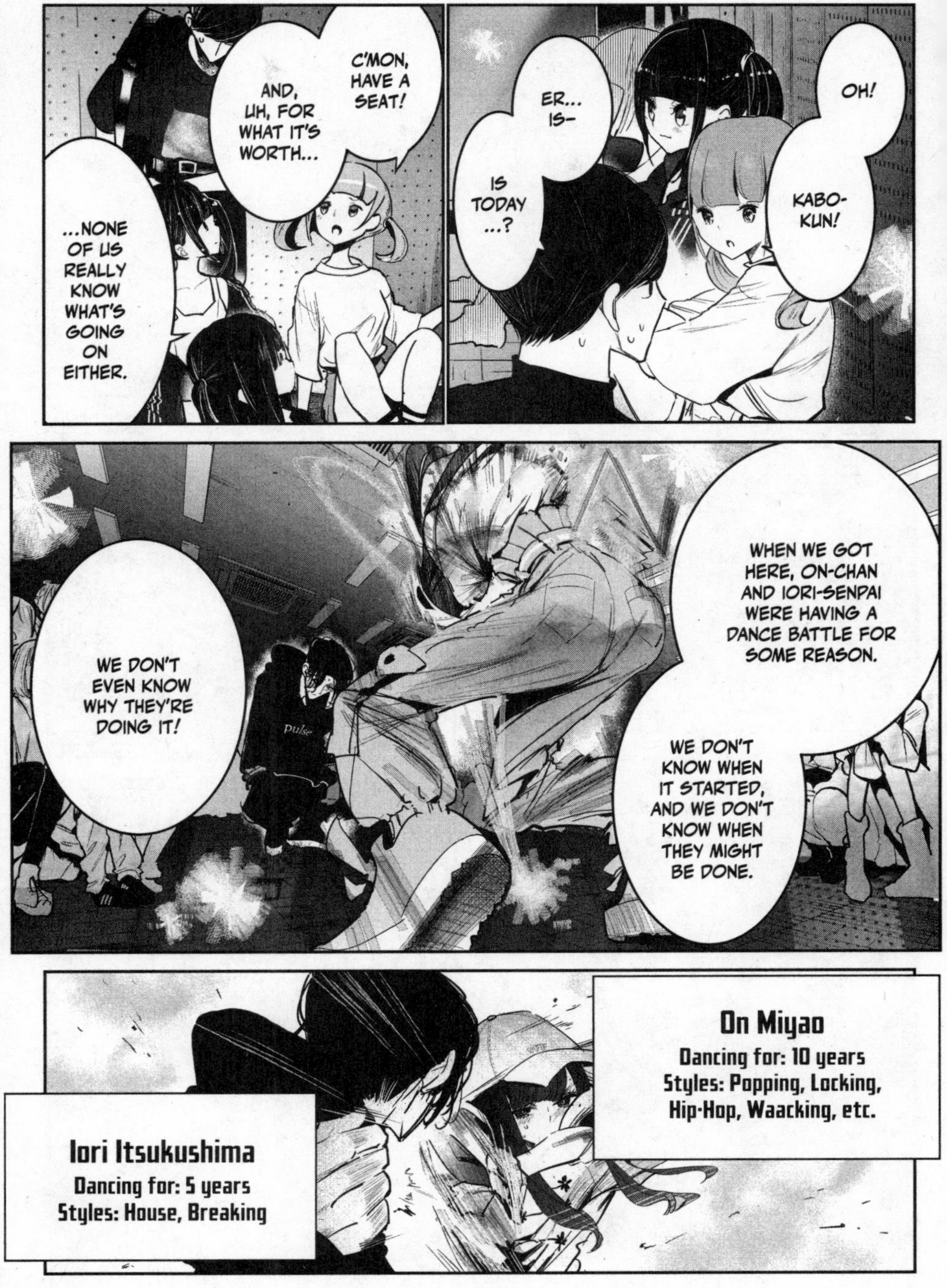
OH!
KABO-KUN!
ER... IS-
IS TODAY ...?
C'MON, HAVE A SEAT!
AND, UH, FOR WHAT IT'S WORTH...
...NONE OF US REALLY KNOW WHAT'S GOING ON EITHER.
WHEN WE GOT HERE, ON-CHAN AND IORI-SENPAI WERE HAVING A DANCE BATTLE FOR SOME REASON.
WE DON'T KNOW WHEN IT STARTED, AND WE DON'T KNOW WHEN THEY MIGHT BE DONE.
WE DON'T EVEN KNOW WHY THEY'RE DOING IT!
On Miyao
Dancing for: 10 years
Styles: Popping, Locking, Hip-Hop, Waacking, etc.
Iori Itsukushima
Dancing for: 5 years
Styles: House, Breaking

♪ Fingadelic - Beat Ya 2 Def (Don't Stop)
pulse
pulse
adidas
adidas

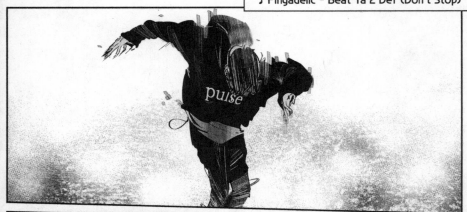

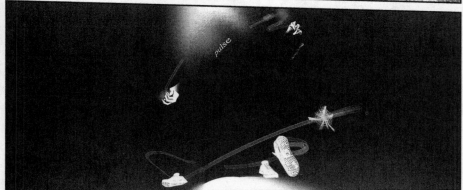

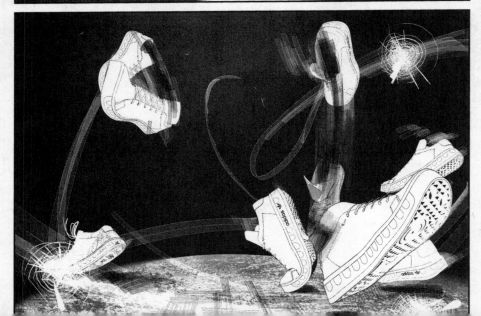

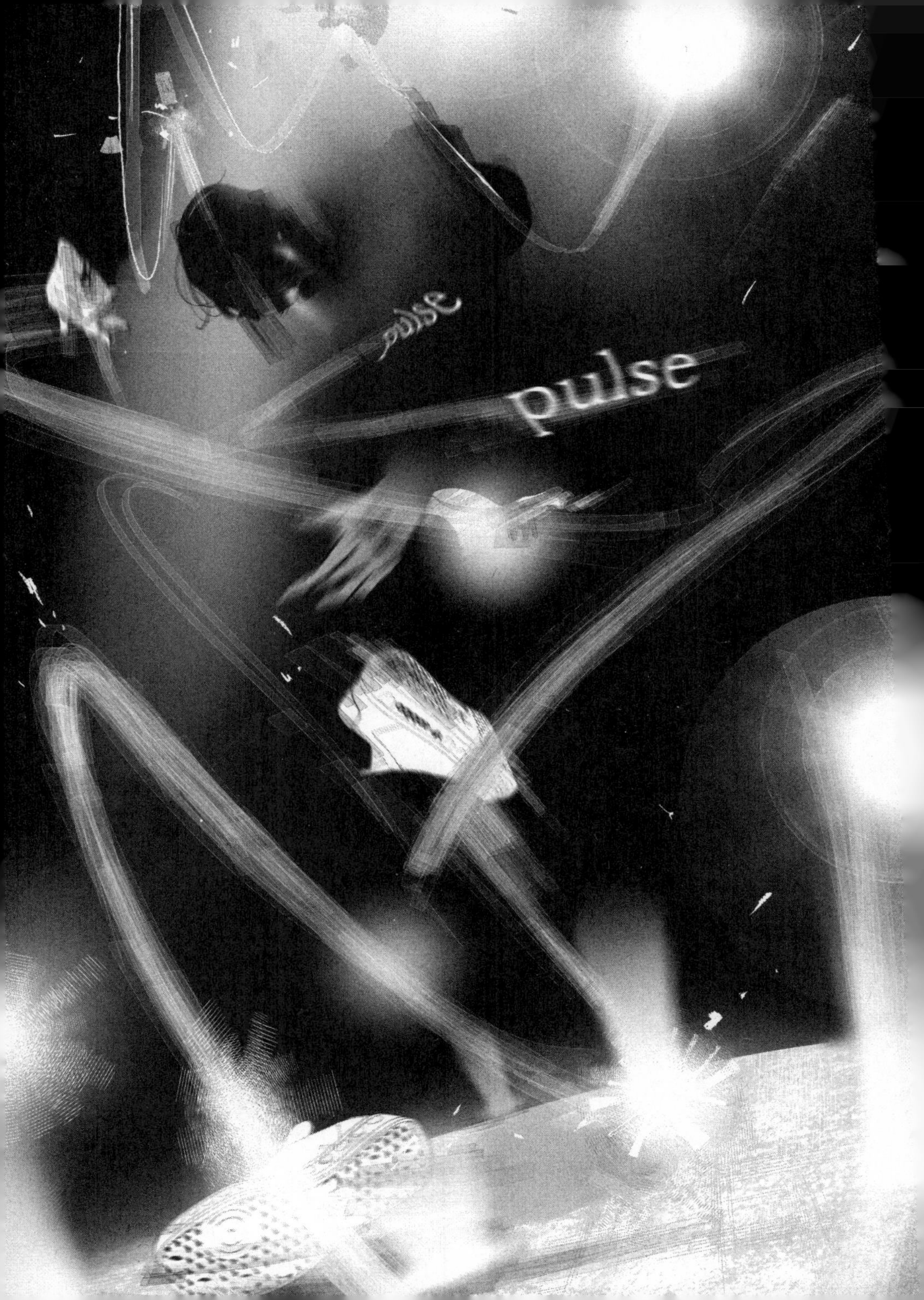
pulse
pulse

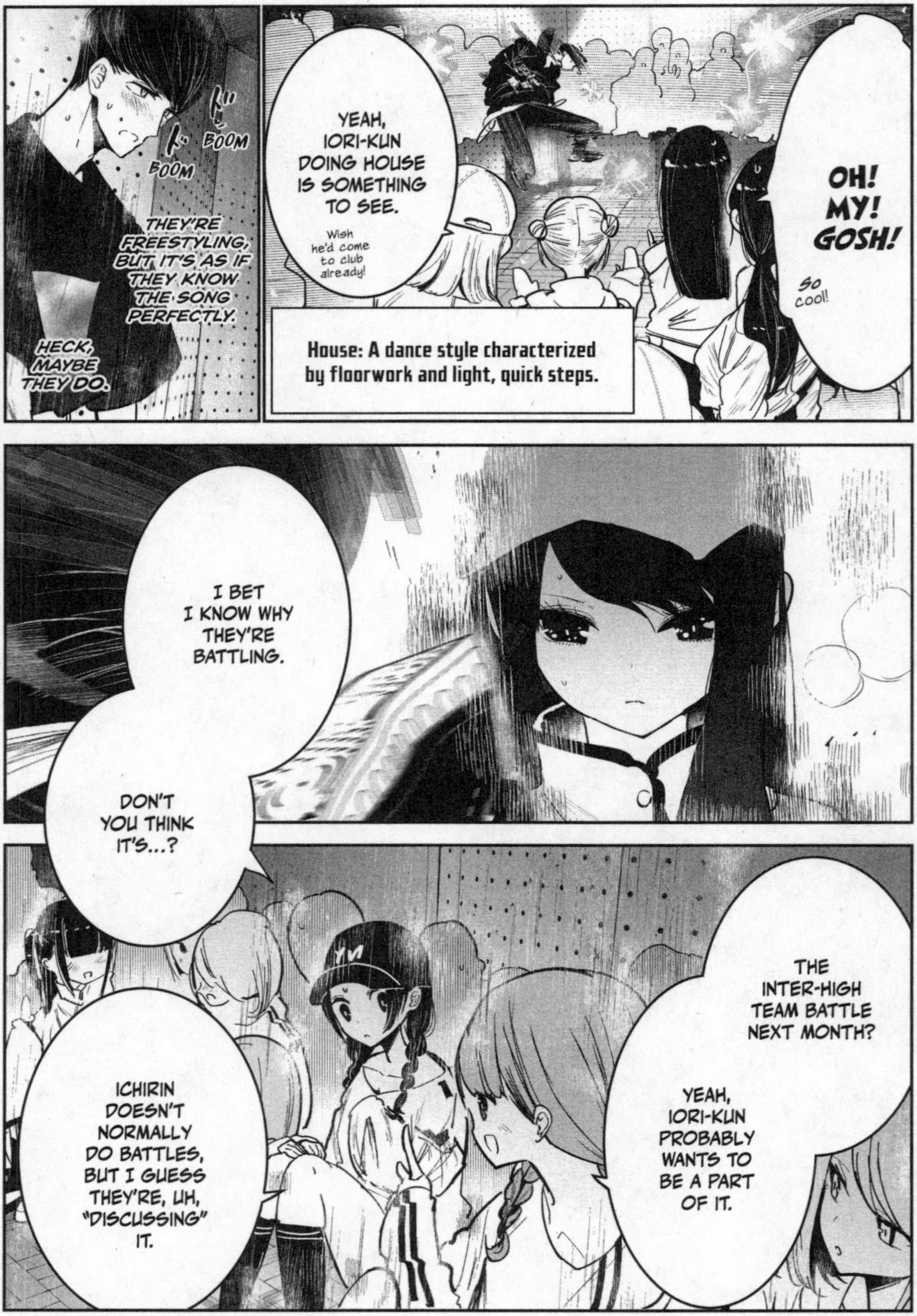
OH! MY! GOSH!
So cool!
YEAH, IORI-KUN DOING HOUSE IS SOMETHING TO SEE.
Wish he'd come to club already!
House: A dance style characterized by floorwork and light, quick steps.
BOOM
BOOM
THEY'RE FREESTYLING, BUT IT'S AS IF THEY KNOW THE SONG PERFECTLY.
HECK, MAYBE THEY DO.
I BET I KNOW WHY THEY'RE BATTLING.
DON'T YOU THINK IT'S...?
THE INTER-HIGH TEAM BATTLE NEXT MONTH?
YEAH, IORI-KUN PROBABLY WANTS TO BE A PART OF IT.
ICHIRIN DOESN'T NORMALLY DO BATTLES, BUT I GUESS THEY'RE, UH, "DISCUSSING" IT.

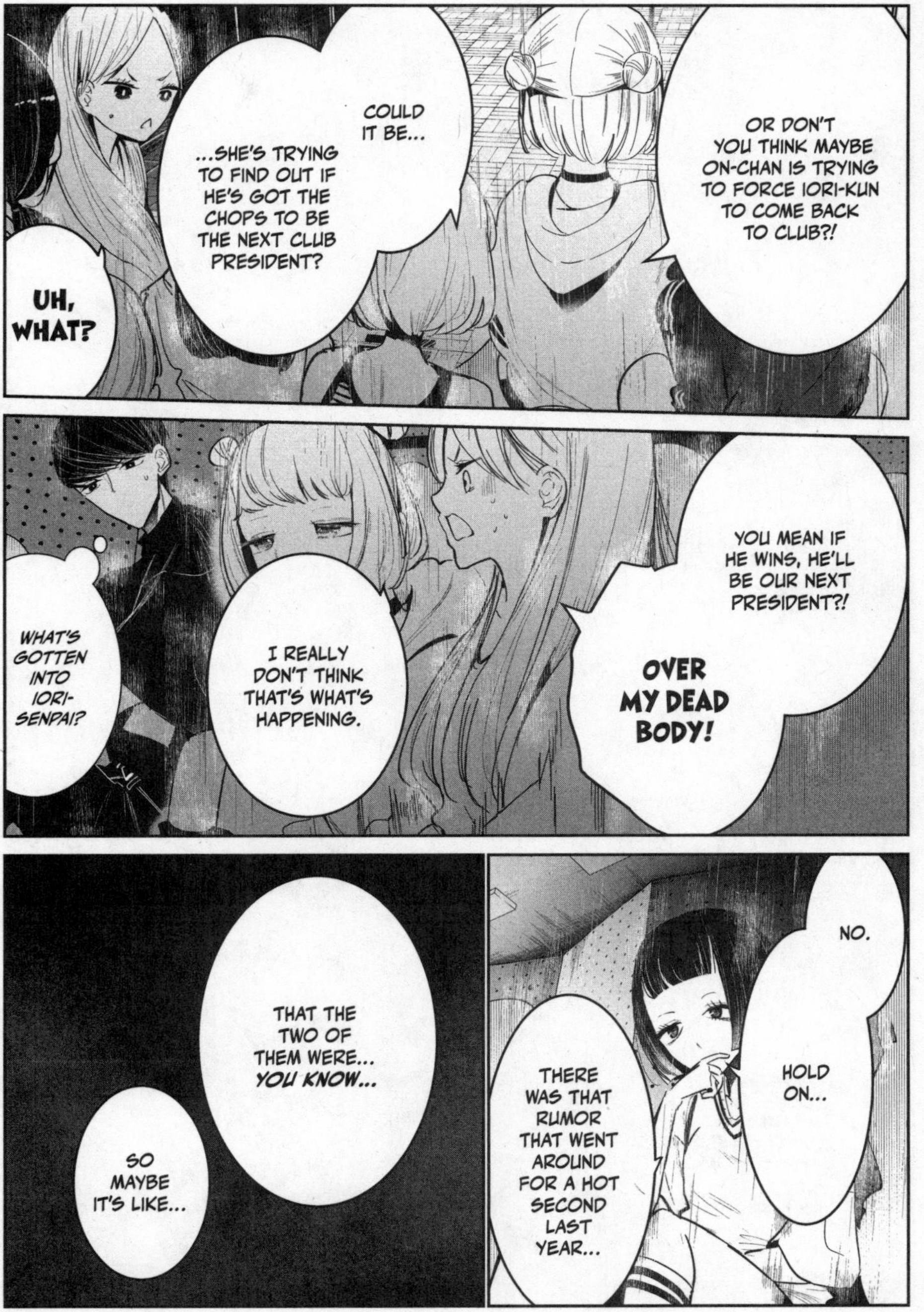
OR DON'T YOU THINK MAYBE ON-CHAN IS TRYING TO FORCE IORI-KUN TO COME BACK TO CLUB?!
COULD IT BE...
...SHE'S TRYING TO FIND OUT IF HE'S GOT THE CHOPS TO BE THE NEXT CLUB PRESIDENT?
UH, WHAT?
YOU MEAN IF HE WINS, HE'LL BE OUR NEXT PRESIDENT?!
OVER MY DEAD BODY!
I REALLY DON'T THINK THAT'S WHAT'S HAPPENING.
WHAT'S GOTTEN INTO IORI-SENPAI?
NO.
HOLD ON...
THERE WAS THAT RUMOR THAT WENT AROUND FOR A HOT SECOND LAST YEAR...
THAT THE TWO OF THEM WERE... *YOU KNOW...*
SO MAYBE IT'S LIKE...

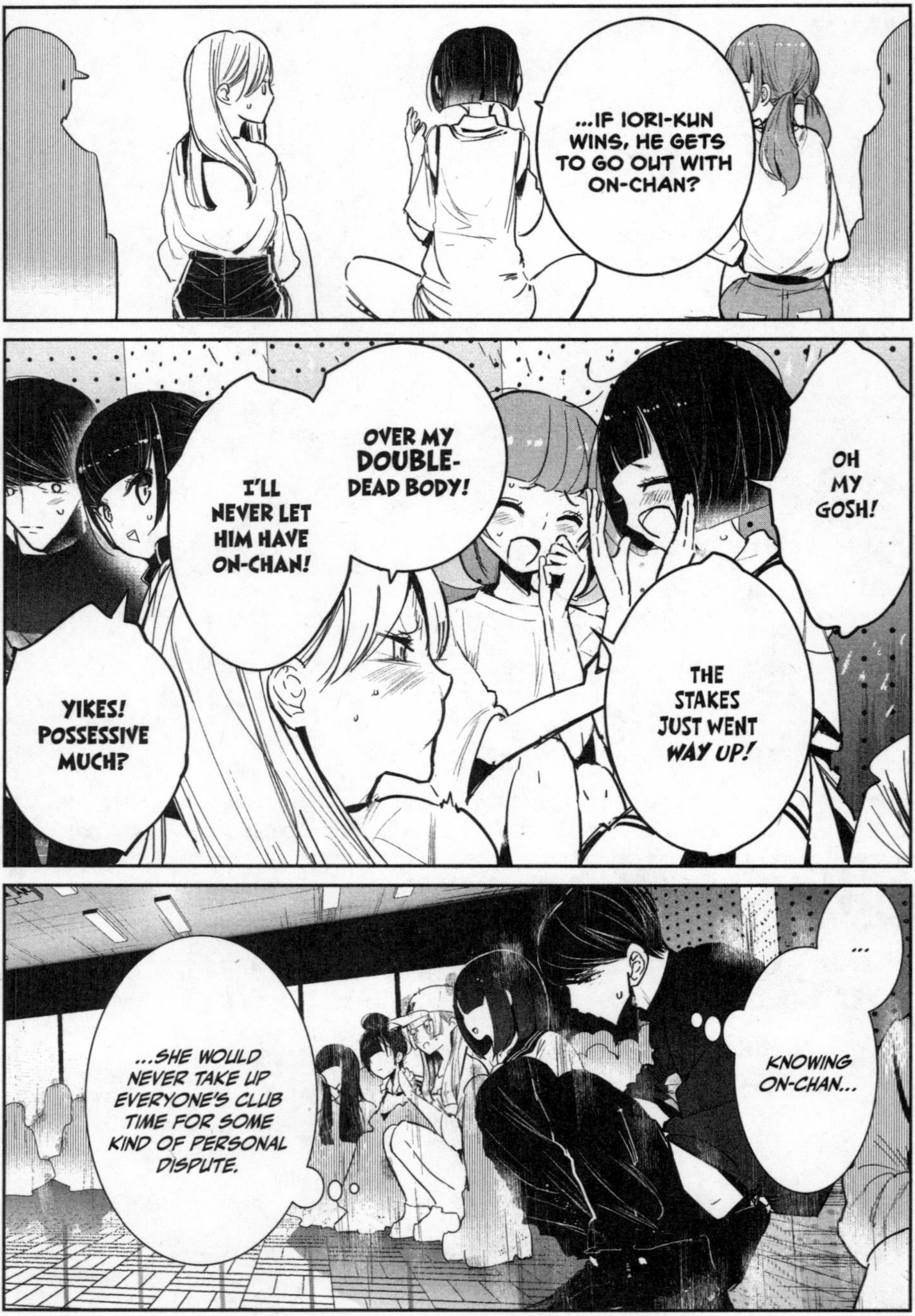
...IF IORI-KUN WINS, HE GETS TO GO OUT WITH ON-CHAN?
OH MY GOSH!
THE STAKES JUST WENT WAY UP!
I'LL NEVER LET HIM HAVE ON-CHAN!
OVER MY DOUBLE-DEAD BODY!
YIKES! POSSESSIVE MUCH?
...
KNOWING ON-CHAN...
...SHE WOULD NEVER TAKE UP EVERYONE'S CLUB TIME FOR SOME KIND OF PERSONAL DISPUTE.

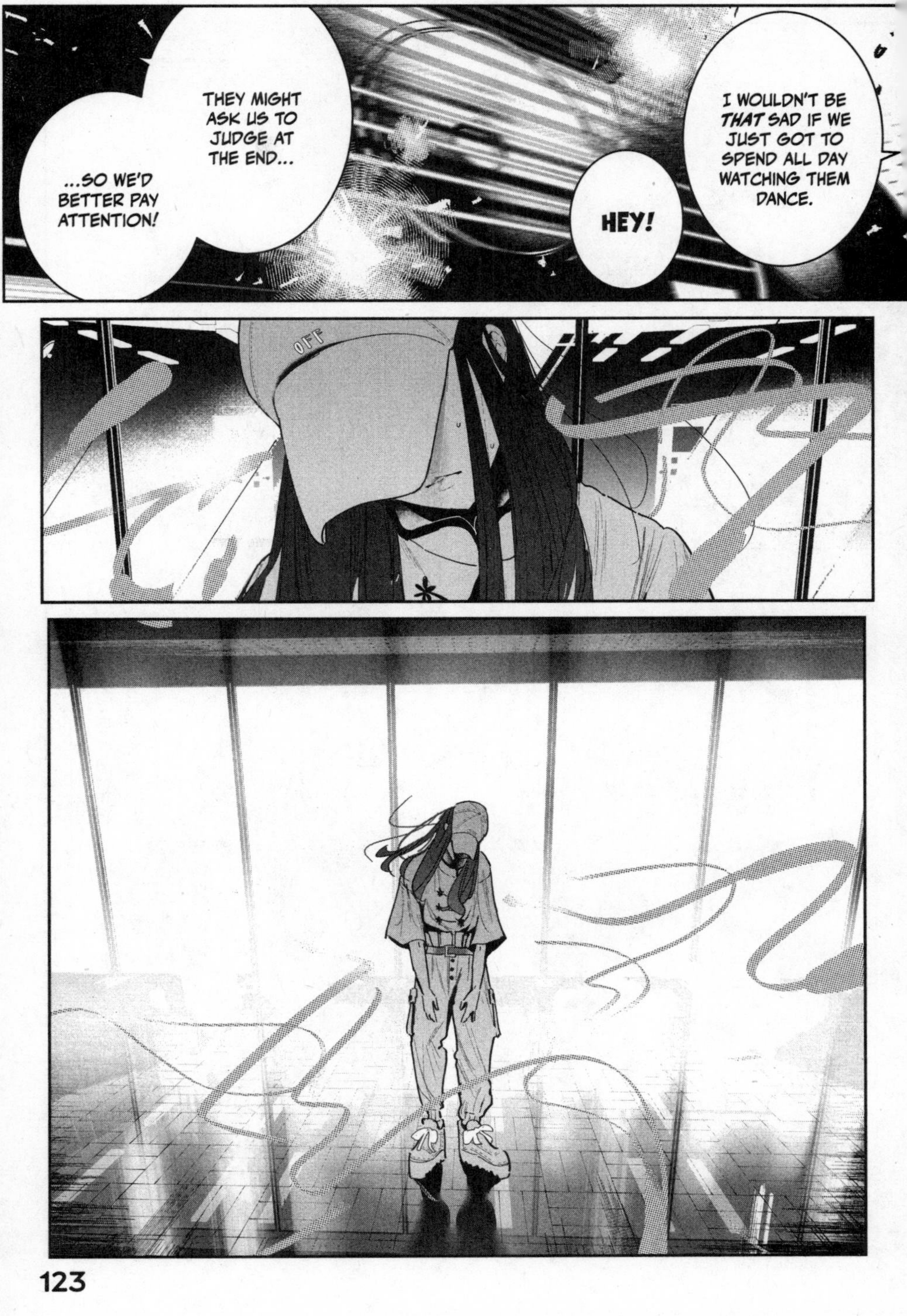
I WOULDN'T BE *THAT* SAD IF WE JUST GOT TO SPEND ALL DAY WATCHING THEM DANCE.
HEY!
THEY MIGHT ASK US TO JUDGE AT THE END...
...SO WE'D BETTER PAY ATTENTION!
OFF

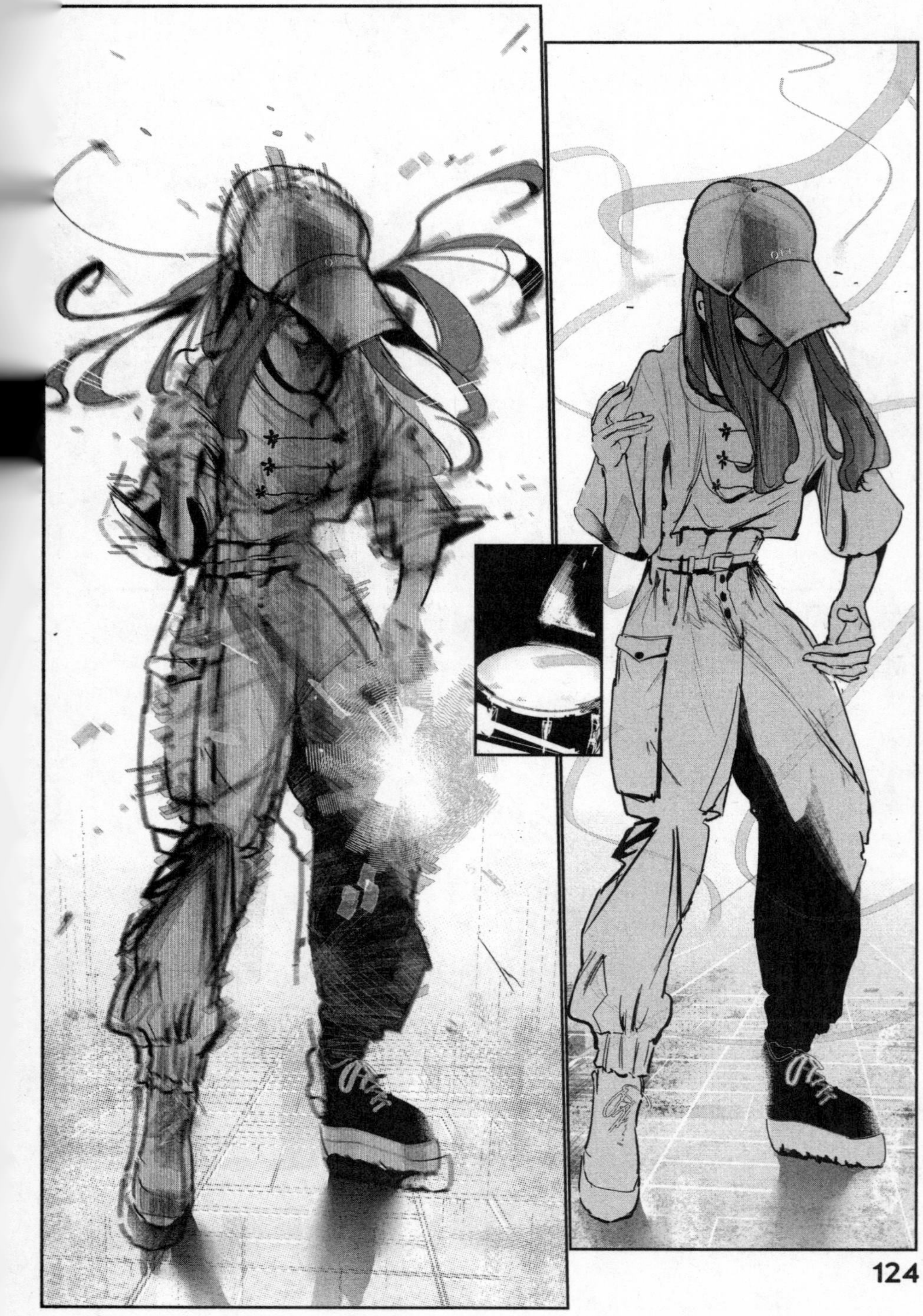

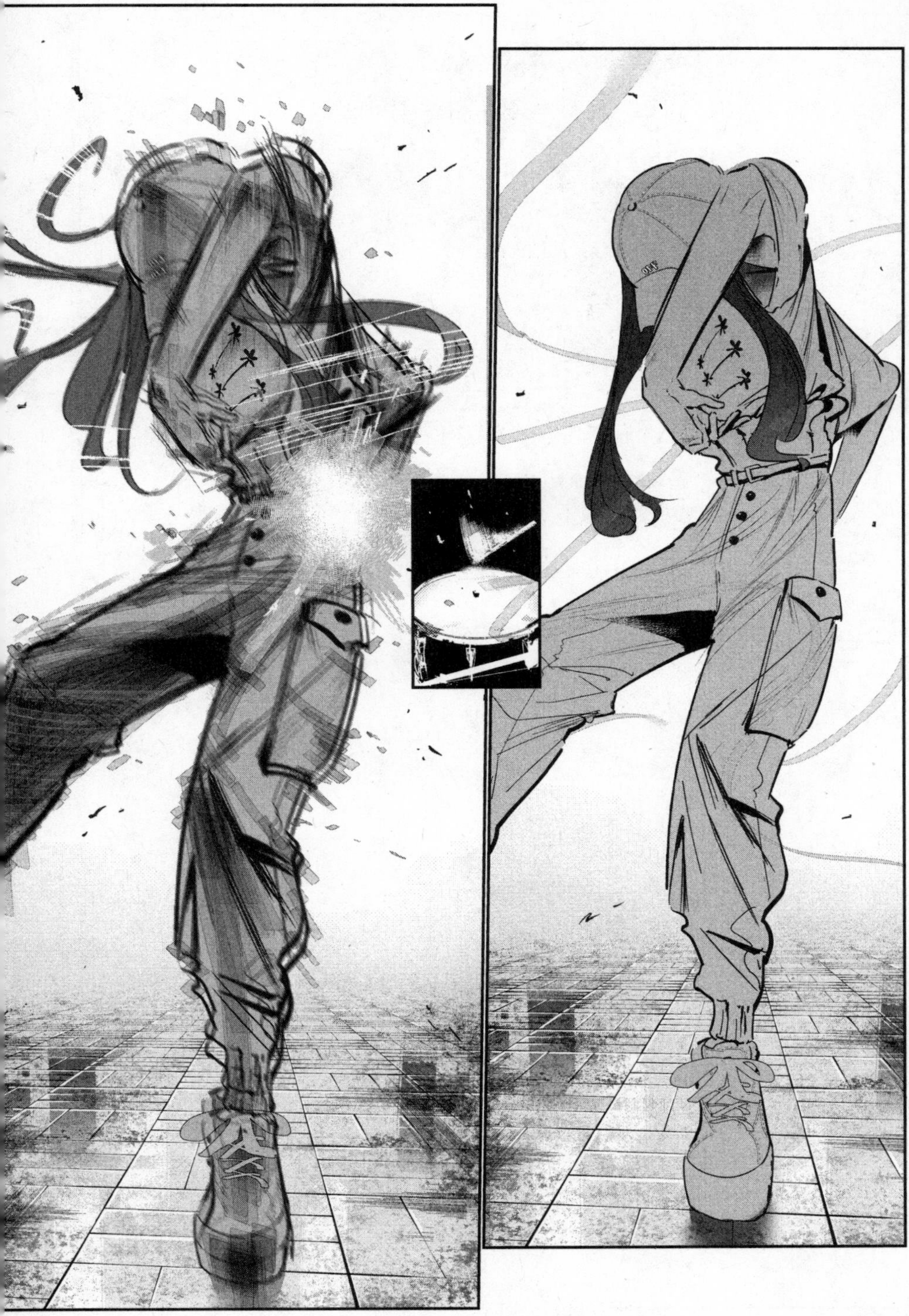

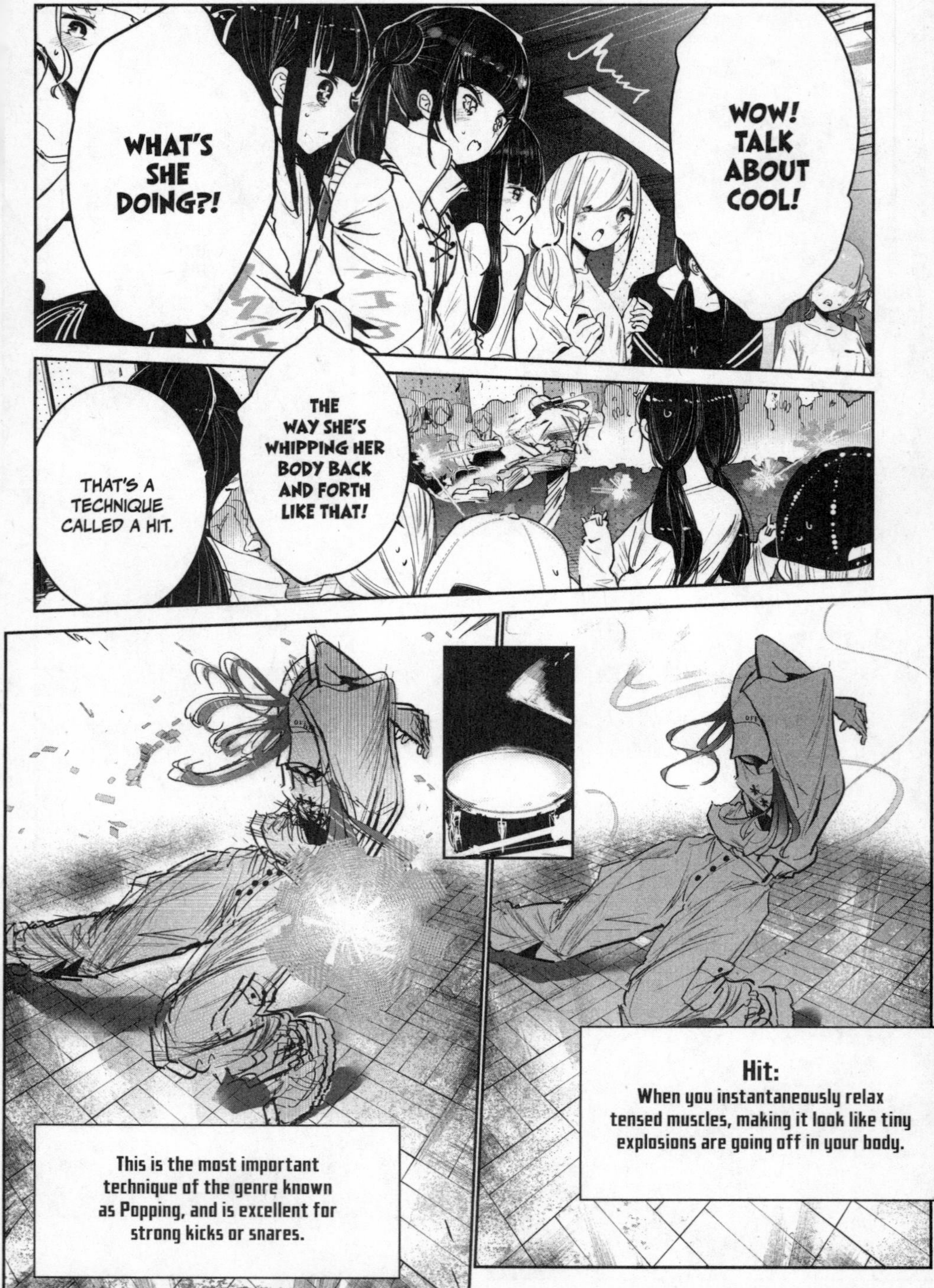
WOW! TALK ABOUT COOL!
WHAT'S SHE DOING?!
THE WAY SHE'S WHIPPING HER BODY BACK AND FORTH LIKE THAT!
THAT'S A TECHNIQUE CALLED A HIT.
Hit:
When you instantaneously relax tensed muscles, making it look like tiny explosions are going off in your body.
This is the most important technique of the genre known as Popping, and is excellent for strong kicks or snares.

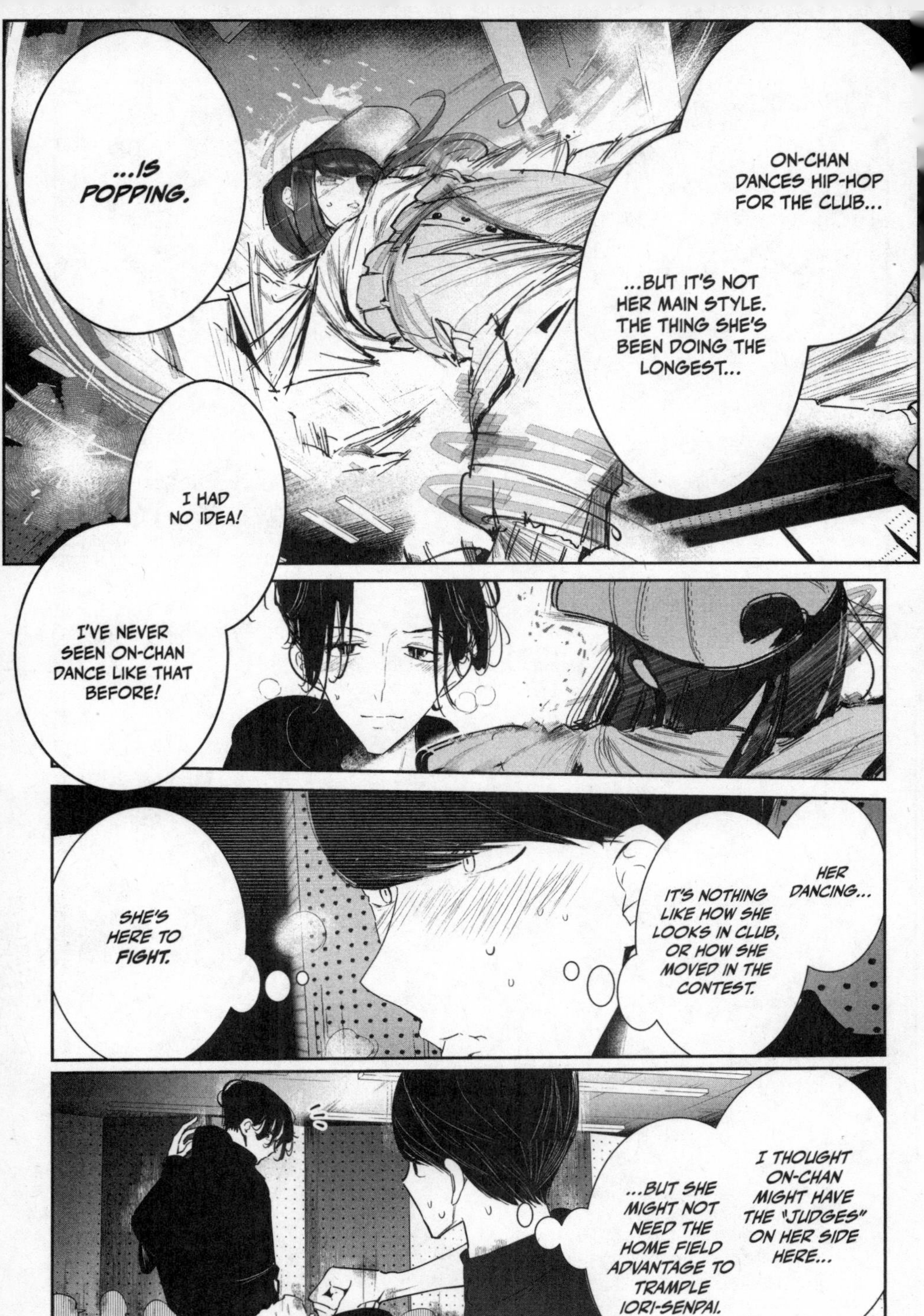
ON-CHAN DANCES HIP-HOP FOR THE CLUB...
...BUT IT'S NOT HER MAIN STYLE. THE THING SHE'S BEEN DOING THE LONGEST...
...IS POPPING.
I HAD NO IDEA!
I'VE NEVER SEEN ON-CHAN DANCE LIKE THAT BEFORE!
HER DANCING...
IT'S NOTHING LIKE HOW SHE LOOKS IN CLUB, OR HOW SHE MOVED IN THE CONTEST.
SHE'S HERE TO FIGHT.
I THOUGHT ON-CHAN MIGHT HAVE THE "JUDGES" ON HER SIDE HERE...
...BUT SHE MIGHT NOT NEED THE HOME FIELD ADVANTAGE TO TRAMPLE IORI-SENPAI.

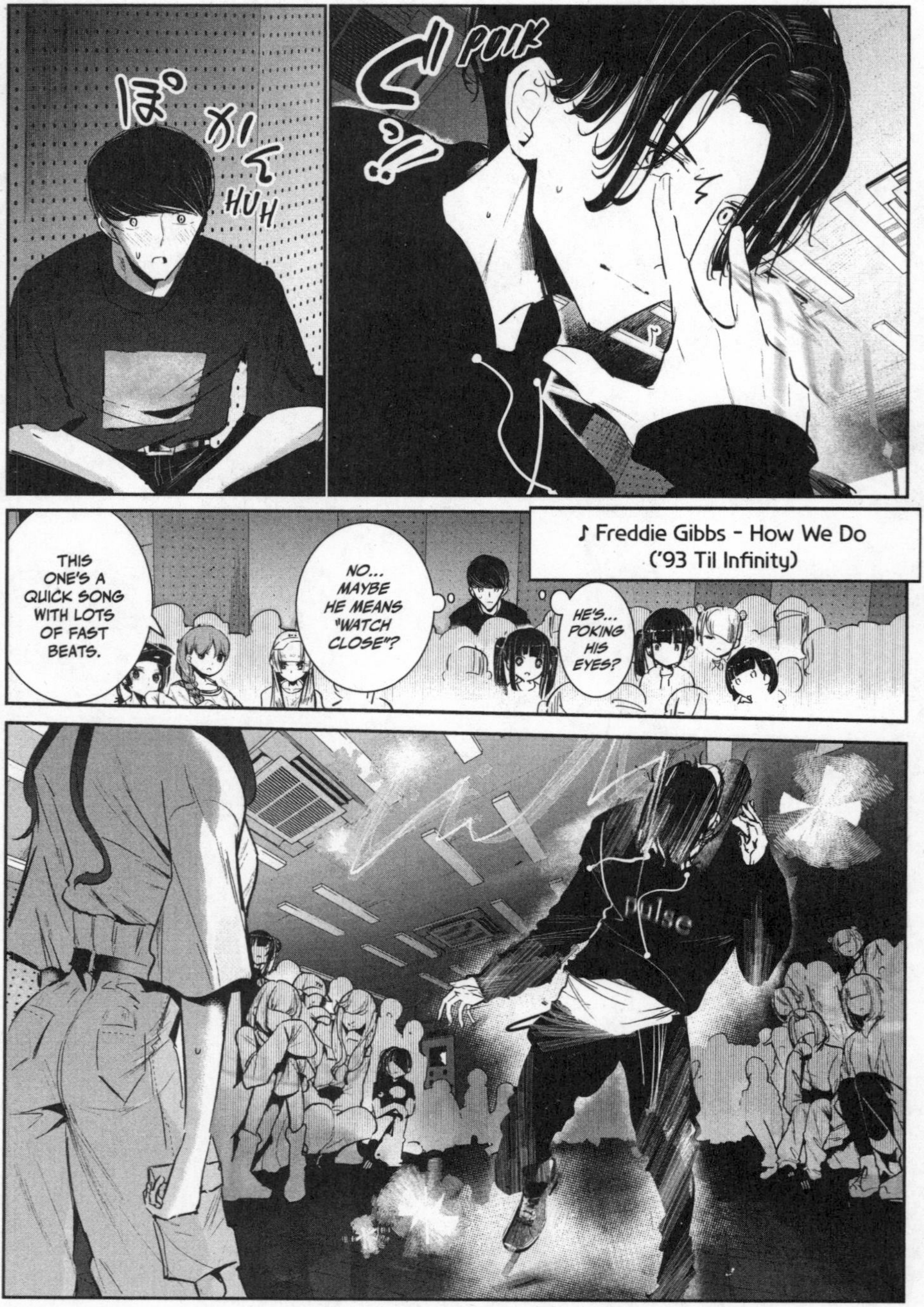

ぐっ!!
POIK
ぽかん
HUH
♪ Freddie Gibbs - How We Do ('93 Til Infinity)
HE'S... POKING HIS EYES?
NO... MAYBE HE MEANS "WATCH CLOSE"?
THIS ONE'S A QUICK SONG WITH LOTS OF FAST BEATS.

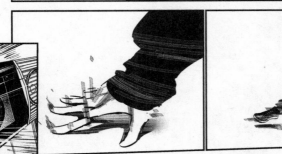

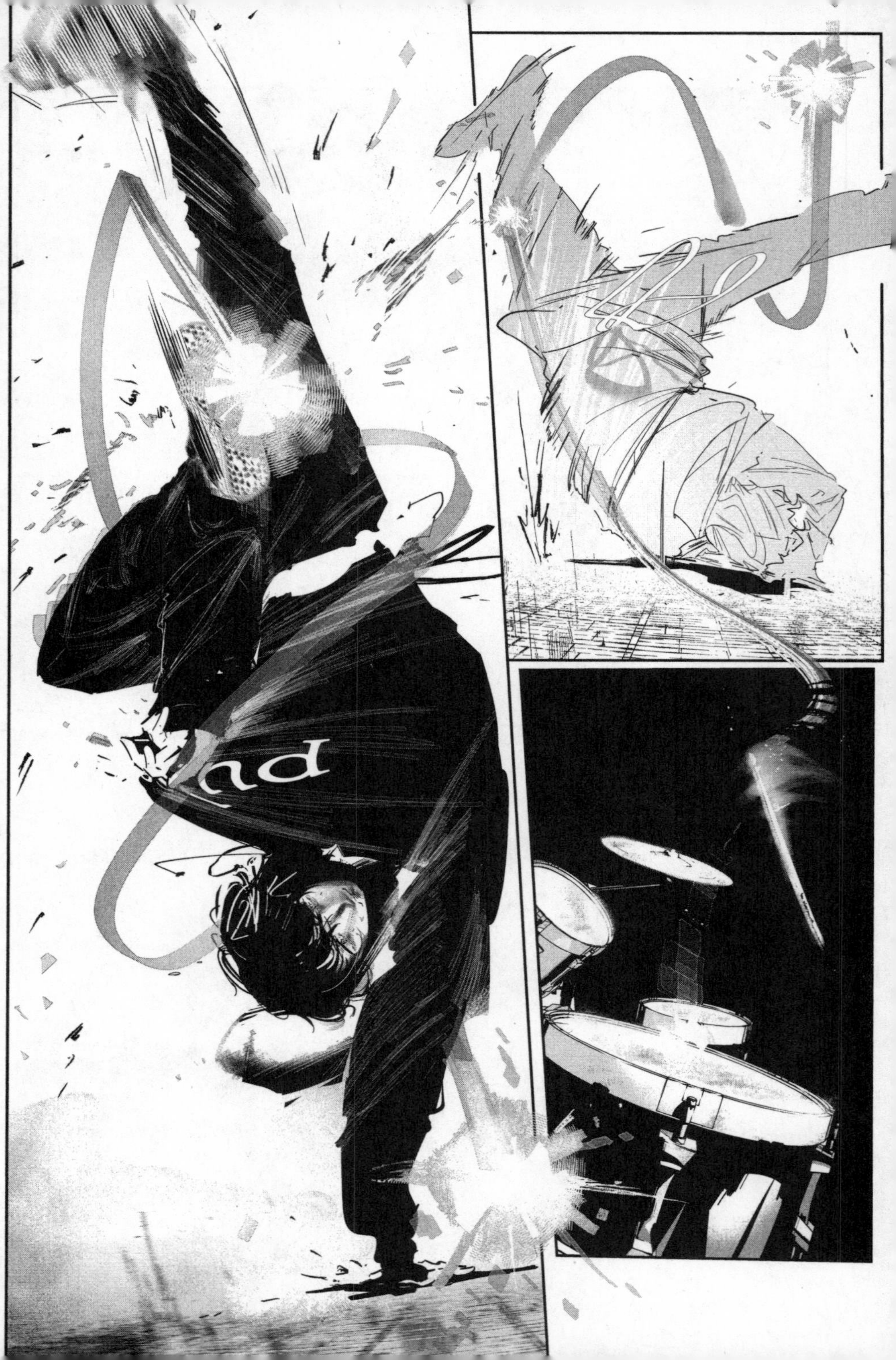

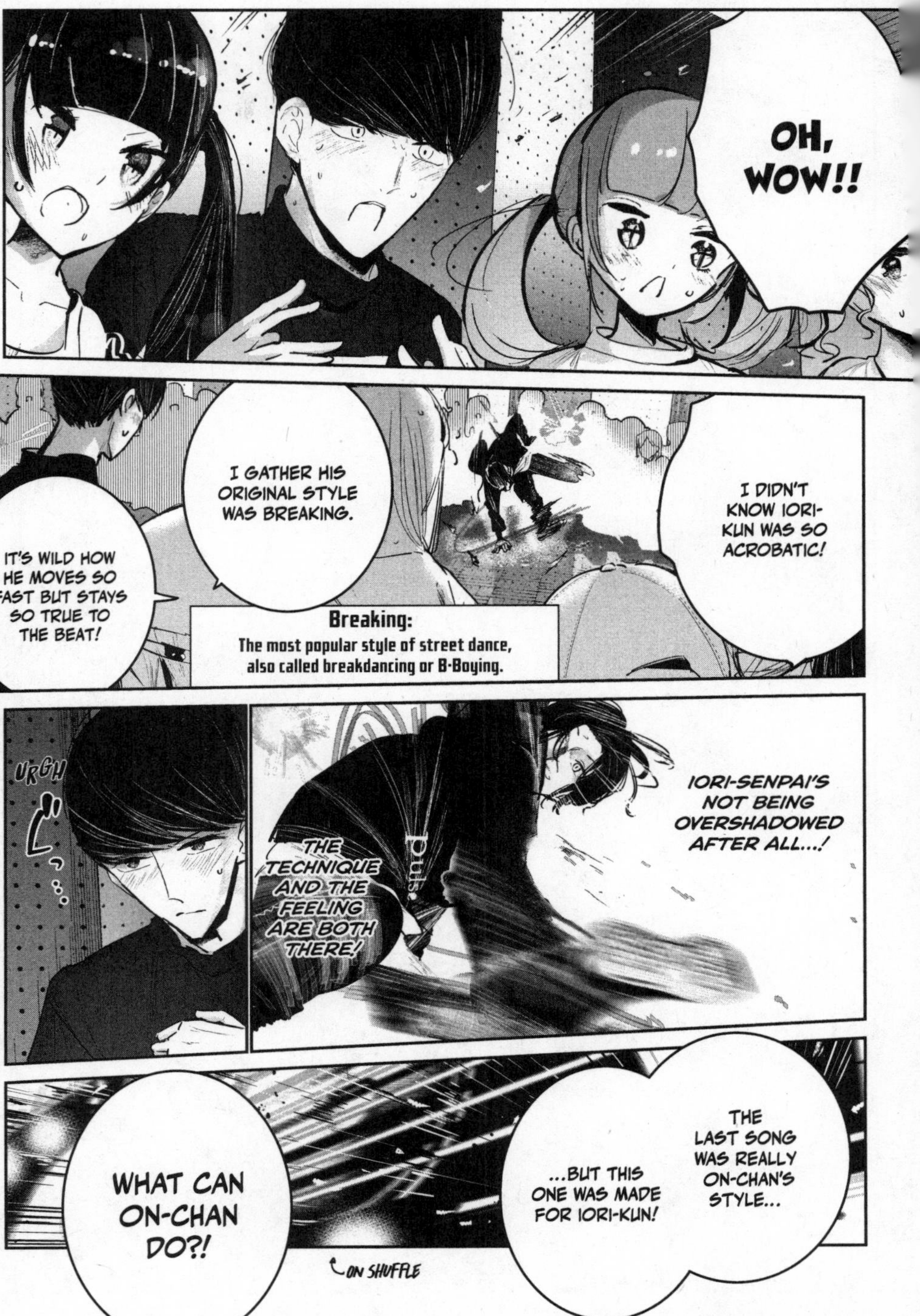
OH, WOW!!
I DIDN'T KNOW IORI-KUN WAS SO ACROBATIC!
I GATHER HIS ORIGINAL STYLE WAS BREAKING.
IT'S WILD HOW HE MOVES SO FAST BUT STAYS SO TRUE TO THE BEAT!
Breaking:
The most popular style of street dance, also called breakdancing or B-Boying.
IORI-SENPAI'S NOT BEING OVERSHADOWED AFTER ALL...!
THE TECHNIQUE AND THE FEELING ARE BOTH THERE!
URGH
THE LAST SONG WAS REALLY ON-CHAN'S STYLE...
...BUT THIS ONE WAS MADE FOR IORI-KUN!
WHAT CAN ON-CHAN DO?!
ON SHUFFLE

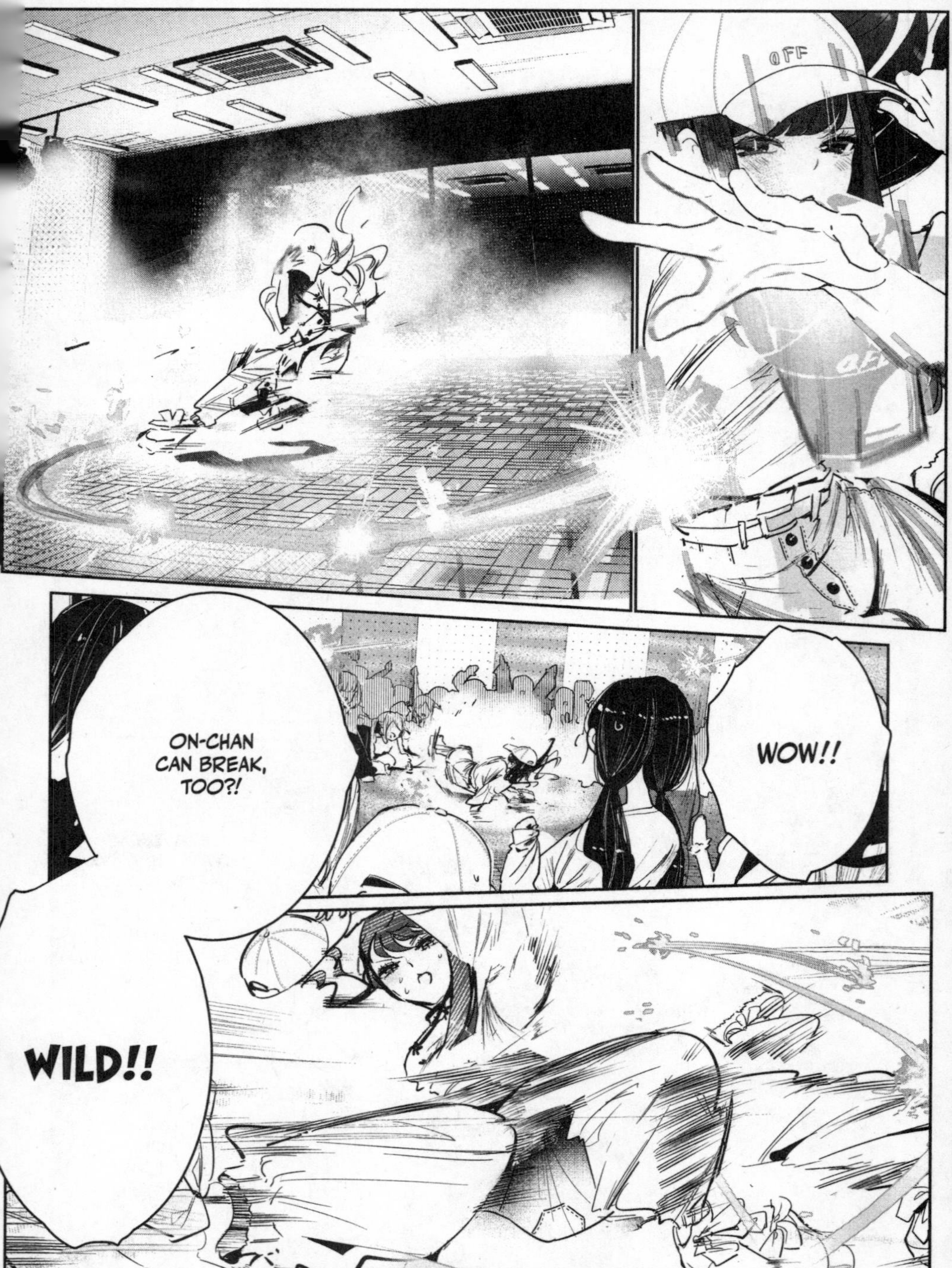
OFF
WOW!!
ON-CHAN CAN BREAK, TOO?!
WILD!!

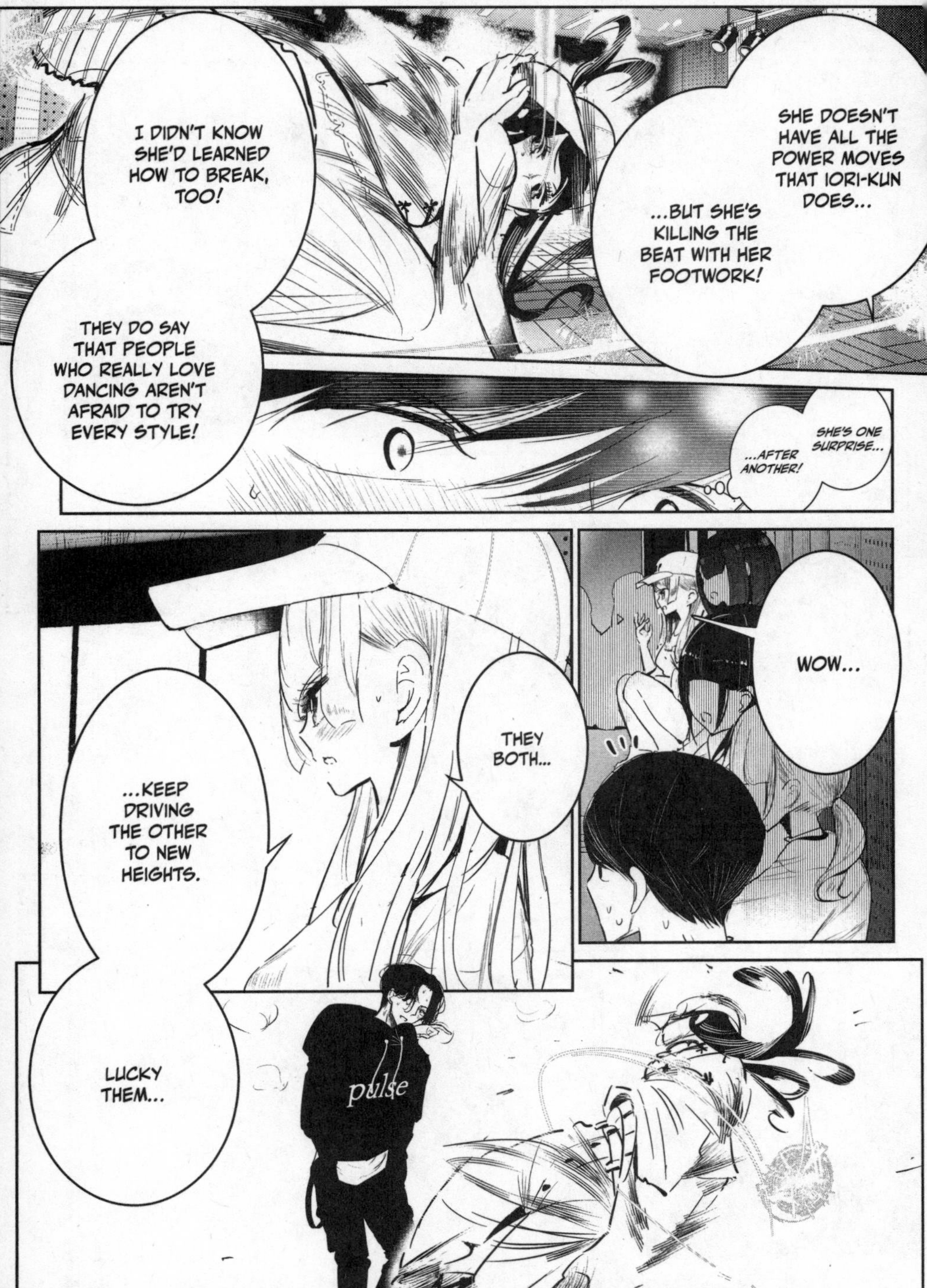
SHE DOESN'T HAVE ALL THE POWER MOVES THAT IORI-KUN DOES...
...BUT SHE'S KILLING THE BEAT WITH HER FOOTWORK!
I DIDN'T KNOW SHE'D LEARNED HOW TO BREAK, TOO!
THEY DO SAY THAT PEOPLE WHO REALLY LOVE DANCING AREN'T AFRAID TO TRY EVERY STYLE!
SHE'S ONE SURPRISE...
...AFTER ANOTHER!
WOW...
THEY BOTH...
...KEEP DRIVING THE OTHER TO NEW HEIGHTS.
LUCKY THEM...
pulse

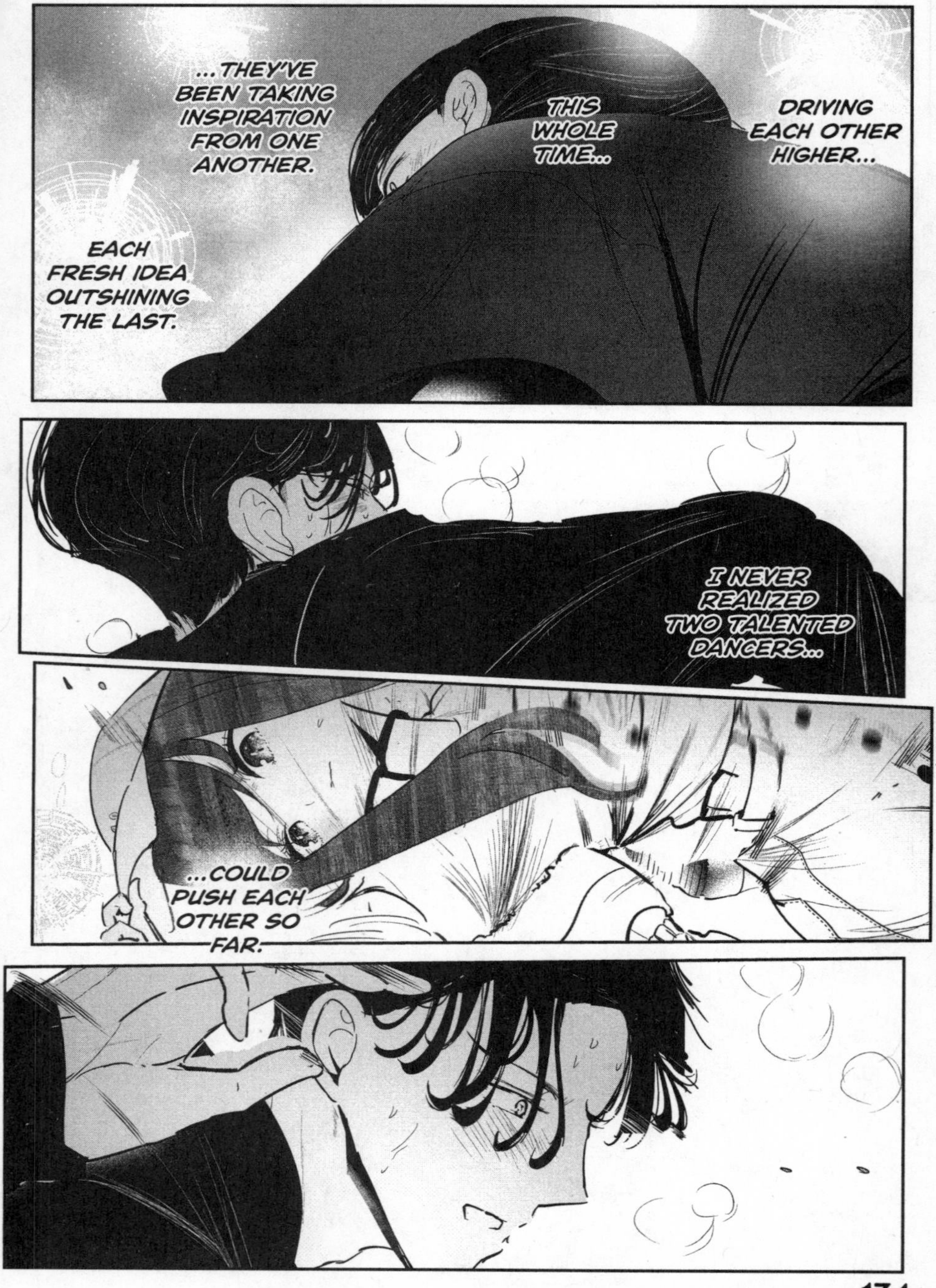
DRIVING EACH OTHER HIGHER...
THIS WHOLE TIME...
...THEY'VE BEEN TAKING INSPIRATION FROM ONE ANOTHER.
EACH FRESH IDEA OUTSHINING THE LAST.
I NEVER REALIZED TWO TALENTED DANCERS...
...COULD PUSH EACH OTHER SO FAR.

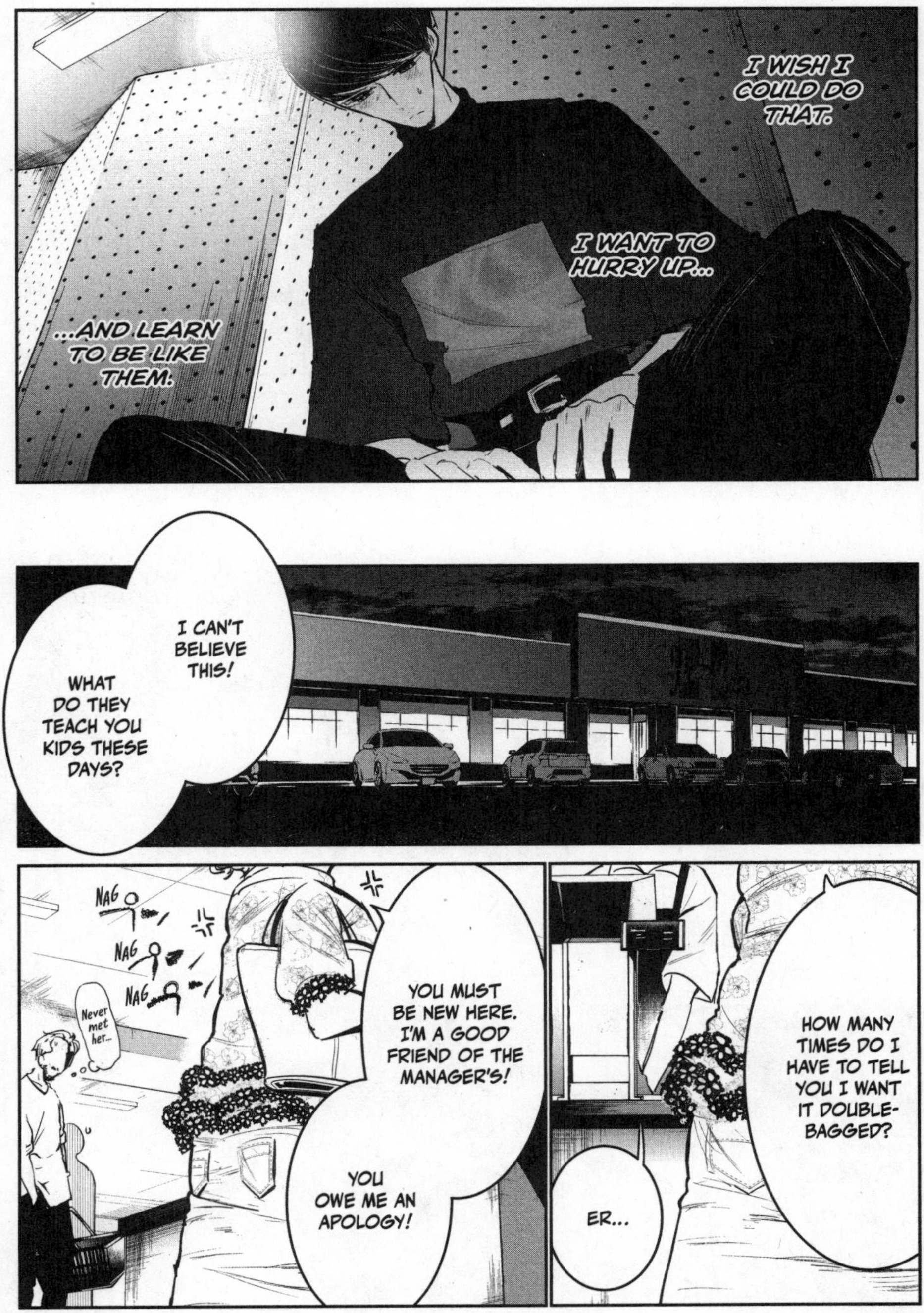
I WISH I COULD DO THAT.
I WANT TO HURRY UP...
...AND LEARN TO BE LIKE THEM.
I CAN'T BELIEVE THIS!
WHAT DO THEY TEACH YOU KIDS THESE DAYS?
HOW MANY TIMES DO I HAVE TO TELL YOU I WANT IT DOUBLE-BAGGED?
ER...
YOU MUST BE NEW HERE. I'M A GOOD FRIEND OF THE MANAGER'S!
NAG
NAG
NAG
Never met her...
YOU OWE ME AN APOLOGY!

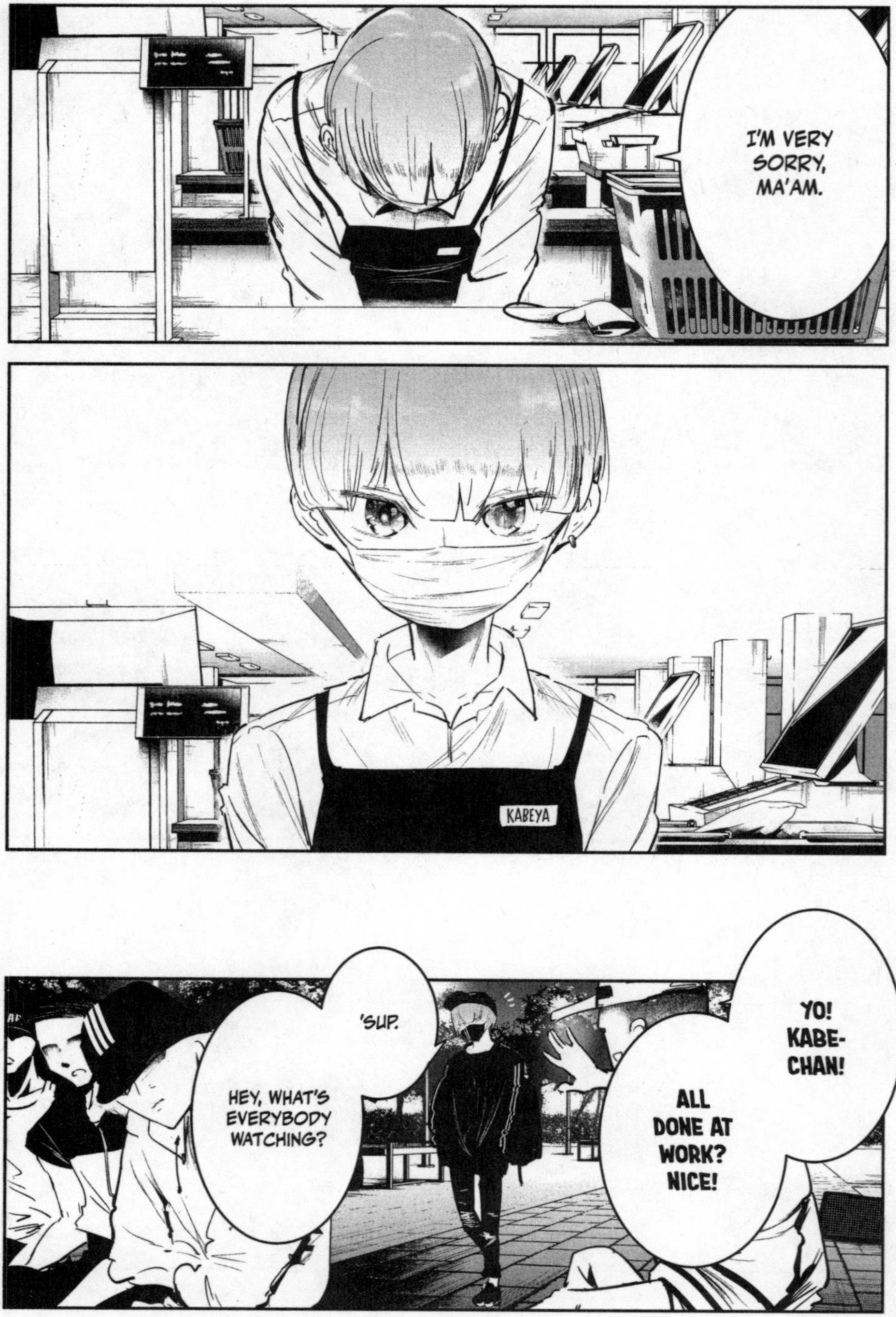
I'M VERY SORRY, MA'AM.
KABEYA
YO! KABE-CHAN!
ALL DONE AT WORK? NICE!
'SUP.
HEY, WHAT'S EVERYBODY WATCHING?

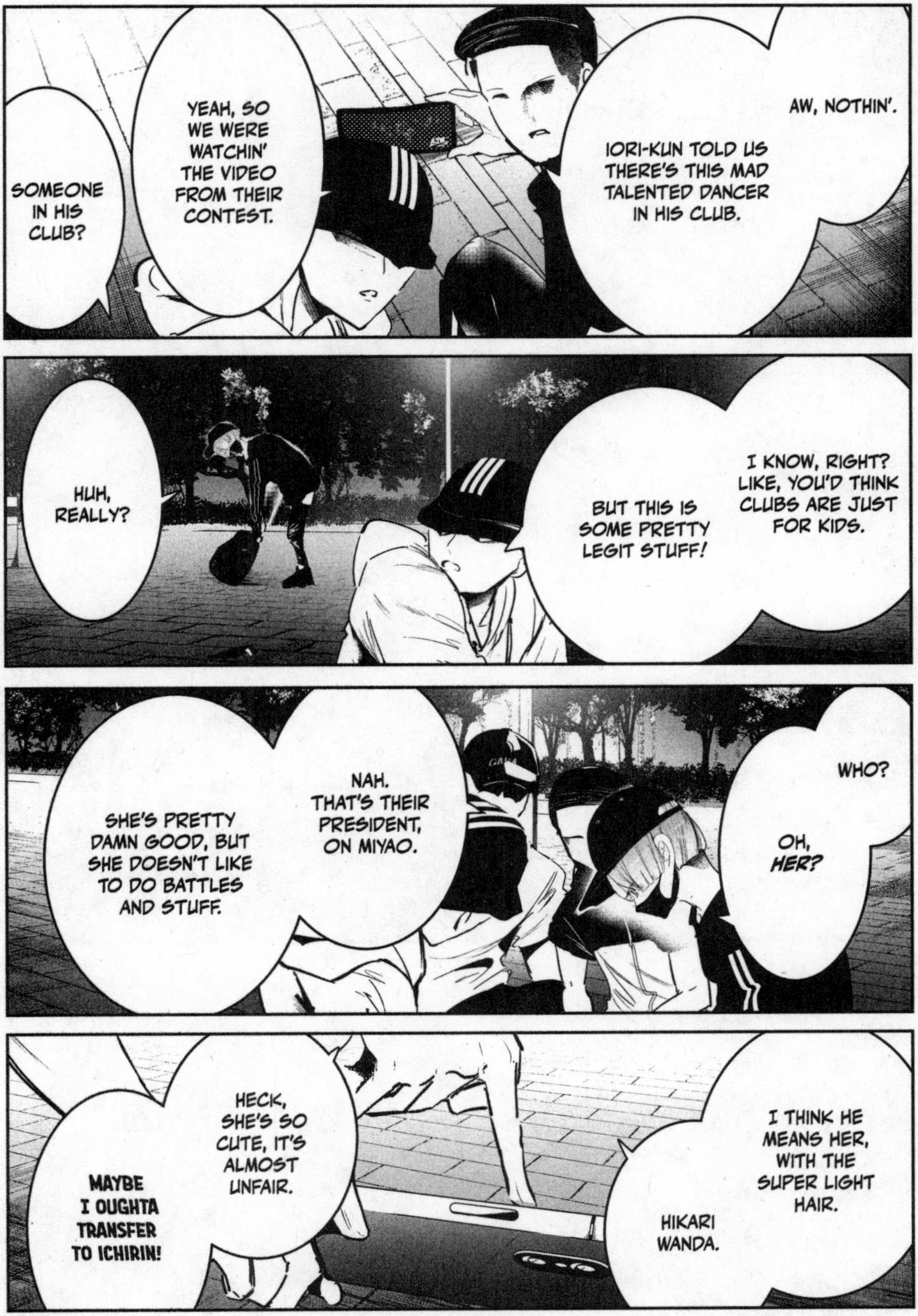
AW, NOTHIN'.
IORI-KUN TOLD US THERE'S THIS MAD TALENTED DANCER IN HIS CLUB.
YEAH, SO WE WERE WATCHIN' THE VIDEO FROM THEIR CONTEST.
SOMEONE IN HIS CLUB?
I KNOW, RIGHT? LIKE, YOU'D THINK CLUBS ARE JUST FOR KIDS.
BUT THIS IS SOME PRETTY LEGIT STUFF!
HUH, REALLY?
WHO?
OH, *HER?*
NAH. THAT'S THEIR PRESIDENT, ON MIYAO.
SHE'S PRETTY DAMN GOOD, BUT SHE DOESN'T LIKE TO DO BATTLES AND STUFF.
I THINK HE MEANS HER, WITH THE SUPER LIGHT HAIR.
HIKARI WANDA.
HECK, SHE'S SO CUTE, IT'S ALMOST UNFAIR.
MAYBE I OUGHTA TRANSFER TO ICHIRIN!

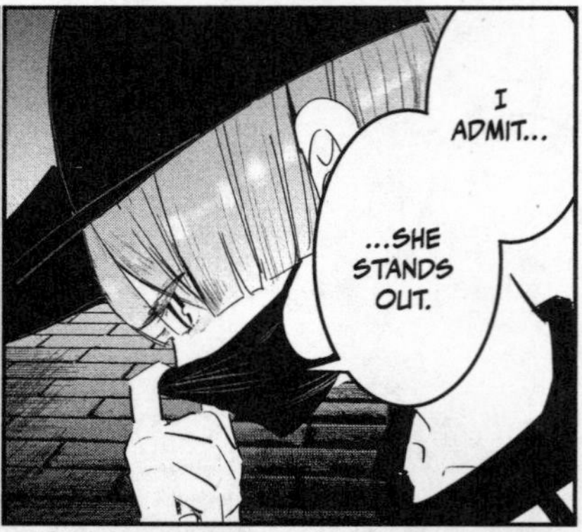
I ADMIT...
...SHE STANDS OUT.

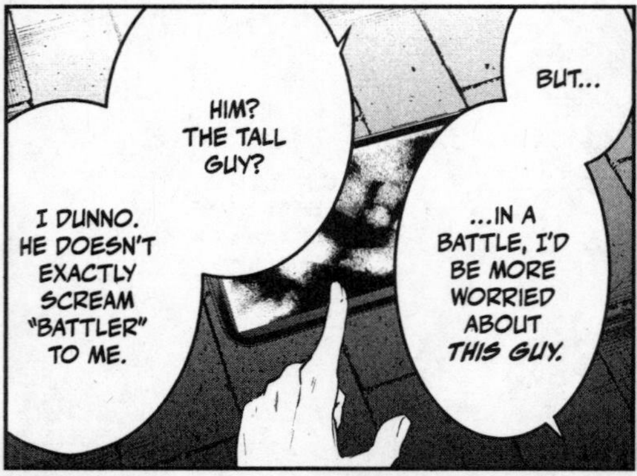
BUT...
...IN A BATTLE, I'D BE MORE WORRIED ABOUT *THIS GUY.*
HIM? THE TALL GUY?
I DUNNO. HE DOESN'T EXACTLY SCREAM "BATTLER" TO ME.

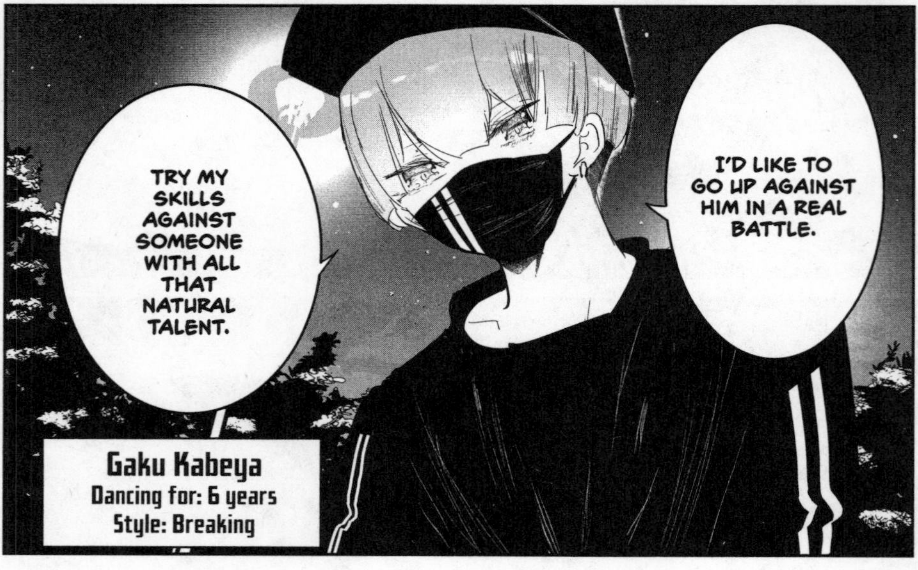
I'D LIKE TO GO UP AGAINST HIM IN A REAL BATTLE.
TRY MY SKILLS AGAINST SOMEONE WITH ALL THAT NATURAL TALENT.
Gaku Kabeya
Dancing for: 6 years
Style: Breaking

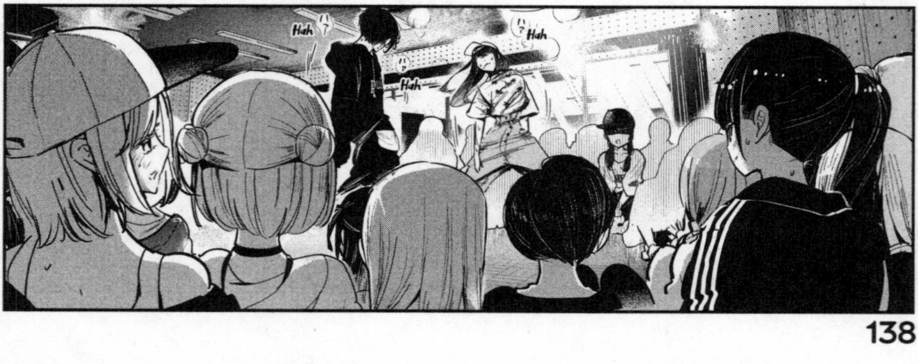
Hah
Hah
Hah

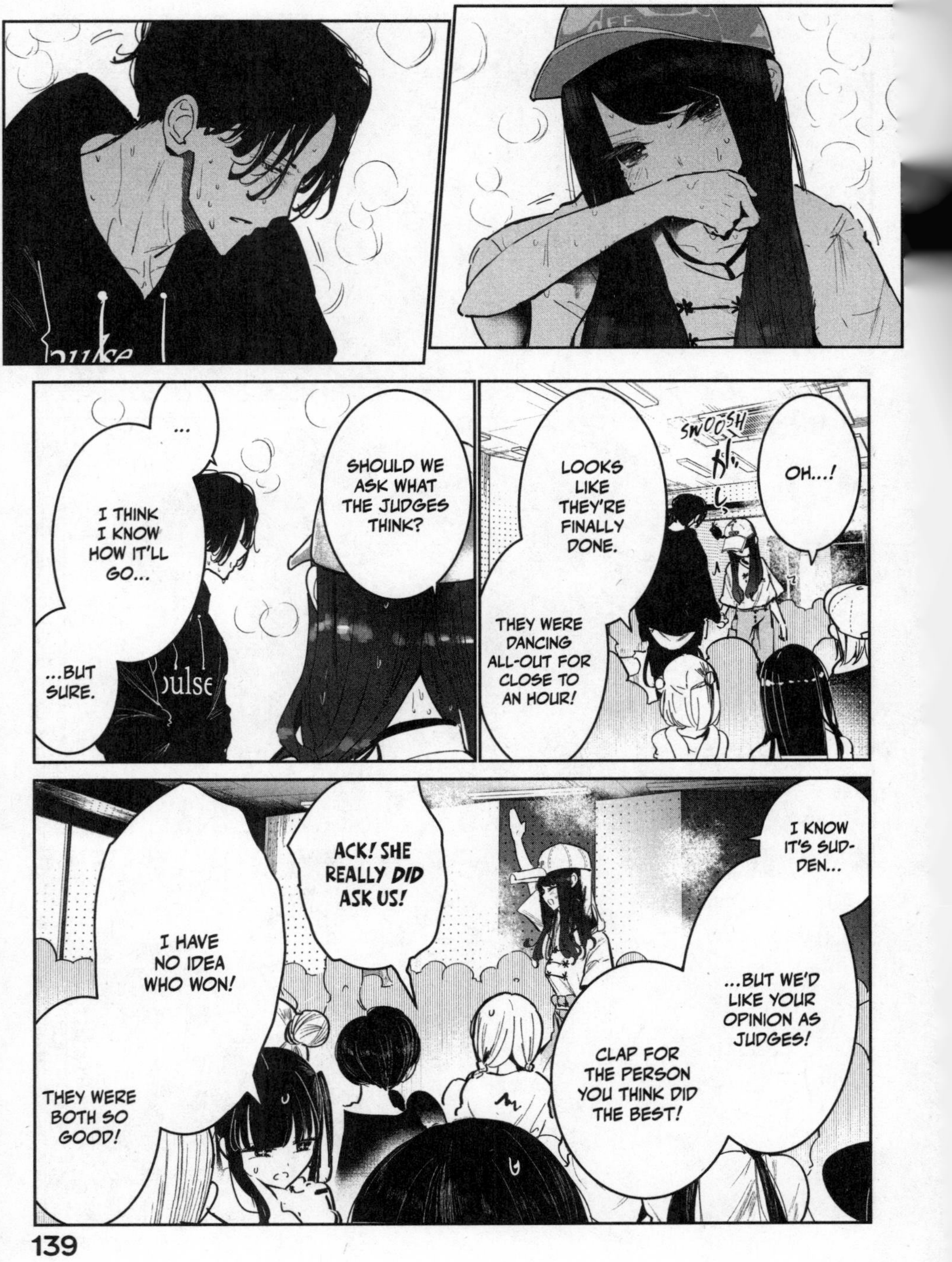
OH...!
SWOOSH
LOOKS LIKE THEY'RE FINALLY DONE.
THEY WERE DANCING ALL-OUT FOR CLOSE TO AN HOUR!
SHOULD WE ASK WHAT THE JUDGES THINK?
...
I THINK I KNOW HOW IT'LL GO...
...BUT SURE.
I KNOW IT'S SUD-DEN...
...BUT WE'D LIKE YOUR OPINION AS JUDGES!
CLAP FOR THE PERSON YOU THINK DID THE BEST!
ACK! SHE REALLY *DID* ASK US!
I HAVE NO IDEA WHO WON!
THEY WERE BOTH SO GOOD!

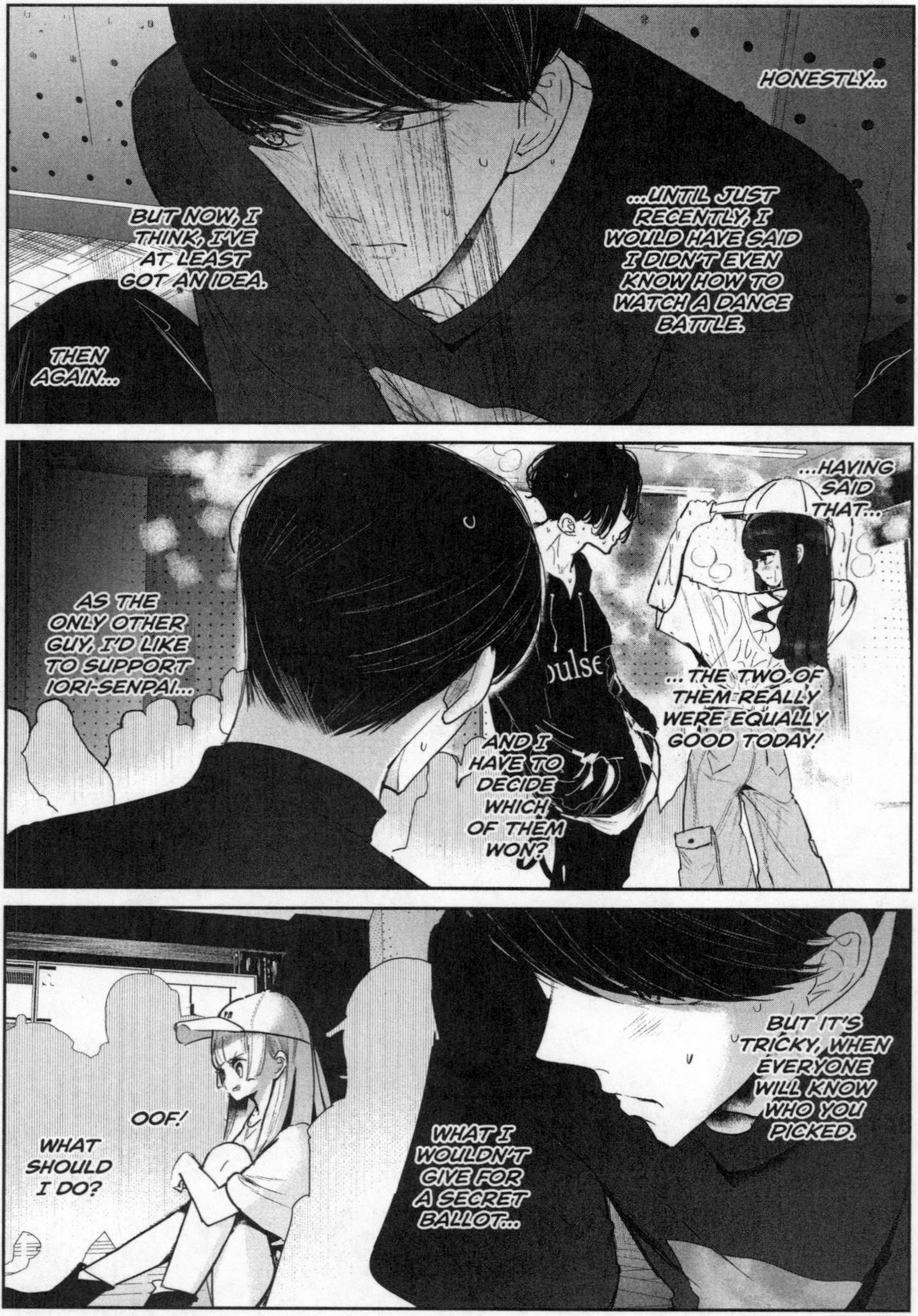
HONESTLY...
...UNTIL JUST RECENTLY, I WOULD HAVE SAID I DIDN'T EVEN KNOW HOW TO WATCH A DANCE BATTLE.
BUT NOW, I THINK, I'VE AT LEAST GOT AN IDEA.
THEN AGAIN...
...HAVING SAID THAT...
... THE TWO OF THEM REALLY WERE EQUALLY GOOD TODAY!
AND I HAVE TO DECIDE WHICH OF THEM WON?
AS THE ONLY OTHER GUY, I'D LIKE TO SUPPORT IORI-SENPAI...
BUT IT'S TRICKY, WHEN EVERYONE WILL KNOW WHO YOU PICKED.
WHAT I WOULDN'T GIVE FOR A SECRET BALLOT...
OOF!
WHAT SHOULD I DO?

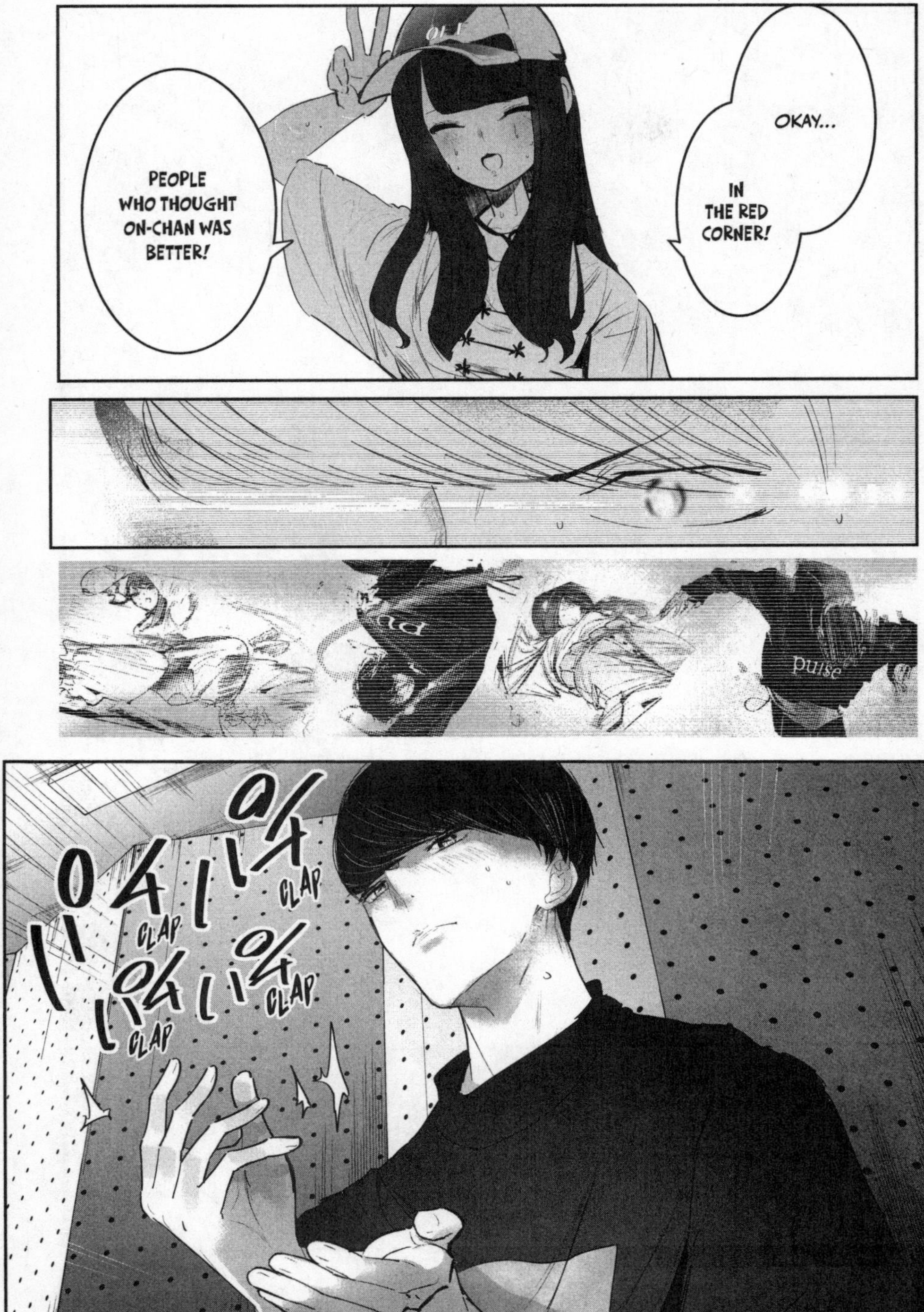
OKAY...
IN THE RED CORNER!
PEOPLE WHO THOUGHT ON-CHAN WAS BETTER!
pulse
CLAP
CLAP
CLAP
CLAP

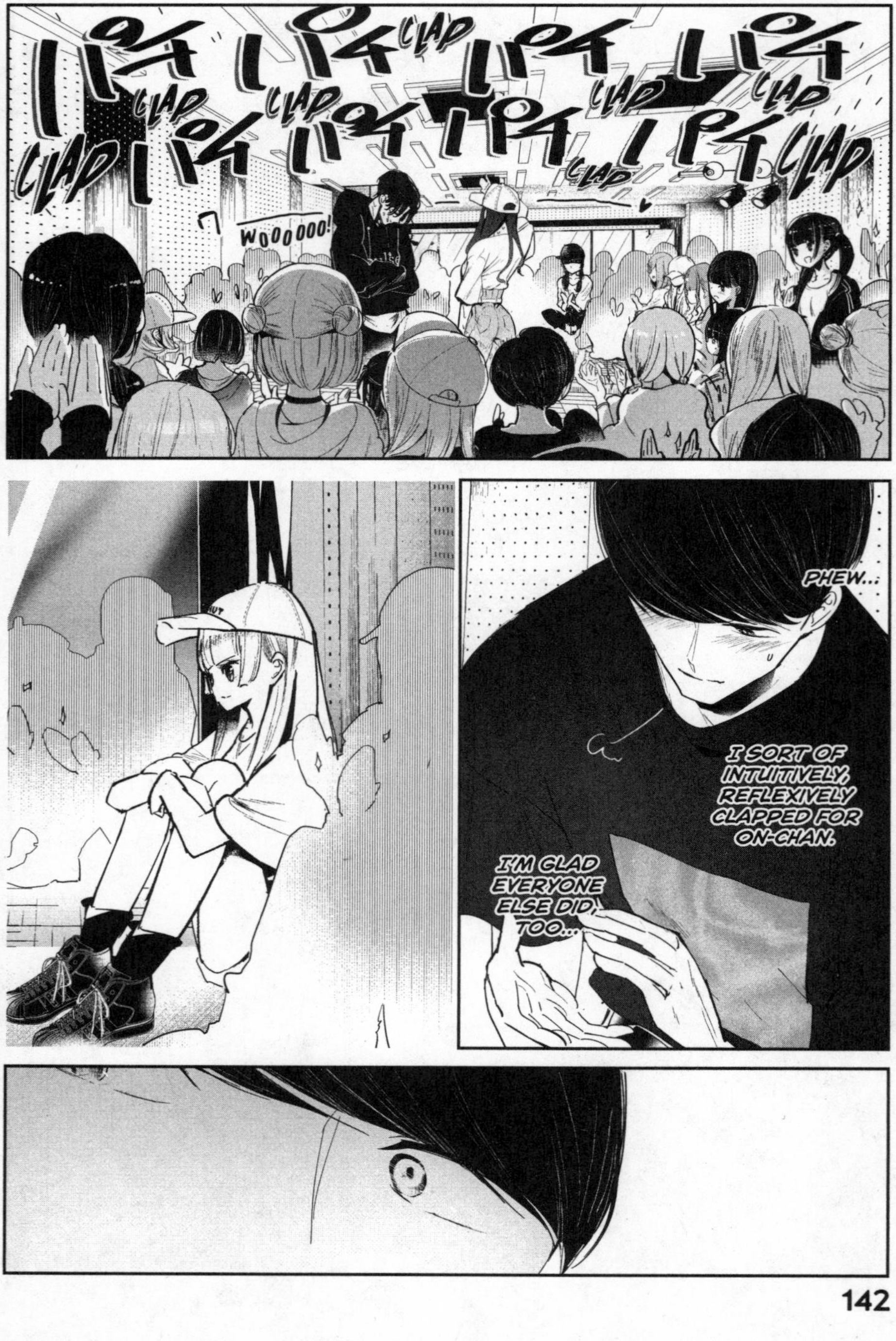
CLAP CLAP CLAP CLAP CLAP CLAP CLAP CLAP
WOOOOOO!
PHEW...
I SORT OF INTUITIVELY, REFLEXIVELY CLAPPED FOR ON-CHAN.
I'M GLAD EVERYONE ELSE DID, TOO...

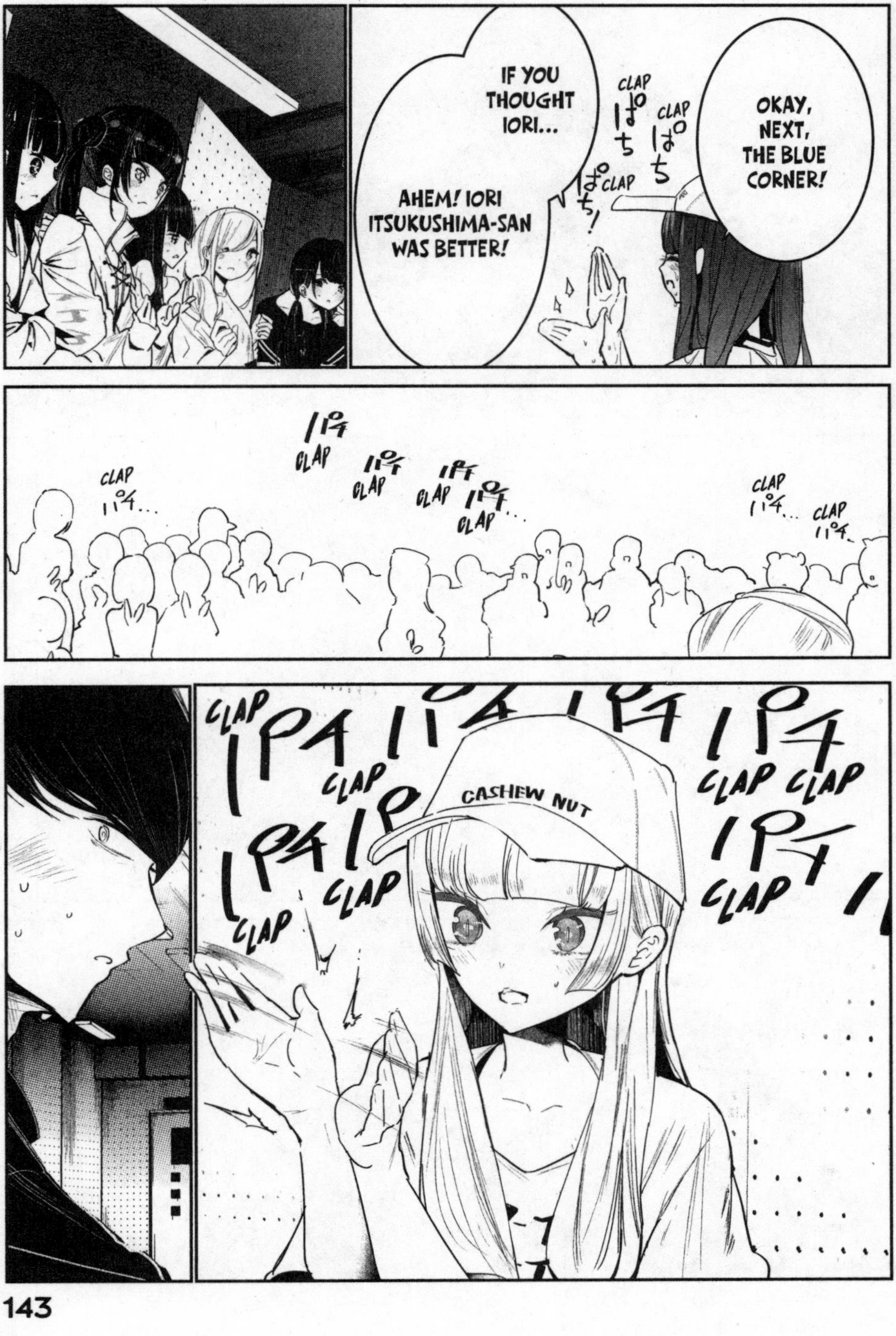
OKAY, NEXT, THE BLUE CORNER!
CLAP ぱち
CLAP ぱち
CLAP ぱち!
IF YOU THOUGHT IORI...
AHEM! IORI ITSUKUSHIMA-SAN WAS BETTER!
CLAP パチ...
CLAP パチ...
CLAP パチ...
CLAP パチ
CLAP パチ
CLAP パチ
CLAP パチ...
CLAP
CLAP
CLAP
CLAP
CASHEW NUT
CLAP
CLAP
CLAP
CLAP

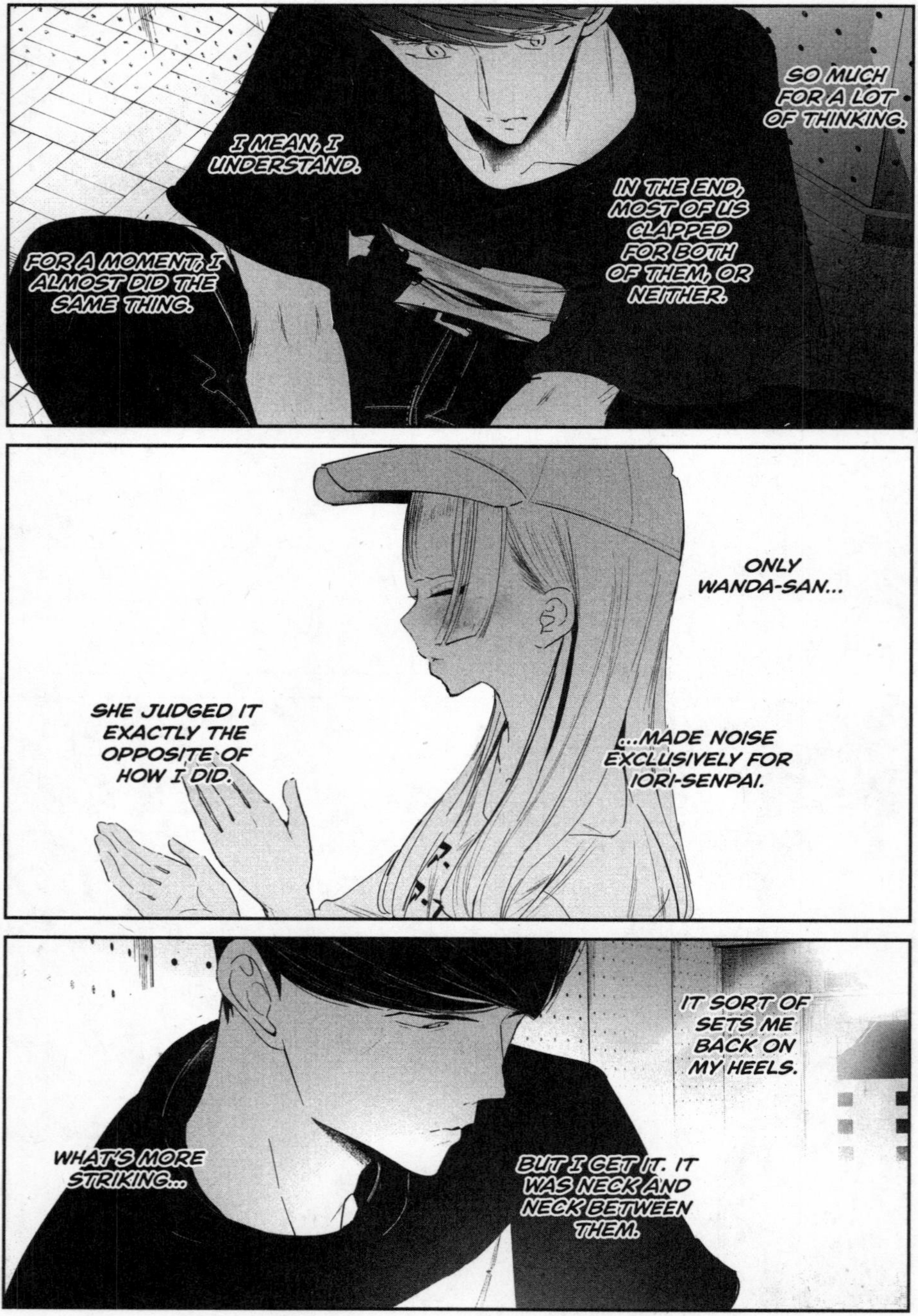
SO MUCH FOR A LOT OF THINKING.
IN THE END, MOST OF US CLAPPED FOR BOTH OF THEM, OR NEITHER.
I MEAN, I UNDERSTAND.
FOR A MOMENT, I ALMOST DID THE SAME THING.
ONLY WANDA-SAN...
...MADE NOISE EXCLUSIVELY FOR IORI-SENPAI.
SHE JUDGED IT EXACTLY THE OPPOSITE OF HOW I DID.
IT SORT OF SETS ME BACK ON MY HEELS.
BUT I GET IT. IT WAS NECK AND NECK BETWEEN THEM.
WHAT'S MORE STRIKING...

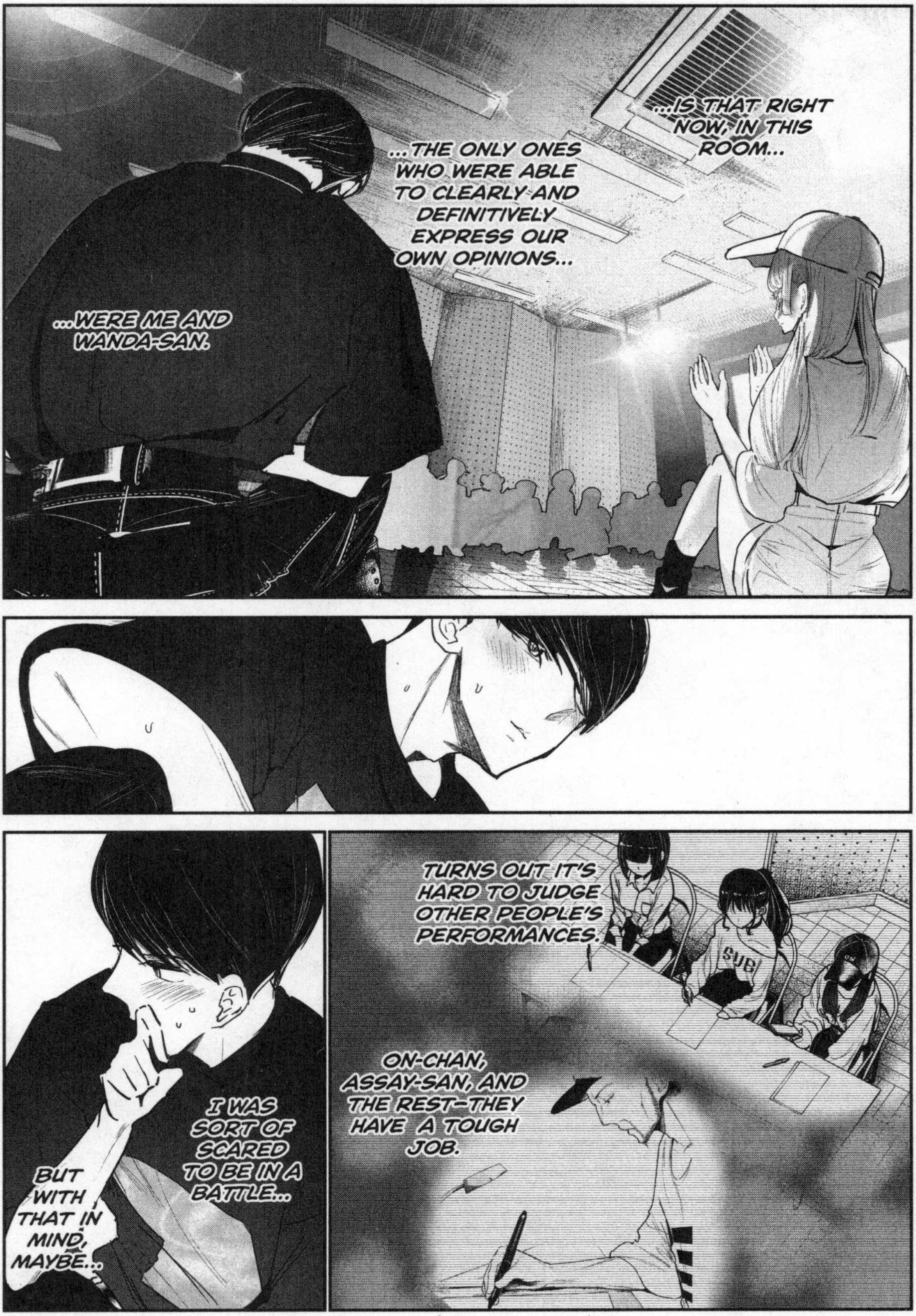
...IS THAT RIGHT NOW, IN THIS ROOM...
...THE ONLY ONES WHO WERE ABLE TO CLEARLY AND DEFINITIVELY EXPRESS OUR OWN OPINIONS...
...WERE ME AND WANDA-SAN.
TURNS OUT IT'S HARD TO JUDGE OTHER PEOPLE'S PERFORMANCES.
ON-CHAN, ASSAY-SAN, AND THE REST—THEY HAVE A TOUGH JOB.
I WAS SORT OF SCARED TO BE IN A BATTLE...
BUT WITH THAT IN MIND, MAYBE...

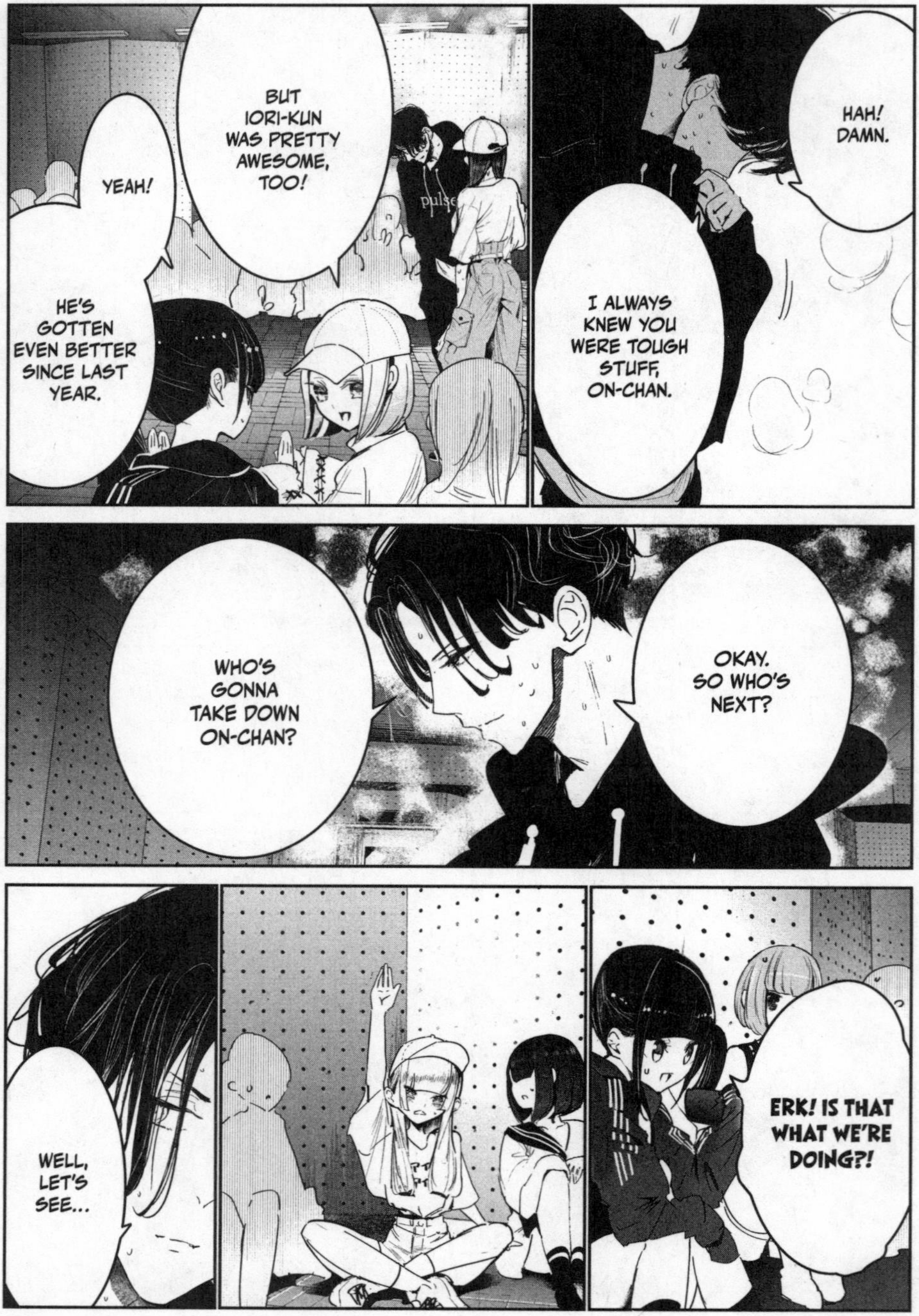
HAH! DAMN.
I ALWAYS KNEW YOU WERE TOUGH STUFF, ON-CHAN.
BUT IORI-KUN WAS PRETTY AWESOME, TOO!
YEAH!
HE'S GOTTEN EVEN BETTER SINCE LAST YEAR.
OKAY. SO WHO'S NEXT?
WHO'S GONNA TAKE DOWN ON-CHAN?
ERK! IS THAT WHAT WE'RE DOING?!
WELL, LET'S SEE...

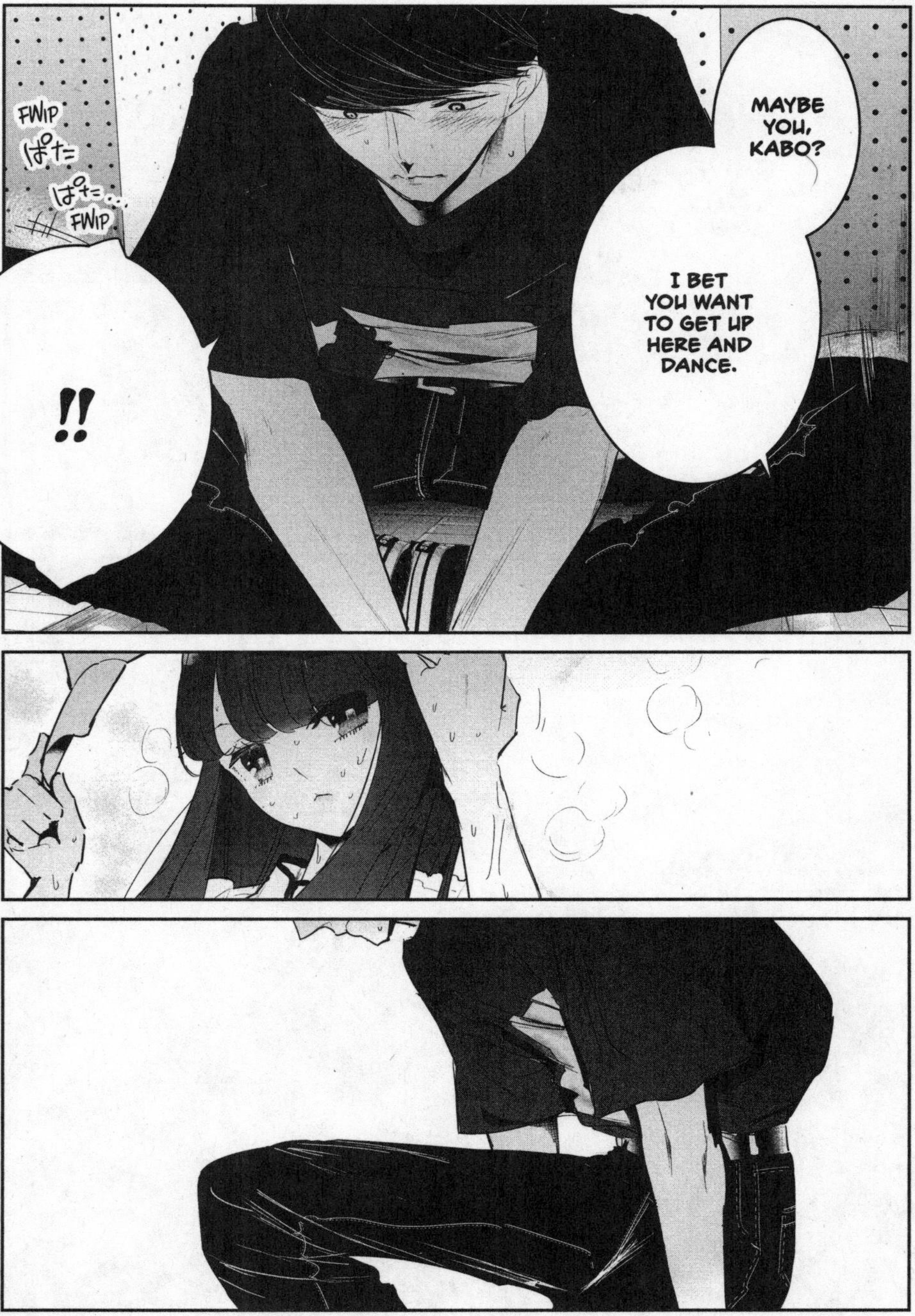
MAYBE YOU, KABO?
I BET YOU WANT TO GET UP HERE AND DANCE.
FWIP
ぱた
ぱた...
FWIP
!!

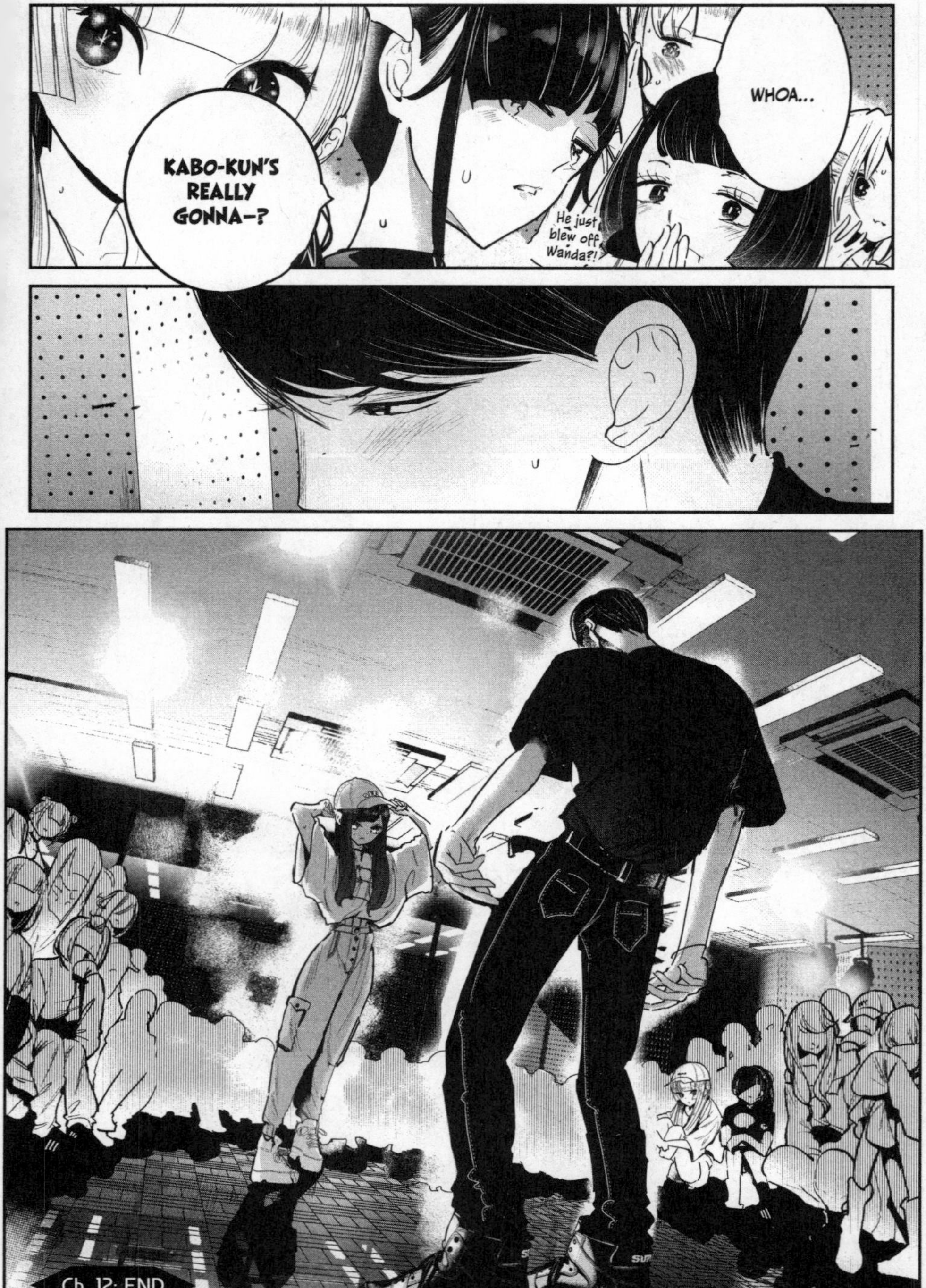
WHOA...
He just blew off Wanda?!
KABO-KUN'S REALLY GONNA–?
Ch. 12: END

WANDANCE

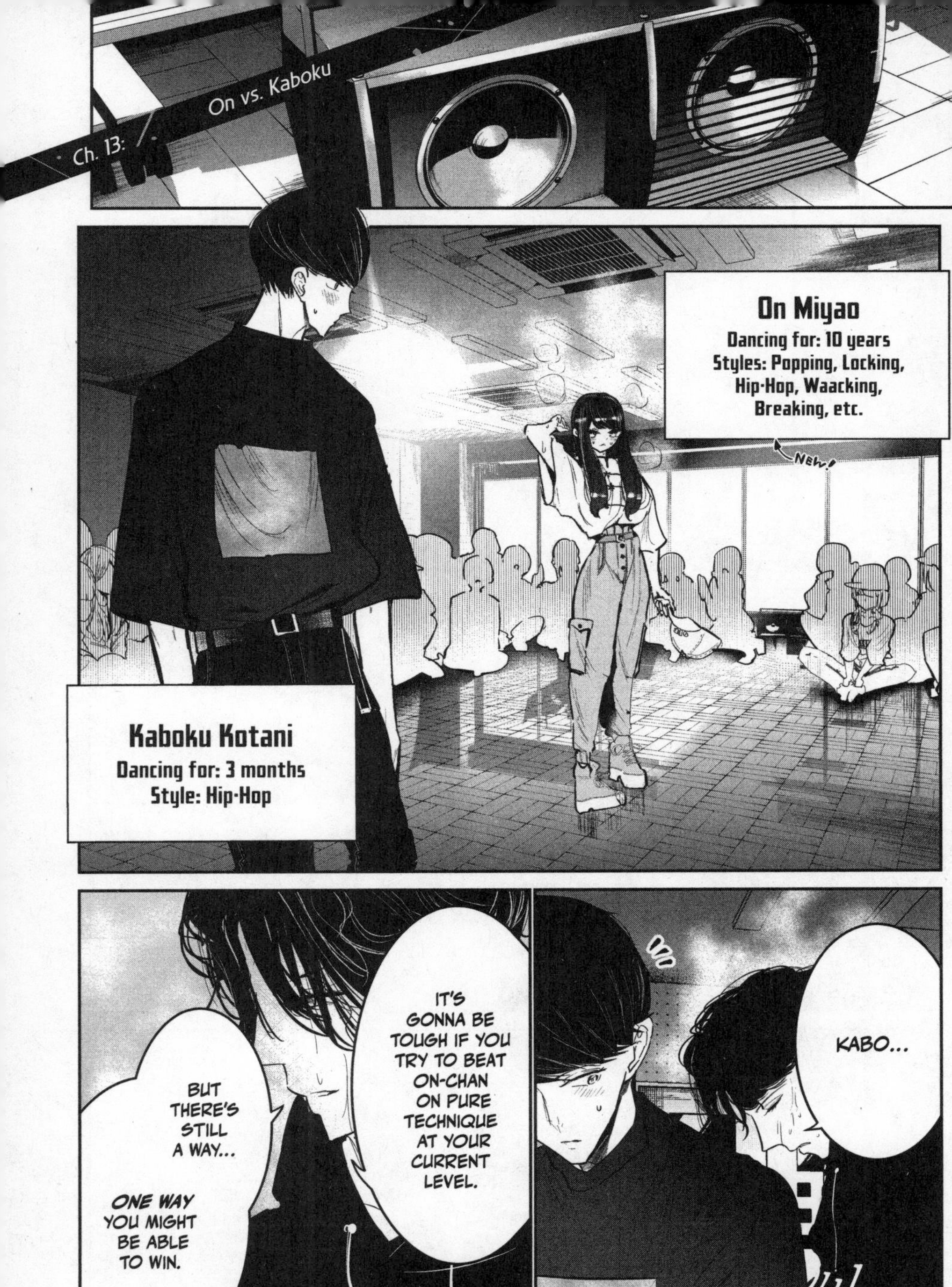
Ch. 13: On vs. Kaboku
On Miyao
Dancing for: 10 years
Styles: Popping, Locking, Hip-Hop, Waacking, Breaking, etc.
NEW!
Kaboku Kotani
Dancing for: 3 months
Style: Hip-Hop
KABO...
IT'S GONNA BE TOUGH IF YOU TRY TO BEAT ON-CHAN ON PURE TECHNIQUE AT YOUR CURRENT LEVEL.
BUT THERE'S STILL A WAY...
ONE WAY YOU MIGHT BE ABLE TO WIN.

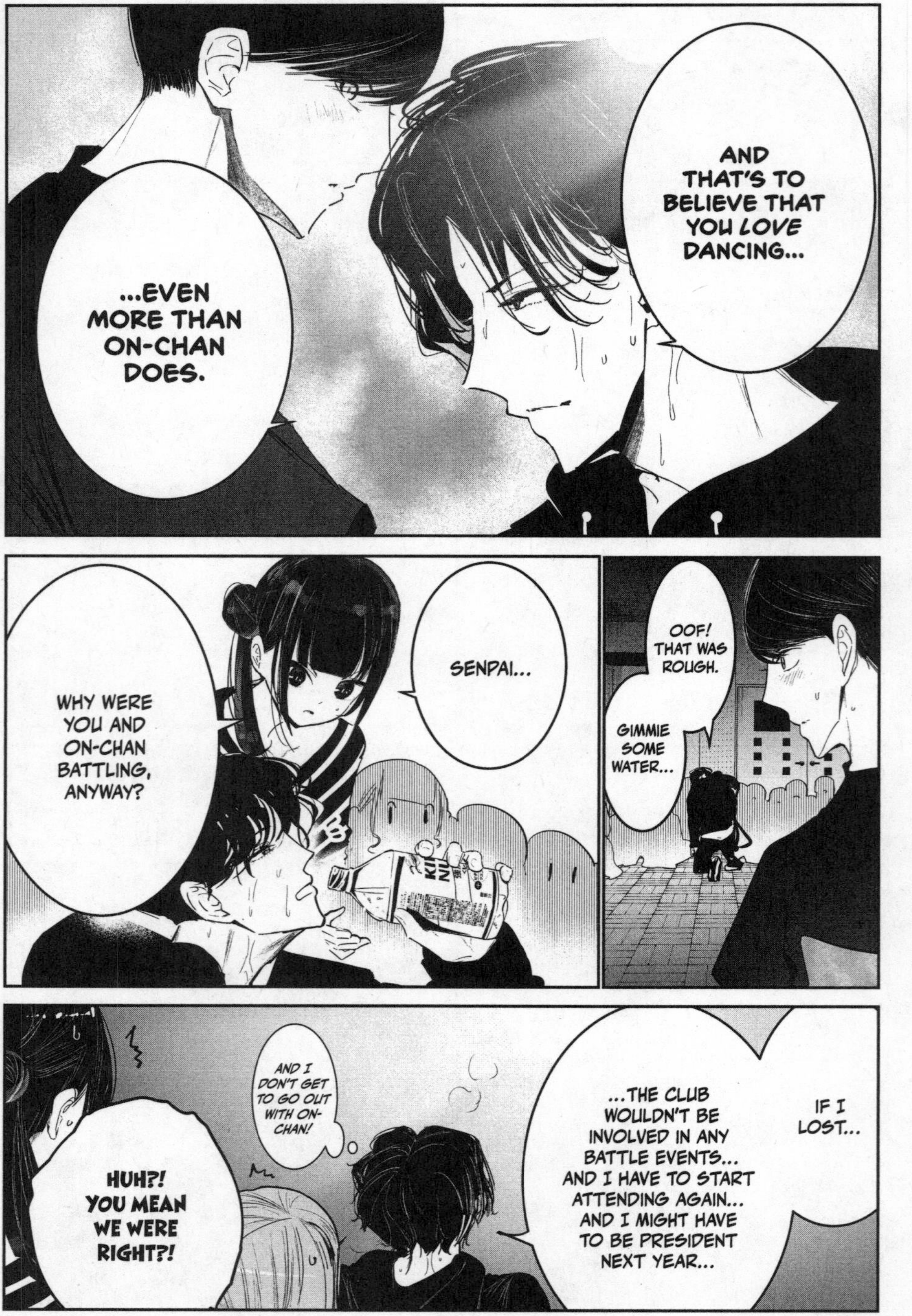
AND THAT'S TO BELIEVE THAT YOU *LOVE* DANCING...
...EVEN MORE THAN ON-CHAN DOES.
OOF! THAT WAS ROUGH.
GIMMIE SOME WATER...
SENPAI...
WHY WERE YOU AND ON-CHAN BATTLING, ANYWAY?
IF I LOST...
...THE CLUB WOULDN'T BE INVOLVED IN ANY BATTLE EVENTS... AND I HAVE TO START ATTENDING AGAIN... AND I MIGHT HAVE TO BE PRESIDENT NEXT YEAR...
AND I DON'T GET TO GO OUT WITH ON-CHAN!
HUH?! YOU MEAN WE WERE RIGHT?!

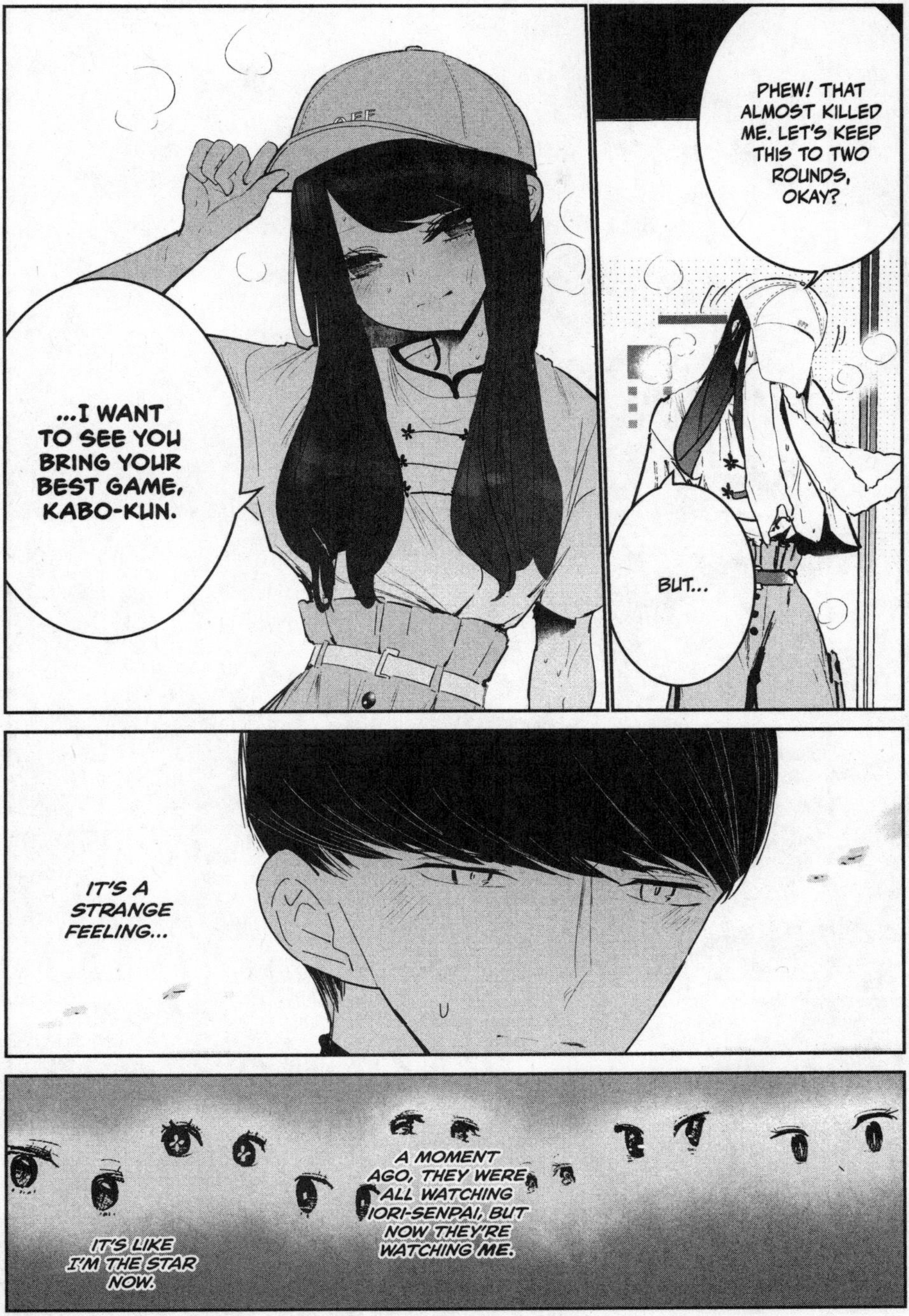
PHEW! THAT ALMOST KILLED ME. LET'S KEEP THIS TO TWO ROUNDS, OKAY?
BUT...
...I WANT TO SEE YOU BRING YOUR BEST GAME, KABO-KUN.
IT'S A STRANGE FEELING...
A MOMENT AGO, THEY WERE ALL WATCHING IORI-SENPAI, BUT NOW THEY'RE WATCHING ME.
IT'S LIKE I'M THE STAR NOW.

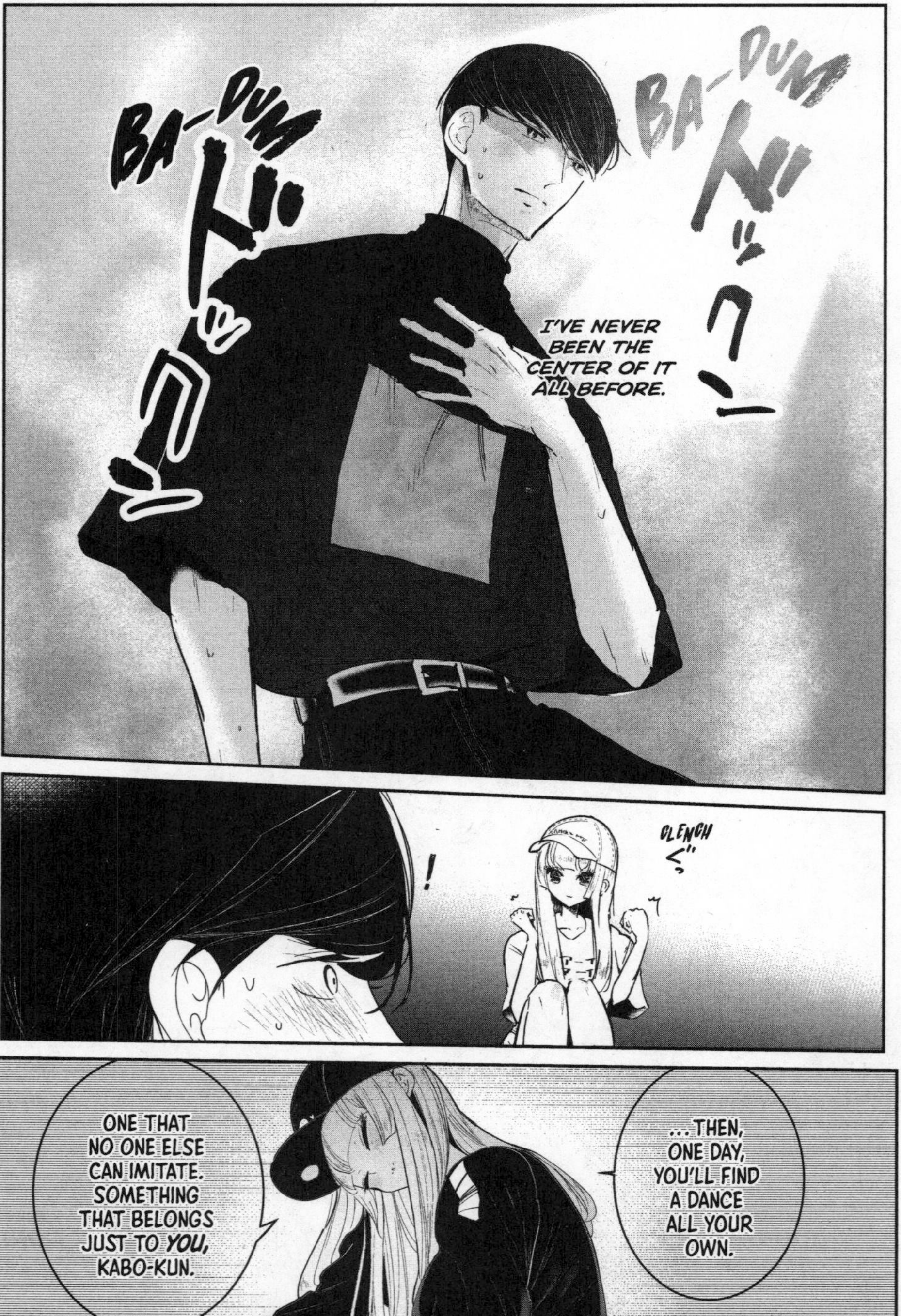
BA-DUM
I'VE NEVER BEEN THE CENTER OF IT ALL BEFORE.
BA-DUM
CLENCH
!
...THEN, ONE DAY, YOU'LL FIND A DANCE ALL YOUR OWN.
ONE THAT NO ONE ELSE CAN IMITATE. SOMETHING THAT BELONGS JUST TO YOU, KABO-KUN.

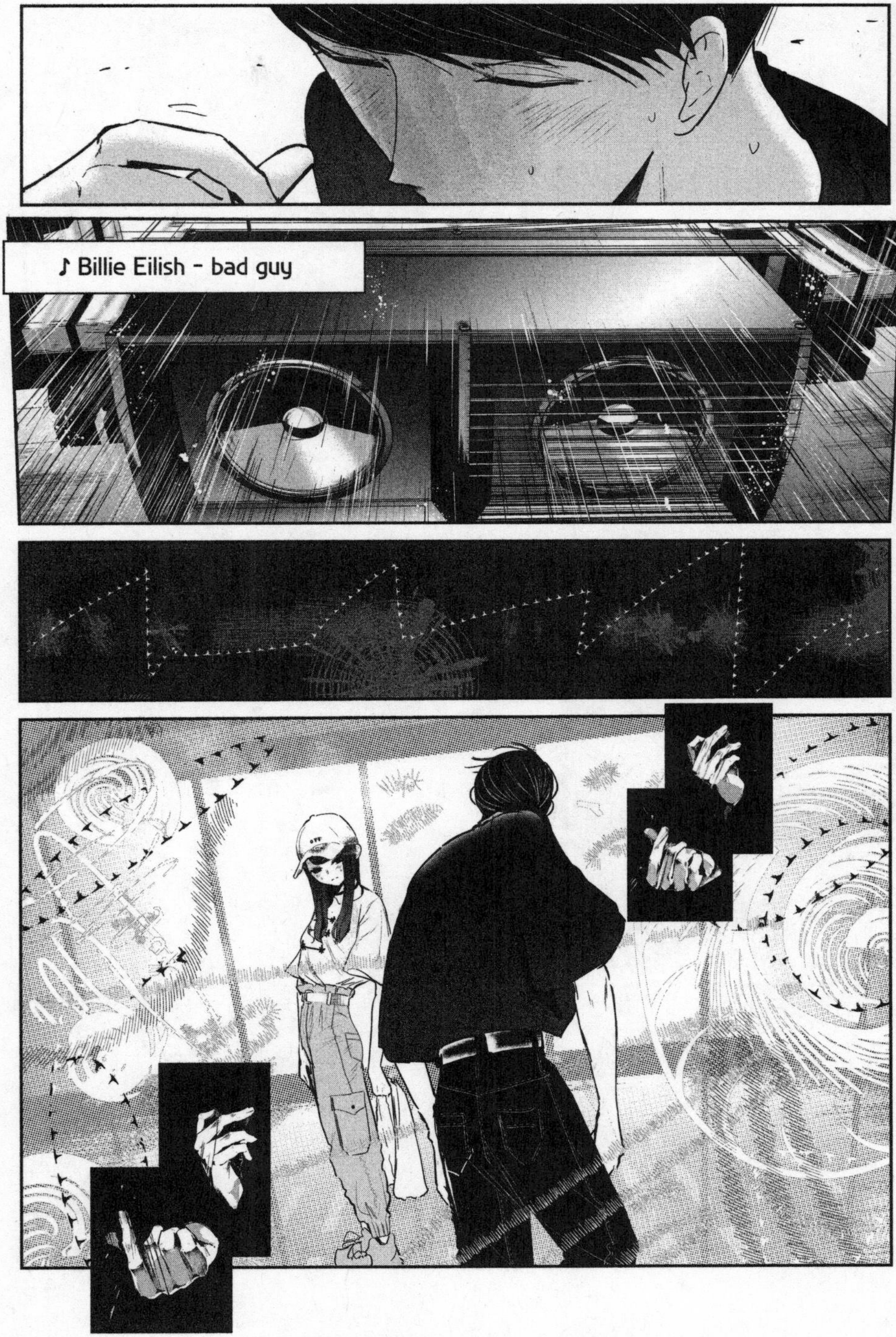
♪ Billie Eilish - bad guy

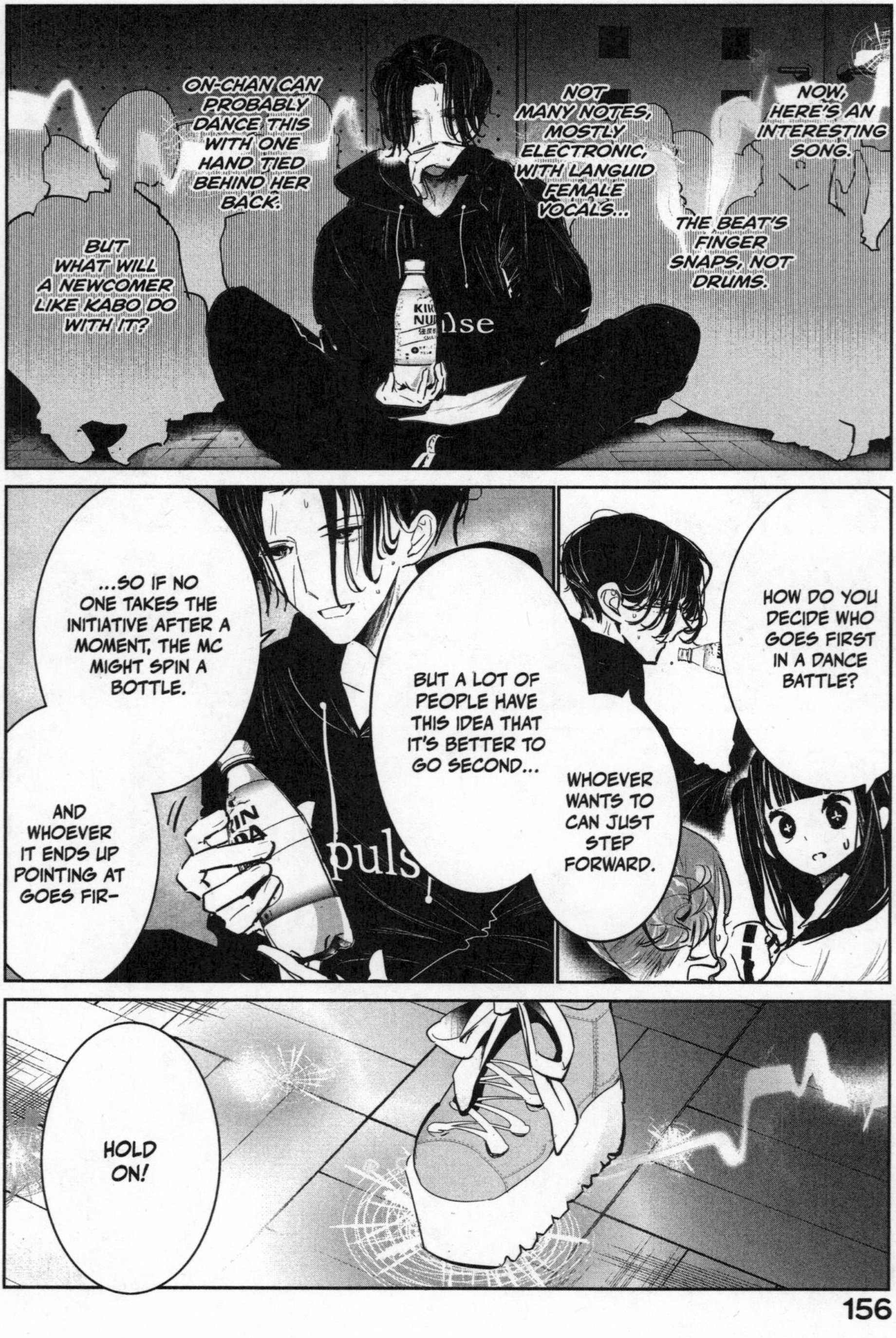
NOW, HERE'S AN INTERESTING SONG.
THE BEAT'S FINGER SNAPS, NOT DRUMS.
NOT MANY NOTES, MOSTLY ELECTRONIC, WITH LANGUID FEMALE VOCALS...
ON-CHAN CAN PROBABLY DANCE THIS WITH ONE HAND TIED BEHIND HER BACK.
BUT WHAT WILL A NEWCOMER LIKE KABO DO WITH IT?
HOW DO YOU DECIDE WHO GOES FIRST IN A DANCE BATTLE?
WHOEVER WANTS TO CAN JUST STEP FORWARD.
BUT A LOT OF PEOPLE HAVE THIS IDEA THAT IT'S BETTER TO GO SECOND...
...SO IF NO ONE TAKES THE INITIATIVE AFTER A MOMENT, THE MC MIGHT SPIN A BOTTLE.
AND WHOEVER IT ENDS UP POINTING AT GOES FIR-
HOLD ON!

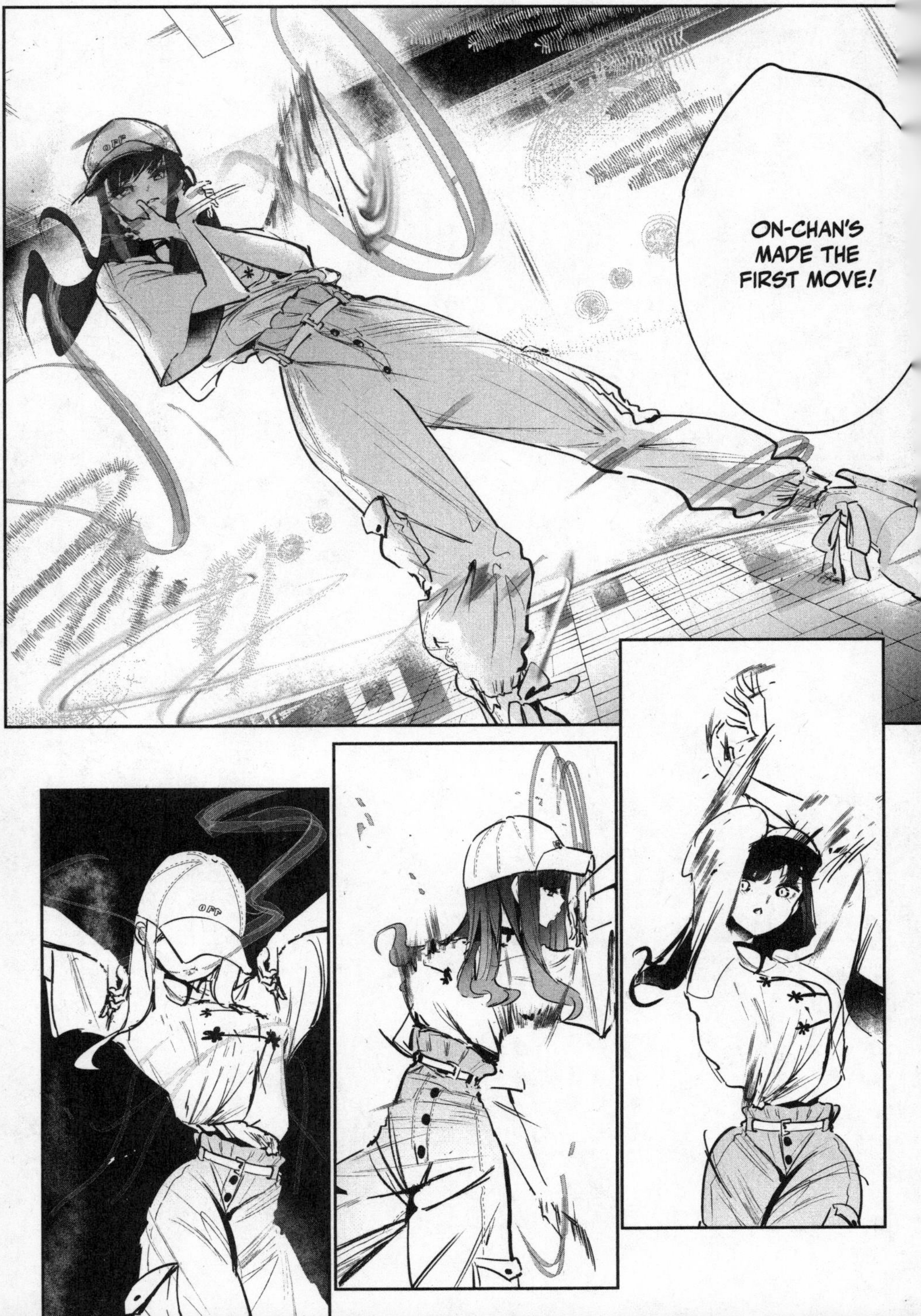
ON-CHAN'S MADE THE FIRST MOVE!

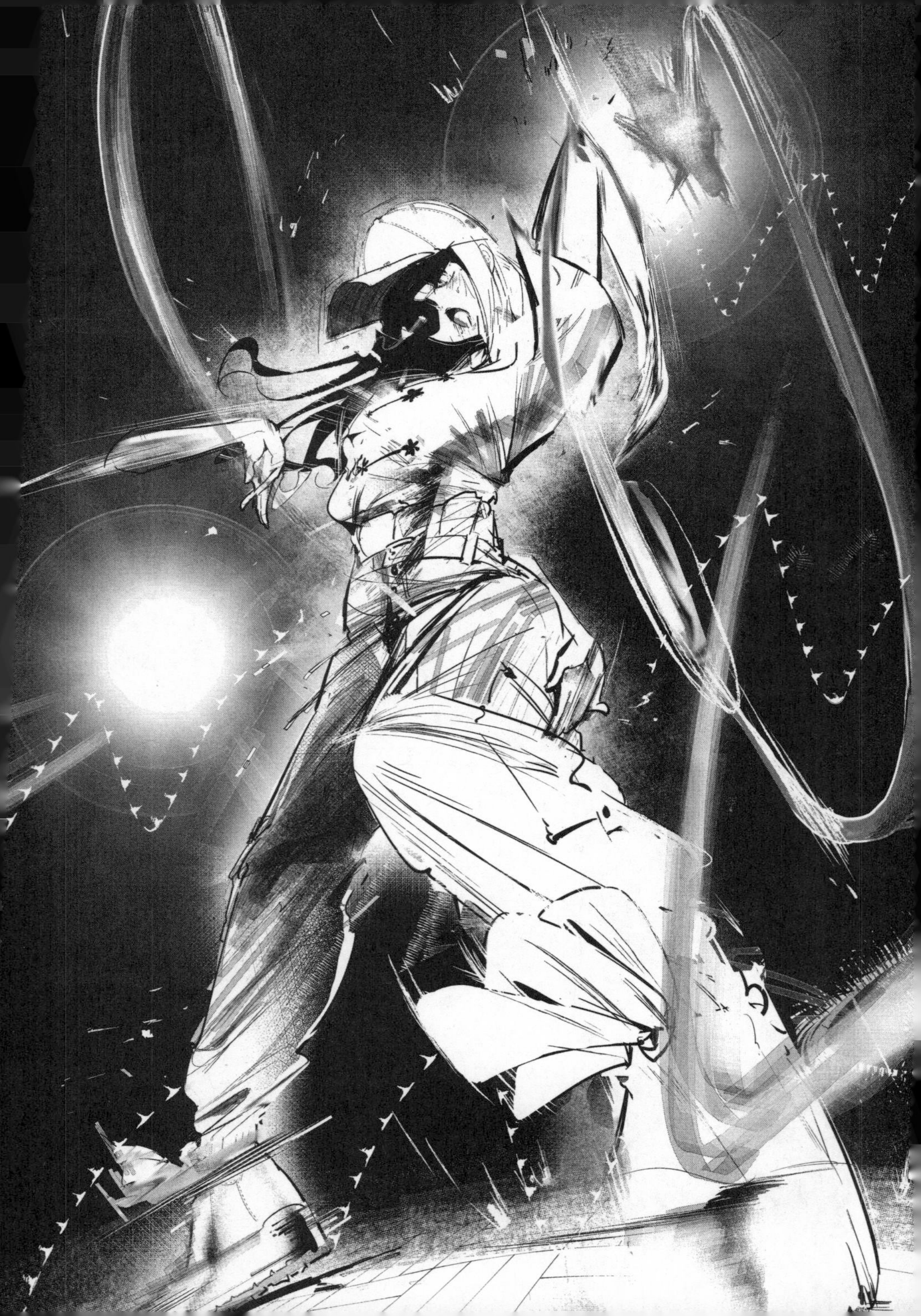

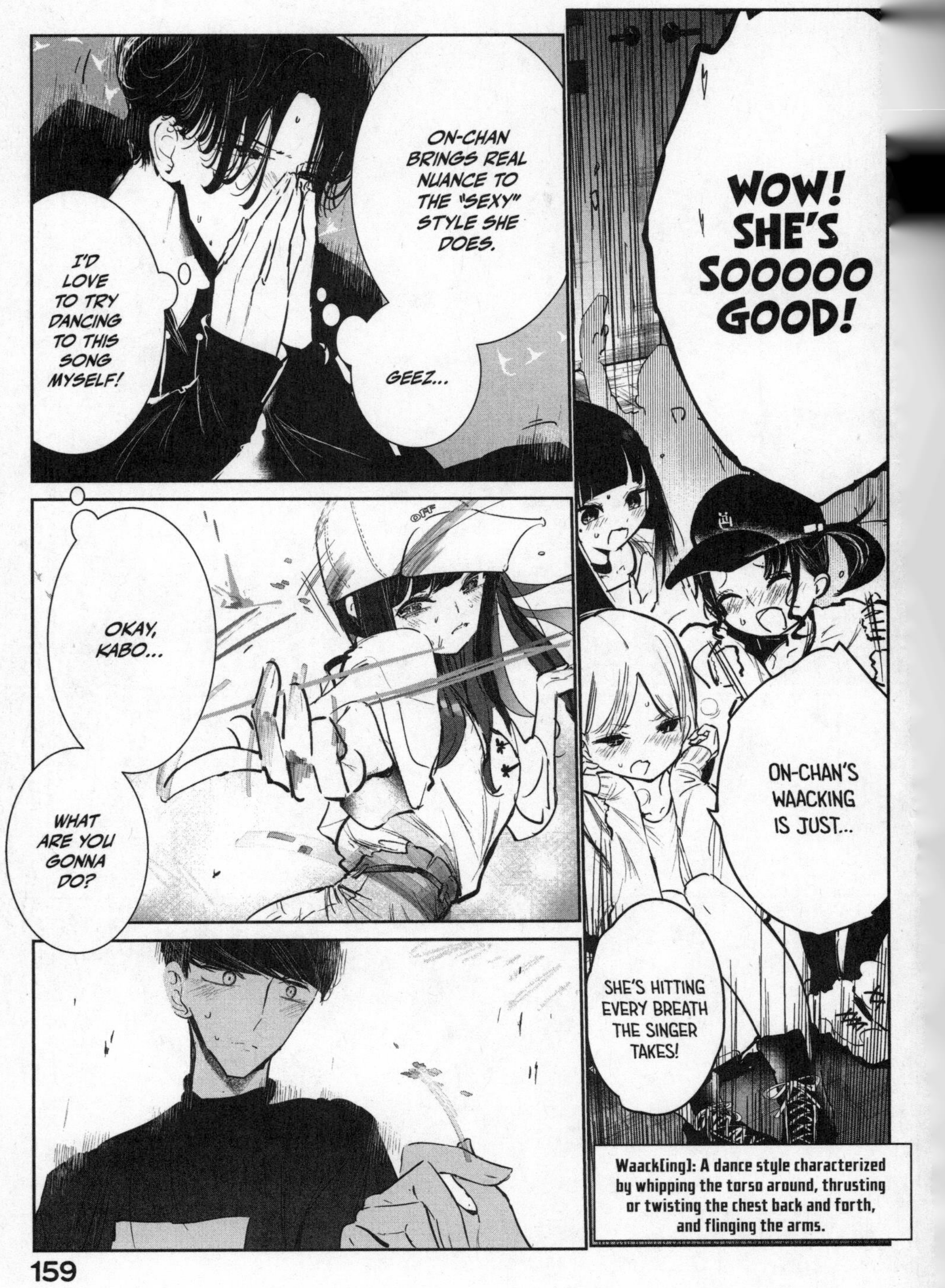
WOW! SHE'S SOOOOO GOOD!
ON-CHAN'S WAACKING IS JUST...
SHE'S HITTING EVERY BREATH THE SINGER TAKES!
Waack[ing]: A dance style characterized by whipping the torso around, thrusting or twisting the chest back and forth, and flinging the arms.
ON-CHAN BRINGS REAL NUANCE TO THE "SEXY" STYLE SHE DOES.
GEEZ...
I'D LOVE TO TRY DANCING TO THIS SONG MYSELF!
OFF
OKAY, KABO...
WHAT ARE YOU GONNA DO?

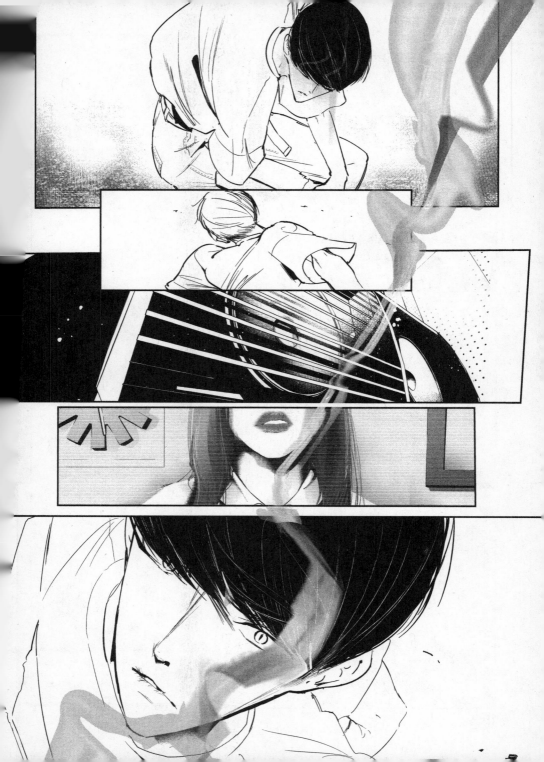

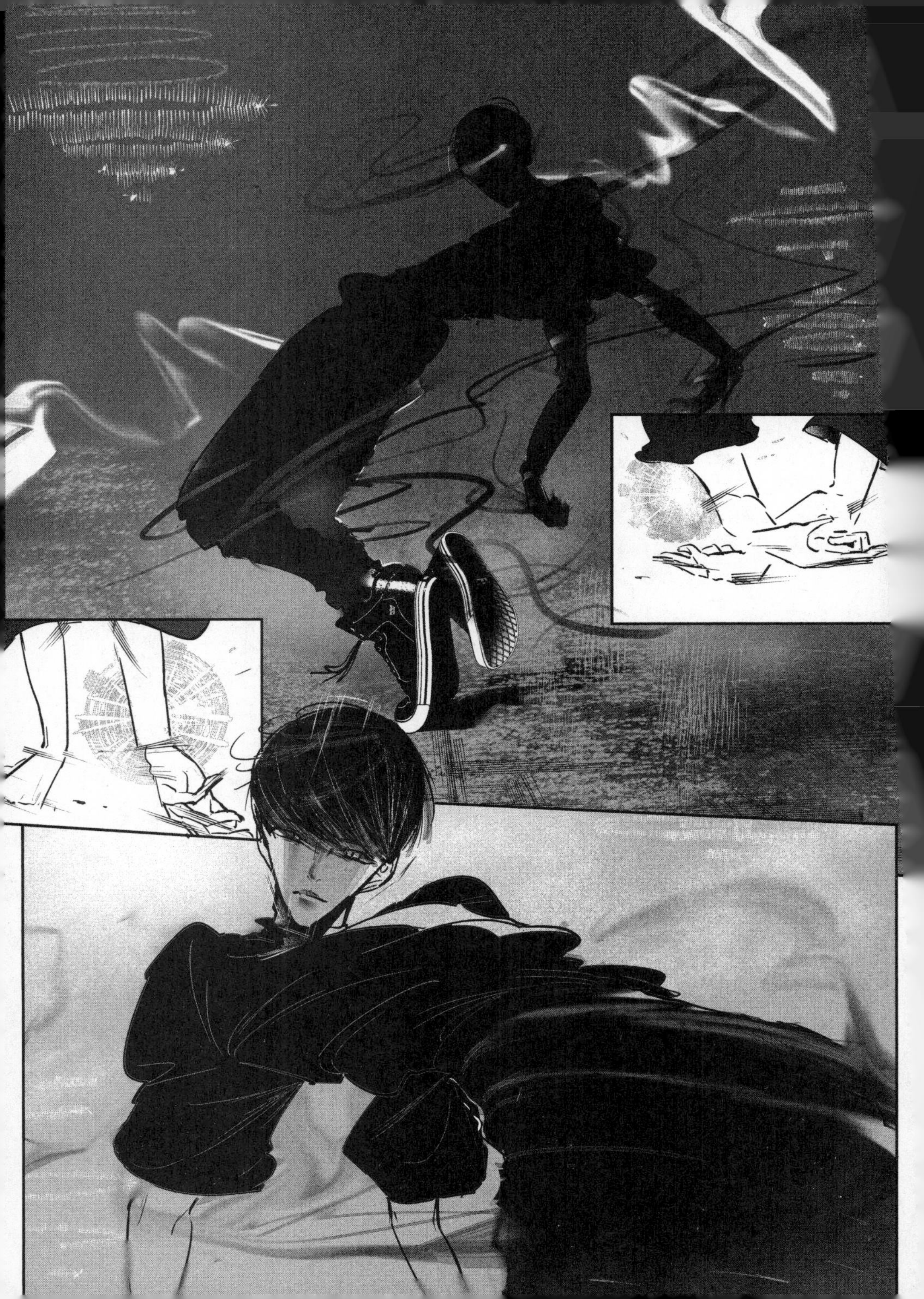

SHOCK
SINCE THE CONTEST...
...I'VE WATCHED MY BATTLE WITH IORI-SENPAI AGAIN AND AGAIN.
I KEPT TRYING TO PRACTICE WHAT I SAW IN THE VIDEO.
AND ONE DAY, MY FUNDAMENTAL PERCEPTION OF RHYTHM JUST... CHANGED.
@macon
DANCE BATTLE RIGHT IN SCHOOL!!
#GACHIDANCE
♪ ORIGINAL SOUND
I COULDN'T EXPLAIN IT IF I TRIED.
OFF
IT'S LIKE THE SOUND IS GOING TO THE DEEPEST PART OF MY BEING.
THE WINNER OF A DANCE BATTLE...
...ISN'T ALWAYS THE MOST EXPERIENCED PERSON...
WATCHING THAT VIDEO MADE ME REALIZE...
...OR THE MOST PHYSICAL...
...OR THE ONE WHO KNOWS THE WILDEST TRICKS.

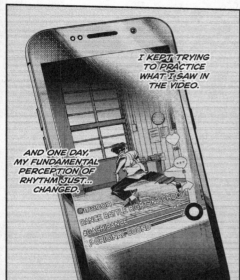

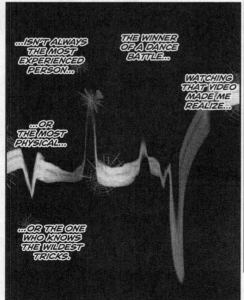

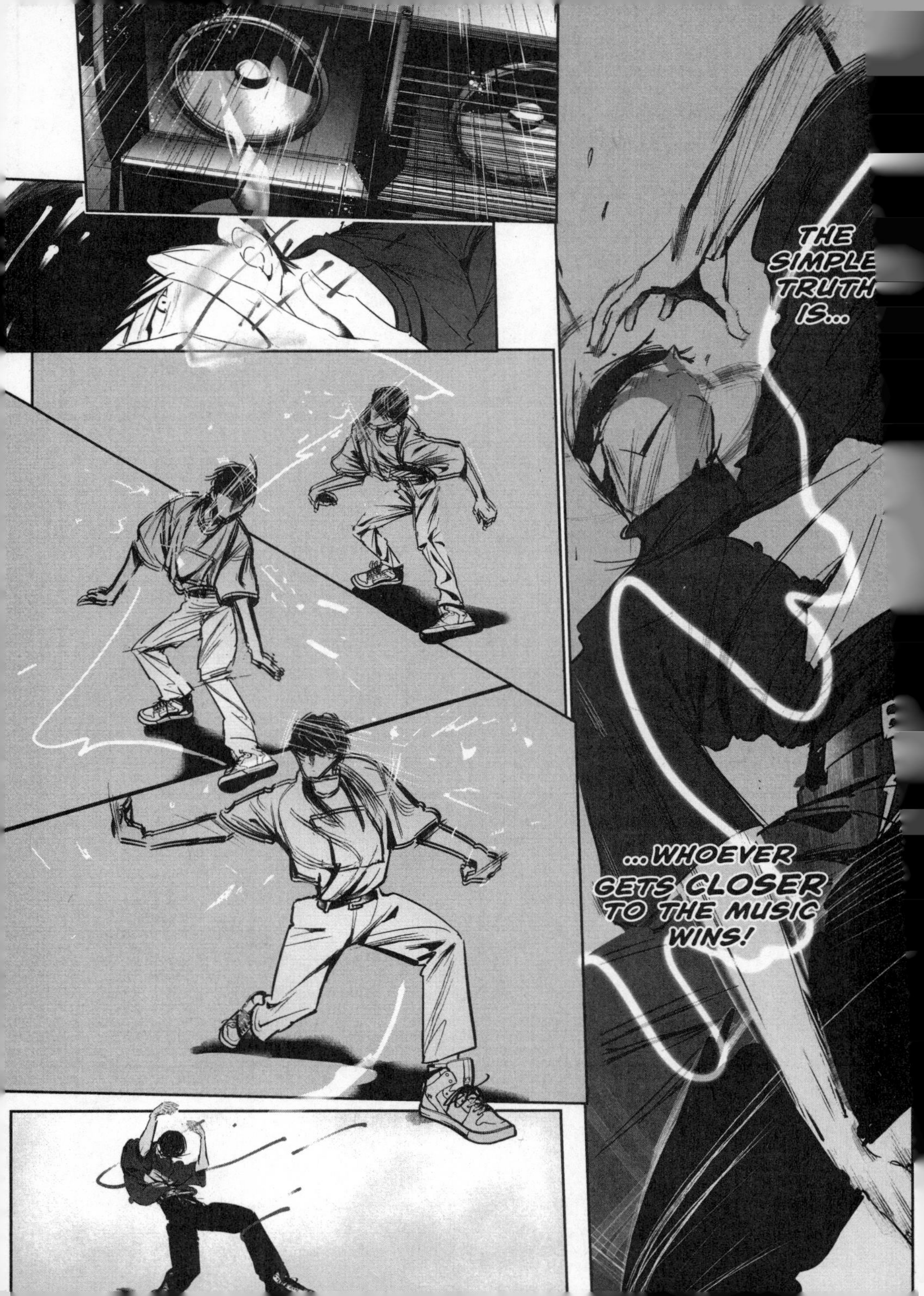
THE SIMPLE TRUTH IS...
...WHOEVER GETS CLOSER TO THE MUSIC WINS!

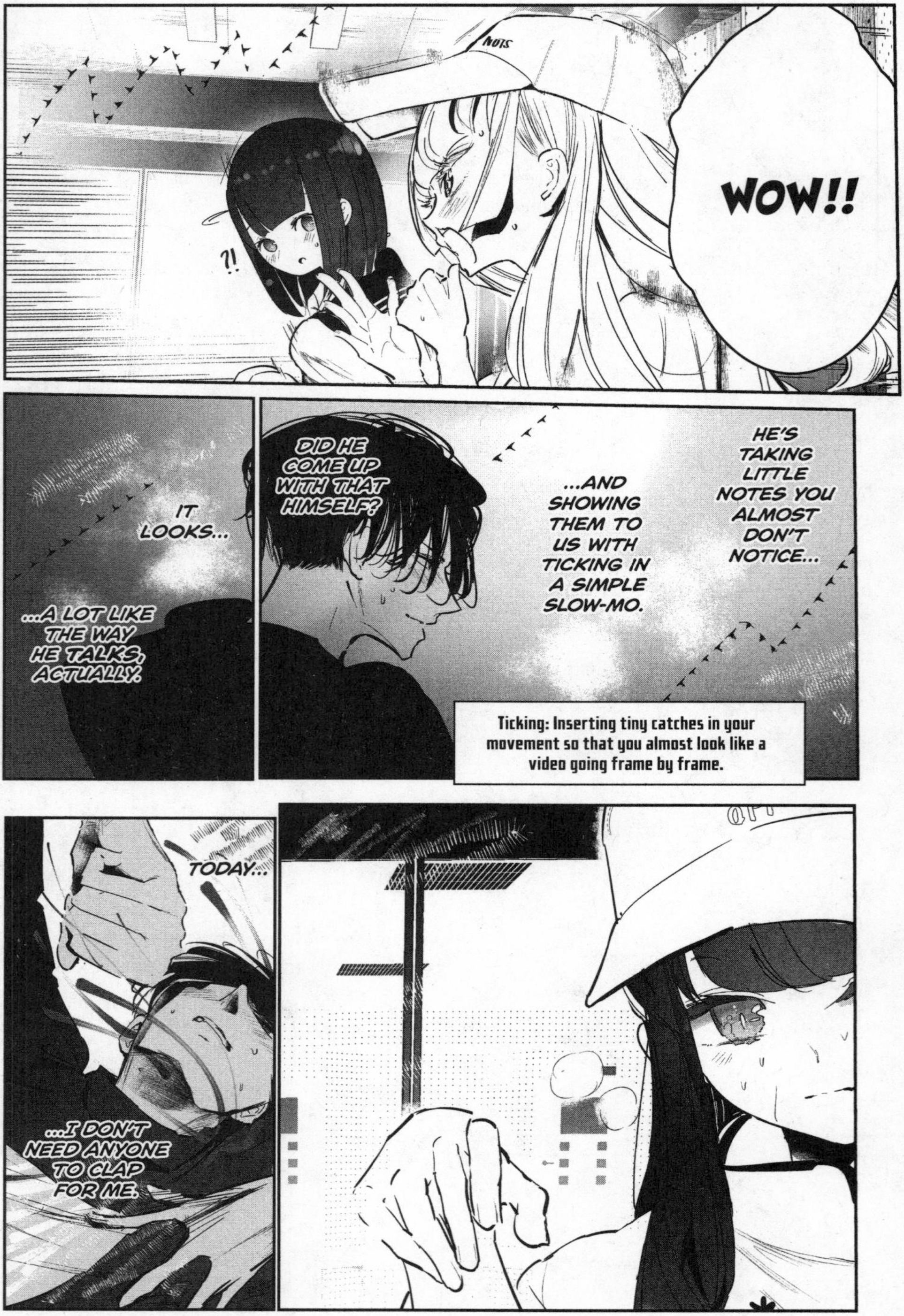
WOW!!
?!
HE'S TAKING LITTLE NOTES YOU ALMOST DON'T NOTICE...
...AND SHOWING THEM TO US WITH TICKING IN A SIMPLE SLOW-MO.
DID HE COME UP WITH THAT HIMSELF?
Ticking: Inserting tiny catches in your movement so that you almost look like a video going frame by frame.
IT LOOKS...
...A LOT LIKE THE WAY HE TALKS, ACTUALLY.
TODAY...
...I DON'T NEED ANYONE TO CLAP FOR ME.

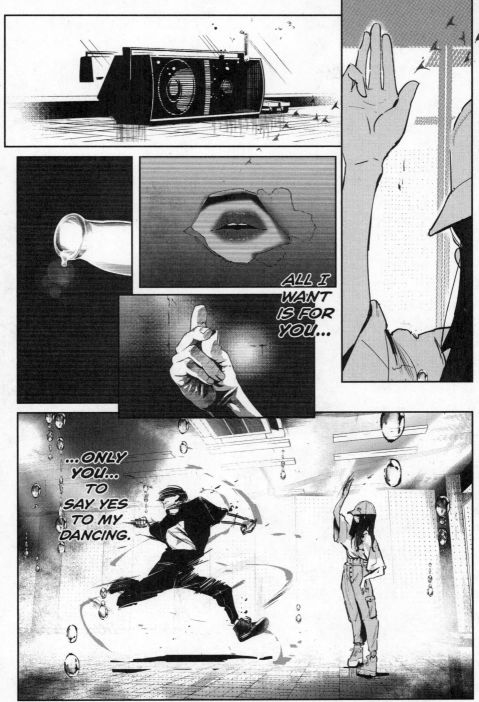

ALL I WANT IS FOR YOU...

...ONLY YOU... TO SAY YES TO MY DANCING.

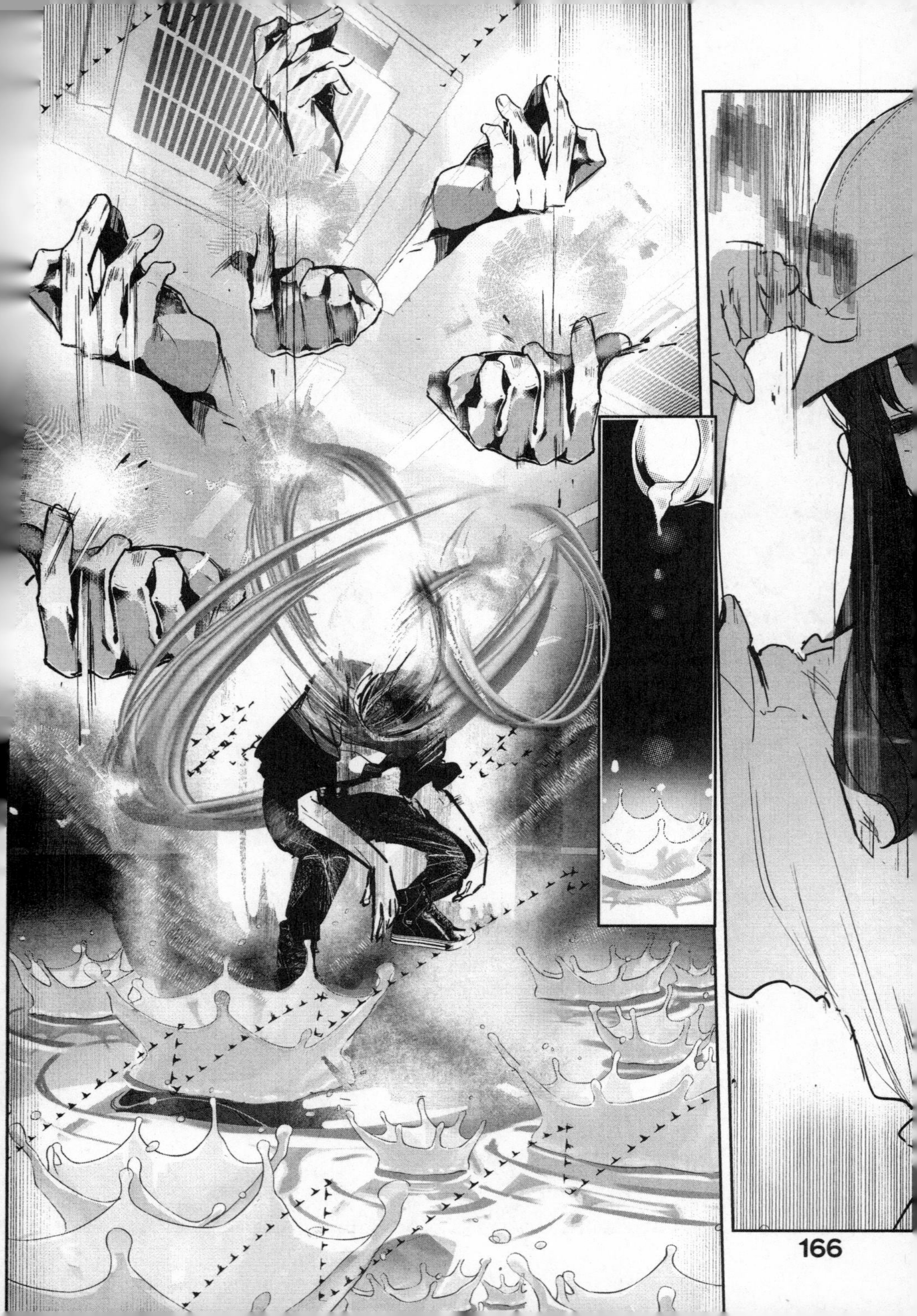

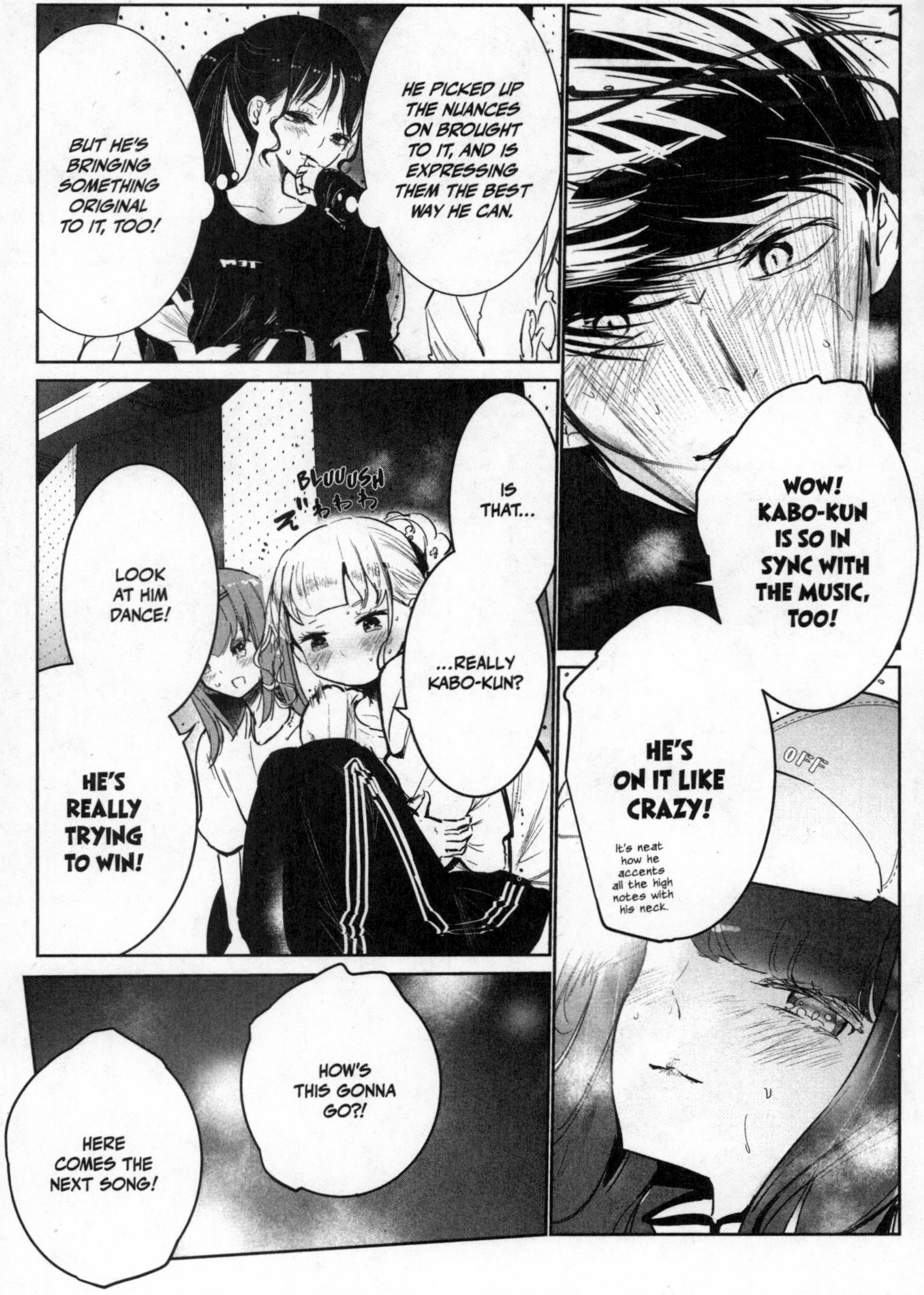
WOW! KABO-KUN IS SO IN SYNC WITH THE MUSIC, TOO!
HE PICKED UP THE NUANCES ON BROUGHT TO IT, AND IS EXPRESSING THEM THE BEST WAY HE CAN.
BUT HE'S BRINGING SOMETHING ORIGINAL TO IT, TOO!
IS THAT...
BLUUUSH
ざわわわ
...REALLY KABO-KUN?
LOOK AT HIM DANCE!
HE'S REALLY TRYING TO WIN!
HE'S ON IT LIKE CRAZY!
It's neat how he accents all the high notes with his neck.
OFF
HOW'S THIS GONNA GO?!
HERE COMES THE NEXT SONG!

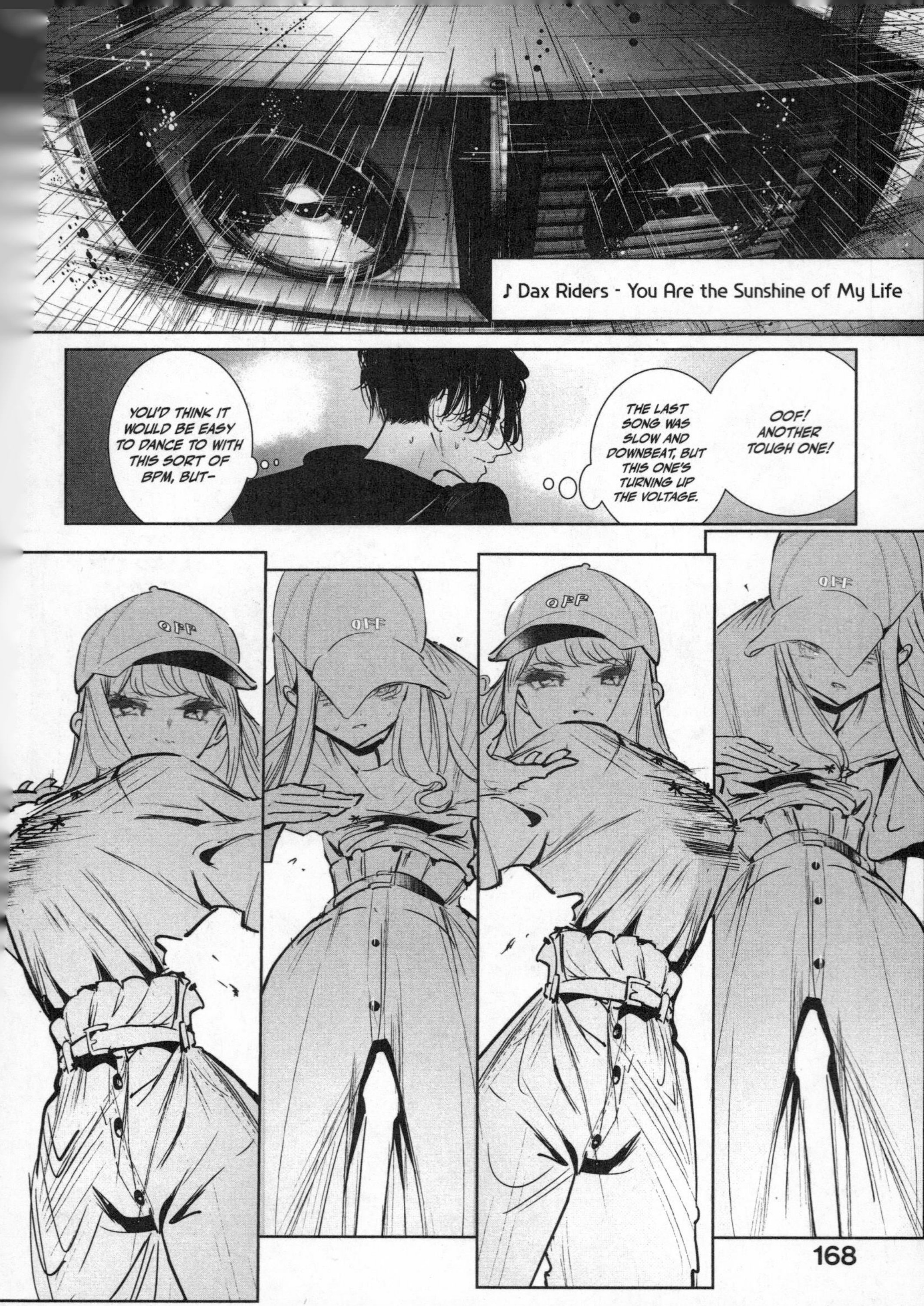
♪ Dax Riders - You Are the Sunshine of My Life
OOF! ANOTHER TOUGH ONE!
THE LAST SONG WAS SLOW AND DOWNBEAT, BUT THIS ONE'S TURNING UP THE VOLTAGE.
YOU'D THINK IT WOULD BE EASY TO DANCE TO WITH THIS SORT OF BPM, BUT-
OFF
OFF
OFF
OFF

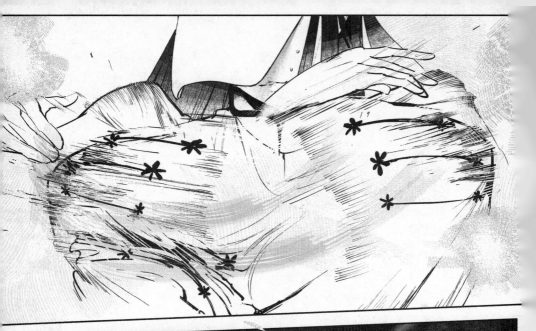

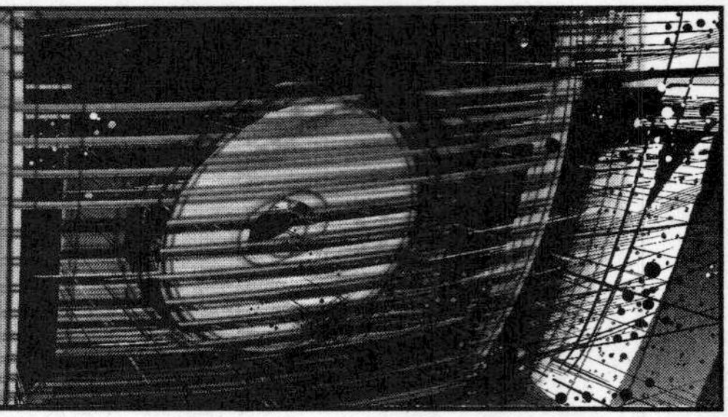
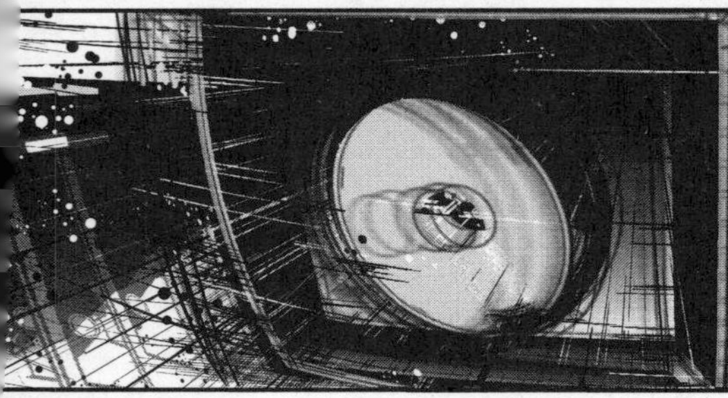
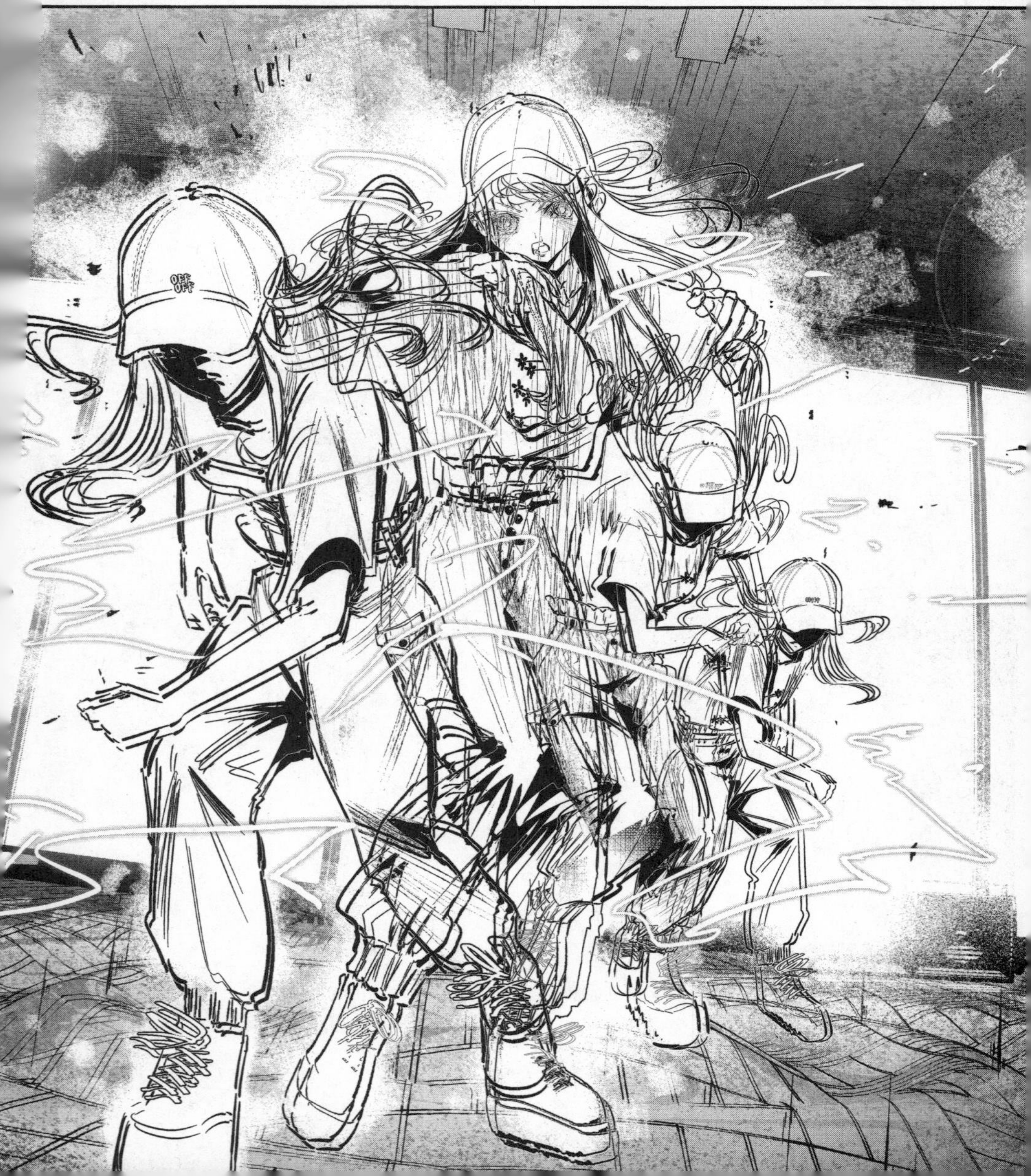
OFF
OFF

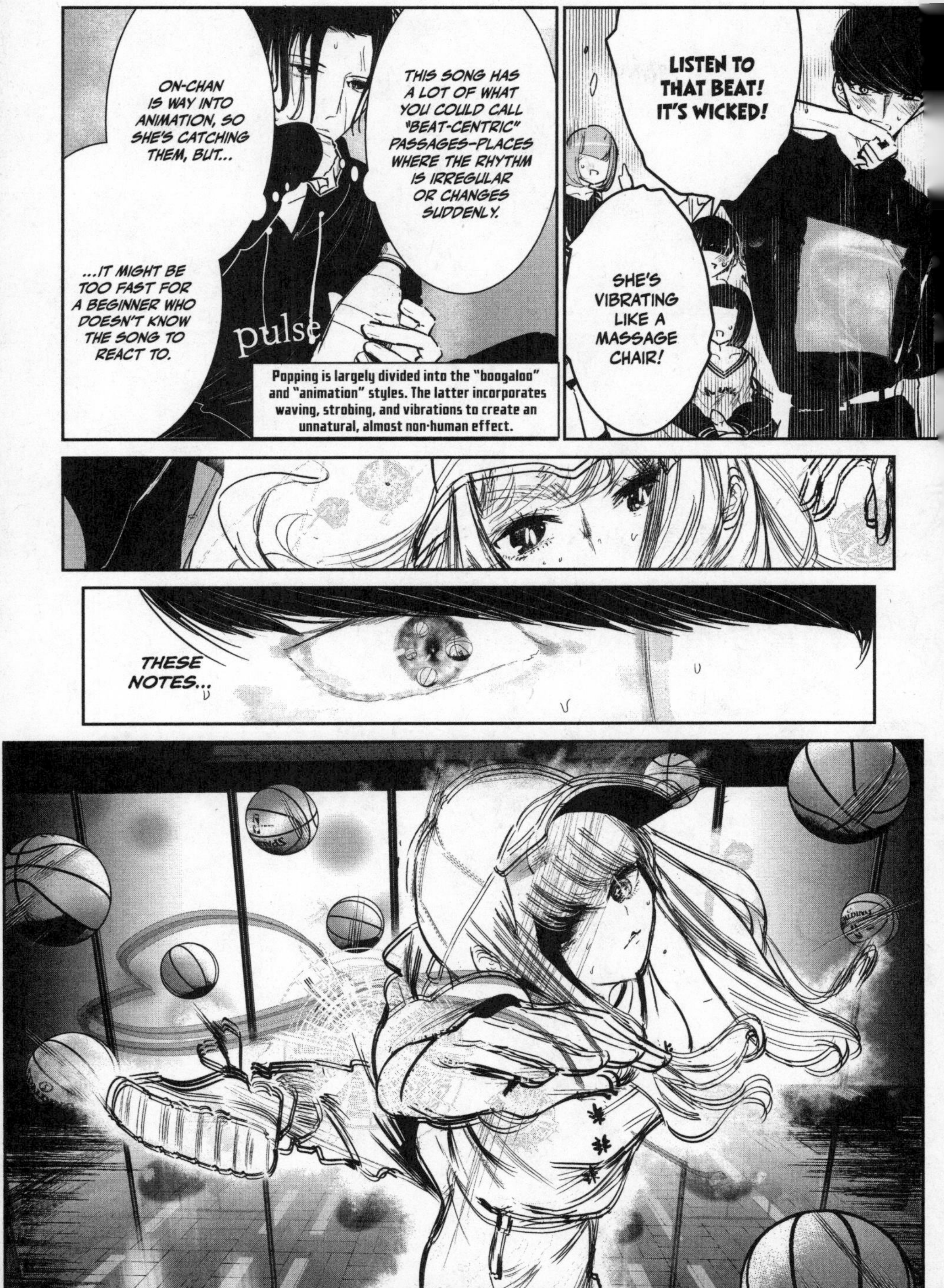
LISTEN TO THAT BEAT! IT'S WICKED!
SHE'S VIBRATING LIKE A MASSAGE CHAIR!
THIS SONG HAS A LOT OF WHAT YOU COULD CALL "BEAT-CENTRIC" PASSAGES—PLACES WHERE THE RHYTHM IS IRREGULAR OR CHANGES SUDDENLY.
ON-CHAN IS WAY INTO ANIMATION, SO SHE'S CATCHING THEM, BUT...
pulse
...IT MIGHT BE TOO FAST FOR A BEGINNER WHO DOESN'T KNOW THE SONG TO REACT TO.
Popping is largely divided into the "boogaloo" and "animation" styles. The latter incorporates waving, strobing, and vibrations to create an unnatural, almost non-human effect.
THESE NOTES...

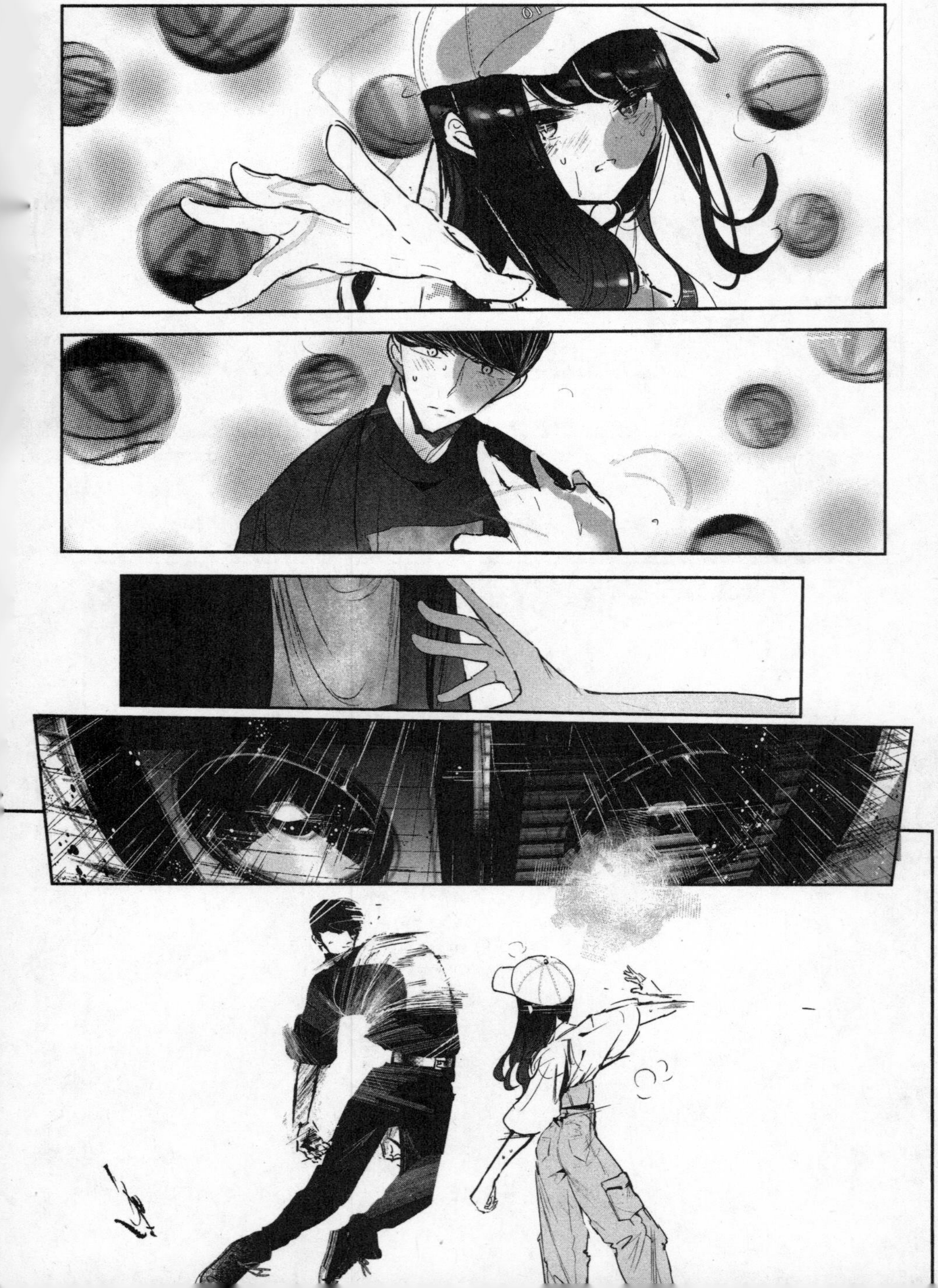

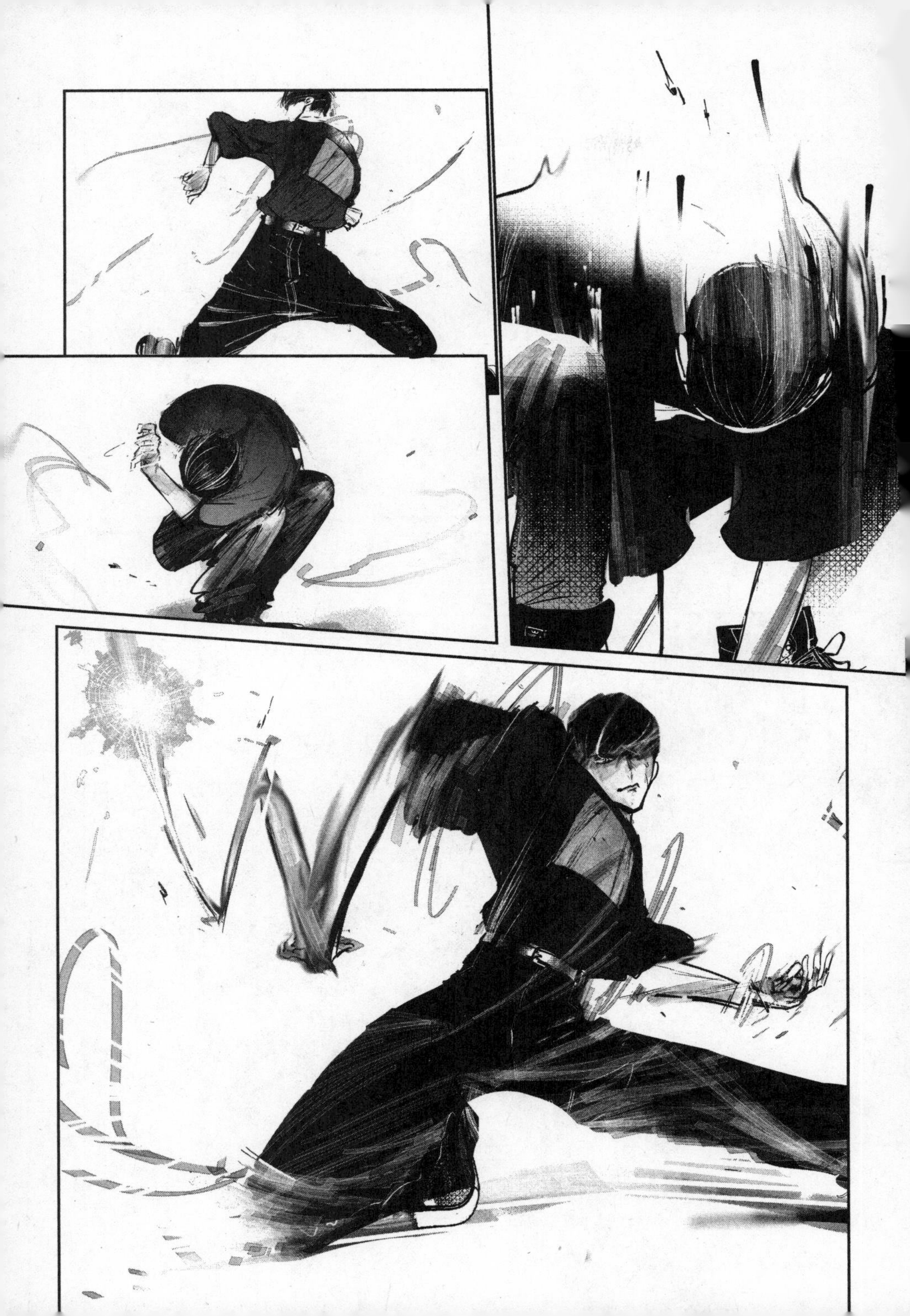

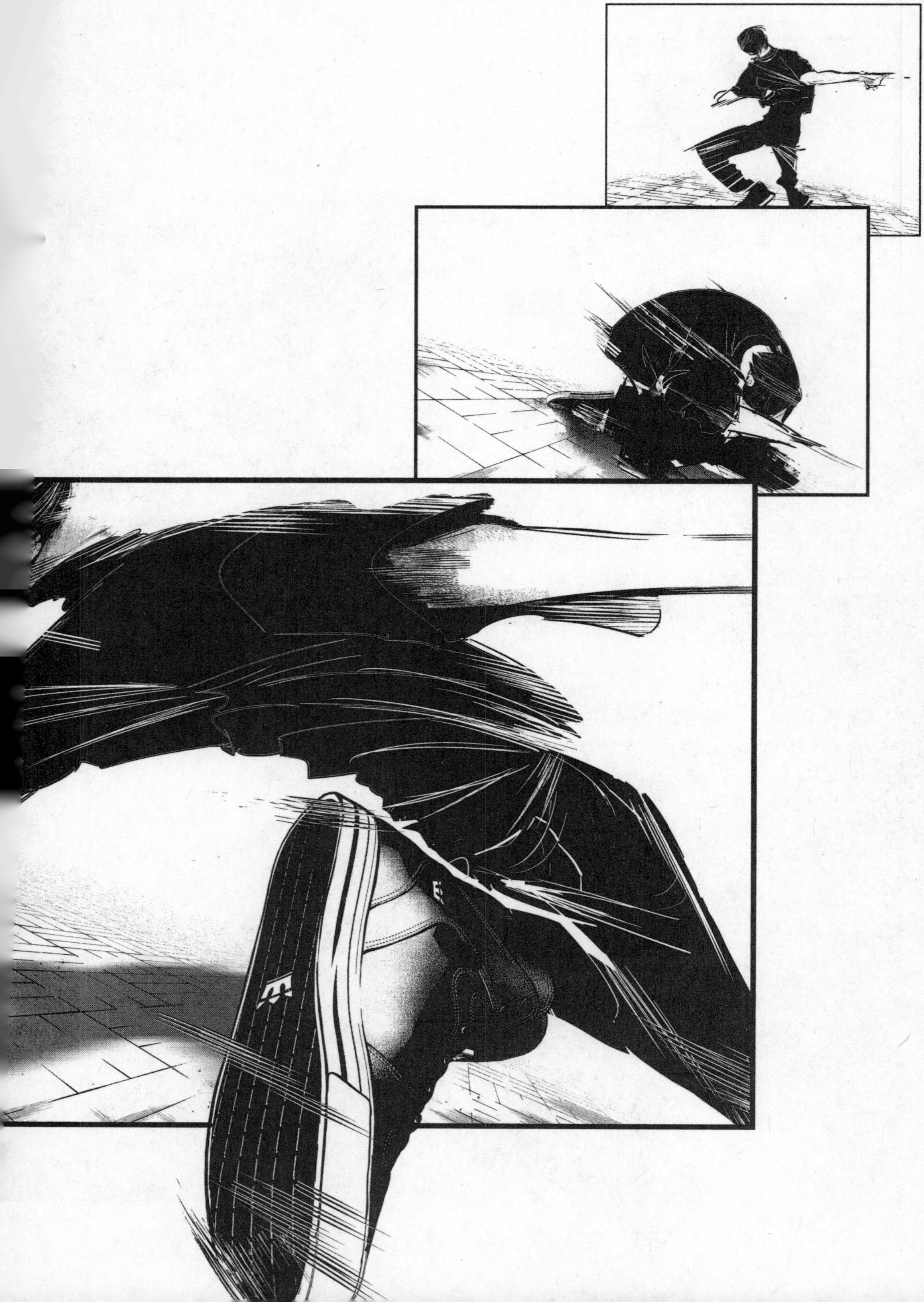

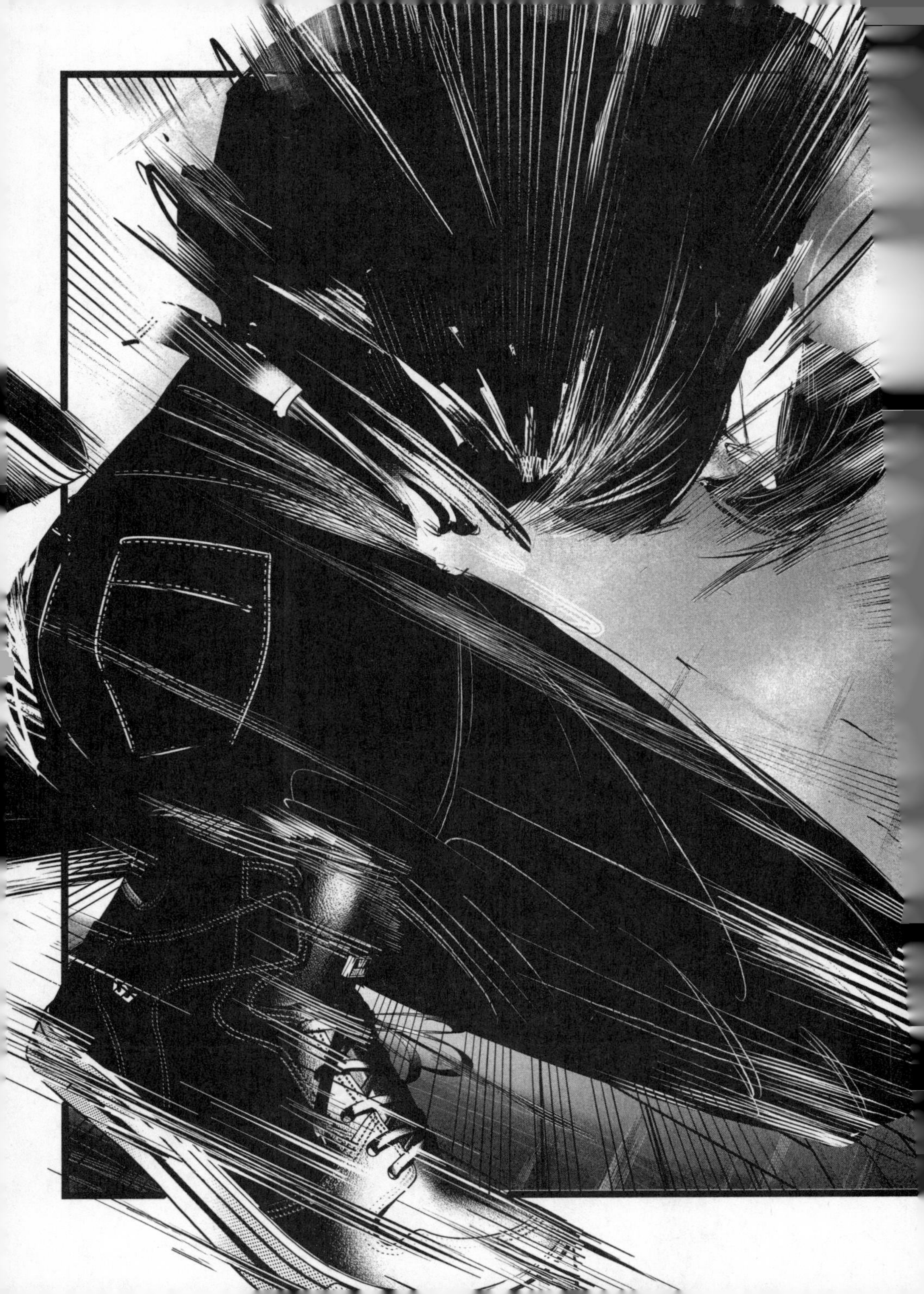

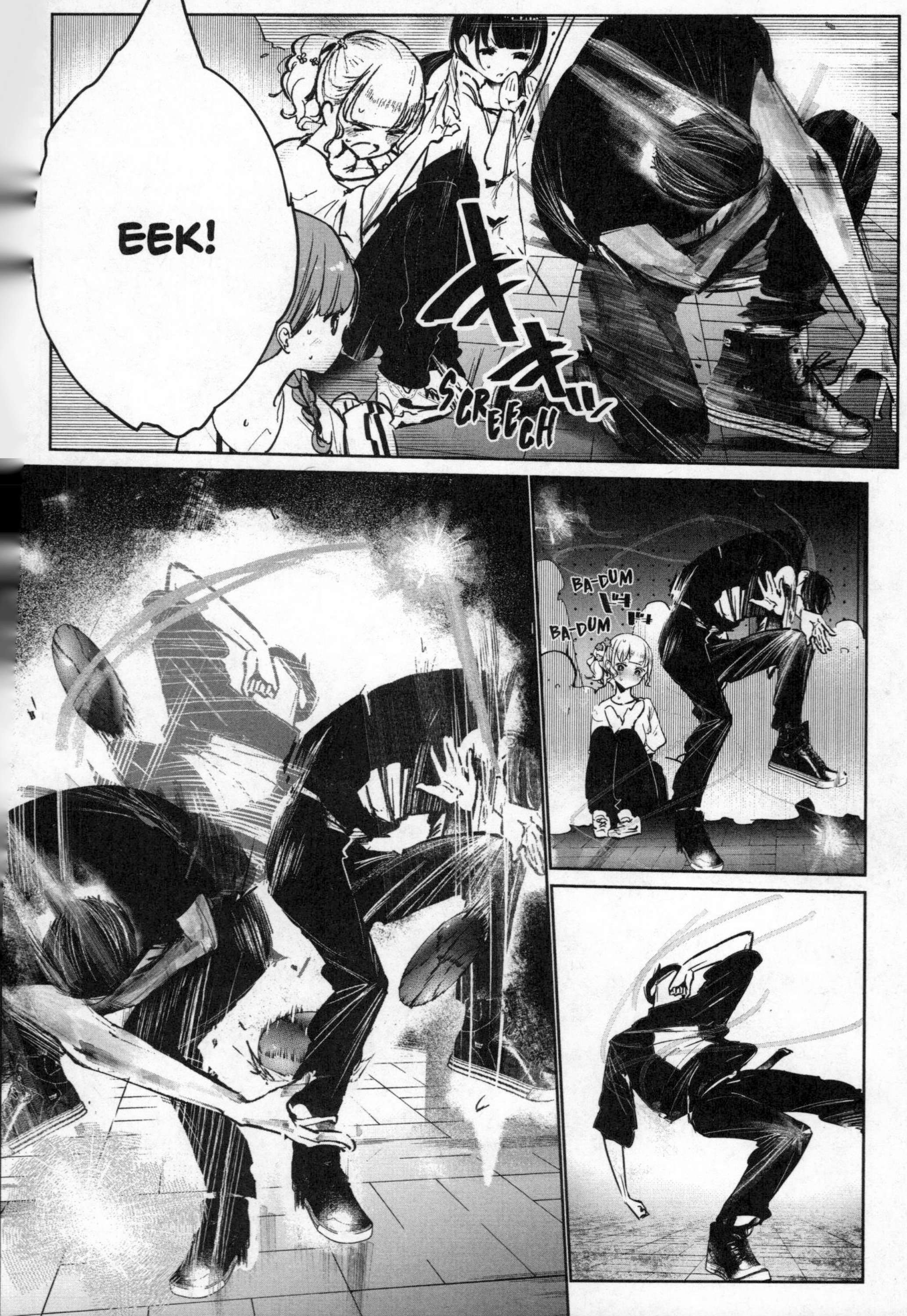
EEK!
SCREECH
BA-DUM
BA-DUM

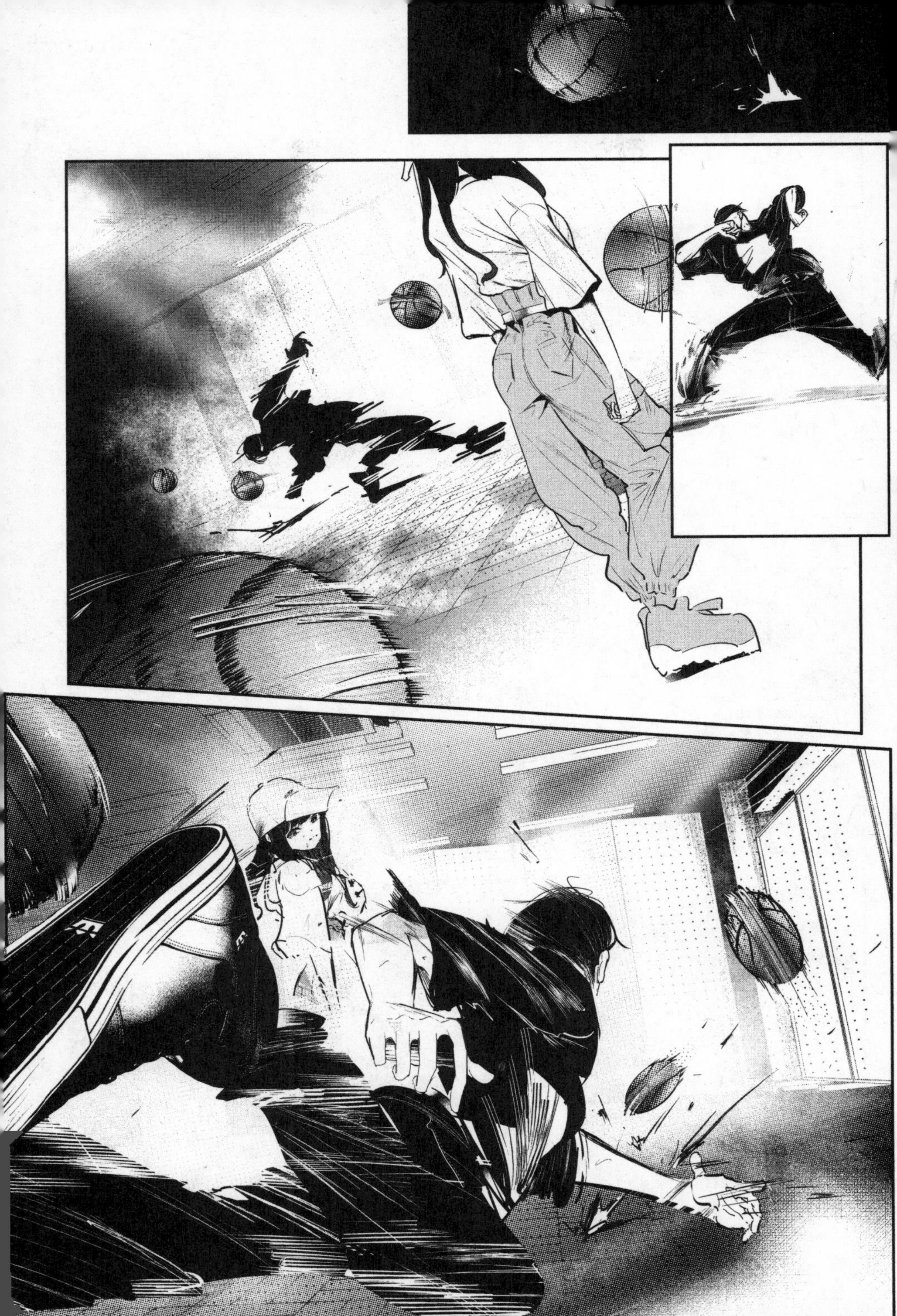

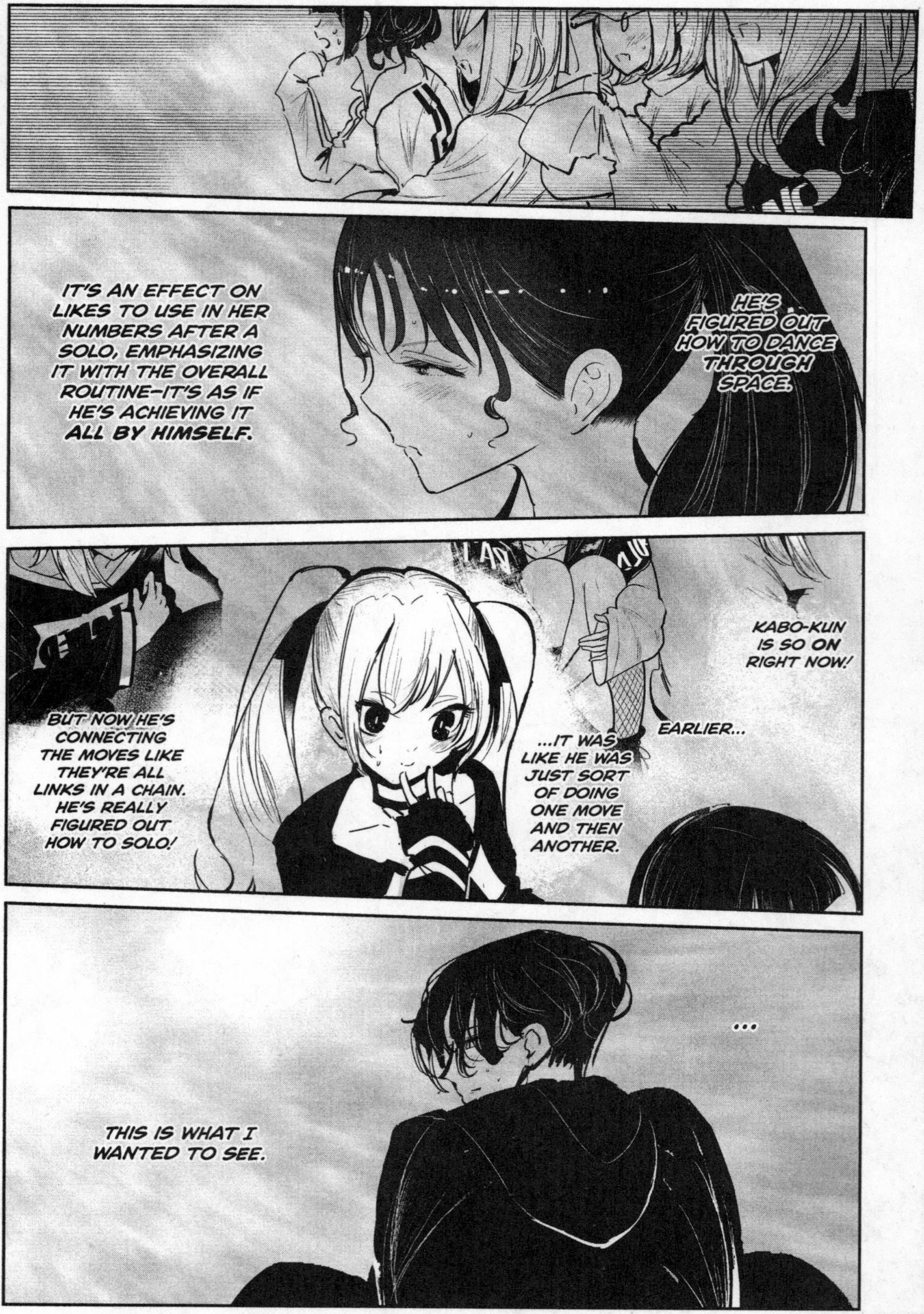
HE'S FIGURED OUT HOW TO DANCE THROUGH SPACE.
IT'S AN EFFECT ON LIKES TO USE IN HER NUMBERS AFTER A SOLO, EMPHASIZING IT WITH THE OVERALL ROUTINE—IT'S AS IF HE'S ACHIEVING IT ALL BY HIMSELF.
KABO-KUN IS SO ON RIGHT NOW!
EARLIER...
...IT WAS LIKE HE WAS JUST SORT OF DOING ONE MOVE AND THEN ANOTHER.
BUT NOW HE'S CONNECTING THE MOVES LIKE THEY'RE ALL LINKS IN A CHAIN. HE'S REALLY FIGURED OUT HOW TO SOLO!
...
THIS IS WHAT I WANTED TO SEE.

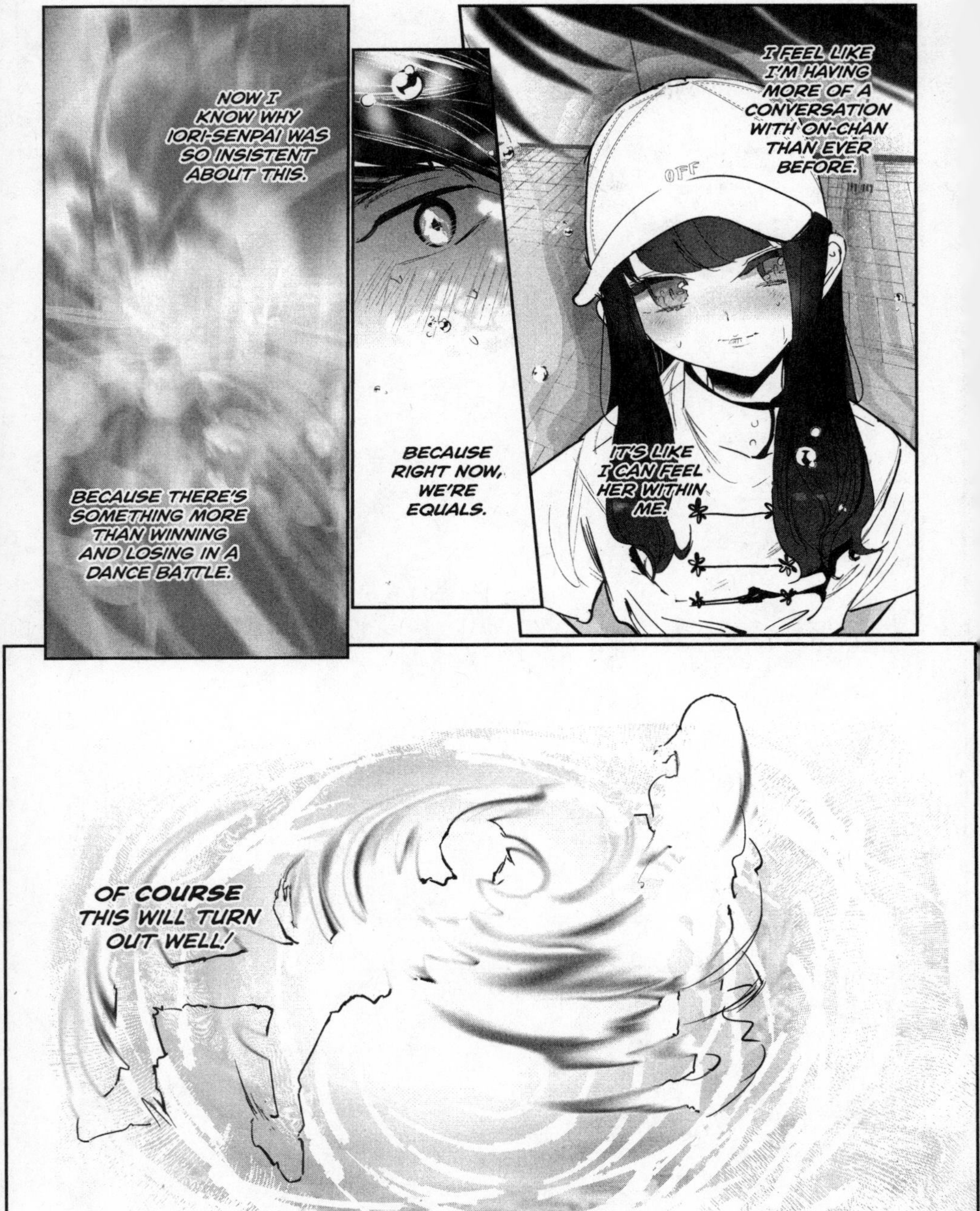
I FEEL LIKE I'M HAVING MORE OF A CONVERSATION WITH ON-CHAN THAN EVER BEFORE.
IT'S LIKE I CAN FEEL HER WITHIN ME.
BECAUSE RIGHT NOW, WE'RE EQUALS.
NOW I KNOW WHY IORI-SENPAI WAS SO INSISTENT ABOUT THIS.
BECAUSE THERE'S SOMETHING MORE THAN WINNING AND LOSING IN A DANCE BATTLE.
OF COURSE THIS WILL TURN OUT WELL!

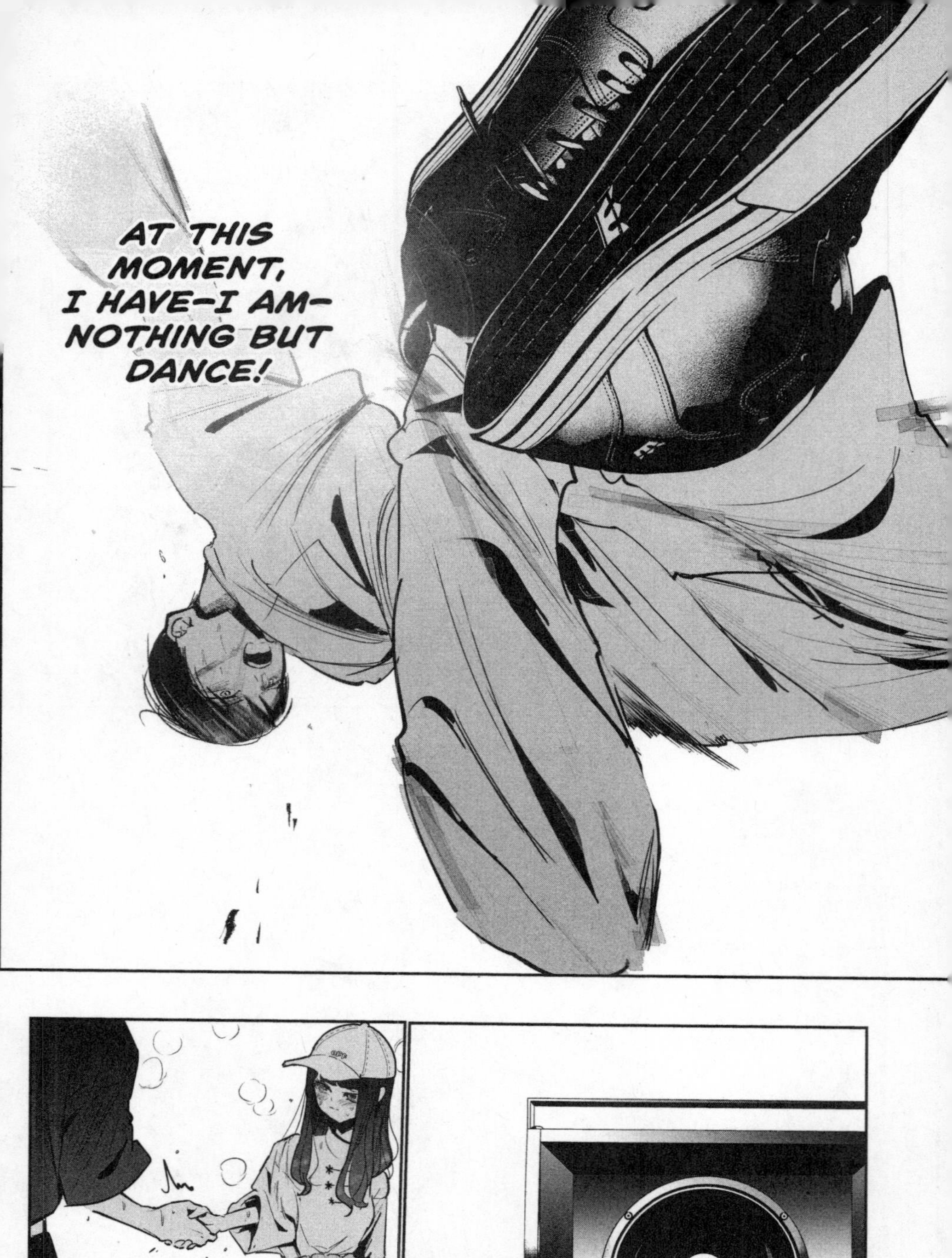
AT THIS MOMENT, I HAVE—I AM—NOTHING BUT DANCE!

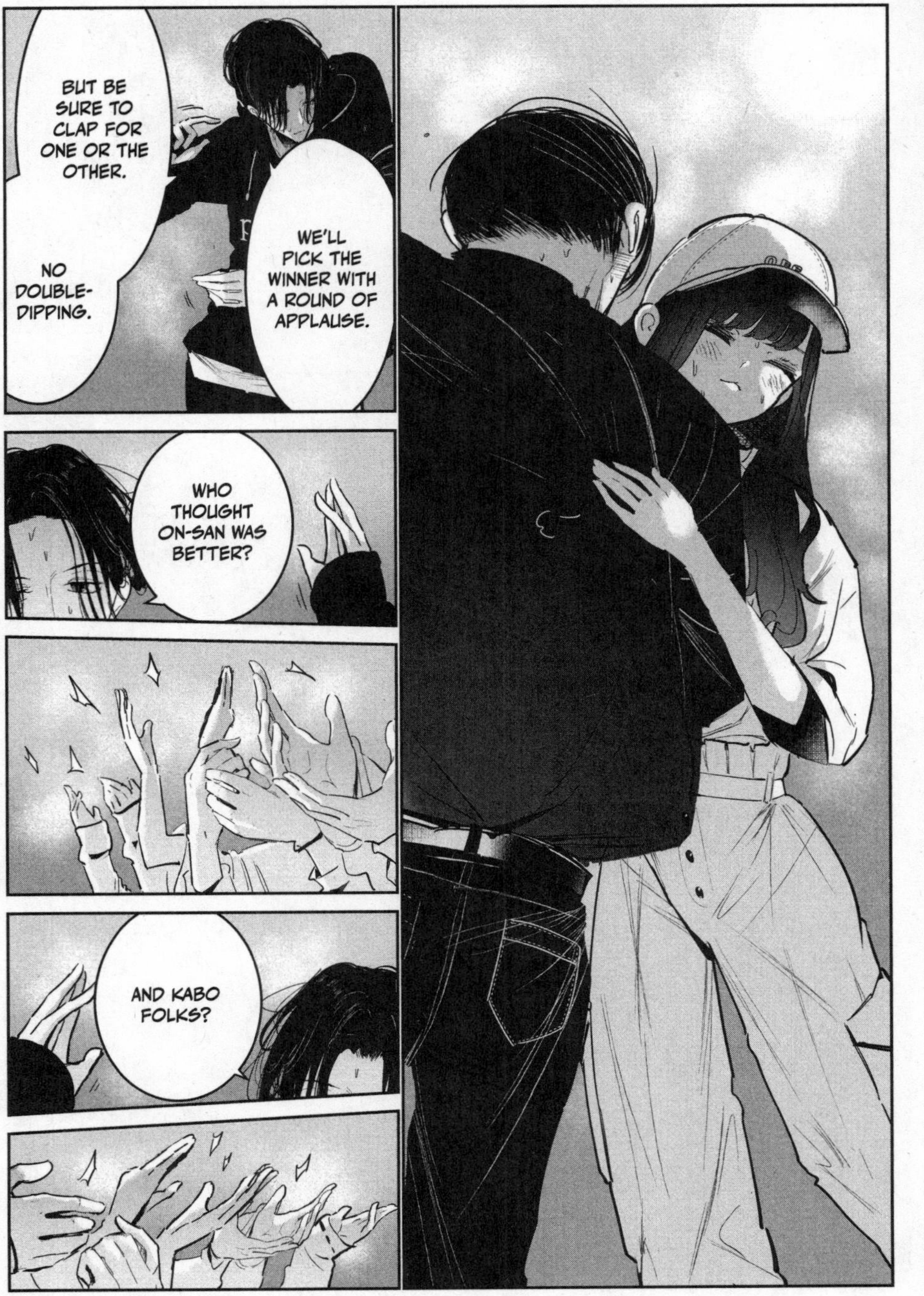
WE'LL PICK THE WINNER WITH A ROUND OF APPLAUSE.
BUT BE SURE TO CLAP FOR ONE OR THE OTHER.
NO DOUBLE-DIPPING.
WHO THOUGHT ON-SAN WAS BETTER?
AND KABO FOLKS?

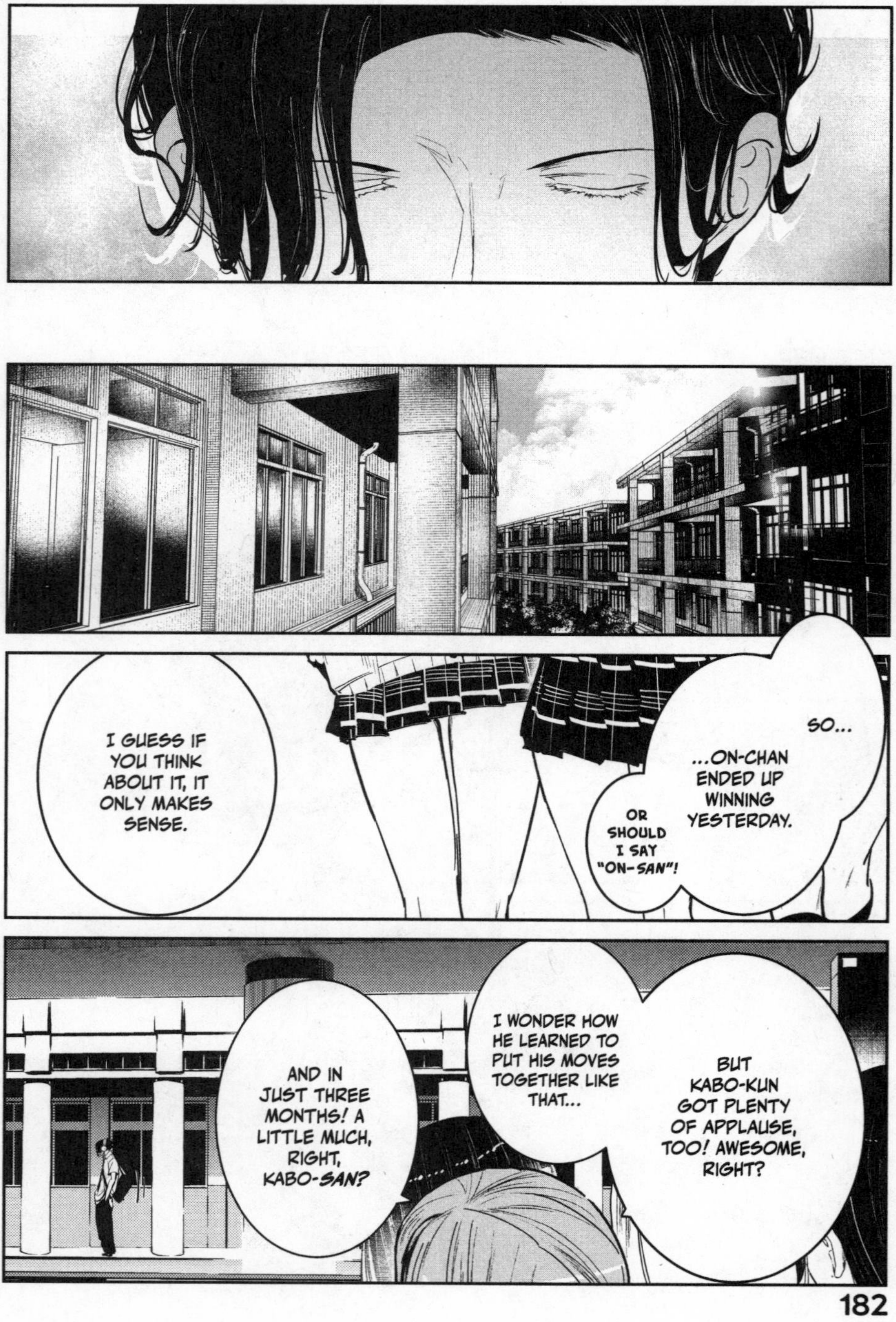
SO...
...ON-CHAN ENDED UP WINNING YESTERDAY.
OR SHOULD I SAY "ON-*SAN*"!
I GUESS IF YOU THINK ABOUT IT, IT ONLY MAKES SENSE.
BUT KABO-KUN GOT PLENTY OF APPLAUSE, TOO! AWESOME, RIGHT?
I WONDER HOW HE LEARNED TO PUT HIS MOVES TOGETHER LIKE THAT...
AND IN JUST THREE MONTHS! A LITTLE MUCH, RIGHT, KABO-*SAN*?

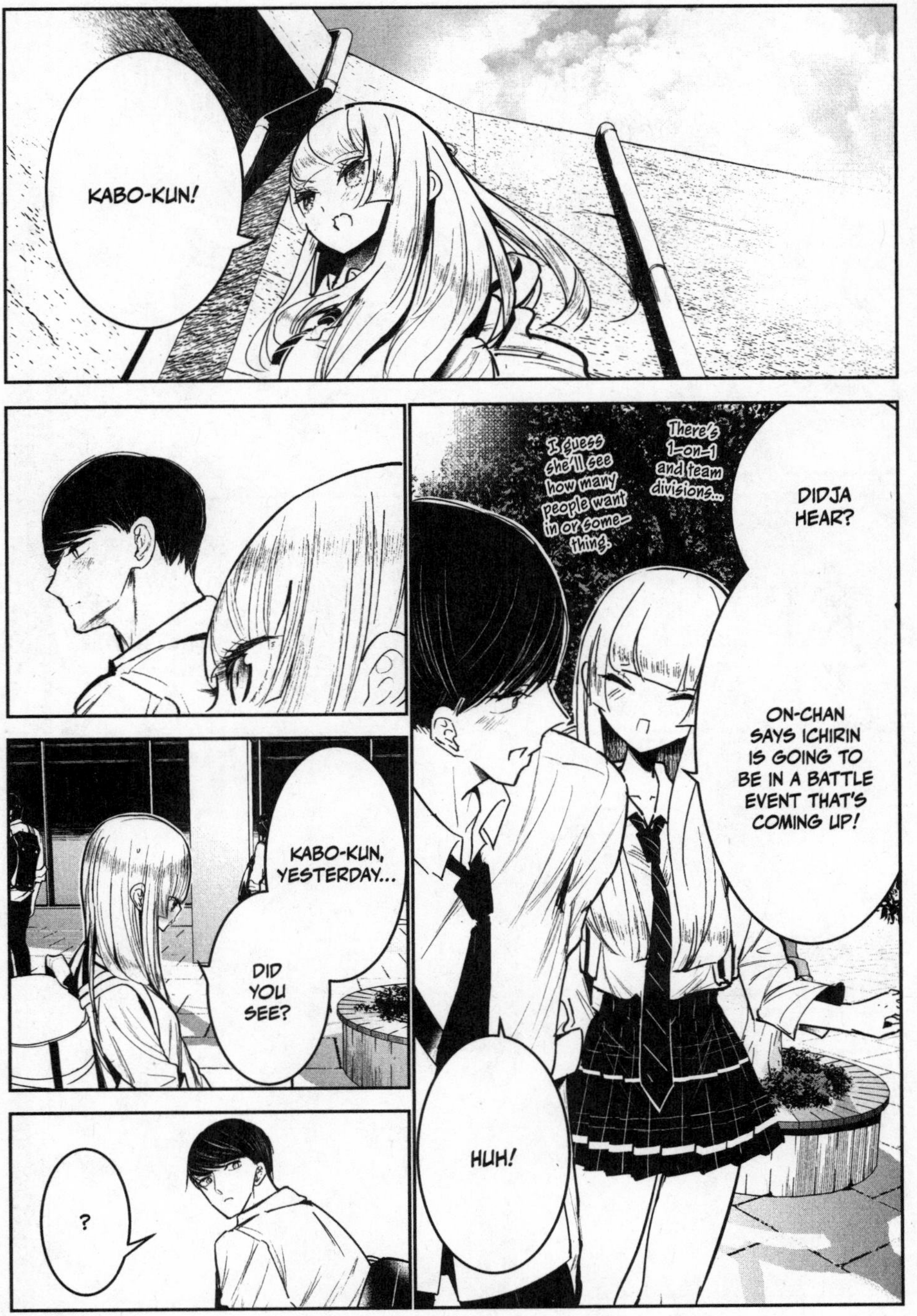
KABO-KUN!
DIDJA HEAR?
There's 1-on-1 and team divisions...
I guess she'll see how many people want in or some-thing.
ON-CHAN SAYS ICHIRIN IS GOING TO BE IN A BATTLE EVENT THAT'S COMING UP!
HUH!
KABO-KUN, YESTERDAY...
DID YOU SEE?
?

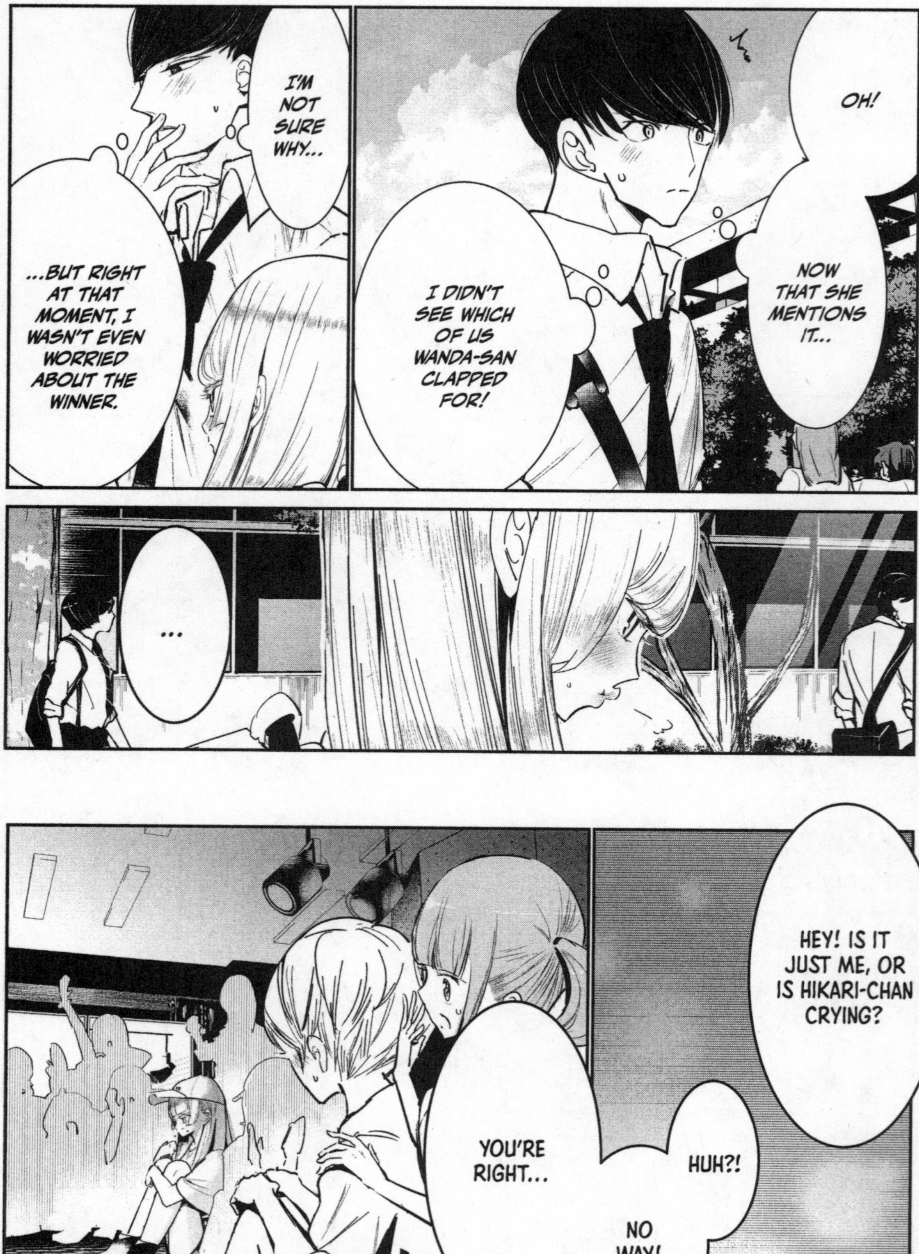
OH!
NOW THAT SHE MENTIONS IT...
I DIDN'T SEE WHICH OF US WANDA-SAN CLAPPED FOR!
I'M NOT SURE WHY...
...BUT RIGHT AT THAT MOMENT, I WASN'T EVEN WORRIED ABOUT THE WINNER.
...
HEY! IS IT JUST ME, OR IS HIKARI-CHAN CRYING?
HUH?!
NO WAY!
YOU'RE RIGHT...

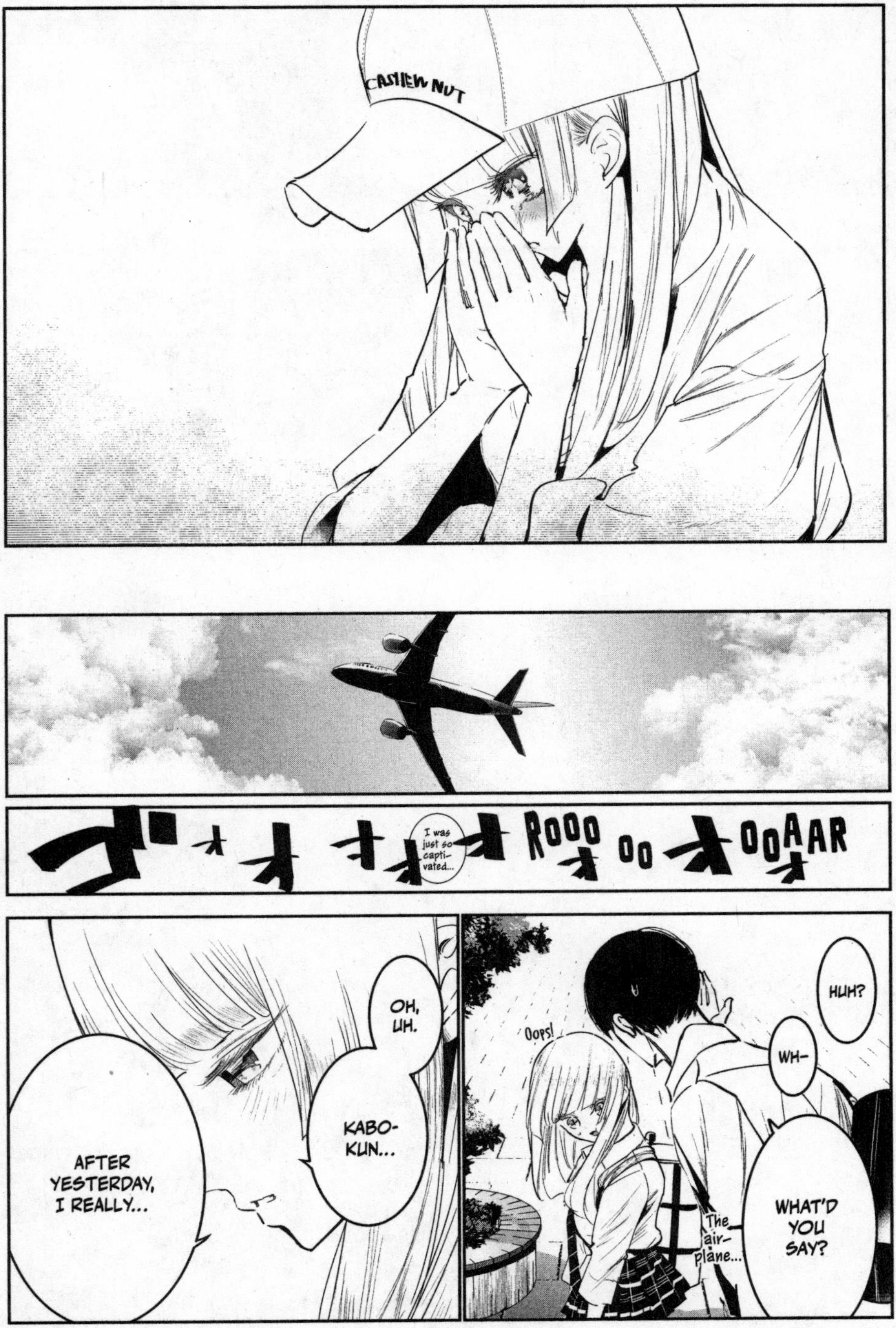
CASHEW NUT
ROOO OO OOAAR
I was just so captivated...
HUH?
WH-
Oops!
WHAT'D YOU SAY?
The air-plane...
OH, UH.
KABO-KUN...
AFTER YESTERDAY, I REALLY...

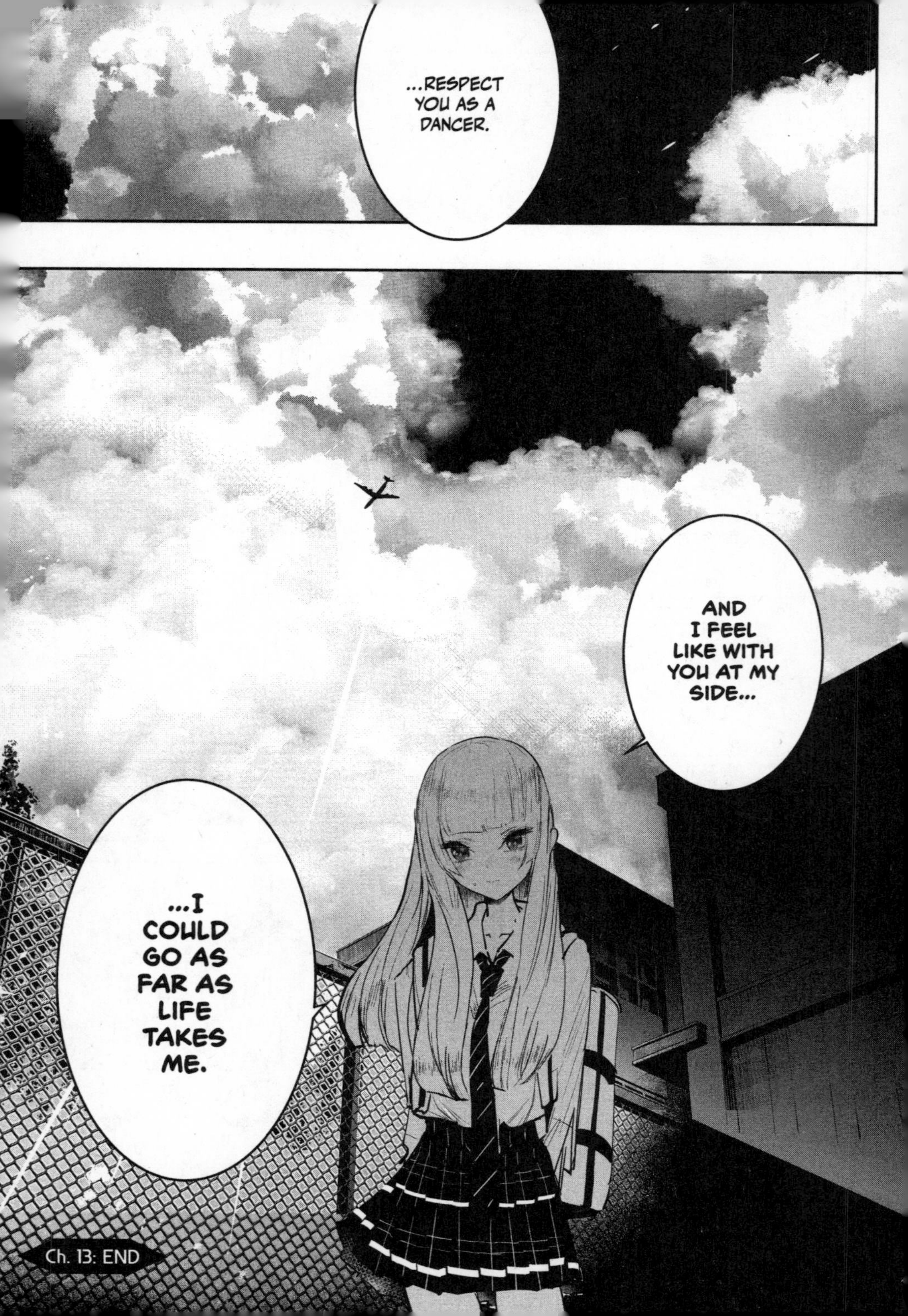
...RESPECT YOU AS A DANCER.
AND I FEEL LIKE WITH YOU AT MY SIDE...
...I COULD GO AS FAR AS LIFE TAKES ME.
Ch. 13: END

Research

YUSUKE-SAMA (Arpeggio, SOUL TRIBE OSAKA, PLAYERS DANCE WORKS)

BEZI-SAMA (BUSTA JAKK BOOGIE)

YUKITOSHI SHIRASAKA-SAMA (The Dancing Math Teacher)

Uenomiya Senior High School Street Dance Club

Art Assistants

Bun'ya Kawaguchi-sama

Ayukan.-sama

Special Thanks

MACHINE HARADA (ADHIP, ANGEL DUST BREAKERS)

TANABON-SAMA (AIR REAL, ADHIP)

MAiKA-SAMA (RUSHBALL, NANIWA HEISEI SISTERS)

KNIT-SAMA (ADHIP, DMJ, New Black-izm)

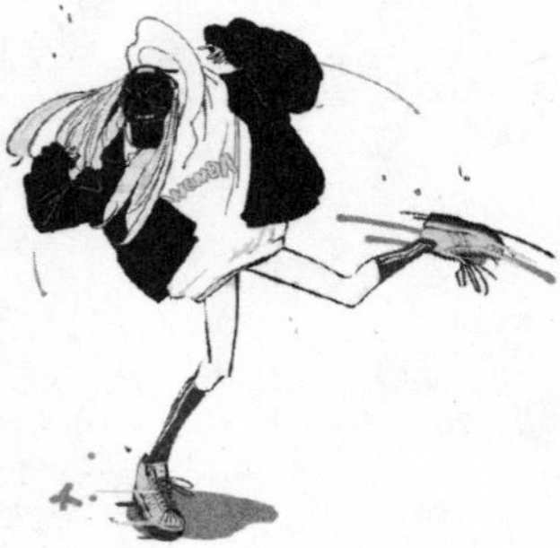

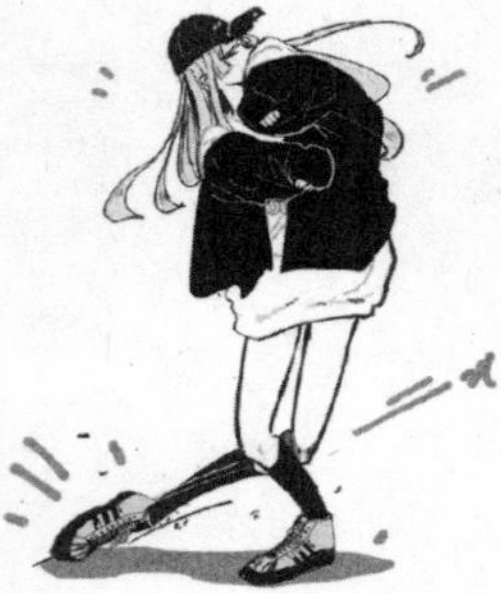

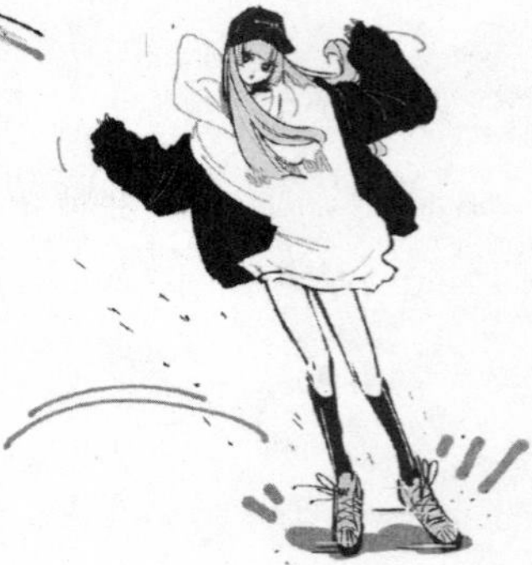

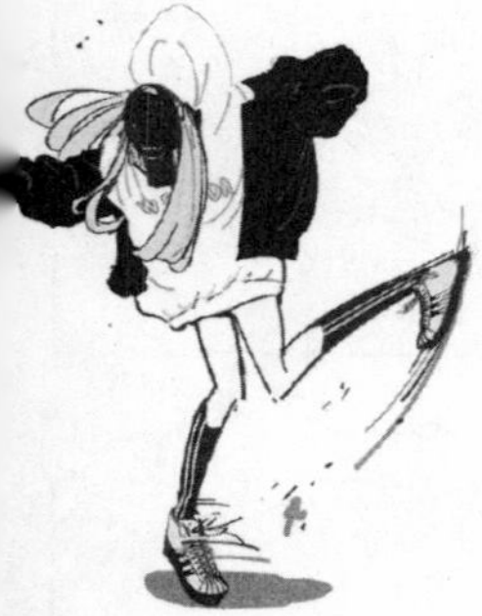

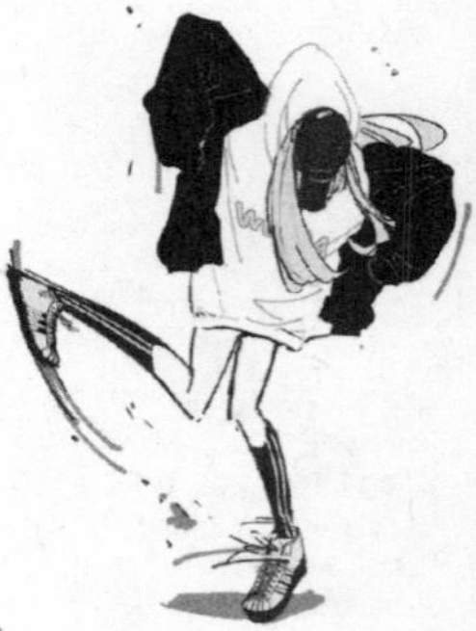

Coffee

I'll show you
what followed from
the dream I had
that day.

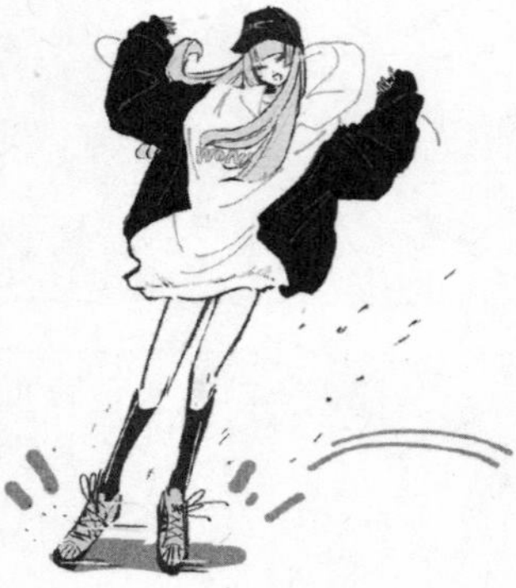

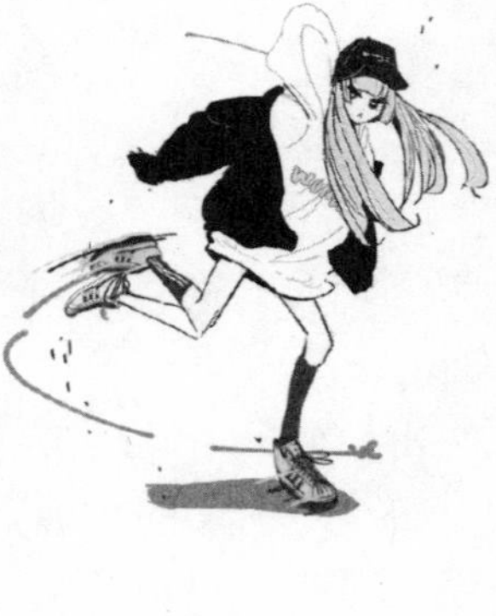

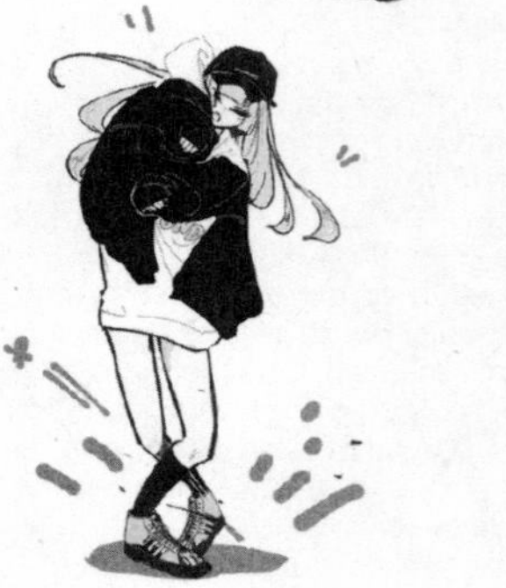

⌜translation notes⌝

"Wan-chaan! C'mere, my perky little puppy!", page 7

It's worth noting that Miyami's nickname for Wanda here, Wan-chan, is not only a shortened form of her name, but can also be interpreted as her calling Wanda a puppy. In Japanese, the onomatopoeia for a barking dog is *wan wan!* (As seen in panel three.) Hence, *wan-chan* (the onomatopoeia *wan* plus the diminutive suffix *-chan)* is sometimes used to refer to puppies. The pun is reinforced by how Miyami tells Wanda to *oide* (Come!) in panel one and offer *o-te* (literally "hand," meaning "shake!" or "paw!") in panel two.

Miyami Seba (Second-Year)
WAN-CHAAAN!
C'MERE, MY PERKY LITTLE PUPPY!
SHAKE!
ARF! ARF!
OHMYGOSH YOU'RE SO CUTE!
I WISH YOU WERE MY PET!

Club Equipment, page 31

80,000 yen is roughly $800, so a little help from the school funds in footing the bill for such equipment would no doubt be welcome.

YOU KNOW THOSE MOVABLE MIRRORS WE USE?
BUT THOSE WEREN'T THERE WHEN I JOINED THE CLUB.
EACH OF THEM COSTS 80,000 YEN.
TH-THAT'S A LOT!
AND WHEN WE DO, WE CAN FINALLY GET THE SCHOOL TO GIVE US SOME DECENT EQUIPMENT!
E... EQUIP-MENT?

Business Card, page 96 and 109

Here, Assay gives Wanda his *meishi, or* business card. Although these cards serve many of the same purposes as business cards in Western settings, such as giving a person's name, job or position, and perhaps contact details, *meishi* are far more prevalent than business cards are in, for example, the United States. Almost every Japanese adult has a supply of *meishi*, and usually carries some around for moments like this, when they need to introduce or identify themselves to someone else. Another person's *meishi* must always be treated with care (notice how Wanda holds Assay's card on page 96; taking something with both hands is considered more respectful than casually grabbing an object with just one hand). It should never be stashed in your pocket, and must absolutely never be crumpled, folded, or sat upon. (Many Japanese people carry a special *meishi* holder, a small box specifically for safely storing cards they receive.) Bonus etiquette tip: Although Assay gives Wanda his card with just one hand (his superior social status and the somewhat informal nature of their meeting allows him to get away with this), you can see in panel 4 of page 96 that he's turned it so that the text is right-side up for her (upside-down from his perspective). This is considered a basic point of politeness when handing any kind of document to another person, the idea being that if they so wish, they can begin to read it immediately without any additional effort.

WHEN I SAW YOU DANCING UP THERE TODAY...
...I THOUGHT, "THERE'S SOMEONE WHO WILL BE DANCING FOR THE REST OF HER LIFE."

WH...
WHAT ABOUT YOU, WANDA-SAN?
ASSAY-SAN GAVE YOU HIS B-B-
BUSINESS CARD...

translation notes

higo Au Lait, page 101

nother of the real-life snack foods and rinks that populate *Wandance,* Ichigo u Lait is a strawberry milk drink from kult.

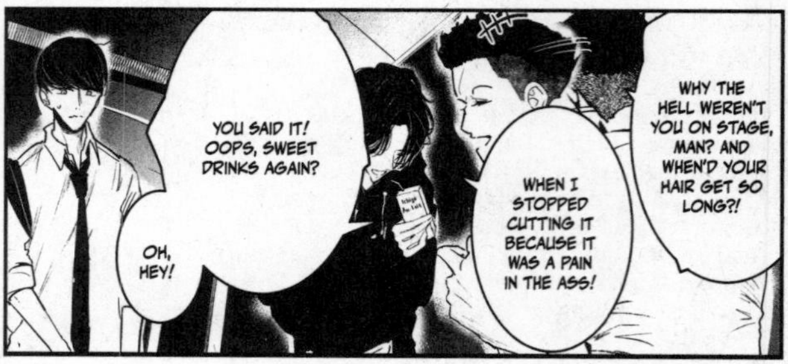
WHY THE HELL WEREN'T YOU ON STAGE, MAN? AND WHEN'D YOUR HAIR GET SO LONG?!
WHEN I STOPPED CUTTING IT BECAUSE IT WAS A PAIN IN THE ASS!
YOU SAID IT! OOPS, SWEET DRINKS AGAIN?
OH, HEY!

'In the red corner!", page 141

Here, On is making a reference to Kohaku Uta Gassen, also simply known as Kohaku, a popular music program that airs in Japan every New Year's Eve. The most popular music artists of the year are invited to perform on Kohaku and are divided into two teams: the red team, or *akagumi,* composed of all female artists (or groups with all female vocals), and the white team, or *shirogumi,* composed of all male artists (or groups with all male vocals). At the end of the program, the show's judges and the audience vote to decide which group is the winner.

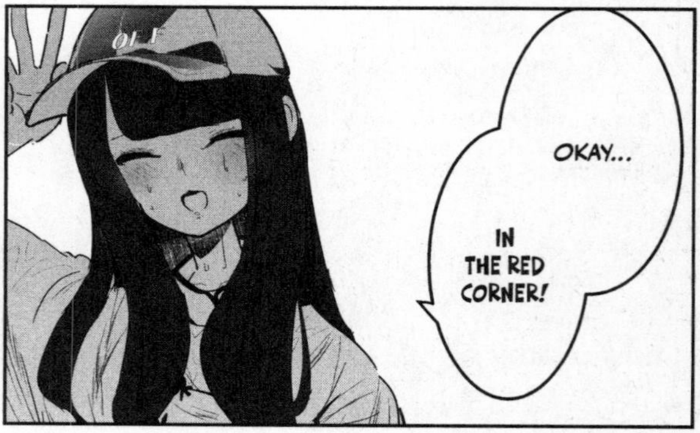
OKAY...
IN THE RED CORNER!

Links in a Chain, page 178

In the Japanese, Monme thinks Kaboku is connecting his moves "like [in] *shiritori.*" Shiritori (literally, "bottom-taking") is a word game in which one player says a word, and then the next player has to come up with a word that starts with the final syllable of the first player's word. So for example, the first player might say *oni* (demon), the second could respond with *niwatori* (chicken), and a third player might then come up with *rikutsu* (logic). The game ends when a player can't come up with a word, or when someone says a word that ends in *-n.* (Although there are plenty of Japanese words that start with n + a vowel, no Japanese word begins with the actual syllable *n.*)

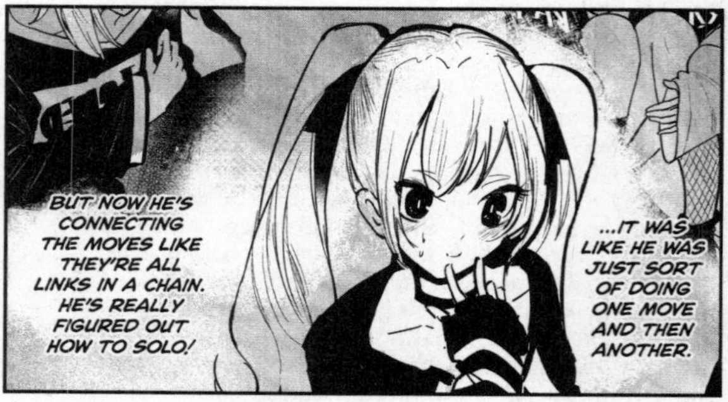
...IT WAS LIKE HE WAS JUST SORT OF DOING ONE MOVE AND THEN ANOTHER.
BUT NOW HE'S CONNECTING THE MOVES LIKE THEY'RE ALL LINKS IN A CHAIN. HE'S REALLY FIGURED OUT HOW TO SOLO!

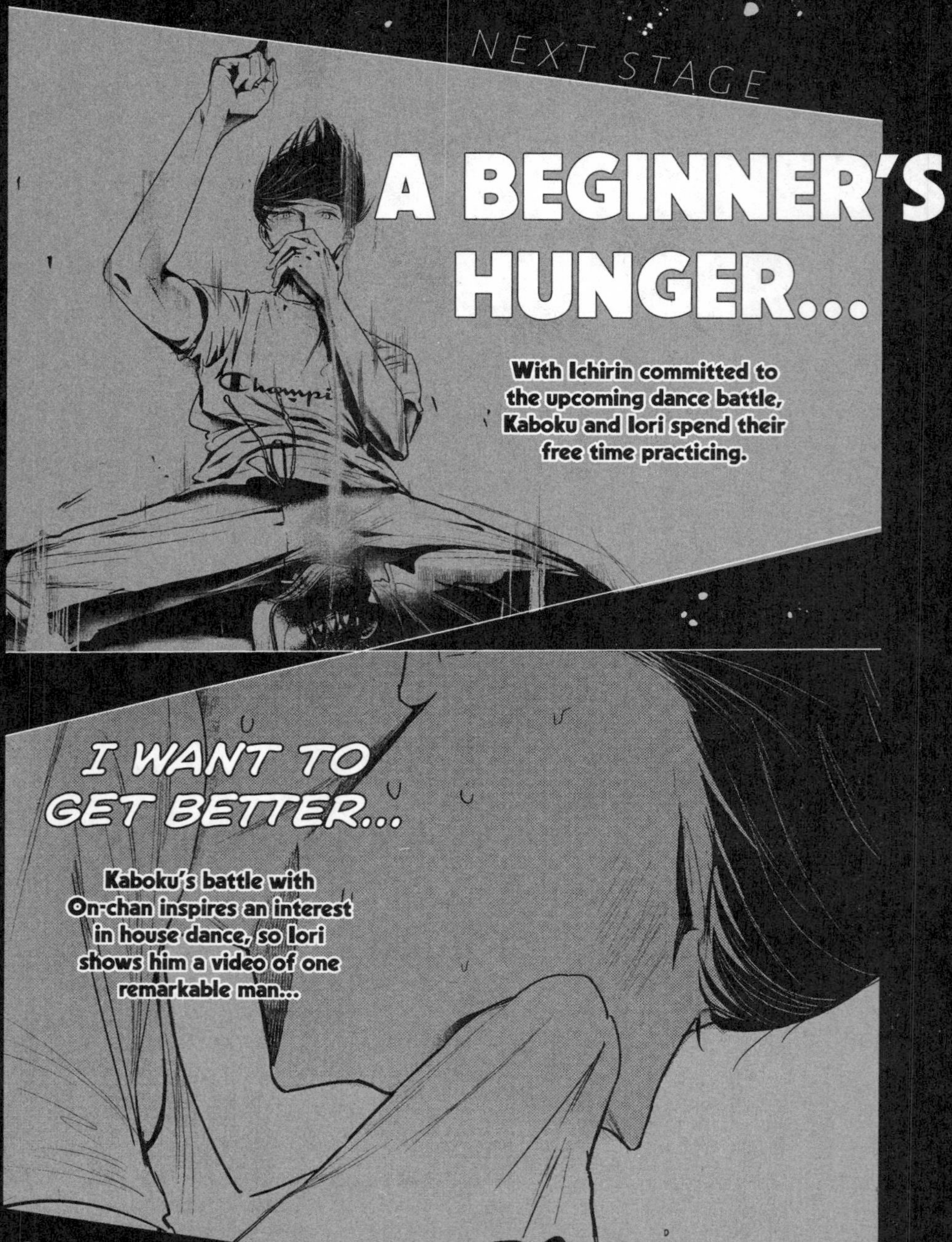
NEXT STAGE
A BEGINNER'S HUNGER...
With Ichirin committed to the upcoming dance battle, Kaboku and Iori spend their free time practicing.
Champi
I WANT TO GET BETTER...
Kaboku's battle with On-chan inspires an interest in house dance, so Iori shows him a video of one remarkable man...

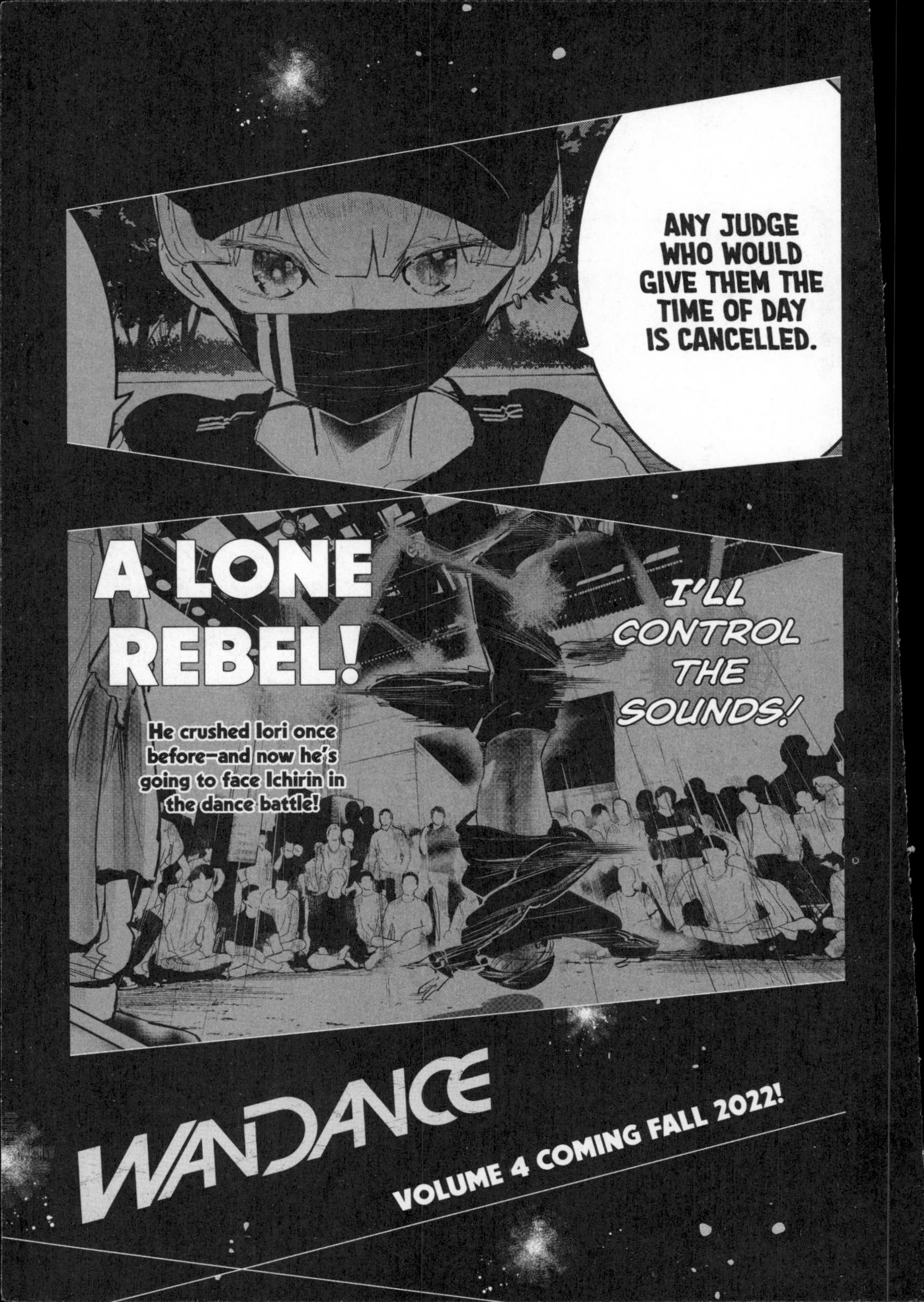
ANY JUDGE WHO WOULD GIVE THEM THE TIME OF DAY IS CANCELLED.
I'LL CONTROL THE SOUNDS!
A LONE REBEL!
He crushed Iori once before—and now he's going to face Ichirin in the dance battle!
WANDANCE
VOLUME 4 COMING FALL 2022!

A SMART, NEW ROMANTIC COMEDY FOR FANS OF *SHORTCAKE CAKE* AND *TERRACE HOUSE*!

A romance manga starring high school girl Meeko, who learns to live on her own in a boarding house whose living room is home to the odd (but handsome) Matsunaga-san. She begins to adjust to her new life away from her parents, but Meeko soon learns that no matter how far away from home she is, she's still a young girl at heart — especially when she finds herself falling for Matsunaga-san.

Knight of the ICE

1

Yayoi Ogawa

Knight of the Ice ©Yayoi Ogawa/Kodansha Ltd.

SKATING THRILLS AND ICY CHILLS WITH THIS NEW TINGLY ROMANCE SERIES!

A rom-com on ice, perfect for fans of *Princess Jellyfish* and *Wotakoi*. Kokoro is the talk of the figure-skating world, winning trophies and hearts. But little do they know... he's actually a huge nerd! From the beloved creator of *You're My Pet* (*Tramps Like Us*).

Chitose is a serious young woman, working for the health magazine *SASSO*. Or at least, she would be, if she wasn't constantly getting distracted by her childhood friend, international figure skating star Kokoro Kijinami! In the public eye and on the ice, Kokoro is a gallant, flawless knight, but behind his glittery costumes and breathtaking spins lies a secret: He's actually a hopelessly romantic otaku, who can only land his quad jumps when Chitose is on hand to recite a spell from his favorite magical girl anime!

Young characters and steampunk setting, like *Howl's Moving Castle* and *Battle Angel Alita*

Beyond the Clouds © 2018 Nicke / Ki-oon

A boy with a talent for machines and a mysterious girl whose wings he's fixed will take you beyond the clouds! In the tradition of the high-flying, resonant adventure stories of Studio Ghibli comes a gorgeous tale about the longing of young hearts for adventure and friendship!

PERFECT WORLD

Rie Aruga

A TOUCHING
NEW SERIES
ABOUT LOVE AND
COPING WITH
DISABILITY

An office party reunites Tsugumi with her high school crush Itsuki. He's realized his dream of becoming an architect, but along the way, he experienced a spinal injury that put him in a wheelchair. Now Tsugumi's rekindled feelings will butt up against prejudices she never considered — and Itsuki will have to decide if he's ready to let someone into his heart...

"Depicts with great delicacy and courage the difficulties some with disabilities experience getting involved in romantic relationships... Rie Aruga refuses to romanticize, pushing her heroine to face the reality of disability. She invites her readers to the same tasks of empathy, knowledge and recognition."
—Slate.fr

"An important entry [in manga romance]... The emotional core of both plot and characters indicates thoughtfulness... [Aruga's] research is readily apparent in the text and artwork, making this feel like a real story."
—Anime News Network

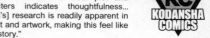

KC
KODANSHA
COMICS

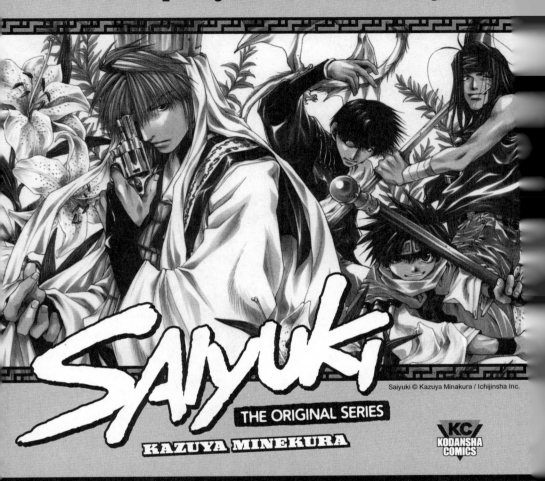

The adorable new odd-couple cat comedy manga from the creator of the beloved *Chi's Sweet Home*, in full color!

Sue & Tai-chan

Konami Kanata

Sue is an aging housecat who's looking forward to living out her life in peace... but her plans change when the mischievous black tomcat Tai-chan enters the picture! Hey! Sue never signed up to be a catsitter! *Sue & Tai-chan* is the latest from the reigning meow-narch of cute kitty comics, Konami Kanata.

THE SWEET SCENT OF LOVE IS IN THE AIR! FOR FANS OF OFFBEAT ROMANCES LIKE *WOTAKOI*

VOL. 1

SWEAT AND SOAP

KINTETSU YAMADA

Sweat and Soap © Kintetsu Yamada / Kodansha Ltd.

In an office romance, there's a fine line between sexy and awkward... and that line is where Asako — a woman who sweats copiously — meets Koutarou — a perfume developer who can't get enough of Asako's, er, scent. Don't miss a romcom manga like no other!

The art-deco cyberpunk classic from the creators of *xxxHOLiC* and *Cardcaptor Sakura!*

CLAMP

CLOVER

COLLECTOR'S EDITION

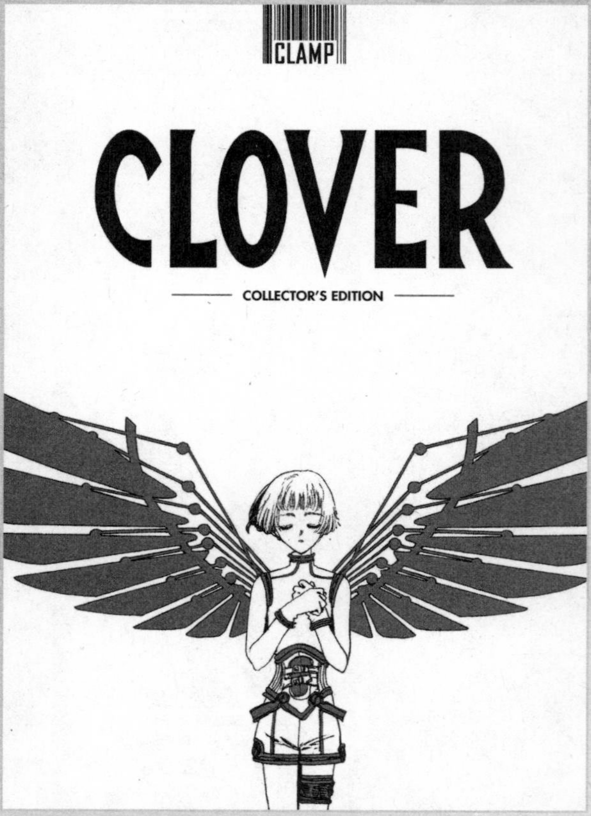

CLOVER ©.CLAMP·ShigatsuTsuitachi CO.,LTD./Kodansha Ltd

Su was born into a bleak future, where the government keeps tight control over children with magical powers—codenamed "Clovers." With Su being the only "four-leaf" Clover in the world, she has been kept isolated nearly her whole life. Can ex-military agent Kazuhiko deliver her to the happiness she seeks? Experience the complete series in this hardcover edition, which also includes over twenty pages of ravishing color art!

KC
KODANSHA COMICS

MAGIC KNIGHT RAYEARTH

25TH ANNIVERSARY EDITION

CLAMP

A BELOVED CLASSIC MAKES ITS STUNNING RETURN IN THIS GORGEOUS, LIMITED EDITION BOX SET!

This tale of three Tokyo teenagers who cross through a magical portal and become the champions of another world is a modern manga classic. The box set includes three volumes of manga covering the entire first series of *Magic Knight Rayearth*, plus the series's super-rare full-color art book companion, all printed at a larger size than ever before on premium paper, featuring a newly-revised translation and lettering, and exquisite foil-stamped covers.

A strictly limited edition, this will be gone in a flash!

KC
KODANSHA COMICS

The beloved characters from *Cardcaptor Sakura* return in a brand new, reimagined fantasy adventure!

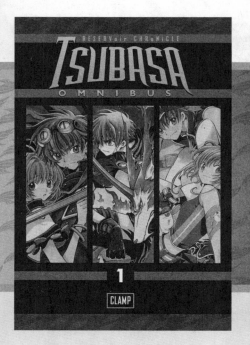

"[*Tsubasa*] takes readers on a fantastic ride that only gets more exhilarating with each successive chapter." —Anime News Network

In the Kingdom of Clow, an archaeological dig unleashes an incredible power, causing Princess Sakura to lose her memories. To save her, her childhood friend Syaoran must follow the orders of the Dimension Witch and travel alongside Kurogane, an unrivaled warrior; Fai, a powerful magician; and Mokona, a curiously strange creature, to retrieve Sakura's dispersed memories!